STEP-BY-STEP
GARDEN
DIY

50 SIMPLE PROJECTS USING
WOOD • STONE • WATER

ALAN & GILL BRIDGEWATER

NEW HOLLAND

Contents

Wood 6

Stone 128

Water 250

Wood

Introduction

One fine summer's day, Gill and I were busy in the workshop enjoying our woodwork, but at the same time desperately wishing that we could be outside in the garden soaking up the sun. Then we realized that we could have the best of both worlds: we could in fact be outside building really adventurous woodworking projects for the garden. We downed tools and wandered around the garden considering the possibilities. I immediately thought about constructing a picnic table I had been dreaming about, and Gill had a Victorian tool shed in her sights. Better still, garden woodwork would be able to make use of relatively low-cost, rough-sawn wood straight from the sawmill, and we would only require basic tools.

The ambition of this book is to share with you all the delights of working with wood to build beautiful creations for the garden. Each project follows the steps of collecting together tools and materials, considering the design, and building. We describe how the component parts are cut and fitted, colourwash illustrations show how the structures are built, and photographs demonstrate how best to achieve the step-by-step procedures; in fact, we take you through all the stages of designing, making and finishing.

So, if you like the idea of spending time out in the garden doing woodwork, which will add to the interest and functionality of your garden, you will get a lot of enjoyment from this book. You may have ambitions to sit on your very own bench to have a coffee, to eat lunch on a picnic table, or to nestle under a romantic arch. You may long for an arbour where you can canoodle with your partner, or perhaps your children have always nagged you for a playhouse. Try one or two projects during the summer, then dream about all the garden woodwork that you are going to build next year!

Best of luck.

Alan & Gill

HEALTH AND SAFETY

Many woodworking procedures are potentially dangerous, so before starting work on the projects, check through the following list:

- Make sure that you are fit and strong enough for the task ahead. If you have doubts, ask your doctor for specific advice.
- When you are building sheds, arbours, pergolas and other large structures, you will need to ask others to help you assemble the components towards the end of the project.

- When operating power tools, read the safety instructions supplied with the tool and wear the appropriate protective gear. A dust-mask and pair of goggles are usually adequate, and if the machine is noisy, wear ear defenders.
- Never operate electric tools, such as a drill or saw, if you are overtired.
- Use power saws extremely carefully. Keep your fingers well away from the blade and use a stick of scrap wood for holding or pushing through short lengths of wood.

Part I: Techniques

Designing and planning

Whatever the size of your garden or its situation, a well thought-out woodwork project will undoubtedly make it a more exciting and dynamic place. You don't have to have loads of experience as a woodworker in order to follow our projects successfully: if you have the correct tools, choose your wood with care, and spend time carefully designing and planning the whole exercise, you will be sure to get good results.

FIRST CONSIDERATIONS

- Do you have a local sawmill, where you can buy rough-sawn, pre-treated wood suitable for building sheds, fences and gates?
- Will the sawmill deliver small quantities of wood, or are you going to fetch it yourself? Do you have a trailer or a suitable rack on the roof of your car?
- Do children and pets use your garden, and if so, is their presence going to affect your choice of project?
- Where are you going to do the woodwork? Are you going to work close to the house, perhaps on a patio or in a yard, or are you going to work on the lawn?
- If you are building a structure such as a shed or arbour, are you going to set it up on levelled blocks or bricks, or are you going to lay a concrete slab?
- Are your neighbours going to be concerned about the siting of a project? If this is a possibility, it's a good idea to involve them at the planning stage.
- Are you going to need help with lifting? If you plan to build the Victorian Tool Shed (see page 110), will you do the construction close to the site, or will you get help to move the panels once they have been built?

Choosing a suitable project

When you have decided what you'd like to build, the next step is to consider the project in terms of the site you have in mind. Is your chosen project perhaps too large for the site? Will you have to move a drain? Will the project upset the way that you and the family currently use the garden?

Are there any narrow gateways that might restrict access when installing a project that you have built away from its eventual site? Are there any shrubs that need to be cut back to allow the project to be put in position? Would it be a good idea to mend and paint your fences before you build a shed? Are there any local restrictions related to the building of sheds?

So, our advice is to choose your projects with great care, and to involve your family (and neighbours if the projects could conceivably affect them, for example the height of your planned structure may obstruct their views) in decision-making, before going ahead and enjoying the building experience.

Planning the project

Whatever your choice of project, whether it is the Rabbit Ark (see page 96) or the Classic Pergola (see page 102), it is vital to plan it out to the last detail, otherwise you can be caught out by unforseen difficulties. If you are thinking about building a large, fixed project such as the Victorian Tool Shed (see page 110), draw a plan of your garden complete with the house, paths, flowerbeds, trees and hedges. Mark in the trajectory of the sun as it arcs across the garden. Will the new shed cast shadows that will affect the flowerbeds? Will it necessitate the building of a new path so the shed can be reached easily from the house?

Keep asking yourself questions. If you have any doubts about how the shed will look when it has been erected, it's a good idea to peg out the site and build a large batten, board and string framework to the size of the shed. When the mock-up is in position, walk around it and consider how it relates to the rest of the garden. Live with it for a few days and see if it affects your family's movement around the garden.

Before you dig deep holes or bang in spiked metal post supports (for a fence, gate or pergola), it is important to avoid potential problems by studying site plans, testing the ground or making trial holes. If you suspect that there might be an underground structure such as a water main, drain or power supply, start by gently and carefully probing the ground with a metal rod. If it slides into the ground easily, the site is clear, but if it meets an obstruction, you must consider digging a trial hole to see what the problem is, or opt to move the project anyway.

Buying the right tools and materials

The best strategy, when building up a tool collection, is to get yourself a basic kit, and then buy specialist tools if the need arises.

When sourcing your materials, on no account consider using pre-packed, planed wood from the local DIY store. Not only would it treble your costs, but its overly smooth finish makes it unsuitable for the projects in this book. You must order rough-sawn wood from a local sawmill. Shop around for the best price and then order in bulk. When you go to the sawmill, ask to see their waste pile, just in case there is a bargain to be had. For example, with the feather-edged boarding, we were able to cut costs dramatically by using wood from a heap of random lengths. When selecting your wood, make sure that the finish is suitable. For instance, you must not use pressure-treated wood for the playhouse, because of the toxic nature of some preservatives.

WOODWORK DESIGNS FOR THE GARDEN

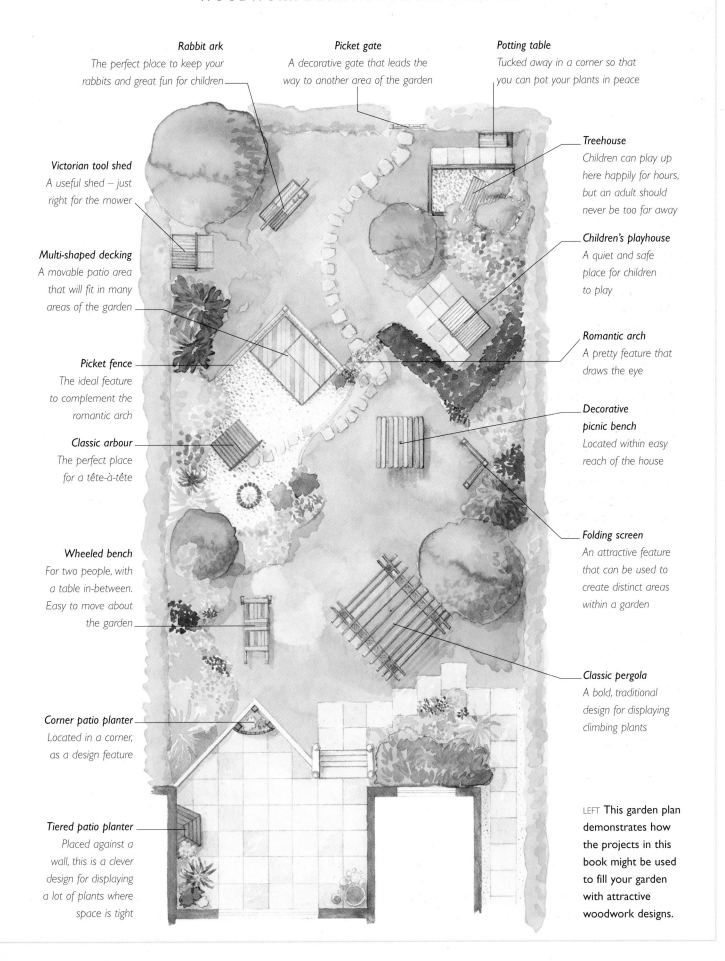

Rabbit ark
The perfect place to keep your rabbits and great fun for children

Picket gate
A decorative gate that leads the way to another area of the garden

Potting table
Tucked away in a corner so that you can pot your plants in peace

Victorian tool shed
A useful shed – just right for the mower

Multi-shaped decking
A movable patio area that will fit in many areas of the garden

Picket fence
The ideal feature to complement the romantic arch

Classic arbour
The perfect place for a tête-à-tête

Wheeled bench
For two people, with a table in-between. Easy to move about the garden

Corner patio planter
Located in a corner, as a design feature

Tiered patio planter
Placed against a wall, this is a clever design for displaying a lot of plants where space is tight

Treehouse
Children can play up here happily for hours, but an adult should never be too far away

Children's playhouse
A quiet and safe place for children to play

Romantic arch
A pretty feature that draws the eye

Decorative picnic bench
Located within easy reach of the house

Folding screen
An attractive feature that can be used to create distinct areas within a garden

Classic pergola
A bold, traditional design for displaying climbing plants

LEFT This garden plan demonstrates how the projects in this book might be used to fill your garden with attractive woodwork designs.

Tools

Always buy tools of the highest quality that you can afford. However, successful garden woodwork relies on controlling the wood while it is worked. To do this, you need a large space such as the lawn, two portable workbenches, and a sheet of plywood for setting out the component parts.

TOOLS FOR MEASURING AND MARKING

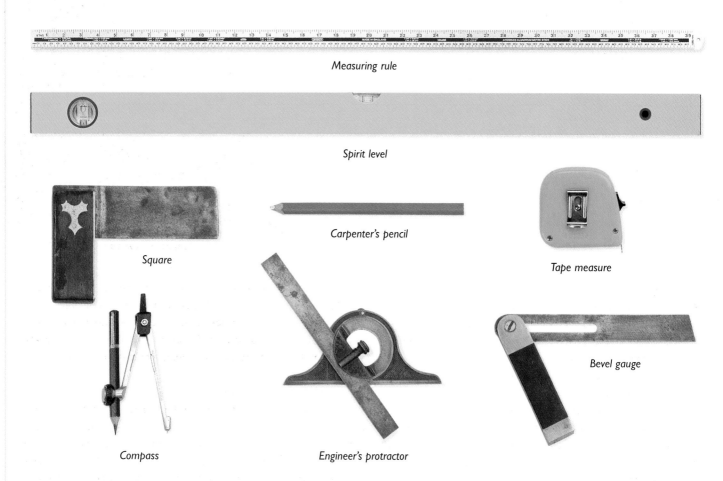

Measuring rule

Spirit level

Square

Carpenter's pencil

Tape measure

Compass

Engineer's protractor

Bevel gauge

Measuring

You need two measuring tools: a wood or metal measuring rule for sizing and marking joints, and a flexible tape measure for setting out the site plan for large projects (such as the Victorian Tool Shed on page 110) and for measuring long lengths of wood. We use an 8-metre tape for all the projects. If you can afford to spend a little extra, it's a good idea to use a fibreglass tape for trailing about the garden, because it is more resilient to the wear and tear of working on wet grass and with damp wood. Always wipe your measuring tool after use and put it away clean and dry.

Marking out

The tools for this are: a square for marking out right angles, a bevel gauge for setting out approximate angles, an engineer's protractor for setting out precise angles, a compass for drawing circles, and a clutch of good-quality carpenter's pencils for drawing on the wood. The flat lead in a carpenter's pencil not only keeps its point longer, but the rectangular section of the lead resists breaking – a really good idea when working on rough-sawn wood. Before you put your tools away, wipe them over with thin oil in order to protect them against damp and corrosion. We use olive oil, but alternatively you could use very thin engine or bicycle oil. On no account use old engine oil.

Levelling

For a project such as a shed, where the ground must be level, you require three tools: a flexible tape for setting out the site, a spade for digging away the earth, and a spirit level for checking vertical and horizontal levels. If you are going to get involved in building a concrete slab, you will also need a shovel and a garden rake.

TOOLS FOR CUTTING WOOD

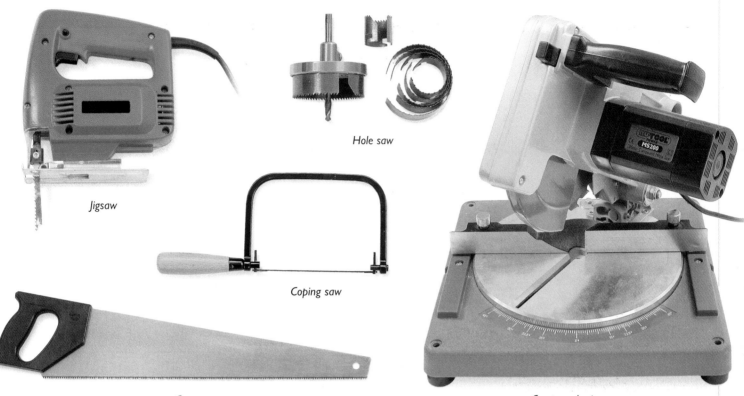

Jigsaw

Hole saw

Coping saw

Crosscut saw

Compound mitre saw

Sawing to size

Assuming that you purchase all your wood ready-sawn to a section size (sawn to the desired width and thickness), all you really need for the projects is a top-quality, hard-toothed, crosscut saw. Buy one that is described as "trade quality", and do not attempt to save money by opting for a bargain or secondhand saw. We purchased ours directly from the sawmill. Sawmill wood is generally green, wet, sappy and sometimes dirty, so it is best to get two crosscut saws – use one for cutting wood to length, and keep the other for cutting joints. To help ensure that the saw blades last, remove sticky sap with white spirit at the end of a day's work, and wipe the blade with olive oil or thin machine oil.

Sawing angles

While you can certainly make all straight and angled cuts with the crosscut saw already described, you can make life much easier – especially when cutting repeat angles – by obtaining an electric compound mitre saw. Not long ago, such saws were quite expensive, but now they are within reach of most people.

To use a compound mitre saw, set it on a level surface, either on a workboard or clamped in the jaws of a portable workbench. Adjust the blade to the desired angle, position the workpiece against the backstop, and then switch on the power and lower the blade to make the cut. Compound mitre saws are great tools for

---

CAUTION

The electric compound mitre saw is potentially an extremely dangerous tool. Never leave it unattended. If you have children, pull out the plug and lock the blade into the "down" position when not in use.

---

tasks such as cutting the tops of the pickets in the Picket Fence project (see page 42). When using a power tool such as this, always read the manufacturer's literature, follow all the safety rules, and work with a helper close at hand.

Sawing curves

The projects use three tools for cutting curves: a hand coping saw for small, tight curves in thin wood; an electric jigsaw for broad curves in thick wood; and an electric drill with a saw-toothed cutter (hole saw) for cutting large-diameter holes. We particularly enjoy using the jigsaw – it is an uncomplicated, very efficient, low-cost tool. To use it, you set the blade close to the start of the cut, with the bed of the tool resting flat on the wood, switch on the power, and then slowly advance the tool so that the cut runs slightly to the waste side of the drawn line. Remember not to snatch the tool from the workpiece while the blade is still moving. When you have made the cut, switch off the power, wait until the blade has come to a standstill, then lift the tool away. Always wear a dust-mask and a pair of safety goggles.

We used an electric drill with a saw-toothed cutter for cutting large-diameter holes in thick wood, but it wasn't an experience that we enjoyed. This tool combination does get the job done, but it is extremely noisy and juddery, and generates a lot of dust. If you feel nervous about using any of the power tools, it's a good idea to ask friends to help you.

TOOLS FOR MAKING JOINTS

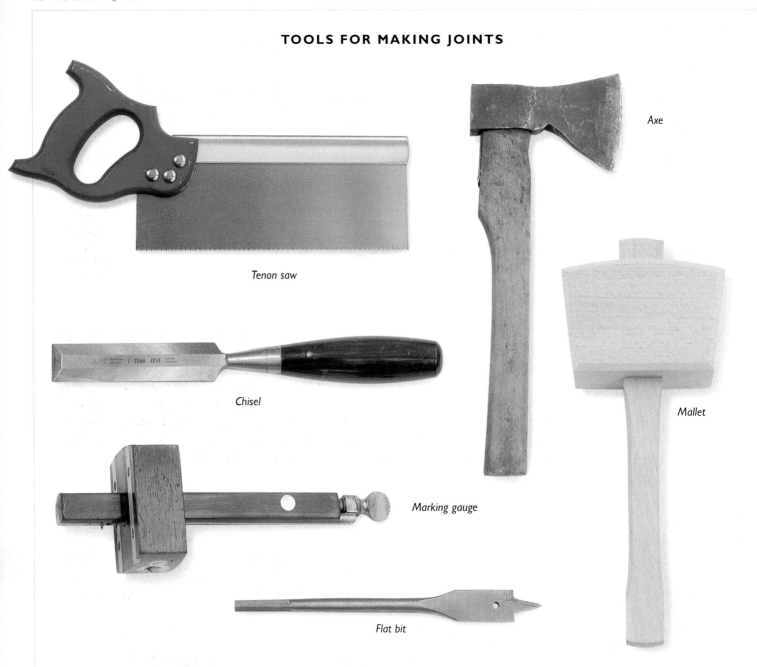

Tenon saw

Axe

Chisel

Mallet

Marking gauge

Flat bit

Marking out and cutting joints

When working outside cutting swift, basic joints in rough-sawn wood, you need these basic tools: a marking gauge, tenon saw, flat drill bit, chisels, mallet and axe.

A large, single-spike marking gauge is used for setting out the joints on the wood, a tenon saw for removing the bulk of the waste, and a flat drill bit for clearing the mortises. When purchasing the marking gauge, get a good, basic model, which will stand up to wear and tear in the garden.

Once the rough has been cleared from the joint with the saw and drill, you need a selection of bevel-edged chisels for shaving the wood down to the mark. Again, choose good-quality solid chisels. Avoid those with cheap wooden handles that are likely to split, and select tools with solid plastic handles moulded to the shank.

CAUTION

Although chisels and axes are potentially dangerous tools, you can cut the risks to almost zero by always holding the tool with a firm grip, cutting away from your body, and applying full concentration to the job.

For large basic joints we also use a mallet and a small axe. The axe is a particularly useful tool. Apart from all manner of splitting and shaving tasks, such as cutting dowels for pegging joints and trimming the bottoms of posts, the axe can also be used in much the same way as a wide-bladed chisel. A tenon is sawn to the waste side of the shoulder-line, and then the blade of the axe is set on the end-grain mark and driven home with a blow from the mallet. Choose a good, heavy-duty axe, with a thin blade that has a bevel on both sides. Avoid the thick-bladed, stainless-steel axes sold for splitting kindling, opting instead for a hand-forged black iron axe. Pay careful attention to safety considerations when using an axe. Always make sure that your body (and anyone else's) is well clear of the path of swing. Do not use your free hand to hold the wood in position.

TOOLS FOR SCREWING AND NAILING

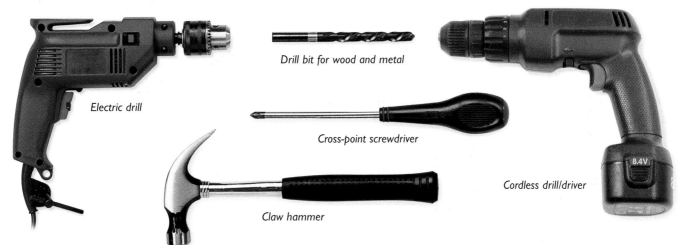

Drill bit for wood and metal

Electric drill

Cross-point screwdriver

Cordless drill/driver

Claw hammer

Screwing

Before a screw is driven into wood, it is best to drill a pilot hole with a twist drill bit. (In most cases, the holes do not need to be countersunk with a pilot-countersink bit: the pine used for the projects is so soft that the screwhead will cut its own counter-sink.) Then use a variable-speed cordless drill fitted with a cross-point screwdriver bit for driving in the screws. Set the torque on the drill to suit the thickness and hardness of the wood, and drive the screw home until the torque slips the clutch.

Nailing

The projects in this book use slender nails for fixing feather-edged boards to frames, and flat-headed nails for roofing felt. To fix the felt, you simply bang the nails home with a claw hammer. With feather-edged boards, however, you need to drill pilot holes for the nails so that you do not split the fragile grain. Small staples are used for fixing rabbit wire. Make sure that all nails and staples are galvanized. Avoid nails and staples described as "black iron", because they bend and stain the wood.

OTHER ESSENTIAL TOOLS

Metal snips

Adjustable spanner

Sledgehammer

Clamp

Utility knife

Electric sander

Paintbrush

Fixing and finishing

Some projects require a sledgehammer, but don't be tempted to buy the biggest one you can find, because a medium-weight one is more than adequate. When using the sledgehammer, make sure that your helper is standing on the opposite side of the post to be driven home, and that his or her hands are out of harm's way.

Once the woodwork is finished, the project is completed by sanding, painting and preserving. You will need an electric sander for removing large splinters and for sculpting surfaces, a clamp for holding parts together, and a brush for applying paint or preserv-ative. Depending upon the project, you might also need an adjustable spanner for tightening up nuts, a pair of metal snips for cutting wire mesh, and a utility knife for cutting roofing felt.

If you really need to cut costs on a project, and do not want to go to the expense of kitting yourself out with the tools we have described, see if you can borrow various items from friends and neighbours. You may also want to consider hiring power tools. If you are going to use an unfamiliar tool, it is always a good idea to have a trial run on some scrap wood, just to make sure that you understand how the tool is best handled.

Materials

We obtained all the rough-sawn softwood from a local sawmill, using four types of wood: wood that had been left in its natural state, wood that had been pressure-treated and had a grey-green finish, wood that had been brush-treated to give it a brown finish, and wood described as "short ends and offcut waste".

USEFUL TIMBER SECTIONS

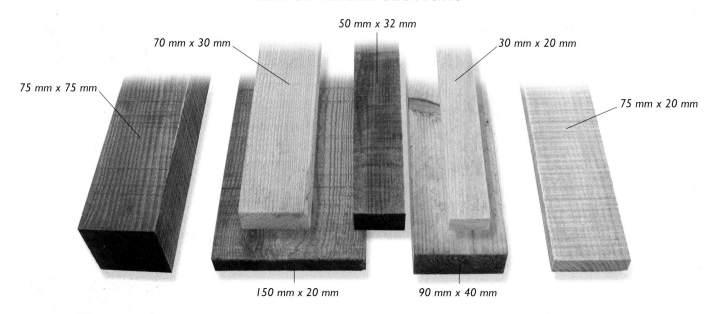

50 mm x 32 mm

70 mm x 30 mm

30 mm x 20 mm

75 mm x 75 mm

75 mm x 20 mm

150 mm x 20 mm

90 mm x 40 mm

Posts, planks and sticks

The sawmill supplied us with rough-sawn softwood intended for garden items such as fences, gates, sheds and screens. We used stick sections ranging from roofing battens about 30 mm wide and 20 mm thick (sold in bundles), through to flat battens 75 mm wide and 20 mm thick (sold to be used for pickets). We purchased posts 75 mm and 100 mm square, planks up to 150 mm wide described as "gravel boards", and all manner of smaller sections.

When you are buying wood, make allowances for inaccuracies in the measurements given by the sawmill. For example, a plank described as being 20 mm thick might actually measure anything from 18 mm through to 23 mm. When you get the wood home, leave it propped up against a wall or fence to dry out for a couple of days, until it feels dry to the touch.

Choosing the right length and section

Most sawmills sell wood in three lengths – 2 m (or 6 ft), 3 m (or 9 ft), and 4 m (or 12 ft). You will need to work out the most economical length for your chosen project. The wood will be sold as square sections, planks, triangular and semicircular rails, grooved decking and cladding. The projects assume that you won't need to cut the wood to a different section size. Be ready to modify the projects to suit the sections sold by your local sawmill. If you are not confident in your ability to adjust the requirements, take your plans to the sawmill and ask for advice.

BUYING TIPS

- Be flexible. If, for example, a project specifies a section 50 mm square, but you are only able to get something 50 mm wide and 25 mm thick, you can screw two sections together.
- Always choose local softwood – it is cheaper and more forest-friendly.
- There are lots of bargains to be had. Go prepared with heavy boots and gloves, and be ready to search through piles of wood that are variously described as trimmings, short ends, offcuts or waney-edged.
- Don't be talked into using imported hardwood or wood that has been overly planed or prepared.
- Remember that while pressure-treated woods are long-lasting, they are also highly toxic (to the extent that your skin might blister on contact). A good option is to buy sawn wood and then treat it with a suitable preservative or paint.
- If you are a woman, be prepared for the fact that most sawmills are run by men and may have a mainly male clientele. Try not to feel intimidated.
- We suggest that you do not take children to the sawmill. But do encourage them to help make the projects, because the planning and building are a good educational experience.

CLADDING

Types of cladding

While we decided to use feather-edged boarding for cladding, most sawmills sell at least two other options. There is ship-lap cladding, which looks a bit like tongue-and-groove boarding, and log cladding, which looks very much like half-logs. In our opinion, the feather-edged cladding is the least expensive, the easiest to work and fit, and the most attractive. The feather edge is also more traditional, and the layering gives a stronger structure.

Nailing feather-edged boards

We always use a jig made from two offcuts screwed together, which is butted against the lower edge of a board to ensure that it overlaps the next one by 35 mm. To avoid splitting the wood, the boards must be drilled prior to fixing, with the holes set so that the nail or screw misses the board that you are just about to lap.

Before fixing the cladding, it is a good idea to have a trial dry run just to make sure that you have enough wood. Arrange each piece so that any knots or splits are clear of the nailing points. When you are driving the nails home, be careful that you do not force the wood to bend into a concave profile, so that it splits.

Log cladding

Feather-edged boarding

OTHER USEFUL SECTIONS AND READY-MADE ITEMS

Triangular section

Decking

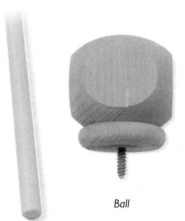

Dowel

Ball

Trellis screen

Triangular section and decking

Triangular sections are designed specifically to be used for fence rails. The rails run horizontally from post to post at the back of the fence and are used to support the vertical boards. The widest face of the section is fixed in contact with the fence.

Decking can either be bought in the form of tiles, or by the metre. We purchased our decking in 3 m lengths. We usually avoid buying pressure-treated wood because of its cost and the toxic nature of the preservative, but decking is an exception. Do not let children play on newly-treated timber, to prevent skin coming into contact with the wood. However, decking is subjected to the full blast of the weather, which soon dispenses with the hazard.

Dowels and balls

Dowelling is bought by the metre according to requirements. Finial balls come in all shapes and sizes. Those with a screw attached just need a pilot hole drilling in the post so the ball can be screwed in place. Some balls require a double-ended screw (half the screw goes into the post and the other end into the ball).

Trellis screens

It is possible to make trellis screens from thin lathes, but they are so tricky to make that it is best to purchase them ready-made. Buy your screens before you buy anything else, and then modify all the other measurements to suit.

FIXINGS AND FITTINGS

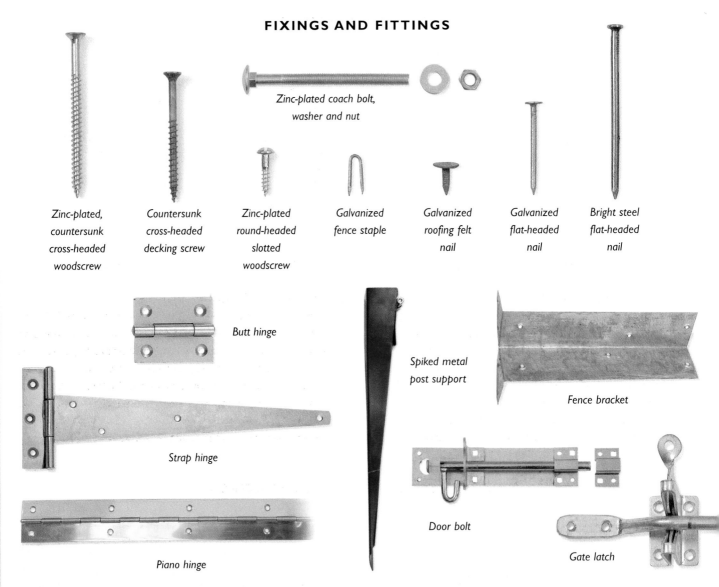

Zinc-plated coach bolt,
washer and nut

Zinc-plated,
countersunk
cross-headed
woodscrew

Countersunk
cross-headed
decking screw

Zinc-plated
round-headed
slotted
woodscrew

Galvanized
fence staple

Galvanized
roofing felt
nail

Galvanized
flat-headed
nail

Bright steel
flat-headed
nail

Butt hinge

Strap hinge

Piano hinge

Spiked metal
post support

Fence bracket

Door bolt

Gate latch

Screws, bolts, nails and staples

We use best-quality, exterior-grade, galvanized or zinc-plated cross-headed screws throughout – because they stay bright and can easily be driven home with a variable-speed, cordless electric drill fitted with a screwdriver bit. Buy boxes of 100 or 200 screws at a time: it is cheaper, and you won't run short of screws.

Coach bolts, with washers and nuts to fit, are used for projects such as the Picket Gate (see page 48). A hole to fit the shank is drilled, the bolt is tapped home until the square section just under the head bites into the hole, and then it is clenched with a washer and nut.

We always buy nails and staples by weight because it is the most cost-effective option. Always specify that they should be galvanized, or at least plated, because then you won't have to worry about rust staining the wood.

Hinges, gate bolts and latches

We use butt door hinges for the Folding Screen (see page 40) and the Rabbit Ark (see page 96), piano hinges for the Children's Playhouse (see page 122), T-strap hinges for the Victorian Tool Shed (see page 110), and heavy-duty reversible hinges for the

Picket Gate (see page 48). The advantage of using piano hinges on a door that children will play with is that the continuous body of the hinge prevents the child from trapping his or her fingers between the door and doorpost. The heavy-duty reversible hinges for the gate are designed to be fixed with both screws and coach bolts, making them even more sturdy.

We also use a latch for the gate and a sliding gate bolt for the tool-shed door. Don't try to cut costs by using cheap metalware. If you have gone to a lot of trouble to build an item, it is a false economy to skimp on the fixings and fittings: always specify that they are galvanized (or at least plated), and always buy the items complete with galvanized bolts and screws to fit.

Post and fence fixings

We use spiked metal post supports for fixing fenceposts and gateposts, because they are very efficient and very easy to fix. The spike is put in position, an offcut is placed on top of the spike, and it is banged home with a sledgehammer. The post is then slid into the containment and held by clamping nuts. The metal fixings for post rails are just as easy to fit. One half is screwed to the triangular-section rail and the other to the post itself.

OTHER MATERIALS

Roofing plywood   Stirling board   Roofing felt   Wire mesh

Plywood, stirling board and felt

To make a board and felt roof, first cover the roof with a sheet of exterior-grade plywood or stirling board. Nail the first sheet of felt in place on the board, paint felt adhesive over the nails, stick the second sheet of felt in place, and so on. The idea is that on the top of the roof at least, the nailed edge of one piece of felt is always covered by the glued edge of the neighbouring piece. It is rather like a tiled roof, where the nailed head end of one tile is covered and protected by the tail end of the neighbouring tile.

Wire mesh and window plastic

We used welded galvanized wire "grid" mesh for the Rabbit Ark (see page 96) rather than woven fence wire, because it keeps its shape and is easier to cut and fit. It is important to buy mesh that is specifically described as being suitable for rabbit cages.

For safety reasons, the window of the Children's Playhouse (see page 122) is glazed with polycarbonate sheet rather than glass. To cut the sheet, score the line of cut with a craft knife – on both sides – and then fold it so that it breaks on the line.

PAINTS, STAINS AND PRESERVATIVES

      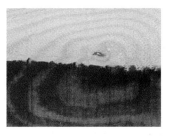   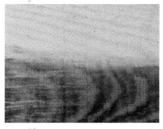

Red stain/preservative on pine   Mauve paint/preservative on pine   Blue stain/preservative on pine   Creosote on pine

Pressure-treated wood

Pressure-treated wood undoubtedly gives the best protection, but it is both expensive and highly toxic. It is fine for projects such as the Victorian Tool Shed (see page 110) and the Multi-shaped Decking (see page 54), but we wouldn't use it for "close-contact" projects such as the Decorative Picnic Table (see page 58), Rabbit Ark (see page 96) or Children's Playhouse (see page 122). The subject is open to debate, but we would not like a child to sleep in a playhouse made from pressure-treated wood.

Exterior paints and stains

We favour using exterior-grade water-based paint, because the colours can be blended, and the paint can be diluted to give a thin wash or

stain. We usually colour the wood with a thin wash, and then protect the whole thing with a coat of clear preservative. Always read the labels on the cans and then you will be able to make a value judgement about the best treatment for your project.

Creosote

Creosote oil is smelly and unpleasant to apply, but the rich brown colour is attractive and it does preserve the wood. It is fine for projects such as the Folding Screen (see page 40), but obviously it's a bad idea for the Children's Playhouse (see page 122), Decorative Picnic Table (see page 58) and the Rabbit Ark (see page 96). Many plants wither if they touch wood that has been protected with creosote.

CAUTION

Always wear gloves when you are handling preservatives and paint. Read the labels carefully. If you are worried, take specific advice.

Working with wood

Immersing yourself in creative woodwork outside in the garden is an exciting and therapeutic activity. A pile of sawn sections can be transformed into attractive and useful items, such as a picnic table or tool shed, in the space of a weekend. If you can use a saw and drive in a screw, you are capable of making all the projects in this book.

STRAIGHT CUTS

ABOVE **Use a square for marking 90° cuts. Hold the wooden handle against the edge of the piece of wood and draw a pencil line.**

To make a straight cut (at right angles to the face or edge of the wood), take a square and pencil and mark the wood. Let's say that you want to cut a 600 mm length off a 150 mm-wide plank. Hold the wooden handle (or "stock") of the square hard against the workpiece, and run a pencil line against the edge of the steel blade. Repeat on all faces and edges of the plank, so the line encircles the wood. Clamp the workpiece in a workbench, take a crosscut saw and place the teeth to the waste side of the drawn line. Perform a few short, dragging strokes, and then use the full length of the saw to make the cut. At the end of the cut, use your free hand to support the waste, making lighter strokes until the wood is sawn through.

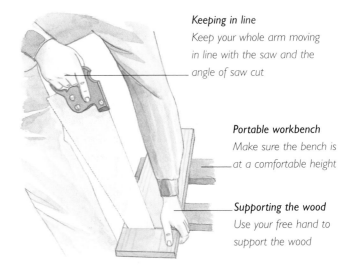

Keeping in line
Keep your whole arm moving in line with the saw and the angle of saw cut

Portable workbench
Make sure the bench is at a comfortable height

Supporting the wood
Use your free hand to support the wood

ABOVE **After marking the length of a piece of wood, use a crosscut saw (for cutting across the grain) to cut it to length. Support the wood on a workbench and saw to the waste side of the pencil line.**

ANGLED CUTS

ABOVE **Use a bevel gauge for drawing angled lines. Set the gauge to the required angle, and use in the same way as a square (shown above).**

To make an angled cut (a straight cut that runs at an angle to the edge of the wood), you can use a crosscut saw or an electric compound mitre saw. For example, imagine that you want to cut an angle across a picket. If are going to use the hand saw, take a bevel gauge, set the angle to suit your needs, hold the handle hard up against the edge of the wood and draw a line against the steel blade. Set the workpiece in the workbench and use the crosscut saw to make the cut as already described. To use the compound mitre saw, first set the blade of the saw to the desired angle and lock it into position. Hold the workpiece hard against the fence, repeatedly lower the blade and nudge the wood until the blade is just to the waste side of the drawn line. Raise the blade, switch on the power, lower the blade and make the cut.

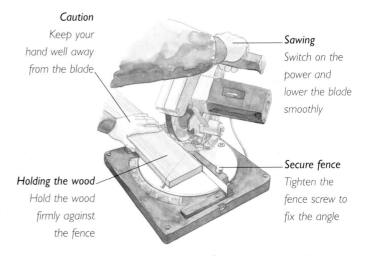

Caution
Keep your hand well away from the blade

Sawing
Switch on the power and lower the blade smoothly

Holding the wood
Hold the wood firmly against the fence

Secure fence
Tighten the fence screw to fix the angle

ABOVE **After marking a straight or angled line, use the compound mitre saw to cut the wood quickly and accurately. The blade can be tilted as well as rotated, so you can also cut compound angles (for example a cut that is 30° across a plank and 20° through it). The saw is especially useful for cutting lots of wood to the same size.**

CUTTING CURVED SHAPES

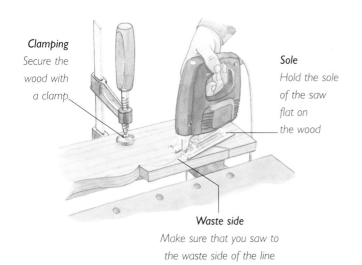

Clamping
Secure the
wood with
a clamp.

Sole
Hold the sole
of the saw
flat on
the wood

Waste side
Make sure that you saw to
the waste side of the line

ABOVE The jigsaw is designed for cutting curves in wood. The narrow blade enables the saw to be rotated to follow tight curves in decorative designs. The sole can be locked in a tilted position to produce an angled, curved cut. Always rotate the saw in the direction of a curve rather than forcing the blade sideways.

We use two procedures to draw curved shapes. For shapes that are made of circles and part-circles, we simply use a compass. For symmetrical cyma curves (the ones that look a little like stylized lips) we draw half of the shape freehand, cut it out, and use this as a template to draw the other half. This way of working ensures that the shape is perfectly symmetrical.

To cut curves, you can use either a coping saw for cutting small, tight curves on or near the edge of thin wood, or a power jigsaw for broad curves in thick wood. To use the coping saw, first make sure that the blade is fitted with the teeth pointing away from the handle. Tighten up the blade until it "pings" when plucked. Secure the workpiece in the jaws of a portable workbench, position the blade to the waste side of the drawn line, and work with a steady stroke to make the cut.

To use the power jigsaw, first bridge the workpiece across a couple of workbenches. Set the bed of the saw on the workpiece (so that the blade is just clear of the wood), switch on the power and slowly advance the tool so that the line of cut runs slightly to the waste side of the drawn line. Hold the tool with a firm grip, in order to stop it juddering and vibrating.

CUTTING MORTISE AND TENON JOINTS

Mortise and tenon joints are made up from two mating halves: the mortise (or hole) and the tenon that fits into the hole. The ideal is a joint that is a tight push-fit.

Making procedure to cut a mortise

1 Use a pencil, ruler, square and marking gauge to carefully set out the lines that make up the mortise.
2 Select a drill bit size that fits within the width of the mortise, and bore out one or more holes to clear the bulk of the waste. Hold the drill upright so that the drilled holes are at right angles to the face of the wood. There are various types of mortise. If it is a through mortise (one that goes right through the thickness of the wood), drill the holes completely through. If it is a blind or stopped mortise (the hole doesn't go through the wood), put a piece of masking tape around the drill bit to mark the depth you want to drill to, and stop when the hole reaches that depth.
3 Use a chisel to pare back the sides of the hole to the drawn lines. Work with a series of skimming cuts.

Making procedure to cut a tenon

1 Use a square, rule, pencil and gauge to draw a tenon that is a tight push-fit for the mortise.
2 Secure the workpiece in the portable workbench at an angle of about 45°. Use the saw to cut down to the shoulder-line. Repeat this procedure for both cuts on both sides of the joint.
3 Set the workpiece flat on the bench and saw down to the waste side of the shoulder-line, so that the piece of waste falls away. Do this on both sides of the tenon.

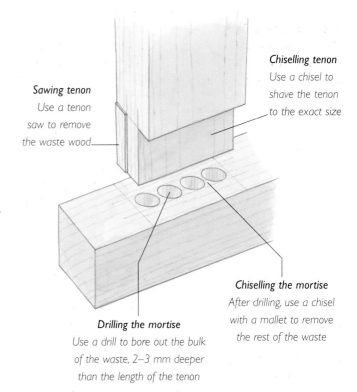

Sawing tenon
Use a tenon
saw to remove
the waste wood

Chiselling tenon
Use a chisel to
shave the tenon
to the exact size

Chiselling the mortise
After drilling, use a chisel
with a mallet to remove
the rest of the waste

Drilling the mortise
Use a drill to bore out the bulk
of the waste, 2–3 mm deeper
than the length of the tenon

ABOVE The mortise and tenon is a traditional joint for joining two pieces of wood, usually at right angles as shown here. Cut the mortise first with a drill bit and chisel(s), and then cut the tenon with a tenon saw. Mortise and tenon joints are hard work to cut by hand but are often stronger, cheaper and more attractive than fixing with screws or special hardware.

Fences and gates

In the Koran it says, "A fence without a gate is a prison, while a fence with a gate is a paradise". This section shows you how to create your own "paradise" by constructing a fence with an integral gate. Strength and stability are watchwords for both items: they must be able to stand up to both the weather and general wear and tear. Gates must be functional and appropriate for their situation, and should open and close without undue hindrance.

FIXING POSTS

Traditionally, wooden fenceposts and gateposts had half their length set below ground, with the below-ground section first charred or tarred, and then supported with a mix of well-tamped clay and rubble. However, the posts in our projects are best supported with concrete, or with a patent metal post support spike. When digging holes or banging in metal spikes, bear in mind that there may be underground power cables, water and drainage pipes lurking in the earth, so dig cautiously.

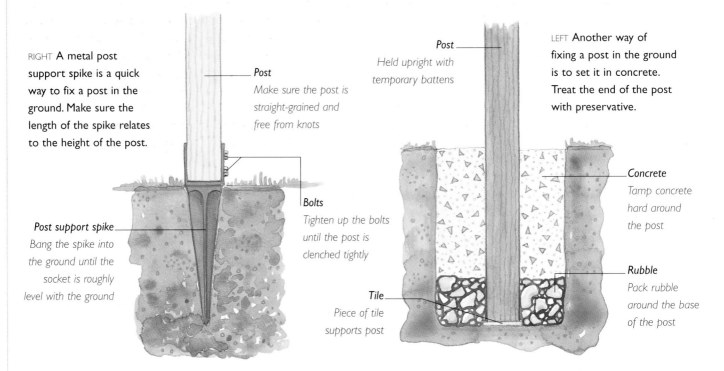

RIGHT A metal post support spike is a quick way to fix a post in the ground. Make sure the length of the spike relates to the height of the post.

Post
Make sure the post is straight-grained and free from knots

Post support spike
Bang the spike into the ground until the socket is roughly level with the ground

Bolts
Tighten up the bolts until the post is clenched tightly

Post
Held upright with temporary battens

LEFT Another way of fixing a post in the ground is to set it in concrete. Treat the end of the post with preservative.

Concrete
Tamp concrete hard around the post

Rubble
Pack rubble around the base of the post

Tile
Piece of tile supports post

Procedure for fixing a post support spike

1 Buy a metal post support spike to suit the length and square section of your post. The taller the post, the longer the length of spike required. Make sure that the spike has a strong bolt-clamp fitting, and that the metal is well protected by being galvanized or painted.

2 Set the support spike on the mark, slide an offcut from your post into the socket at the top of the spike, and give it a little tap with a sledgehammer to insert it just into the ground.

3 Adjust the spike so that it is upright, and bang it down into the ground with the sledgehammer. Continue until the bottom of the socketed top is positioned just above ground level.

4 Finally, set the post in the socket, make adjustments until it is vertical, and clench the bolts with a spanner.

Procedure for fixing a post with concrete

1 Use a spade to dig out a hole about 400 mm deep and 300 mm square. Remove the waste earth from the site.

2 Put a piece of broken tile into the bottom of the hole, position the post on the tile, and tamp a small amount of rubble around the bottom 100 mm of the post.

3 Prop the post upright with three temporary battens (nail the battens near the top of the post and angle them down to make a tripod) and make adjustments until the post is perfectly vertical. Make checks with a spirit level.

4 Make a concrete mix of 1 part Portland cement, 2 parts sharp sand, and 3 parts coarse aggregate (gravel). Tamp it into the hole.

5 Remove the temporary battens after four days. The concrete will not achieve its full strength until about three weeks later.

TYPES OF FENCE

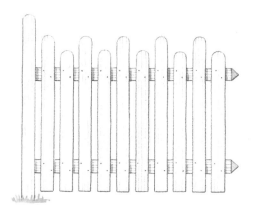

ABOVE A traditional picket fence with rounded ends. The gap between the pickets should be no greater than the width of a picket.

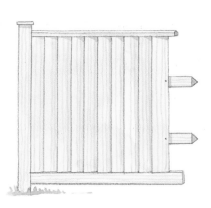

ABOVE A closeboard fence – feather-edged boards framed by the posts, capping rail and bottom board.

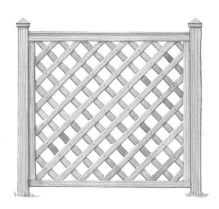

ABOVE A diamond trellis (overlapping lathes contained within a batten frame) set between capped posts.

There are various things to take into consideration when planning a fence. Do you need to keep children or livestock in, or wildlife out? Would you like the fence to look attractive and welcoming? Do you want a strong fence that discourages invaders, or a tall fence that prevents prying eyes?

In this book we show you how to make a traditional picket fence (see page 44). The word "picket" comes from the French word *piquer*, meaning "to prick". A picket fence has now come to mean a fence made up from a number of pointed slats; however the word once meant the pointed part of a palisade or wicket. From one country to another, the terms picket, wicket and palisade are more or less interchangeable and loosely used to describe many other types of wooden fence. There are closeboard fences made up from overlapping feather-edged boards, trellis fences made from a woven web of thin sections, and woven willow fences. Ranch-style fences are made from large-section cleft wood, and the rails are dominant; chestnut fences are made from cleft sticks and the posts are dominant.

TYPES OF GATE

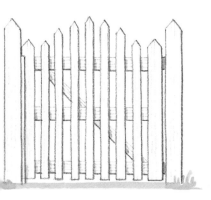

ABOVE A traditional picket gate in an arched pattern, held together with three horizontal rails and a diagonal brace.

ABOVE A gate made from riven wood (split, not sawn) is a good choice for an informal rustic garden. The split wood has a rough texture and varies in width and thickness, giving the gate an unmistakable hand-crafted appearance.

ABOVE Closeboard gates such as this are long-lasting and will prevent pets wandering in and out of your garden.

Gates have much the same history and design variations as fences, but they are more complex structures in that they have additional members such as stiles, braces and posts. Within the basic gate, the vertical side members are called stiles, the horizontal members are called rails, and the diagonal member is called a brace (and of course the gate frame is covered with additional vertical or horizontal members).

The gate is set between two posts – hinged to one and latched to another. Though designs vary, the one constant is that the brace always runs uphill from the hinge side of the gate through to the latch side. If the brace were to be set the other way around, the gate would sag down from the hinge side. A main factor in the strength of a gate is its hinges, and the hinge stile and the hinge post are often built from large-section wood.

Benches, chairs and decking

Every garden needs benches and seats scattered around so that you can enjoy the changing seasons during fine weather throughout the year. If their design includes decorative touches, they are lifted above mere practicality and can become attractive garden features. If your garden is in need of small areas of hard standing, wooden decking is a good-looking solution, which can create a softer effect than stone or concrete.

GARDEN SEATING CONSIDERATIONS

Garden seats must be attractive and well built, and should be positioned to take advantage of sun or shade as required. They can be made to a variety of designs to suit a selection of purposes. We have chosen three different options: a Decorative Picnic Table (see page 58), a Wheeled Bench (see page 70) and a small bench seat set within a Classic Arbour (see page 64). The picnic table can be used for family meals or entertaining. The wheeled bench has been designed for a small garden, incorporating wheels so that it can be moved with ease. It has an integral table, which is a useful place to put a drink. The arbour provides a sheltered spot to sit.

TYPES OF SEATING

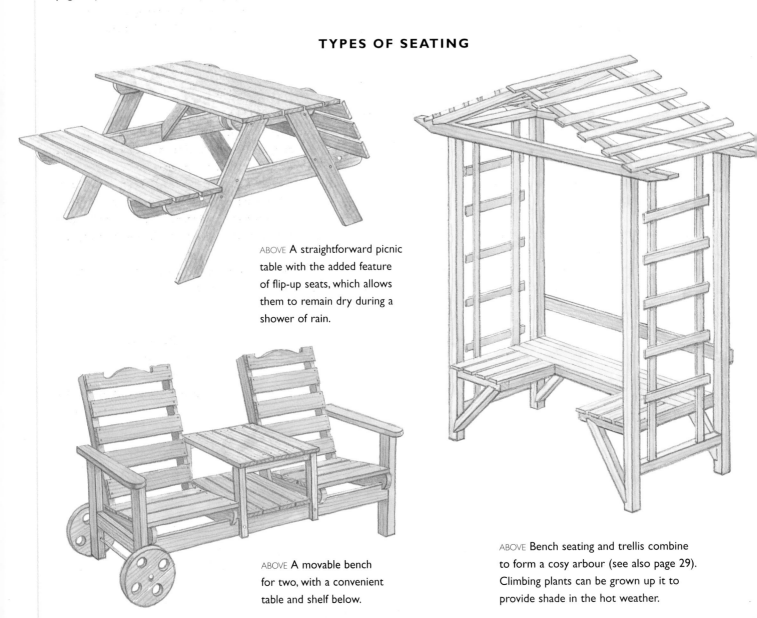

ABOVE A straightforward picnic table with the added feature of flip-up seats, which allows them to remain dry during a shower of rain.

ABOVE A movable bench for two, with a convenient table and shelf below.

ABOVE Bench seating and trellis combine to form a cosy arbour (see also page 29). Climbing plants can be grown up it to provide shade in the hot weather.

TYPES OF CHAIR

ABOVE **A traditional painted pine chair with slatted seat and strong mortise and tenon joints.**

ABOVE **An oriental-style teak chair, ideal for outdoor dining and general use. Heavyweight and long-lasting.**

ABOVE **A folding chair for occasional use, which can be brought in from the garden during the wet weather.**

DECKING

Wooden decking is a great idea for the garden – perfect when you want a level patio without going to all the time, trouble and expense of laying a concrete or stone paved area complete with a massive hardcore and concrete foundation. Furthermore, if you might conceivably want to move the patio from one year to the next, or you have a difficult sloping site, wooden decking is a good contender. There are also aesthetic considerations – perhaps you enjoy the sight and feel of wood – a decked area feels alive and springy, quite different from stone or brick. Also, by building a raised decking, you can achieve an area that gives the impression of a balcony or jetty, which extends and enhances your home.

Procedure for levelling decking

1 Rake the site smooth and cover it with a plastic membrane.
2 Rake a layer of gravel or bark chippings over the plastic, completely covering it to a thickness of about 100 mm.
3 Mark the position of the decking legs on the ground, set each paving slab on a bed of mortar, and wait for the mortar to set.
4 Lift the decking module into position, with each leg resting on a slab. Test to see whether it is level with a spirit level, selecting one leg to become a constant reference point.
5 Make adjustments by adding slabs under one or all of the remaining legs, to make the decking level.

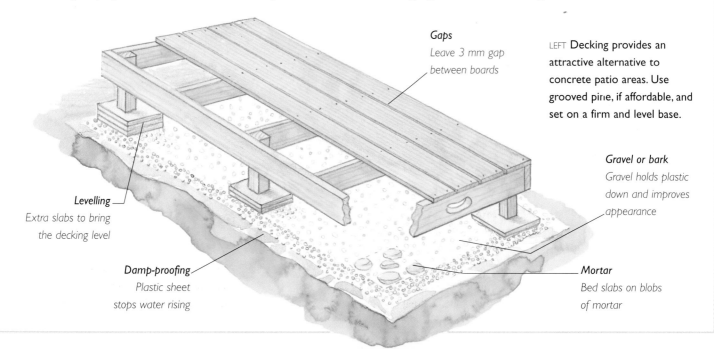

Gaps
Leave 3 mm gap between boards

LEFT **Decking provides an attractive alternative to concrete patio areas. Use grooved pine, if affordable, and set on a firm and level base.**

Gravel or bark
Gravel holds plastic down and improves appearance

Levelling
Extra slabs to bring the decking level

Damp-proofing
Plastic sheet stops water rising

Mortar
Bed slabs on blobs of mortar

Sheds, houses and arbours

A shed is invaluable for storing all the paraphernalia required for tending the garden. Summerhouses and arbours

are beguiling and exciting structures which can enhance a garden, adding texture to the backdrop of plant life.

They are functional too, providing a sheltered spot to sit. You can sit and enjoy looking at a cheerful display of bulbs

on a fresh spring morning, or appreciate blazing leaf colours on a chilly autumn afternoon.

FOUNDATIONS

All these structures require firm foundations, although you do not necessarily need to go to the trouble of laying a concrete base slab, which involves lots of digging, tamping hardcore, mixing concrete and so on. If the ground is wet and boggy, there is no option other than to lay concrete; otherwise a base made from concrete paving slabs set on a bed of sand is more than adequate.

Procedure for laying a concrete base
1 Skim off the topsoil to a depth of about 100 mm.
2 Position, peg out and level a foundation frame (made from rough-sawn wood 80 mm wide and 25 mm thick).
3 Fill the area within the frame with builder's rubble or a mixture of crushed stone and gravel, to a depth of about 100 mm.
4 Top up the frame with concrete (1 part Portland cement, 2 parts sharp sand, 3 parts aggregate, water); level and tamp with a plank.
5 Remove the wooden frame and rub the sides of the slab with a piece of scrap wood to remove the sharp edges.
6 When dry, lay pads of heavy-duty plastic or felt on the concrete to go under the shed's base bearers.

Procedure for laying concrete slabs
1 Dig away the topsoil to a depth of about 100 mm.
2 Fill the recess with a layer of sharp sand, to a depth of 100 mm, then rake it smooth and level it off.
3 Set the concrete paving slabs on generous wedges of mortar (1 part Portland cement, 6 parts building sand, 1 part hydrated lime, water). Level the first slab with a spirit level and then make sure that all subsequent slabs relate to it.
4 When the mortar has set (two days to harden completely), sit the shed's base bearers on pads of heavy-duty felt or plastic sheet.

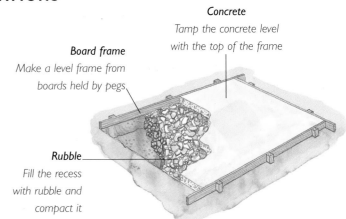

Concrete
Tamp the concrete level with the top of the frame

Board frame
Make a level frame from boards held by pegs

Rubble
Fill the recess with rubble and compact it

ABOVE If the ground is unstable, sheds, garden houses and arbours require a foundation consisting of hardcore and concrete.

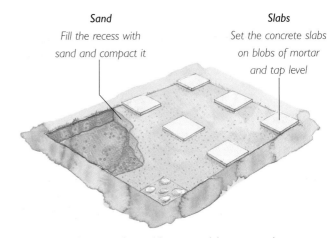

Sand
Fill the recess with sand and compact it

Slabs
Set the concrete slabs on blobs of mortar and tap level

ABOVE Where the ground is stable, paving slabs are an adequate foundation for sheds, arbours and other lightweight structures.

TYPES OF SHED

Sheds are defined and described by the shape of their roof. There are two basic types: the A-frame apex roof, which slopes down from a central ridge board, and the pent roof, which has a single gentle slope. A pent roof is cheaper and easier to build than an apex roof, because it can be made from large sheets of board. When planning a shed, you need to consider the head height required inside the shed, and the way the roof sits in relation to the door. For example, some structures are designed with the slope of the roof running forwards rather than backwards. Certainly the rain drips off at the front, so you get wet going in and out, but on the other hand, the low front prevents driving rain from getting inside the shed.

LEFT **A** simple, small garden tool shed with an apex roof.

LEFT **A** pent-roofed shed (the roof is a single slope).

SUMMERHOUSES AND OUTDOOR ROOMS

A summerhouse is a retreat, which allows you to get away from your everyday home. It is an opportunity to let your imagination run riot. If you have always harboured fantasies about living in a Wild West cowboy bunkhouse, Swiss cottage or log cabin, your summerhouse is an opportunity to satisfy these urges. Basically, there are two types of summerhouse: the small day room that is just big enough for a couple of chairs and a table, and the room that is large enough to double up as a spare guest room.

ABOVE **A** Swiss-style summerhouse complete with fancy gable boards, double doors and integral matching window boxes.

ABOVE This Victorian-design octagonal summerhouse has arched windows and a roof vent.

ABOVE **An** elaborate summerhouse with a lovely verandah, thistle-pattern banister rails and decorative woodwork on the gable.

ARBOURS

Generally speaking, an arbour is no more than a roof supported on poles – an open-sided structure that is just about big enough for a couple of seats. Arbours are very similar to gazebos in that they are often used to support scented climbing plants such as honeysuckle. Our Classic Arbour (see page 64) has a solid back and a waterproof roof, the idea being that it can be built in a small garden and pushed up against a wall or fence to be used as a bower, rather like a miniature summerhouse.

LEFT **An** arched arbour in an American design of the early nineteenth century.

LEFT **A** corner arbour with pergola beams and trellis sides.

LEFT **A** Victorian-style arbour with plenty of ornate details.

Pergolas, trellises and planters

If you want to add an eye-catching feature to your garden, you will find this section useful. Pergolas and trellises provide a support for plants and add a vertical dimension to the geography of the garden. If you would like to create stunning seasonal displays of flowers, our two patio planters (see pages 36 and 84) provide solutions.

TYPES OF PERGOLA

A pergola is best defined as a pattern of beams supported by a collection of posts, rather like a basic hut frame. In essence, there are four types of pergola design. A traditional rustic frame is made from poles cut straight from the tree and nailed together. A straightforward pergola is made from sawn square sections notched and screwed together. A slightly more elaborate variation on this has the ends of the crossbeams shaped and profiled. Finally, a lean-to pergola is designed to be built up against a wall.

The rustic pergola is exciting to build, but the actual jointing is made more difficult by the fact that the sections are round. Our design for the Classic Pergola (see page 102) is something of a hybrid, with the cross beams made by laminating pairs of planks.

Whatever the design, the structure must be strong and stable enough to withstand high winds. The best way to do this is to fix it with screws, wait for the structure to settle, and then run galvanized bolts through the primary joints.

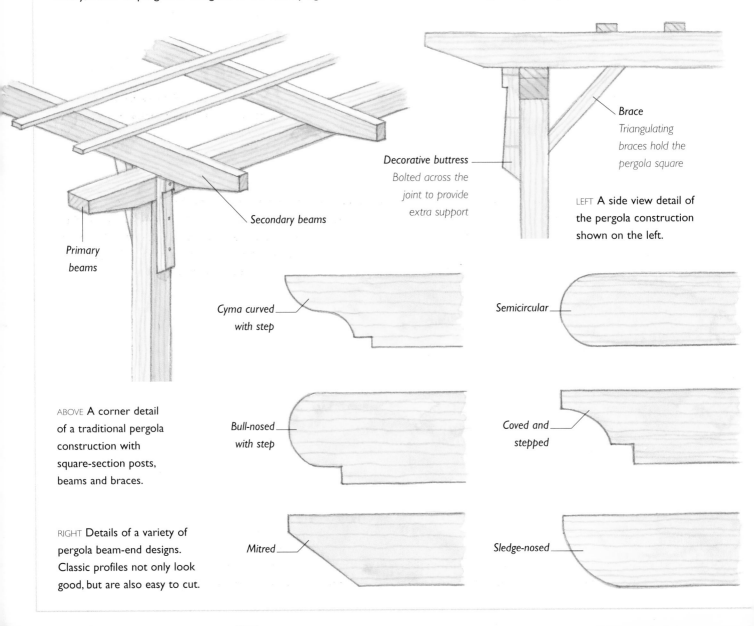

Secondary beams

Primary beams

Brace
Triangulating braces hold the pergola square

Decorative buttress
Bolted across the joint to provide extra support

LEFT **A side view detail of the pergola construction shown on the left.**

ABOVE **A corner detail of a traditional pergola construction with square-section posts, beams and braces.**

RIGHT **Details of a variety of pergola beam-end designs. Classic profiles not only look good, but are also easy to cut.**

Cyma curved with step

Bull-nosed with step

Mitred

Semicircular

Coved and stepped

Sledge-nosed

TRELLISES

Trellises are traditionally made from sawn lathes arranged in a square or diamond grid pattern. The trellis is either contained within a frame or fixed to a stronger support, and then mounted on a wall, used as a space filler between two posts, or fixed between a wall and a post.

Naked trellis can be used as an effective design motif, but it is mostly used as a support for climbing plants. If you want to use trellis as a plant support, make sure, when purchasing, that it has been treated with a plant-friendly preservative. Some

trellises are painted with toxic preservatives that kill plants on contact. Perhaps the most attractive type of trellis is one described as "riven", which means that the lathes are split rather than sawn, giving the structure a curvy appearance. The highest quality of trellis you can buy is made by hand from riven hardwood such as oak or hazel, and the intersections are fixed with bent and clenched copper nails.

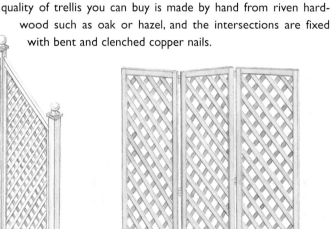

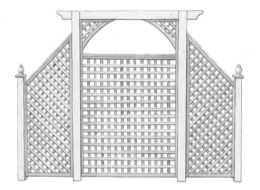

ABOVE A Victorian patio trellis with neo-Japanese beam design. Trellises of this type were traditionally used as freestanding backdrop features at the end of walkways.

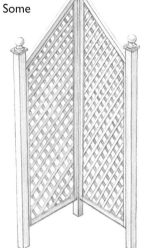

ABOVE Book-fold trellis – this is designed to be used in a corner area.

ABOVE A traditional folding trellis: this can also be used in a conservatory.

PLANTERS

Planters are best defined as self-contained plant-holders. The plants within it have no contact with the ground underlying the planter. Some planters hold earth, but our Corner Patio Planter (see page 84) is designed as a repository for a number of potted plants. Position it on your patio, balcony, or conservatory. The air

space underneath the planter ensures that the structure remains sound and free from rot. When individual plants have passed their best, or you would simply like a change, remove or add plants as desired. The Tiered Patio Planter project (see page 36) gives you the opportunity to create a really dramatic display.

ABOVE A planter with integral trellis and finial posts is a stylish structure.

ABOVE A traditional English design – usually displayed in pairs by a doorway.

ABOVE Pickets are adaptable components, which can be used for constructing various planters. Small ones are suitable for window boxes; larger versions are good for grander patio containers.

Finishing

In the context of garden woodwork, the term "finishing" has very little to do with bringing the surface of the wood to a smooth, shiny finish – as you would do when building fine furniture. Rather, it is the procedure of finishing a project by ensuring a satisfactory colour and surface texture, which is suitably protected or preserved.

SANDING

Sanding or rubbing down is the process of using sandpaper to smooth wood to a textural finish that suits your requirements. The degree of sanding is a matter of personal choice. For example, while you might want to sand the handles and arms of the Wheeled Bench (see page 70) to a really butter-smooth finish, you might well do no more than remove large splinters from the sides of the Classic Arbour (see page 64). We employ a power sander because it is so quick and easy to use. When fitted with a coarse sandpaper, it is possible to sculpt wood to shape – as shown by the handles of the Rabbit Ark (see page 96).

APPLYING PAINTS, STAINS AND PRESERVATIVES

RIGHT Deciding how to paint and/or preserve garden woodwork is not always straightforward. Bright colours, although appealing, may be too dominant in your garden, particularly in winter, so choose carefully. Always read the directions for applying paint and preservative and wear protective gloves.

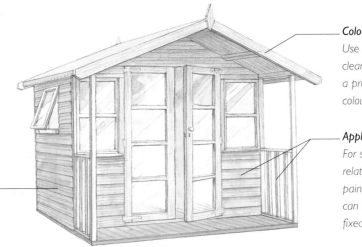

Colour
Use exterior paint over a clear preservative, or choose a product that preserves and colours in one go

Application
For speed, use brush sizes that relate to the size of area you are painting – smelly preservatives can be applied using a brush fixed to the end of a stick

Preserving
Most exterior woodwork should be painted with preservative

Colourwashing
Colourwashing is the technique of diluting a water-based paint with water, and painting the resulting wash over the wood. This can then be rubbed through in places if desired, to reveal the underlying wood. We like this finish for many reasons – it is possible to mix an unlimited range of subtle colours, it is very cheap, it is non-toxic, and the finish blends in with nature. When choosing your paints, make sure that they are the water-based type specifically designed for exterior use.

Painting
Unlike interior painting, where you nearly always need to sand wood to a smooth finish first, or the exterior painting of woodwork such as doors and windows, for which spirit-based gloss paints are mostly used, painting garden woodwork involves very little sanding and is done with water-based paints. All we do is rub down the wood to remove the worst of the splinters and then brush on the paint. The more textured the wood, and the thicker the paint, the more exciting and dynamic the finish achieved. When the paint is dry, we favour rubbing though areas of paint to create a worn and weathered appearance.

Preserving
Not so long ago, the only product for preserving garden wood-work was dark brown creosote, but now there are many other options. You can buy wood that has been pre-treated with a clear or coloured preservative, or apply a preservative yourself. Alternatively, you can paint the wood and then give the item a coat of clear preserva-tive. For structures such as gates and fencing, which you do not come into close contact with, a good coat of creosote takes a bit of beating. But for items such as tables and benches, and particularly the Children's Playhouse (see page 122), you must ensure that a non-toxic preservative is used.

> **USEFUL TIP**
>
> If you want to avoid using paints and preservatives altogether, opt for a long-lasting wood such as Western red cedar.

Maintenance

Maintenance is the procedure of keeping garden woodwork in good order and fit for its intended purpose. Every autumn and spring, make sure that fixings are firm and have not rusted, check that wood is sound, and apply paint or preservative if necessary. You will then be able to enjoy your wooden items for many years to come.

REPAIRING AND REPLACING

Repairing and replacing

The forces of nature and normal wear and tear mean that garden woodwork is under constant attack. Metal may rust, wood may go mouldy, or structures may break from misuse. If you want your projects to last for more than a couple of seasons, you do need to spend time repairing and replacing fixings that are less than sound.

You will need to oil hinges and latches, make sure screws are free from rust, replace pieces of rotten or broken wood, renew torn or pierced roof felt, add more bolts, and so on. The best time to do these tasks is in the early spring (after the wind and rain of winter and before the peak garden season of summer) and then again in the autumn (after a summer's use and before the winter). By following this routine conscientiously, you can expect most of the projects to last for up to ten years.

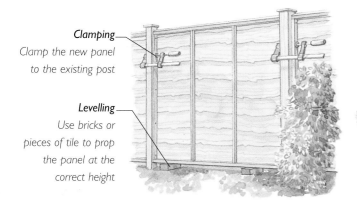

Clamping
Clamp the new panel to the existing post

Levelling
Use bricks or pieces of tile to prop the panel at the correct height

ABOVE Replacing a damaged fence panel. Fences made from thin wood, resembling this one, will need regular maintenance.

Procedure for mending a fence panel

1 Remove dying foliage and tie plants back so that you are able to move freely around the fence panel. Discuss the situation with your neighbour if it is a boundary fence.

2 Remove the broken panel along with any clips or fixings, and make sure that both posts are sound and in good order. Give the posts a generous coat of a suitable preservative.

3 Take your replacement panel and position it between the two posts. Check the level and make height adjustments by standing the panel on bricks or tiles.

4 Clamp the panel in place. Drill holes from the edge of the panel through into the post and fix with galvanized screws.

Procedure for mending feather-edged cladding

1 Wedge the overlapping board out of the way, and use a pair of long-nosed pliers or a wire cutter to snip the nails or screws so that the damaged piece of wood falls away.

2 Buy a length of feather-edged board to match the damaged piece and cut it to fit.

3 Ease the new board up under the overlapping board and use a clamp to hold it in place. Remove the wedge.

4 Drill pilot holes through the new board and its underlying piece and fix in place with galvanized screws.

Procedure for mending a felt roof

1 Cut around the hole in the roof and remove the damaged felt, together with any accumulated grit and debris.

2 Daub a generous amount of felt adhesive in and around the hole and let it dry completely.

3 Daub more adhesive over the first layer, then stick a patch of new felt over the damage and fix with flat-headed galvanized nails.

4 Finally, stick a larger patch of felt over the first patch, which covers all the nail heads with a generous overlap.

Fixing
Glue and nail the first patch and then glue the top patch over the first

Ladder
A board under the ladder stops it sinking into the ground

ABOVE Felt roofs can suffer after a bout of hot or severe weather. The double-patch procedure avoids nailing through the exposed felt.

Part 2: **Projects**

Tiered patio planter

If you have ever stared enviously at the stunning displays of flowers exhibited at professional flower shows, and wondered how the designers manage to achieve such beautiful cascading tiers of blooms, this project tells you how. To create a similar effect, you need to display flowers on a purpose-built tiered planter.

TIME

Two days' work (about a day to mark out and cut the wood, and the rest of the time for putting together and finishing).

USEFUL TIP

An electric compound mitre saw can be used instead of a mitre saw. This is a relatively inexpensive tool, which is really good for cutting repeat angles in small-section wood.

EXPLODED VIEW OF THE TIERED PATIO PLANTER

Shelf
207 mm x 100 mm x 20 mm

668 mm long

Shelf support
321 mm x 50 mm x 30 mm

369 mm long

Bracket piece
235 mm x 50 mm x 30 mm

1.048 m long
Top face positioned 720 mm from base

397 mm long

559 mm long

511 mm long

1.48 m long
Top face positioned
360 mm from base

612 mm long

Leg
1.3 m x 100 mm x 20 mm

40 mm gap between shelves

774 mm long

727 mm long

Leg
1.285 m x 100 mm x 20 mm

YOU WILL NEED

Materials *for a planter 1.1 m high, 1.5 m wide and 690 mm deep. (All rough-sawn pine pieces include excess length for wastage.)*
- Pine: 7 pieces, each 3 m long, 100 mm wide and 20 mm thick (shelves, legs and braces)
- Pine: 6 pieces, each 2 m long, 50 mm wide and 30 mm thick (shelf supports)
- Zinc-plated, countersunk cross-headed screws: 100 x 38 mm no. 8, 50 x 50 mm no. 10,
- Acrylic paint, colour to suit
- Clear preservative

Tools
- Pencil, ruler, tape measure, marking gauge and square
- Portable workbench and G-clamp
- Plywood workboard about 1 m square
- Crosscut saw
- Cordless electric drill with a cross-point screwdriver bit
- Drill bits to match the screw sizes
- Electric compound mitre saw
- Electric sander with a pack of medium-grade sandpaper
- Paintbrush: 40 mm

A HIGH-RISE DISPLAY

This planter is designed to be pushed against a wall, with the flowers being viewed from the front. However, the height of the stand and the fact that it is based on a hexagon also mean that the display will be cone-like in form – so if you were to arrange 50 potted plants on it, you would see a towering hill of blooms.

The tiered shelves enable you to design a display where the focus is directed towards the plants rather than their pots. We have painted the wood a rich red colour, so that when there are gaps in the display and the supporting skeleton peeks through, it looks attractive. The structure stands well over a metre high, but even so, the splay of the legs allows it to be fully loaded without any danger of it tipping forward.

Because you are likely to be watering the plants daily, we have given the wood extra protection by sealing the paint with a coat of clear preservative. You may prefer to go for a brown colour rather than the red we have used, but do not use a high-odour preservative such as creosote, because the plants will not like it.

Step-by-step: **Making the tiered patio planter**

Workboard
*Square the top support
with the workboard*

Screwholes
*Drill holes for the screws to
avoid splitting the wood*

*Parallel
supports*
*Make sure
that the three
shelf supports
are parallel to
one another*

Cordless driver
*Charge the
driver the
day before
you start
the project*

Supports
*Butt the
supports
together so
that they
meet on the
centre-line*

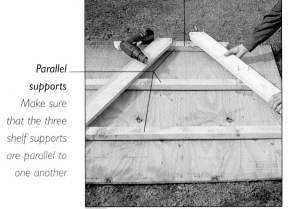

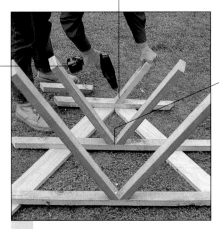

1 Take the two legs that make the primary back frame and centre them on top of the three primary shelf supports. Butt the legs together at the top, check the angles and squareness, and drive 38 mm screws through into the legs.

2 Turn the back frame over so that the shelf supports are uppermost, and screw the secondary supports in place with 50 mm screws – so that they angle out at 60° from the centre. Take care: the structure is fragile at this stage.

Screwing
*Position the
screws to
avoid knots*

3 Set the secondary legs in place, so that they meet at top centre, and screw them to the side of the supports with one 38 mm screw at each intersection. Check the angles and positioning and then drive in the second screws.

Helpful hint

If you find that the whole structure is difficult to support while you work, you could either ask a friend to help or secure the various components with clamps.

Power cable
Make sure the power cable is clear of the saw

Screw position
Make sure you do not put a screw close to the end of the support

Caution
Switch off the power before moving the workpiece

Shelf centre
Align the ends of the shelves with the centre-line of the supports

Shelf position
Butt the shelves together on the centre-line

 4 Clamp the electric compound mitre saw on the portable workbench, check that it is stable, and set the machine to cut at an angle of 60°. Cut all the shelves to length.

5 Starting at the bottom tier and working upwards, set the shelf boards in place on the supports, with the butted ends of the shelves meeting the centre-line of the supports. Screw in place with 38 mm screws.

6 Fix the two bracket pieces in place in the angle on the underside of the top shelf, using 50 mm screws. Finally, rub down the wood to remove the splinters, give it a thin wash of acrylic paint and brush on the clear preservative.

Screwdriver
You might need to use a hand screwdriver at this stage if your cordless driver is too big

Angled support
Drive the screw home so that the bracket is a tight fit

Folding screen

A folding screen is a very useful item for the garden. It can be used to create a separate space or "room", which might be used for relaxing, or for a dining area, or even for a children's play corner. If you yearn for somewhere to sneak off to and read a book, find a nice quiet part of the garden or yard, preferably by lots of flowers or a favourite plant, and site the screen so that you have your own private space. Even greater privacy is available if you clothe the screen in climbing plants.

TIME

Two long days' work (most of the time for building the screen, and about an hour to get it sited).

USEFUL TIP

If you decide to open the screen wider than 90°, it will need to be secured with pegs or spiked post supports.

YOU WILL NEED

Materials *for a screen 1.174 m square and 2.289 m high. (All rough-sawn pine pieces include excess length for wastage.)*

- Pine: 4 pieces, each 3 m long and 70 mm square (main posts)
- Pine: 4 pieces, each 2 m long and 70 mm square (main horizontal rails)
- Ready-made pine trellis screens: 2 screens, 1.86 m high and 930 mm wide
- Pine dowel: 8 pieces of 10 mm dowel, each 70 mm long (for pegging the joints)
- Pine turned balls: 4 balls with screws to fit (post finials)
- Galvanized steel fence panel U-clips: 12 with screws to fit
- Galvanized steel large butt door hinges: 2 with screws to fit
- Clear preservative

Tools

- Pencil, ruler, tape measure, marking gauge and square
- Portable workbench
- Mallet
- Bevel-edged chisel, 30 mm wide
- Crosscut saw
- Small axe
- Claw hammer
- Electric drill with a 10 mm flat bit
- Cordless electric drill with a cross-point screwdriver bit
- Drill bits to match the screw sizes
- Electric sander with a pack of medium-grade sandpaper
- Paintbrush: 40 mm

EXPLODED VIEW OF THE FOLDING SCREEN

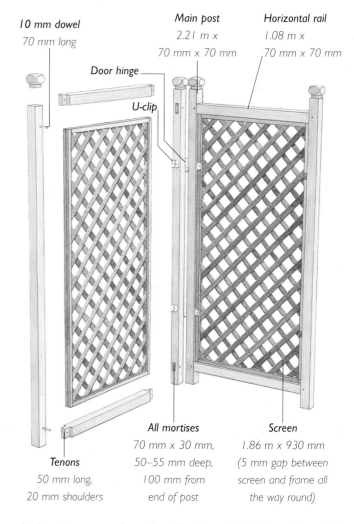

10 mm dowel 70 mm long

Door hinge

U-clip

Main post 2.21 m x 70 mm x 70 mm

Horizontal rail 1.08 m x 70 mm x 70 mm

Tenons 50 mm long, 20 mm shoulders

All mortises 70 mm x 30 mm, 50–55 mm deep, 100 mm from end of post

Screen 1.86 m x 930 mm (5 mm gap between screen and frame all the way round)

A COSY, QUIET CORNER

The folding screen is portable, but it is not terribly easy to move, so the idea is that it is installed in the garden in the spring, and stored away in the winter. The way it folds allows you to set it up at an angle that is greater than 90°.

You may decide to use the screen as a permanent feature, for example as a backdrop for a wall mask fountain, with the lattice being employed to disguise the workings of the fountain. Alternatively, it could become a support for a vine or other climbing plant. In either case, the feet need to be held secure in spiked post supports for safety. The frame is held together with tenons on the ends of the rails and mortises in the posts. The ready-made trellis screens are fitted with panel U-clips. The shop-bought ball finials are simply screwed into the top of the posts.

Because we chose to use contrasting materials for this project – brown-stained trellis screens and natural finish posts – we decided to protect the wood with a clear preservative to retain the freshness of the colour contrast.

Step-by-step: **Making the folding screen**

Mallet size
Choose a solid mallet
with a square-faced head

Chisel grip
Hold the chisel
firmly and keep
it upright

1 Set out the blind mortises on all four main posts – 100 mm along from the ends, 30 mm wide and 70 mm long – and chop them out with the mallet and chisel. Aim to cut the mortises slightly over 50 mm deep.

On target
Make sure the mallet hits the
axe head and not the handle

Grain
If the wood is
not straight-
grained, use a
saw rather
than the axe

2 Set out the tenons on the ends of all four main horizontal rails, making them 50 mm long and 30 mm wide, with 20 mm-wide shoulders to the sides. Next, saw down to the waste side of the shoulder-line, then clear the waste wood using the axe and chisel.

Hole alignment
Align the holes
and gently tap
the dowel into
place (avoid
hitting it too
hard, which
may damage
the dowel or
the frame)

3 Knock the joint together, then drill a 10 mm hole right through the joint and peg it with a length of dowel. Screw the finial balls in place.

Helpful hint

If you damage a dowel while knocking it into the hole – or the dowel breaks off – use a hammer with a screwdriver to drive the dowel through the joint and out the other side. Check that the drilled hole is big enough for the dowel before trying again.

Equal gap
Maintain a 5 mm gap between trellis and frame all the way round

4 Screw six U-clips on each frame, bending the tabs out and fitting the trellis in place, then bending the tabs back and screwing the clips to the frame.

Trellis
The best trellis is either stapled or nailed at the intersections

U-clips
Choose galvanized clips made from thin metal, which is easy to bend

5 Position the two frames side by side and on edge so that the spine posts are uppermost. Screw the hinges in place (you can either recess the hinges or surface-mount them). Finally, rub down the screen with sandpaper and lay on a coat of clear preservative.

Alignment
Make sure that the two frames are perfectly aligned before you screw the hinges on

Hinge position
Position the hinges to avoid knots

Picket fence

White-painted picket fences conjure up images of country cottages and flower-filled gardens. If you are fed up with your mass-produced garden fence – whether it is ungainly chicken wire or ugly concrete blocks – a picket fence is an attractive solution. (See also the Picket Gate project on page 48.)

(See also the Picket Gate project on page 48.)

TIME

A day for every 2-metre length of fence.

USEFUL TIP

You can adjust the height of the pickets to suit your own requirements.

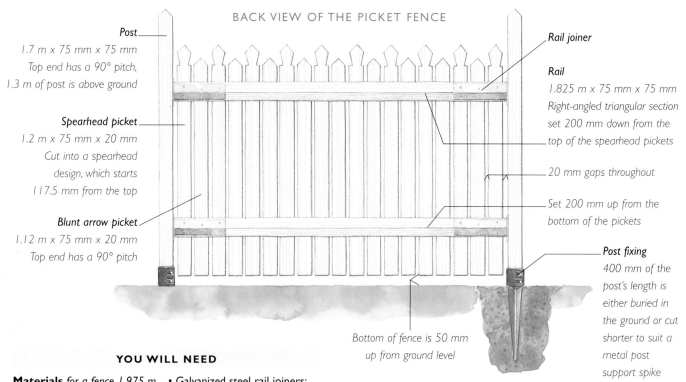

BACK VIEW OF THE PICKET FENCE

Post
1.7 m x 75 mm x 75 mm
Top end has a 90° pitch,
1.3 m of post is above ground

Spearhead picket
1.2 m x 75 mm x 20 mm
Cut into a spearhead
design, which starts
117.5 mm from the top

Blunt arrow picket
1.12 m x 75 mm x 20 mm
Top end has a 90° pitch

Rail joiner

Rail
1.825 m x 75 mm x 75 mm
Right-angled triangular section
set 200 mm down from the
top of the spearhead pickets

20 mm gaps throughout

Set 200 mm up from the
bottom of the pickets

Post fixing
400 mm of the
post's length is
either buried in
the ground or cut
shorter to suit a
metal post
support spike

Bottom of fence is 50 mm
up from ground level

YOU WILL NEED

Materials *for a fence 1.975 m long and 1.3 m high. (All rough-sawn pine pieces include excess length for wastage.)*
- Pine: 10 pieces, each 3 m long, 75 mm wide and 20 mm thick (spearhead pickets and blunt arrow pickets)
- Pine: 2 pieces 75 x 75 mm right-angled triangular section, each 2 m long (rails)
- Pine: 1 piece, 2 m long, 30 mm wide and 20 mm thick (temporary batten)
- Pine: 2 pieces, each 2 m long and 75 mm square (posts)
- Zinc-plated, countersunk cross-headed screws: 200 x 38 mm no. 8

- Galvanized steel rail joiners: 4 to suit your rail size and section
- Matt white exterior-quality paint

Tools
- Pencil, ruler, tape measure, bevel gauge and square
- Crosscut saw
- Two portable workbenches
- Cordless electric drill with a cross-point screwdriver bit
- Drill bit to match the screw size
- Electric sander with a pack of medium-grade sandpaper
- Paintbrush: 40 mm

A COUNTRY COTTAGE FENCE

The fence is made up from two picket designs: the blunt arrows have a finished length of 1.12 m and the spearheads reach 1.2 m. The posts are 1.7 m long, with 400 mm of this set in the ground. The bottom of the fence is positioned about 50 mm up from ground level. The top rail is set 200 mm down from the top of the spearheads, while the bottom rail is set 200 mm up from the bottom of the pickets. We have allowed 50 mm on the length of each picket for cutting waste.

In many ways, this is a kit fence, with the rail and the rail joiners as standard; however the design of the pickets is most certainly something that you can chop and change to suit your own needs. The rails are triangular in cross-section, with the short sides measuring about 75 x 75 mm and the hypotenuse 100 mm. When you come to putting the fence together, the pickets are screwed to the 100 mm face of the rails, the galvanized joiner plates are screwed to the ends of the rails, and the flaps of the joiners are screwed to the posts. Finally, the fence is sanded to remove splinters and painted white.

Step-by-step: **Making the picket fence**

First picket
Screw the first picket 20 mm along from the end of the rails

1 Cut the pickets as described on page 50. Lay the two triangular rails on the workbenches (so that they are parallel and 600 mm apart) and screw a spearhead picket in position 20 mm along from each end of the rail. Screw the temporary batten to the bottom ends of the pickets.

Triangular jig
Use scraps of triangular section to make a cradle for each rail

Spacer
Set a picket on edge as a spacer

2 Using a picket as a spacer, screw the pickets in place so that their ends butt up against the temporary batten. Continue until you have used up all the pickets. Saw the rails to length.

Helpful hint

Stagger the positioning of the screws on each picket – one towards the top of the rail, the other towards the bottom. This avoids splitting the wood. Remember that the rails are triangular, so do not screw near their edges, otherwise the screw will break out of the wood.

Pilot holes
Run pilot holes through the plate holes and into the wood

Drill angle
Hold the drill so that the bit is at 90° to the plate

3 Screw the galvanized joiner plates in position on the triangular rails so that the flaps are flush with the cut ends. Be careful, because the edges of the plates are sharp.

Alignment
Align the face of the flaps with the end of the rail

Angled top
Make two 45° cuts to create the 90° pitched top

Picket pattern
The shoulders of the spearhead pickets should align with the corners of the blunt arrow pickets

Saw cut
Start the saw cut with several strokes pulling towards you

Screw angle
Run the screw in at a slight angle so that it avoids the edge of the post

Rail joiner
The joiner becomes stronger when all the screws are in position

4 Take the two posts and set out the top ends with a 90° pitch. Saw off the waste and use the sander to give the sawn faces a quick rub-down – just enough to remove the splinters and rough edges.

5 Align the fence with the posts (so that the joiner plate flaps are aligned with the back edge of the post) and screw it into position. Fix the posts as described on page 51. Finally, sand off the splinters and paint the whole fence white.

Picket gate

Of all the projects in the book, the picket gate is, at one and the same time, one of

the prettiest, easiest to build, and most eye-catching. If you are looking to create a

garden with the appeal of a traditional cottage plot, which will be complemented by

a little gate that invites opening, this is the project for you. The gate can, of course,

be incorporated into the Picket Fence project on page 44.

be incorporated into the Picket Fence project on page 44.

TIME

A weekend (a long day for building the gate and a day to get it into position).

USEFUL TIP

Don't be tempted to cut costs on the hinges: they need to be heavy-duty and galvanized.

YOU WILL NEED

Materials *for a gate 995 mm wide and 1.3 m high. (All rough-sawn pine pieces include excess length for wastage.)*

• Pine: 9 pieces, each 1.185 m long, 75 mm wide and 20 mm thick (spearhead pickets)
• Pine: 1 piece, 3 m long, 100 mm wide and 20 mm thick (horizontal rails and diagonal brace)
• Pine: 2 pieces, each 2 m long and 75 mm square (gateposts)
• Pine: 1 piece, 2 m long, 30 mm square (gate stop)
• Painted steel post support spikes: 2 complete with bolts (to support the gateposts)
• Heavy-duty, galvanized steel reversible strap hinges: 2 with screws and coach bolts to fit
• Galvanized steel latch: 1 with screws to fit

• Zinc-plated, countersunk cross-headed screws:
100 x 38 mm no. 8
50 x 50 mm no. 8
• Matt white exterior-quality paint

Tools

• Pencil, ruler, tape measure, bevel gauge and square
• Portable workbench
• Plywood workboard about 1.5 m square
• Jigsaw
• Cordless electric drill with a cross-point screwdriver bit
• Drill bits to match the screw sizes
• Crosscut saw
• Sledgehammer
• Spanner to fit your chosen coach bolts
• Electric sander with a pack of medium-grade sandpaper
• Paintbrush: 40 mm

BACK VIEW OF THE PICKET GATE

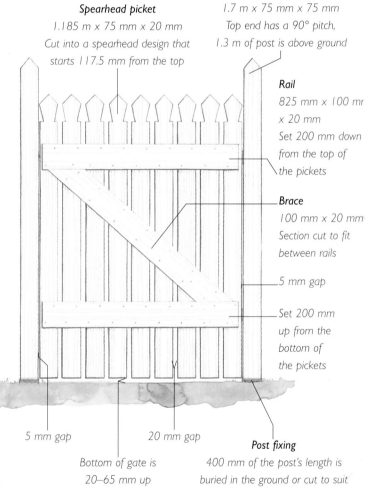

Spearhead picket
1.185 m x 75 mm x 20 mm
Cut into a spearhead design that starts 117.5 mm from the top

Post
1.7 m x 75 mm x 75 mm
Top end has a 90° pitch,
1.3 m of post is above ground

Rail
825 mm x 100 mm x 20 mm
Set 200 mm down from the top of the pickets

Brace
100 mm x 20 mm
Section cut to fit between rails

5 mm gap

Set 200 mm up from the bottom of the pickets

5 mm gap

20 mm gap

Bottom of gate is 20–65 mm up from ground level

Post fixing
400 mm of the post's length is buried in the ground or cut to suit a metal post support spike

PICTUREBOOK PICKET GATE

Although the gate is designed to complement the picket fence, we have varied the design slightly by using spearhead pickets throughout. You do not have to follow suit, but this shows that it is possible to change the emphasis of the design simply by opting for one arrangement of pickets rather than another.

The 75 mm-wide pickets are spaced 20 mm apart and screwed to the 100 mm-wide horizontal rails, and then the arrangement is braced with a single diagonal. Note how the brace – with this gate or any gate – is always fitted so that the bottom end is on the hinge side, and also how the rails are cut slightly shorter than the total width of the gate. We opted for using the

post support spikes for three good reasons. Not only are they wonderfully easy to fit – you just bang them in and the job is done, but they instantly make the posts firm, and the whole operation can be managed without the need to mess up the site by digging holes. The gate is naturally quite strong, but the galvanized strap hinges greatly increase its strength, because the screws and coach bolts clench the layers together tightly.

Step-by-step: **Making the picket gate**

First cut
Cut inwards from the side first

Clamp
Secure the workpiece with a clamp

Jigsaw
Cut to the waste side of the drawn line

1 Take the 1.185 m-long pickets and set out the spearheads with 90° tops. Position the shoulders 117.5 mm down. Fret out the shape with the jigsaw.

Right angles
Make sure that the rails cross the pickets at right angles

2 Place the spearhead pickets on the workboard, cross them with the horizontal rails, check the alignment and spacing, and fix with two 38 mm screws at each crossover intersection.

Helpful hint

To double-check that the gate is square, you can use the workboard (which should be square) as a guide. First drive in one screw at each joint, align the gate with a corner of the workboard (pushing it into a square shape if needed) and then drive in the second lot of screws.

Angled joint
Butt the diagonal hard
up against the rail

3 Using the crosscut saw, cut the diagonal brace to length so that it fits the diagonal. Trim the ends to fit the angles, and then butt it in place and fix with 38 mm screws. Use two screws for each intersection.

Screwing
Use two screws
to fix each
picket to the
diagonal brace

Adjustments
You may need
to make
adjustments to
the angle on
the ends of the
diagonal brace

Post offcut
Put a post offcut in the post support spike
while you are hitting it into the ground

Hinge type
Use heavyweight
galvanized hinges

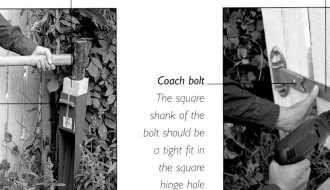

Bolt position
Position the
spike so that
you will be
able to reach
the bolt

Coach bolt
The square
shank of the
bolt should be
a tight fit in
the square
hinge hole

Gate height
Use a scrap of
wood to prop
up the gate at
the correct
height

4 Cut the two gateposts to shape as shown on page 47. Use the sledgehammer to bang the two post support spikes into place so that they are flush with the ground. Trim the bottom of the posts to fit and bolt them in position.

5 Rub down the gate and gateposts with the sander and paint them white. Hang the gate in position, complete with strap hinges and latch. Using 50 mm screws, fix the gate stop to the catch post and paint it white.

Inspirations: Decorative gates

Garden gates hint at what lies beyond them. A gate needs to be functional, but it should also express a message. It might say, "Please come in", "Welcome", or perhaps "This part of the garden is a haven, the perfect place to sit and ponder." The design can be straightforward and inexpensive to realize, or you may prefer to embellish your garden with a customized design that makes use of more expensive varieties of wood and carefully crafted details.

ABOVE **A beautiful oak gate complete with finials, lapped and pegged joints, chamfered details and forged iron strap hinges. Its** artistic appearance complements the formal clipped hedges that border it and suggests an interesting garden beyond.

LEFT **A simple picket gate is the perfect partner for this pretty country garden. It is low in height, strong enough to keep children and pets in, and above all it is welcoming. If you want to make an inexpensive gate, this is a good type to choose.**

ABOVE **A beautifully constructed gate, with vertical square-section staves contained within a simple frame. Each rail is made from two components that have been cut, stepped and bolted together to sandwich the staves.**

Multi-shaped decking

If your garden is the focus for an ever-changing programme of activities – an area for

the children to play and a place for hosting family barbecues or entertaining friends,

all of which would benefit from a hard standing – our super modular decking is a

good option. The decking can be shaped to suit your needs.

TIME

A weekend (about a day to make the three frames and the rest of the time for fixing the decking).

USEFUL TIP

You can cut the decking with a hand saw, but it is much easier to use an inexpensive electric compound mitre saw.

YOU WILL NEED

Materials *for 3 decking shapes 1 m wide and 2 m long. (All rough-sawn pine pieces include excess length for wastage.)*
- Pine: 6 pieces, each 2 m long, 150 mm wide and 20 mm thick (long side frame boards)
- Pine: 5 pieces, each 3 m long, 150 mm wide and 20 mm thick (short end frame boards and dividing support planks)
- Pine: 24 pieces, each 3 m long, 95 mm wide and 18 mm thick (grooved decking)
- Pine: 4 pieces, each 2 m long and 100 mm square (legs)
- Zinc-plated, countersunk cross-headed screws: 200 x 38 mm no. 8, 100 x 50 mm no. 10

- Green acrylic paint
- Clear preservative

Tools
- Pencil, ruler, tape measure, compass, bevel gauge and square
- Two portable workbenches
- Crosscut saw
- Electric drill with a 50 mm-diameter saw-toothed cutter to fit
- Electric jigsaw
- Cordless electric drill and cross-point screwdriver bit
- Drill bits to match screws
- Electric compound mitre saw
- Electric sander with a pack of medium-grade sandpaper
- Paintbrush: 40 mm

HIGH AND DRY AND SITTING COMFORTABLY

This is, without doubt, one of the simplest projects in the book. In essence, it is no more than three frames (each the size of a single bed), which are clad with grooved decking boards. Each frame is made up from six 200 mm-long legs, with the four side boards and three dividing boards all put together in such a way that the finished frame makes a module precisely 1 m wide and 2 m long. The idea of the decking is that the three frames can variously be fitted end to end, side by side, end to side, or in any combination to create a surface that always measures a number of whole metres in width and depth. The spacing of the grooved decking allows good airflow, and the handle holes make it easy to lift.

The middle legs are centred on the long side frame board; the middle dividing support plank is screwed to one side of the middle leg, with the other two dividing planks set to quarter the total length. We painted the side and end frame boards green, but you might prefer a natural finish or perhaps a more startling colour.

EXPLODED VIEW OF THE MULTI-SHAPED DECKING

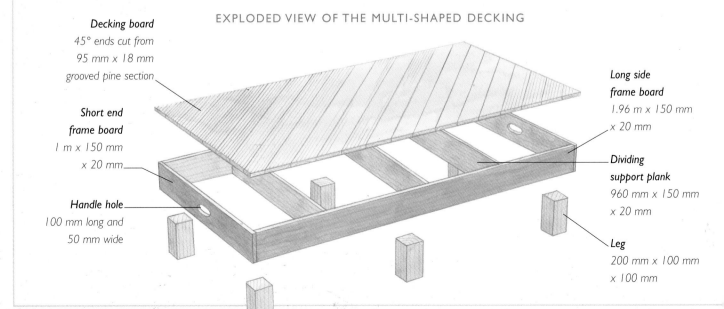

Decking board
45° ends cut from 95 mm x 18 mm grooved pine section

Short end frame board
1 m x 150 mm x 20 mm

Handle hole
100 mm long and 50 mm wide

Long side frame board
1.96 m x 150 mm x 20 mm

Dividing support plank
960 mm x 150 mm x 20 mm

Leg
200 mm x 100 mm x 100 mm

Step-by-step: **Making the multi-shaped decking**

Saw-toothed cutter
Hold the drill perfectly upright

Clamping
You may want to use a clamp to hold the board still

Spacer
Use a spare piece of 20 mm-thick board as a spacer to help you position the leg

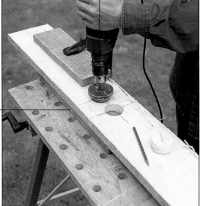

Waste board
Put a piece of waste board under the hole to be drilled

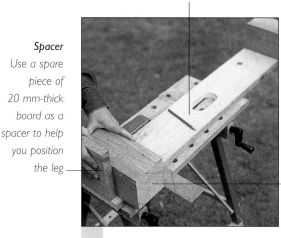

Flush fit
Slide the leg down until the top is flush with the board

1 Use the crosscut saw to cut the short end frame boards to size (1 m long). Draw out the handle holes, making them 100 mm long and 50 mm wide, and clear the waste with the electric drill and saw-toothed cutter, and the jigsaw.

2 Cut the 100 mm-square wood for the legs into eighteen 200 mm lengths – one for each leg. Set two legs 20 mm in from the ends of the short end frame boards, check that they are square and fix them with 50 mm screws.

Middle leg
Position the leg halfway along the board

3 Cut the long side frame boards to a length of 1.96 m and fix the middle leg in position with 50 mm screws. Butt the end of each board in place on the side of the corner legs and hard up against the inside face of the short end frame board, and fix with 50 mm screws.

Helpful hint

Search out a level area of lawn to work on. Ask a friend to help hold the frame upright while you work, or clamp the frame to a workbench.

Clamping
Clamp the end of the frame in the jaws of the vice

Divider position
Screw the middle divider to one side of the leg

4 Bridge the frame across the two workbenches and fix the three 960 mm-long dividing support planks in place. Screw the middle divider to the legs with 38 mm screws, and fix the quarter dividers with 50 mm screws running through the long side board.

Screw fixing
Locate the divider by screwing through the long side frame boards and into the end of the divider

5 Set the electric compound mitre saw to an angle of 45° and set to work cutting the decking to length. Cut the longest boards first and fill in the corners with the various offcuts. Sand all the boards. Paint the long side frame and short end frame boards green. Seal the completed decking module with a coat of clear preservative.

Screws
Use two 38 mm screws at each end of the lengths of decking

Screws
Use one or two 38 mm screws at the points where the decking crosses the dividing support planks

Decorative picnic table

There is something really enjoyable about eating outdoors. There are fewer worries about etiquette or spillages when you gather to eat around a picnic table, guaranteeing that any meal is a relaxed affair. The beauty of this table is that it can live outside all year, and doesn't have to be dragged out and assembled to make the most of a sunny day in spring, summer or winter.

YOU WILL NEED

Materials *for a picnic table 1.625 m wide, 1.826 m deep and 720 mm high. (All rough-sawn pine pieces include excess length for wastage.)*
- Pine: 12 pieces, each 2 m long, 150 mm wide and 22 mm thick (tabletop and seat boards; cross supports)
- Pine: 2 pieces, each 2 m long, 100 mm wide and 50 mm thick (legs)
- Pine: 4 pieces, each 2 m long, 75 mm wide and 20 mm thick (diagonal braces and cross tie boards)
- Galvanized coach bolts: 16 bolts, 85 mm long, with 16 nuts and washers to fit
- Zinc-plated, countersunk screws: 100 x 38 mm no. 8 100 x 50 mm no. 8
- Clear preservative

Tools
- Pencil, ruler, tape measure, compass, bevel gauge and square
- Two portable workbenches
- Crosscut saw
- Large clamp
- Electric jigsaw
- Plywood workboard about 1 m square
- Spanner to fit the nuts
- Cordless electric drill with a cross-point screwdriver bit
- Drill bits to match the screw sizes, bolt holes and decorative holes
- Electric sander with a pack of medium-grade sandpaper
- Paintbrush: 40 mm

PICNIC TIME

This table is strong, sturdy, decorative and can seat up to eight. It's longer and wider than most tables, with a central hole for a sun umbrella, and lots of curves and curlicues to make it attractive and user-friendly. We have rounded off all the corners so people will not scrape their shins. The frame is clenched with lots of coach bolts, so it stands absolutely firm. We went out of our way to use boards pre-treated with a water-based, non-toxic preservative: this is vital for a surface where food will be served. We chose to use sawn timber, because we like the texture, but rubbed down all edges and surfaces to a smooth, non-splintering finish.

EXPLODED DETAIL OF THE DECORATIVE PICNIC TABLE

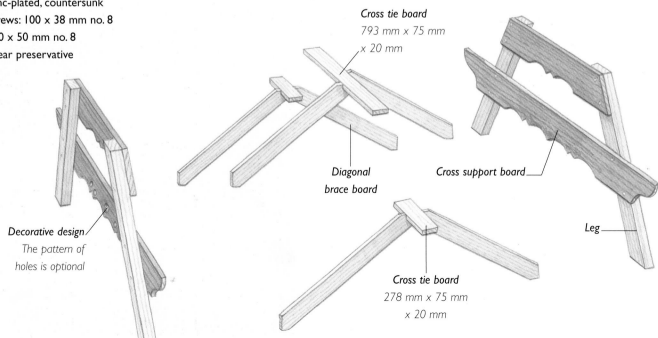

Cross tie board
793 mm x 75 mm x 20 mm

Diagonal brace board

Cross support board

Leg

Decorative design
The pattern of holes is optional

Cross tie board
278 mm x 75 mm x 20 mm

Decorative picnic table

END VIEW OF THE DECORATIVE PICNIC TABLE

Cross support board
1 m x 150 mm x 22 mm
59° ends

Spaced 150 mm apart

1 grid square
equals 20 mm

Cross support board
1.783 m x 150 mm x 22 mm
59° ends

1 grid square
equals 20 mm

Leg
880 mm x 100 mm x 50 mm
59° ends

Diagonal brace board
646 mm x 75 mm x 20 mm
Same joints as the diagonal
brace below

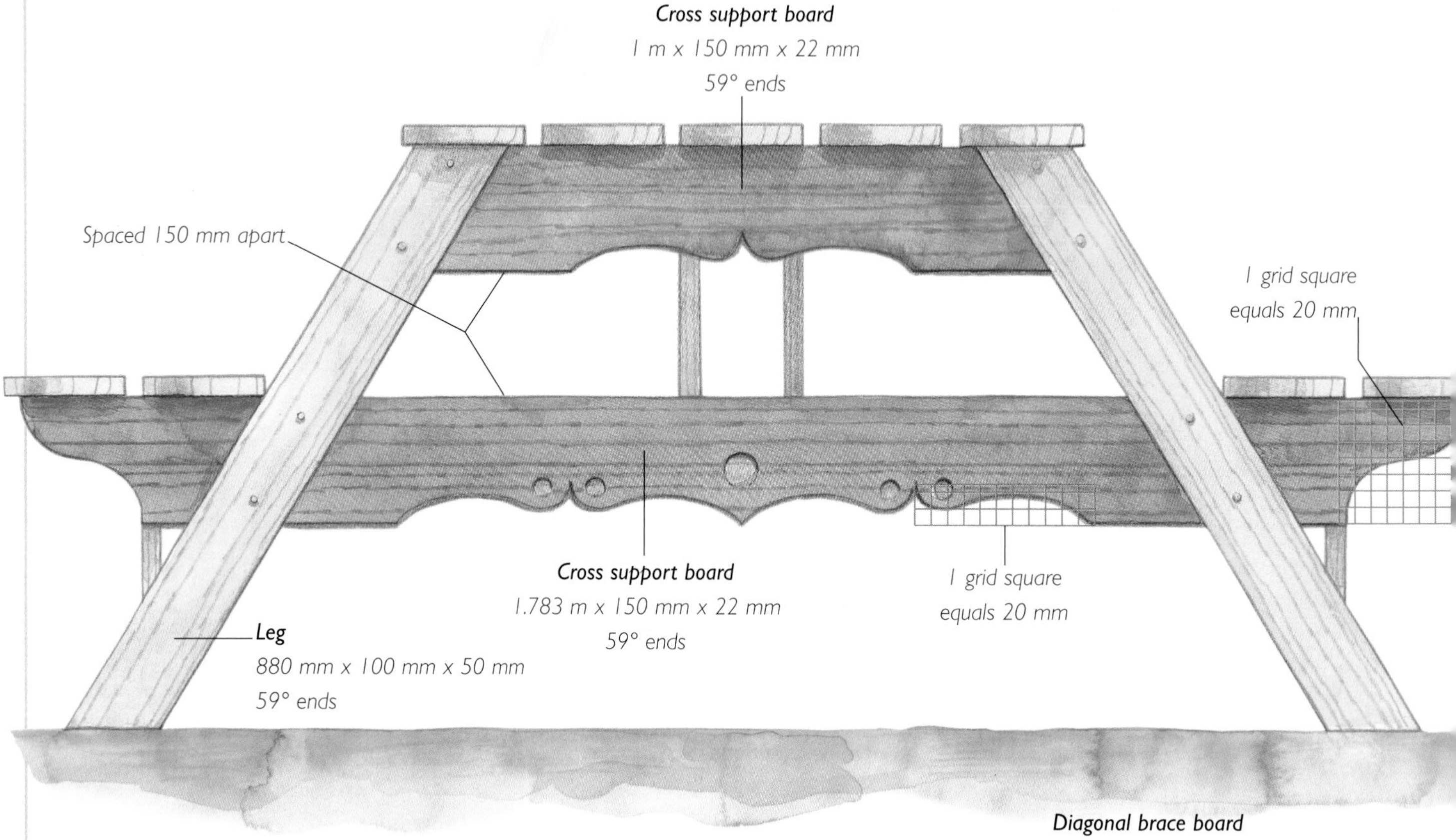

FRONT VIEW OF THE
DECORATIVE PICNIC TABLE

1 grid square
equals 20 mm

Diagonal brace board
671 mm x 75 mm x 20 mm

1 grid square
equals 20 mm

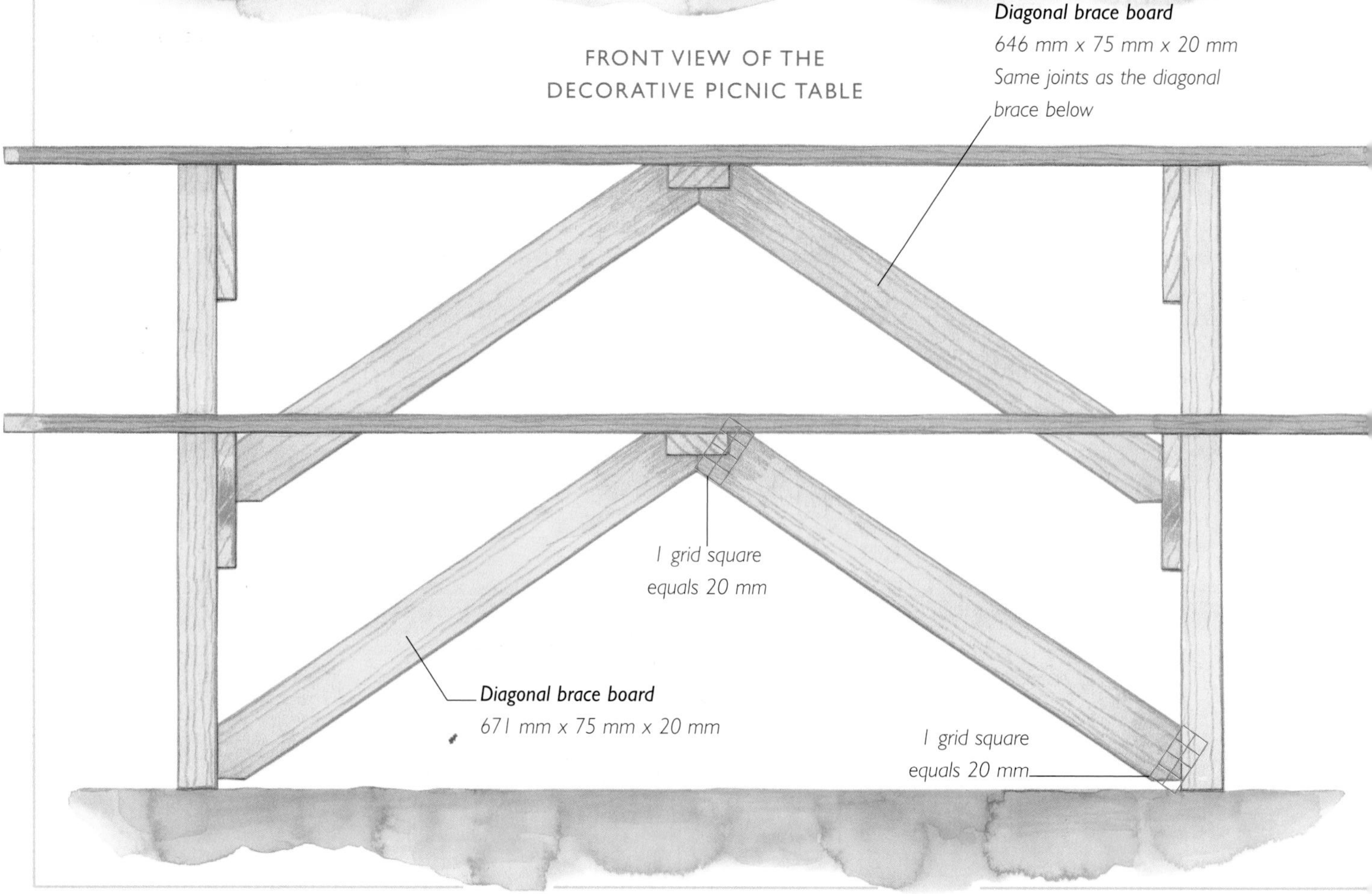

PLAN VIEW OF THE DECORATIVE PICNIC TABLE

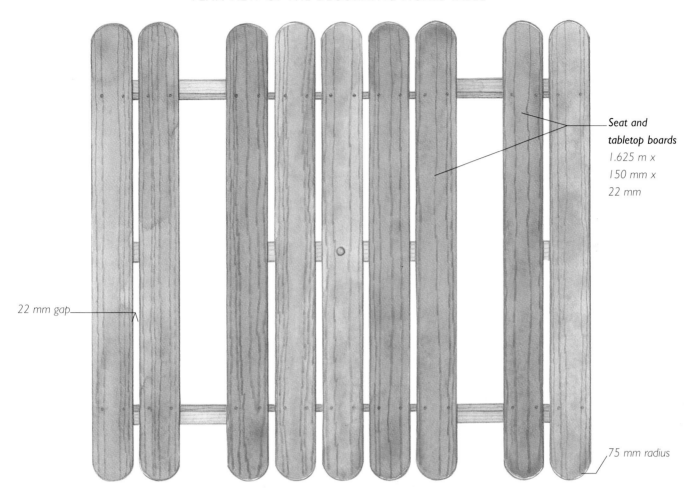

Seat and
tabletop boards
*1.625 m x
150 mm x
22 mm*

22 mm gap

75 mm radius

DETAIL OF HOW THE BRACES ARE FIXED UNDER THE TABLETOP

Tabletop board

Cross tie board

Notched joint
37.5 mm x 20 mm

Diagonal brace board

Step-by-step: **Making the decorative picnic table**

Cutting the curves
Rotate the saw in the direction of the
cut, rather than forcing it sideways

1 Cut the boards to length with the crosscut saw and draw out the imagery. Clamp each workpiece to the workbench and fret out the curves with the jigsaw. Work from side to centre in order to achieve a crisp central cleft.

Clamp position
Put the handle of the clamp under the bench so that it does not get in your way

Board position
Set up the board so that the area to be cut hangs over the bench

2 Set the plywood workboard flat on the ground to support the components, and carefully bolt the legs and the cross supports together. Check the arrangement with a square. Note how the components have been spaced with the aid of a 150 mm-wide board.

Hole size
Check that the hole is large enough for the bolt to pass through easily

Board spacer
Use an offcut of 150 mm-wide board as a spacer

Diagonals
If the diagonal measurements are identical, the table is square

Central hole position
Keep all the screws well away from the centre

Seat board
Butt the seat board against the side of the angled leg

Cross tie board
The cross tie board needs to be positioned centrally and squarely

Screws
Avoid driving the screws below the surface of the wood as they may break through on the other side

3 Link the legs by screwing the two outer seat boards in place with a single 50 mm screw at each joint. Ease the frame until its squareness is confirmed by identical diagonal measurements, and then drive in the other 50 mm screws. Screw all the other seat and tabletop boards in place with 50 mm screws.

4 Screw a cross tie board in place across the underside of the tabletop, using 38 mm screws, with the screws positioned well clear of the actual centre-point, and then bore out a hole for the sun umbrella. Screw the diagonal braces in place with 50 mm screws.

Notched braces
All the braces align with the edge of a plank

5 With 38 mm screws, fix the cross tie boards under the seat boards, and then cut and notch the two diagonal braces so that they butt joint at the centre. Screw the brace boards in place with 50 mm screws. Sand the table to a splinter-free finish and brush on the preservative.

Helpful hint

If you are having trouble fitting the notched braces accurately – maybe the ones you have cut are too long – keep trimming the end of one until it fits perfectly, and then use this as a template for cutting the opposite brace.

Classic arbour

An arbour is not only a practical idea (a perfect way of providing a sheltered seat),

but a beautiful and decorative structure in its own right. With climbing plants grown

up its sides, particularly scented varieties such as jasmine and honeysuckle, you can

create a delightful nook to escape to. Use it as a quiet place to read a book, or make

it a corner for a romantic rendezvous – it's up to you.

YOU WILL NEED

Materials *for an arbour 1.492 m wide, 1.114 m deep and 2.738 m high. (All rough-sawn pine pieces include excess length for wastage.)*
- Lattice screens: 4 screens, 1.83 m x 303 mm (sides)
- Pine: 4 pieces, each 2 m long, 75 x 75 mm square section (main posts)
- Pine: 15 pieces, each 3 m long, 50 mm wide and 32 mm thick (roof and back panels, seat supports and A-brace)
- Pine: 6 pieces, each 3 m long, 150 mm wide and 22 mm thick (top and bottom side boards, seat, decorative barge boards)
- Pine feather-edged board: 20 pieces, each 3 m long, 100 mm wide and 10 mm thick (back panel and roof)

- Zinc-plated countersunk cross-headed screws: 100 x 50 mm no. 8, 100 x 60 mm no. 10, 20 x 89 mm no. 10
- Galvanized wire nails: 1 kg 40 mm x 2.65 mm
- Clear preservative

Tools
- Pencil, ruler, tape measure, compass, bevel gauge and square
- Two portable workbenches
- Cordless electric drill with a cross-point screwdriver bit
- Selection of drill bits to match screw sizes
- Crosscut saw
- Hammer
- Four large clamps
- Electric jigsaw
- Electric sander with a pack of medium-grade sandpaper
- Paintbrush: 40 mm

SIDE VIEW OF THE CLASSIC ARBOUR

Seat support 1.08 m x 50 mm x 32 mm Top face positioned 400 mm from the base

Seat support 1.08 m x 50 mm x 32 mm Top face positioned 1 m from the base

Seat support 1.08 m x 50 mm x 32 mm Front face positioned 200 mm from the back of the seat planks

Seat support 1.08 m x 50 mm x 32 mm Top face positioned 300 mm from the base

CONTEMPLATIVE SEAT FOR TWO

This project is built around four slender lattice screens. Buy the screens first, as you may only be able to obtain them in a slightly different size to that we have quoted, and make adjustments to other materials if necessary. Basically, the arbour is a seat for two enclosed on three sides, with a roof over the top. We have designed the project so that it can be made as six knockdown units – the two lattice sides, the back panel, the two roof panels and the seat – with various other pieces used to support and decorate. The feather-edged boards are lapped in such a way that they channel rain off the roof and back panel. The strength and stability of the overall structure are guaranteed by diagonal braces fixed to both the back panel and the roof. When we went to purchase the materials, the only available lattice screens and 150 mm boards were pre-treated with rather heavy brown wood preservative, so we decided to lift the design by leaving all the other components in their natural colour.

Classic arbour

EXPLODED VIEW OF THE CLASSIC ARBOUR

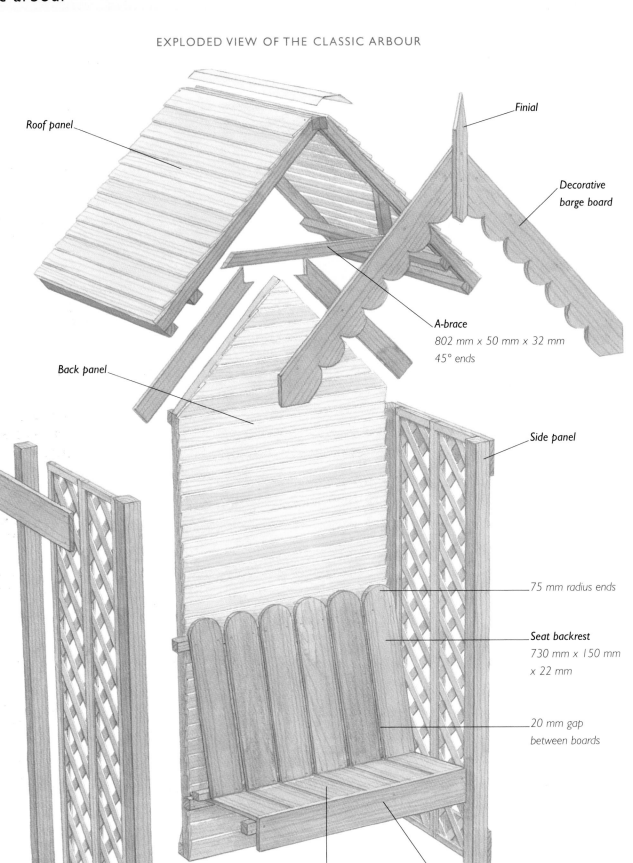

Roof panel

Finial

Decorative
barge board

A-brace
*802 mm x 50 mm x 32 mm
45° ends*

Back panel

Side panel

75 mm radius ends

Seat backrest
*730 mm x 150 mm
x 22 mm*

*20 mm gap
between boards*

Seat boards
610 mm x 150 mm x 22 mm

Seat apron board
1 m x 150 mm x 22 mm

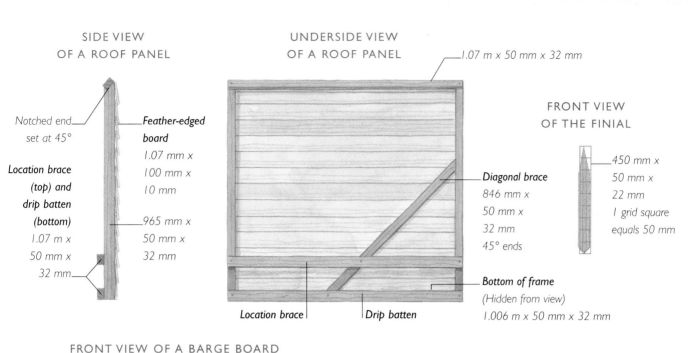

SIDE VIEW OF A ROOF PANEL

Notched end set at 45°

Feather-edged board 1.07 mm x 100 mm x 10 mm

Location brace (top) and drip batten (bottom) 1.07 m x 50 mm x 32 mm

965 mm x 50 mm x 32 mm

UNDERSIDE VIEW OF A ROOF PANEL

1.07 m x 50 mm x 32 mm

Diagonal brace 846 mm x 50 mm x 32 mm 45° ends

Bottom of frame (Hidden from view) 1.006 m x 50 mm x 32 mm

Location brace

Drip batten

FRONT VIEW OF THE FINIAL

450 mm x 50 mm x 22 mm 1 grid square equals 50 mm

FRONT VIEW OF A BARGE BOARD

1.131 m x 150 mm x 22 mm 1 grid square equals 50 mm 45° ends

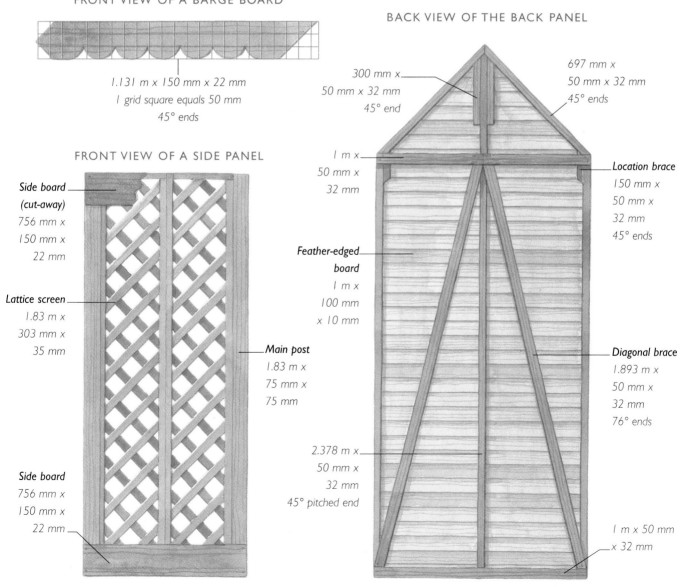

FRONT VIEW OF A SIDE PANEL

Side board (cut-away) 756 mm x 150 mm x 22 mm

Lattice screen 1.83 m x 303 mm x 35 mm

Main post 1.83 m x 75 mm x 75 mm

Side board 756 mm x 150 mm x 22 mm

BACK VIEW OF THE BACK PANEL

300 mm x 50 mm x 32 mm 45° end

697 mm x 50 mm x 32 mm 45° ends

1 m x 50 mm x 32 mm

Location brace 150 mm x 50 mm x 32 mm 45° ends

Feather-edged board 1 m x 100 mm x 10 mm

Diagonal brace 1.893 m x 50 mm x 32 mm 76° ends

2.378 m x 50 mm x 32 mm 45° pitched end

1 m x 50 mm x 32 mm

Step-by-step: **Making the classic arbour**

Screwing
Drive the screws through the side of the lattice

Block joints
Pre-drill the blocks to prevent splitting

Lattice
Arrange the two screens side by side so that the pattern is aligned

Strengthening
Use long offcuts to strengthen the ridge joint

1 Sandwich the lattice screens between the main posts and screw them in place with 50 mm screws. Set a 150 mm-wide board at top and bottom and screw these to the posts with 50 mm screws. Re-run this procedure so that you have two identical side panels.

2 Use the 50 mm x 32 mm section to make the back frame. Cut the parts to size with the crosscut saw and fix them with 60 mm screws. Screw blocks of waste at the angles to help firm up the joints.

Nailing
Use one nail at each end of the board

Feather-edged board
The boards are lapped so that water runs off the back of the arbour

Overlapping
Make sure that the boards are overlapped in the correct way

Clamping
Set the clamps so that they are away from screw positions

3 Cut the feather-edged board into 1 m lengths and position these on the back frame so that they lap over from top to bottom, ensuring that rain will be thrown off the back of the arbour. Drill pilot holes and fix the strips to the frame with the 40 mm nails.

4 Clamp the two side panels to the back panel and fix with the 60 mm screws. Drive the screws through the edges of the panel and into the posts. Check the structure for squareness and then add the additional horizontal and diagonal braces to the back panel.

Seat support
The planks that form the seat backrest are fixed to two battens

Drip batten
Drill holes for the screws when you are working near the end of a piece of wood

Location brace
The brace locates the roof on the posts and needs to be positioned accurately

Sanding
Sand the seat boards to remove sharp corners and splinters

Diagonal brace
The diagonal brace is used to set the roof panel square

5 Position and fit the base for the seat, and then build off the seat to make the backrest. Fit the seat support battens with 50 mm screws. Use the jigsaw to cut the 75 mm radius curves on the top of the backrest boards. Leave a 20 mm space between the boards on both the seat and the backrest.

6 Build and clad the two roof panels in much the same way as the back panel, and then fix additional strengtheners in place with 60 mm screws – a diagonal brace, a drip batten, and a location brace (see the working drawing).

Location
Centre the location brace on top of the post

Positioning
Set the top edge of the barge board so that it is higher than the roof strips

Screwing
Angling the screw allows you to fix the roof panel to the post

Clamping
Use a clamp to hold the board in postion while you work

A-brace
This horizontal bar prevents the roof from spreading

7 Set the two roof panels in place, so that the location batten is more or less centred on the post (at all four corners) and fix with the 89 mm screws. Run the screws up at an angle, with at least two screws for each post.

8 With 50 mm screws, fix the A-brace to link the two roof panels. Draw the shape of the barge boards and fret them out with the jigsaw. Clamp the boards in place and fix with 50 mm screws. Fit the finial spike to cover the joint. Finally, sand everything to a splinter-free finish and give the arbour a coat of preservative.

Wheeled bench

Imagine going out into the garden on a beautiful morning to sit and enjoy the sunshine. Unfortunately, as soon as the sun moves, you will be left shivering in the shade. However, if you were sitting on our beautiful wheeled bench, you would simply take hold of its handles and move it to a sunny location.

YOU WILL NEED

Materials *for a bench 1.898 m wide, 775 mm deep and 877 mm high. (All rough-sawn pine pieces include excess length for wastage.)*

- Pine: 3 pieces, each 3 m long, 90 mm wide and 40 mm thick (main handle beams, legs, stretchers, axle blocks)
- Pine: 2 pieces, each 2 m long, 150 mm wide and 20 mm thick (arms and shaped backrest boards)
- Pine: 2 pieces, each 3 m long, 50 mm wide and 30 mm thick (table supports, table front horizontal, back rail)
- Pine: 8 pieces, each 3 m long, 100 mm wide and 20 mm thick (seat slats, back slats and tabletop)
- Pine: 4 pieces, each 2 m long, 75 mm wide and 20 mm deep (seat and back supports)
- Pine: 1 piece, 2 m long, 40 mm wide and 20 mm thick (underarm supports)
- Plastic wheels: 2 wheels, 200 mm in diameter, 20 mm holes in centres
- Galvanized threaded rod: 1 m long and 20 mm in diameter (size to suit wheel holes), with 6 washers and 6 nuts to fit
- Zinc-plated, countersunk screws:
  100 x 48 mm no. 8,
  100 x 70 mm no. 10

- Matt green acrylic paint
- Clear preservative

Tools
- Pencil, ruler, tape measure and square
- Portable workbench
- Crosscut saw
- Cordless electric drill with a cross-point screwdriver bit
- Drill bits to match the screw sizes
- Electric jigsaw
- Electric sander with a pack of medium-grade sandpaper
- Electric drill with a 20 mm flat bit and a 10 mm twist bit
- Spanner to fit the nuts
- Paintbrush: 40 mm

A SEAT IN THE SUN

This bench is built with butt joints throughout. There are no complex saw cuts to make or expensive fixings to buy – the bench is created by lots of straight cuts and put together with a generous number of screws. However, the strength of the main joints (where all the 90 x 40 mm sections come together at the corners) relies on the joints being tight. Therefore it is vital that all your measurements and saw cuts are as accurate as possible.

Note how at all the important structural intersections, for example where the legs pass through the frame, the screws are always run into strong face grain, rather than into weak end grain. While the components that make up the main frame are square to each other, the seat and back supports are, for reasons of comfort, canted back at a slight angle. The bottoms of the legs on the wheel side of the bench are reduced in height by 15 mm and the corners chamfered to allow the bench to be tilted up and pushed along. We painted the finished bench with a wash of green acrylic paint, and when it was dry rubbed it down to cut through the paint on edges and corners. The whole bench was then given a coat of clear preservative.

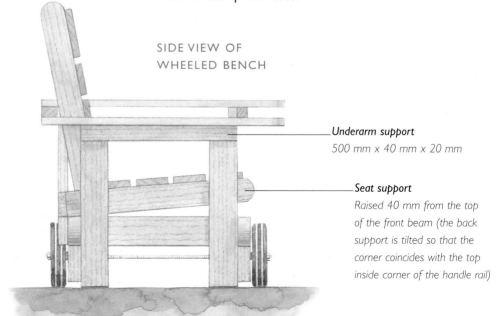

SIDE VIEW OF
WHEELED BENCH

Underarm support
500 mm x 40 mm x 20 mm

Seat support
Raised 40 mm from the top of the front beam (the back support is tilted so that the corner coincides with the top inside corner of the handle rail)

Wheeled bench

EXPLODED VIEW OF THE WHEELED BENCH

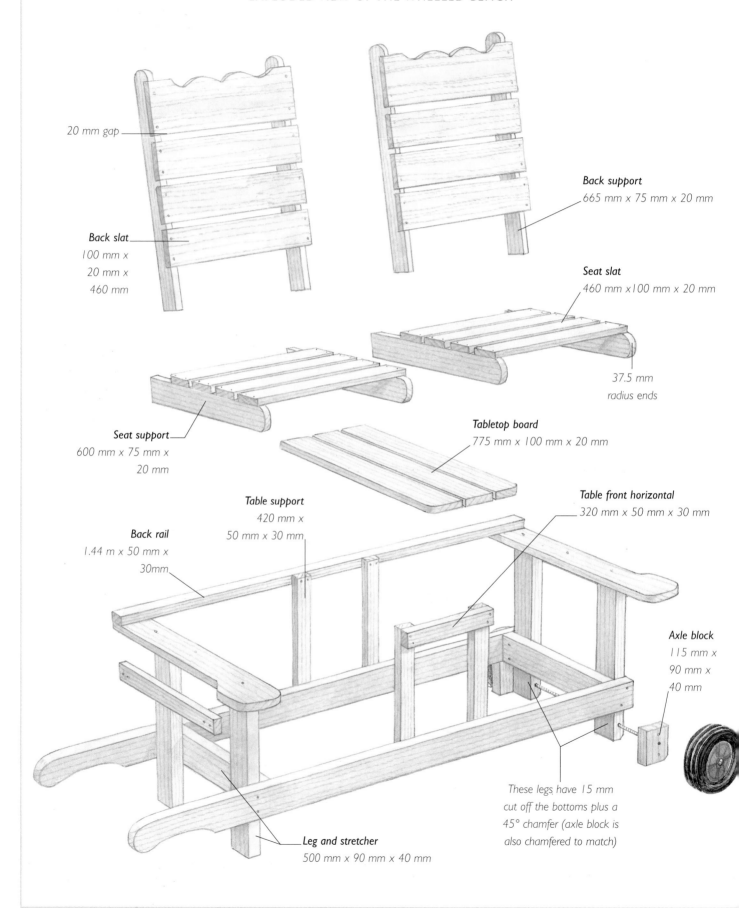

20 mm gap

Back slat
100 mm x
20 mm x
460 mm

Back support
665 mm x 75 mm x 20 mm

Seat slat
460 mm x100 mm x 20 mm

37.5 mm
radius ends

Seat support
600 mm x 75 mm x
20 mm

Tabletop board
775 mm x 100 mm x 20 mm

Table support
420 mm x
50 mm x 30 mm

Back rail
1.44 m x 50 mm x
30mm

Table front horizontal
320 mm x 50 mm x 30 mm

Axle block
115 mm x
90 mm x
40 mm

These legs have 15 mm
cut off the bottoms plus a
45° chamfer (axle block is
also chamfered to match)

Leg and stretcher
500 mm x 90 mm x 40 mm

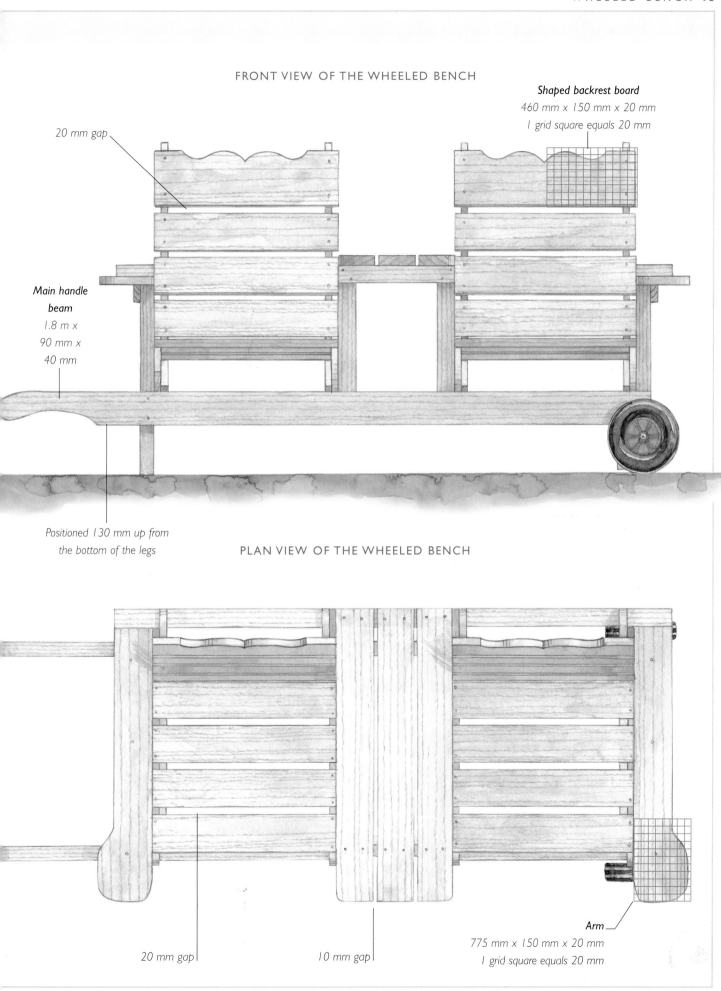

FRONT VIEW OF THE WHEELED BENCH

Shaped backrest board
460 mm x 150 mm x 20 mm
1 grid square equals 20 mm

20 mm gap

*Main handle
beam
1.8 m x
90 mm x
40 mm*

Positioned 130 mm up from
the bottom of the legs

PLAN VIEW OF THE WHEELED BENCH

20 mm gap

10 mm gap

Arm
775 mm x 150 mm x 20 mm
1 grid square equals 20 mm

Step-by-step: **Making the wheeled bench**

Legs
Make sure that the legs are parallel to each other

Sawing the handle
Work slowly as the wood is very thick

Sanding
Use the electric sander to soften the edges of the handle

Right angle
Check that the leg is square to the stretcher

Beam position
Position the beam so that the line of cut is unobstructed

1 With the crosscut saw, cut the legs and the stretchers to length (all at 500 mm), establish the position of the crossover, and fix with one 70 mm screw at each joint. Check for squareness and then drive in a second 70 mm screw.

2 Cut the handle beams to a length of 1.8 m with the crosscut saw. Next, draw the shape of the handle and fret out the profile with the jigsaw. Work in the direction of the end of the handle, to avoid cutting directly into end grain.

Tabletop position
Screw on one tabletop board to establish the middle of the table

Screw position
Make sure that the screws are centred in the thickness of the underarm support

Underarm support
Screw the support so that it is flush with the top of the legs

Marking
Use a square to mark in the position of the two flanking planks

Flush fit
Have the inside edge of the arm flush with the inside of the legs

3 Link the arms with the back support and screw it in place. Using 48 mm screws, screw on the table supports, fix the middle tabletop board to establish the centre of the table and then flank it with another tabletop board at each side.

4 Cut the arms to shape and sand them to a smooth finish. Using 48 mm screws, fix the underarm supports to the top of the legs (so the legs are set parallel) and then screw the arms in place with screws running into the supports.

Back support
Ease the bottom of the board forward to make the back angle

End of cut
Run the cut to finish in the central cleft

Clamping
Position and clamp the board so that the cutting line is unobstructed

Template
Use the waste from cutting the first half of the design to mark out the other half

Screw position
Drive the screws through both boards and into the legs

5 Take the two boards that go to make the seat supports, establish the correct canted angle, and fix them with 48 mm screws at the front end and the intersection of the two boards. Use a 70 mm screw (recessed in a 10 mm hole by 30 mm) from the back rail through into the edge of the back support.

6 Draw half of the cyma curve at the centre of the shaped backrest board and fret out with the jigsaw. Use the waste piece as a template to establish the other half of the design, and to create the total shape on the other shaped backrest board.

Back slats
Use waste pieces of board as spacers

Threaded rod
Drill a hole for the rod (it should not be a tight fit)

Fixing wheels
The order for fixing the wheels is washer, nut, washer, wheel, washer, nut and a final nut to lock

Spacer
Use two thicknesses of waste board to bring the first board up to the correct height

Leg blocks
Chamfer the corner of the blocks and legs with a saw

7 Screw the seat and back slats in place with 48 mm screws. Ensure that the spacing is correct by sliding pieces of waste wood between neighbouring boards.

8 Cut away the lower outside corners of the legs. Drill holes, 20 mm in diameter, through both the leg blocks and the legs, and then slide the axle in place. Finally, sand everything to a smooth finish, lay on a thin wash of paint and give the bench a coat of preservative.

Inspirations: Benches and chairs

Dreams about my childhood often feature an old oak bench in a neglected, overgrown orchard, dappled sunshine, buzzing insects and a rich carpet of fallen fruit! You may dedicate a lot of time to working on your garden to create a leafy heaven, but it is important to spend time actually sitting and enjoying the changing seasons and their cast of plants and flowers. A good selection of seats is vital.

RIGHT Swinging benches are a great place to while away an afternoon. Incorporating one into an arbour makes a delightful feature, which is very pleasant to sit in when surrounded by scented climbers.

ABOVE A grand bench and a modern push-along lounger provide a variety of seating options on this patio, to suit both mood and weather.

LEFT A well-worn rocker nestles in a glade of rough grass, surrounded by foraging hens. Its weathered appearance suits the informal backdrop perfectly.

Romantic arch

This project really comes into its own in summer – there is something gloriously exciting about a wooden arch heavy with clematis and honeysuckle, and it makes a really beautiful feature. Position it at the entrance point to a garden area, where it will frame the vista behind it, or site it midway along a path to add a romantic touch.

TIME

A full weekend (about twelve hours for the woodwork, and four hours for putting together and finishing).

USEFUL TIP

Avoid using a wood treatment such as creosote, because it will cause some plants to shrivel on contact. Use a water-based finish – for example matt white paint.

YOU WILL NEED

Materials *for an arch 1.150 m wide, 440 mm deep and 2.250 m high. (All rough-sawn pine pieces include excess length for wastage.)*
- Pine: 4 pieces, each 2 m long, 75 mm square (posts)
- Pine: 20 pieces, each 2 m long, 50 mm wide and 30 mm thick (cross ties)
- Pine: 1 piece, 1 m long, 75 mm x 75 mm triangular section (capital cross ties)
- Pine: 4 pieces, each 2 m long, 150 mm wide and 20 mm thick (arch laminations)
- Galvanized and painted spiked post supports: 4 (one for each post)
- Zinc-plated, countersunk screws:
  100 x 38 mm no. 8,
  100 x 65 mm no. 10
- Exterior-quality matt white paint

Tools
- Pencil, ruler, tape measure, compass, engineer's protractor, bevel gauge and square
- Two portable workbenches
- Plywood workboard, about 1 m square
- Electric jigsaw
- Large clamp
- Cordless electric drill with a cross-point screwdriver bit
- Drill bits to match the screw sizes
- Electric sander with a pack of medium-grade sandpaper
- Crosscut saw
- Mallet
- Bevel-edged chisel: 50 mm
- Sledgehammer
- Spanner to fit the post support nuts
- Paintbrush: 40 mm

UNDERNEATH THE ARCHES

The clever thing about this structure is the way that the arch tops consist of a number of identical components. Each is made up of eight curvy-shaped boards (one cut in half), which are cut from 150 mm-wide board and laminated together with screws. Once made, the arches are screwed into the half-laps at the top of the posts, and the whole thing is held together and braced with cross ties. We used ties 50 mm wide and 30 mm thick for running up the sides of the posts and over the arch, and two triangular-section ties to act as capitals at the point where the arched top joints into the posts. Finally, just to make sure that the structure stays put, the four posts are located in spiked post supports. The finished arch is an ideal structure for hanging a gate – see the Picket Gate project on page 48.

FRONT VIEW OF THE ROMANTIC ARCH

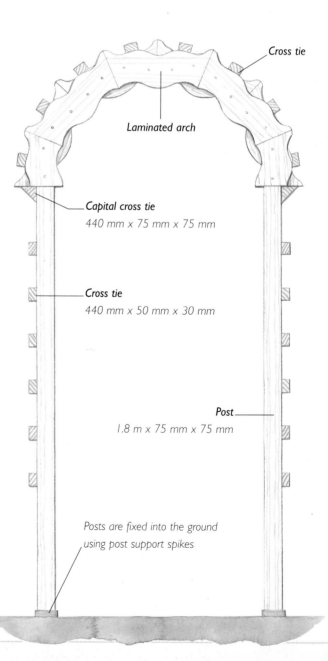

Cross tie

Laminated arch

Capital cross tie
440 mm x 75 mm x 75 mm

Cross tie
440 mm x 50 mm x 30 mm

Post
1.8 m x 75 mm x 75 mm

Posts are fixed into the ground using post support spikes

Romantic arch

THE PIECES THAT MAKE UP THE INNER LAYER OF ONE ARCH

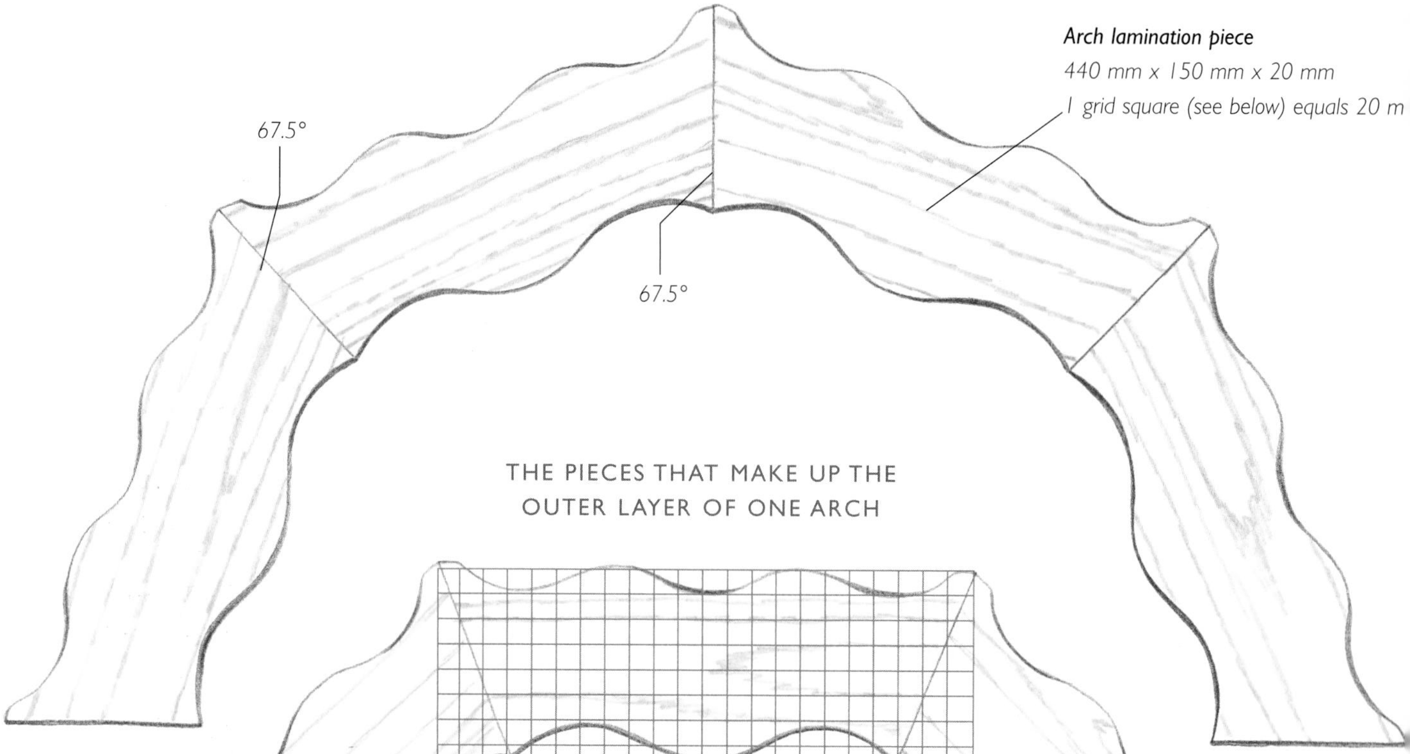

Arch lamination piece
440 mm x 150 mm x 20 mm
I grid square (see below) equals 20 m

67.5°

67.5°

THE PIECES THAT MAKE UP THE
OUTER LAYER OF ONE ARCH

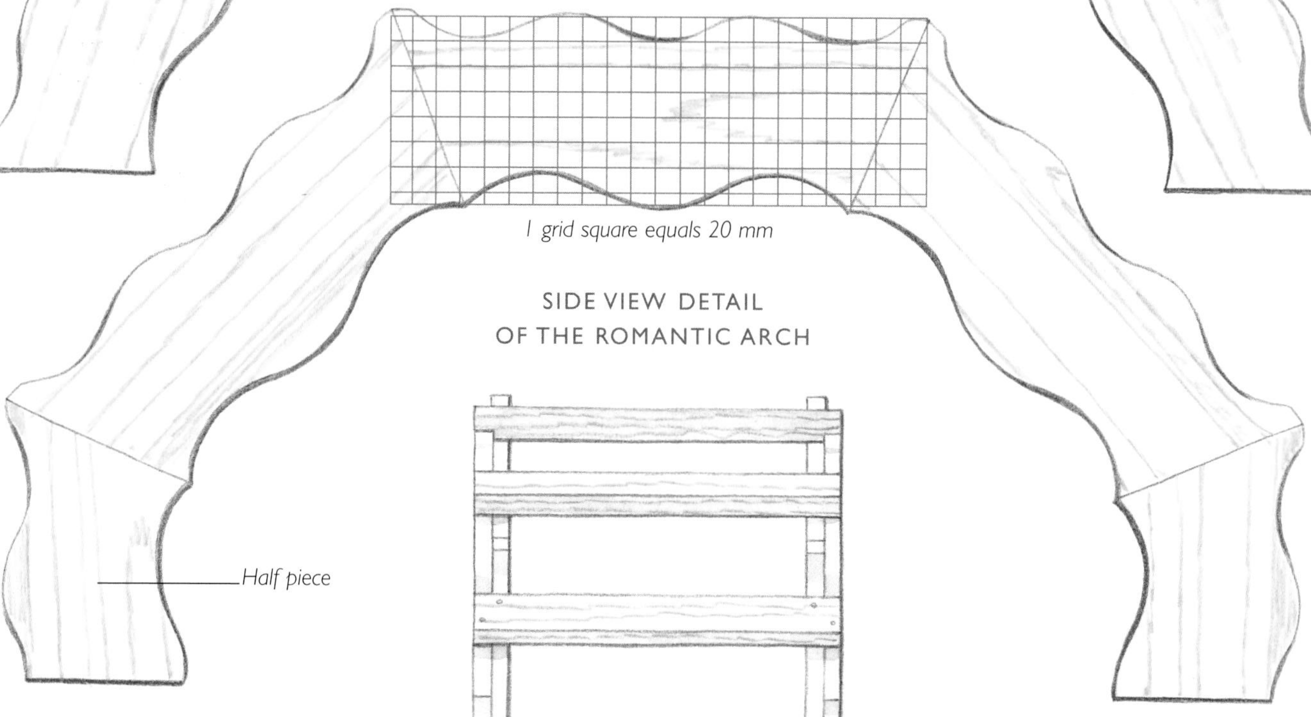

I grid square equals 20 mm

SIDE VIEW DETAIL
OF THE ROMANTIC ARCH

Half piece

Cross tie
440 mm x 50 mm x 30 mm

Capital cross tie
440 mm x 75 mm x 75 mm
Right-angled triangular section

EXPLODED VIEW OF THE ROMANTIC ARCH

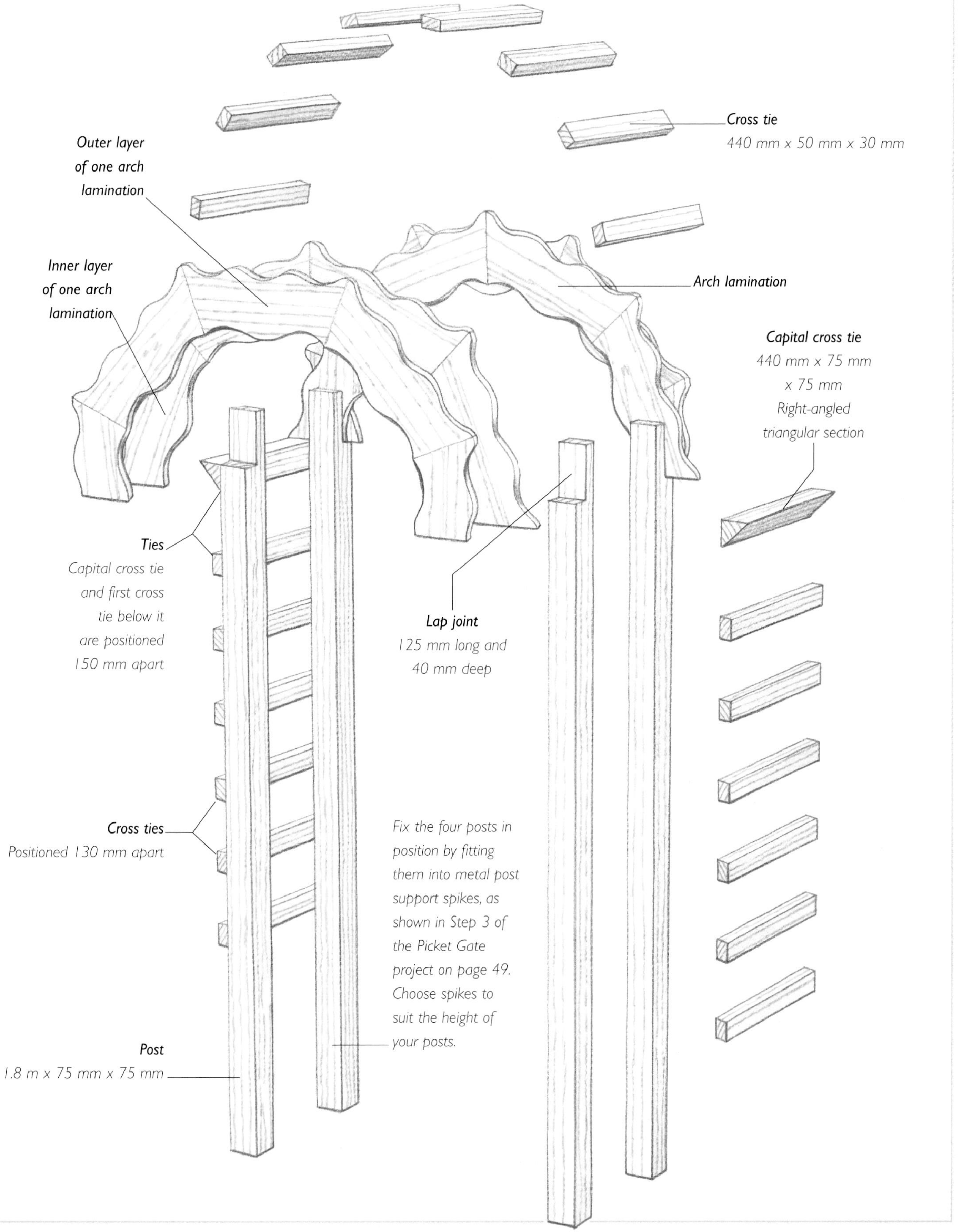

**Outer layer
of one arch
lamination**

**Inner layer
of one arch
lamination**

Cross tie
440 mm x 50 mm x 30 mm

Arch lamination

Capital cross tie
*440 mm x 75 mm
x 75 mm
Right-angled
triangular section*

Ties
*Capital cross tie
and first cross
tie below it
are positioned
150 mm apart*

Lap joint
*125 mm long and
40 mm deep*

Cross ties
Positioned 130 mm apart

*Fix the four posts in
position by fitting
them into metal post
support spikes, as
shown in Step 3 of
the Picket Gate
project on page 49.
Choose spikes to
suit the height of
your posts.*

Post
1.8 m x 75 mm x 75 mm

Step-by-step: **Making the romantic arch**

Sawing square
Hold the saw at right angles to the wood

Template
Use the piece of waste as a template

Cutting angle
Neighbouring boards share the same 67.5° cut

Holding firm
If you can't hold the wood with your hand, use a clamp to hold it down

1 Fix the engineer's protractor to an angle of 67.5° and set out the sixteen boards that make up the arch laminations for the top of the arch. The longest side of each board should measure 440 mm from point to point.

2 Draw the curved profile of the arch lamination on one board and use the jigsaw to fret it out. Use the waste pieces as templates to help you draw the shapes on the other fifteen boards.

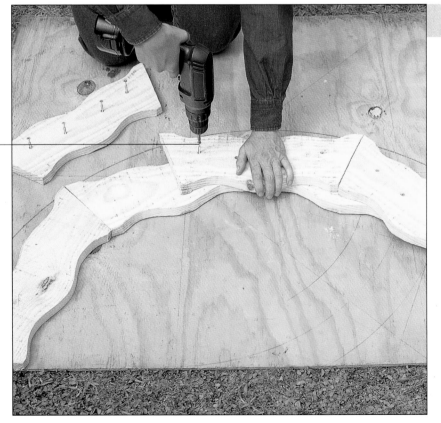

Screwing
Run four screws in from one side

3 Sandwich and clamp the boards together to make the double-thickness shape and fix together with 38 mm screws. You will need two half-boards to complete each form.

Helpful hint

When you have lots of pieces to fit together, as in this design, you may find that inaccuracies in marking out and cutting are amplified. To avoid problems, arrange the pieces that make up the arch (without screwing them), check they fit well and make adjustments as necessary.

Lapped ends
The end of the arch fits squarely
against the top of the post

4 Set out the top of the posts with laps at 125 mm long and 40 mm deep, and cut them out with the crosscut saw, mallet and chisel. Screw the arch in place in the lap with 65 mm screws. Repeat this sequence for the other arch.

Waste block
Use the lap waste to lift the arch up to the correct height

Flush fit
The face of the arch must be flush with the face of the post

Angled screws
Run the screws in at a slight angle

Tie position
Centre the cross ties between humps

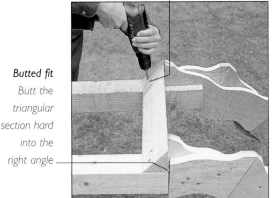

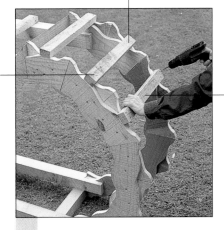

Butted fit
Butt the triangular section hard into the right angle

Screwholes
Drill holes for the screws

Parallel ties
Ensure that the cross ties are parallel to each other

5 Cut the triangular section for the capital cross ties into two lengths of 440 mm and use 65 mm screws to fix them in place so that they are butted hard up against the underside edge of the bottom of the laminated arch.

6 Using 38 mm screws, fix all the cross ties up the posts and over the arch. Rub down the arch to remove splinters, give it a generous coat of white paint, and fix in the spiked supports as shown in the Picket Gate project (see page 48).

Corner patio planter

If your patio is dotted with a colourful collection of little pot plants, which are forever

being knocked over by children or pets, this is the perfect project for you. Gather up

your plants, arrange them in the planter, and you have an enviable patio feature that

keeps the area tidy and displays the plants attractively.

YOU WILL NEED

Materials *for a planter 565 mm high and 950 mm square. (All rough-sawn pine pieces include excess length for wastage.)*
- Pine: 1 piece, 2 m long and 75 mm square (main posts)
- Pine: 7 pieces, each 2 m long, 100 mm wide and 25 mm thick (back and front pickets)
- Pine: 4 pieces, each 2 m long, 150 mm wide and 20 mm thick (front rails, floorboards, post capitals)
- Pine: 2 pieces, each 2 m long, 50 mm wide and 35 mm thick (back rails)
- Zinc-plated, countersunk cross-headed screws: 100 x 38 mm no. 8
- Acrylic paint in colour to suit
- Clear preservative

Tools
- Pencil, ruler, tape measure, compass, bevel gauge and square
- Portable workbench
- Flexible metal metre rule
- Electric jigsaw
- Crosscut saw
- Tenon saw
- Cordless electric drill and cross-point screwdriver bit
- Drill bit, 20 mm wide (for boring out the mortises)
- Mallet
- Bevel-edged chisel, 35 mm wide
- Drill bits to match screws
- Electric sander with a pack of medium-grade sandpaper
- Paintbrush: 30 mm wide

COMPLETELY CORNERED

The design brief for this project was six-fold. The planter had to be raised up off the ground, it had to fit into a right-angled corner, it had to present a curved front, it had to look good alongside a picket fence, it had be scaled and detailed so it suited a cottage garden, and it had to be strong.

In many ways, the resulting design is very straightforward – really it is just a right-angled box with pickets to the sides. However, the curved front rails and the mortise and tenon joints make it a little more complex. The front rails are slightly unusual in that the tenons run at a skewed angle into the mortises. The joints aren't particularly difficult to cut, but you do need to spend longer than usual at the setting out stage. When we came to painting the finished piece, we decided that the only way to achieve a subtle colour was to water down the acrylic paint to a thin wash, and then to top this with a coat of clear preservative.

FRONT VIEW OF THE
CORNER PATIO PLANTER

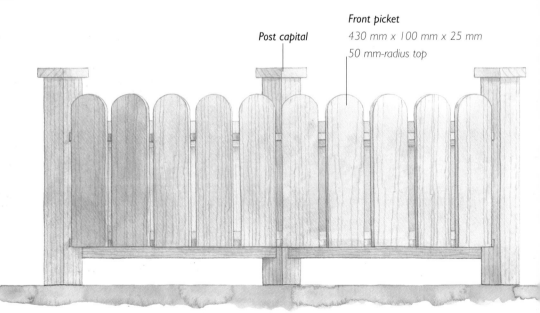

Post capital

Front picket
430 mm x 100 mm x 25 mm
50 mm-radius top

Corner patio planter

SIDE VIEW OF THE CORNER PATIO PLANTER

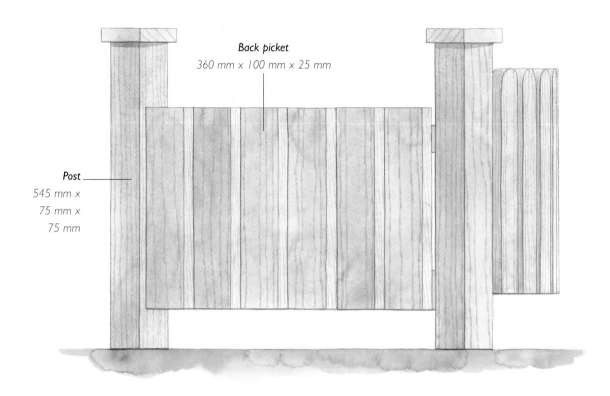

Back picket
360 mm x 100 mm x 25 mm

Post
*545 mm x
75 mm x
75 mm*

PLAN VIEW OF THE CORNER PATIO PLANTER

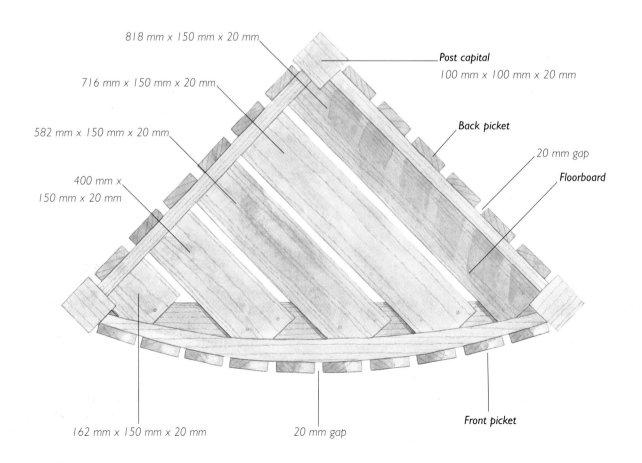

818 mm x 150 mm x 20 mm

716 mm x 150 mm x 20 mm

582 mm x 150 mm x 20 mm

*400 mm x
150 mm x 20 mm*

Post capital
100 mm x 100 mm x 20 mm

Back picket

20 mm gap

Floorboard

162 mm x 150 mm x 20 mm

20 mm gap

Front picket

EXPLODED VIEW OF THE CORNER PATIO PLANTER

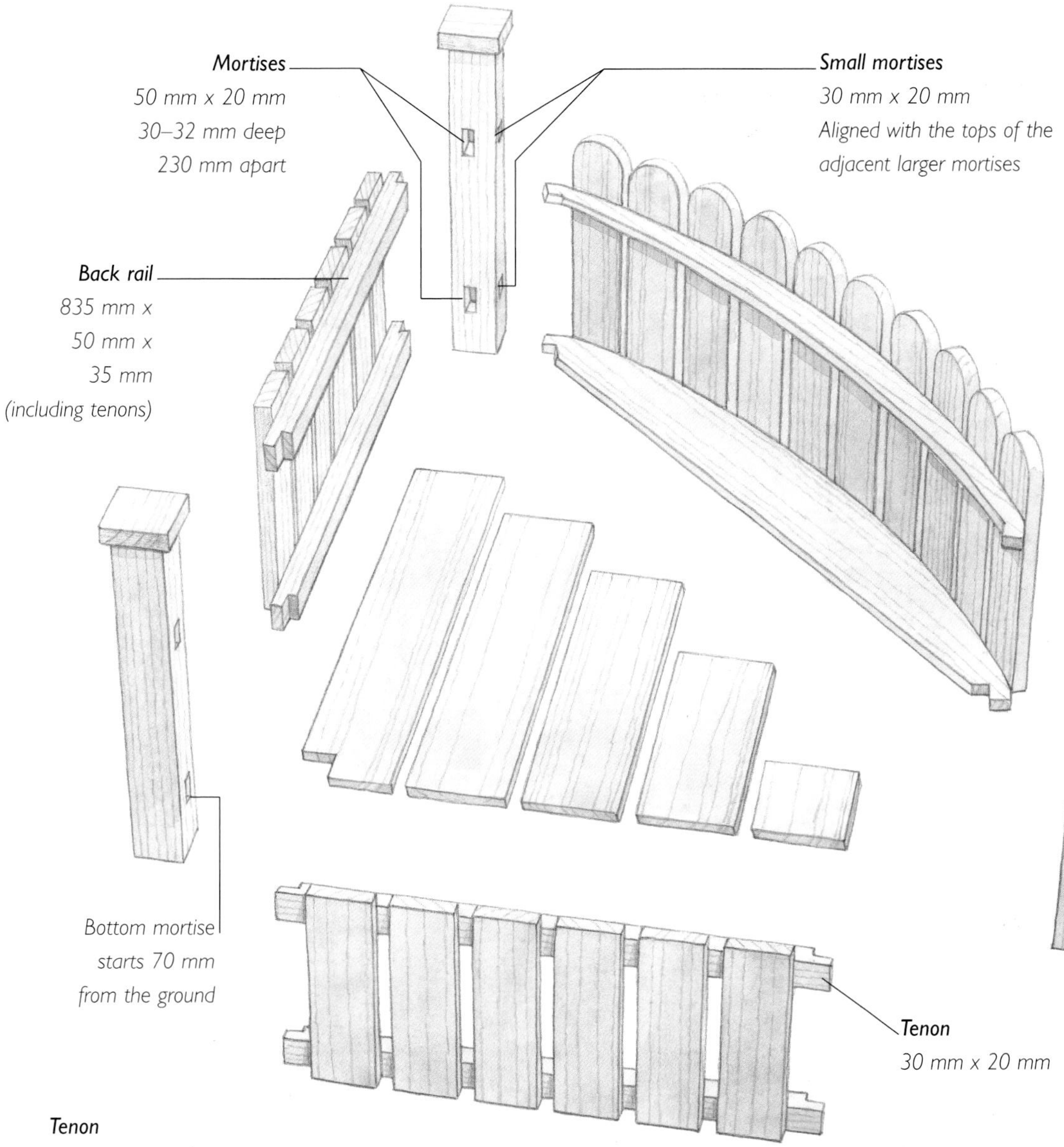

Mortises
50 mm x 20 mm
30–32 mm deep
230 mm apart

Small mortises
30 mm x 20 mm
Aligned with the tops of the
adjacent larger mortises

Back rail
835 mm x
50 mm x
35 mm
(including tenons)

Bottom mortise
starts 70 mm
from the ground

Tenon
30 mm x 20 mm

Tenon
30 mm x
20 mm

DETAIL OF THE TOP CURVED FRONT RAIL

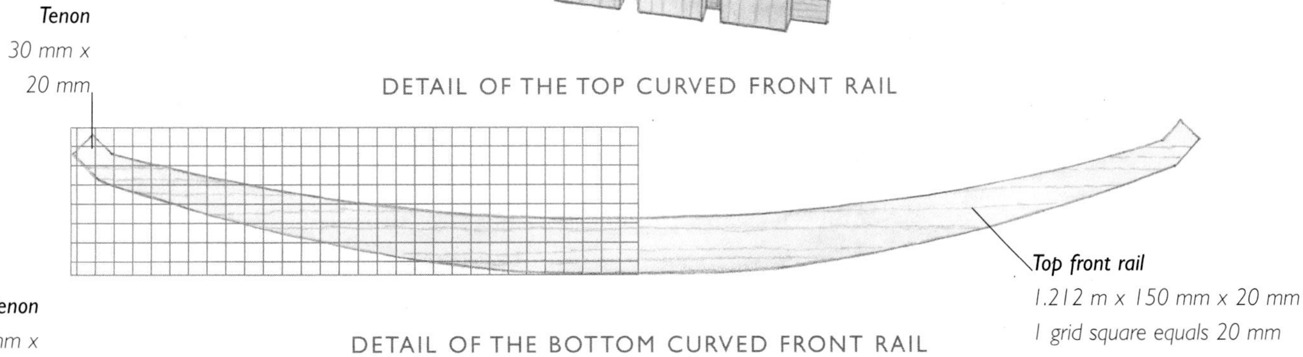

Top front rail
1.212 m x 150 mm x 20 mm
1 grid square equals 20 mm

Tenon
30 mm x
20 mm

DETAIL OF THE BOTTOM CURVED FRONT RAIL

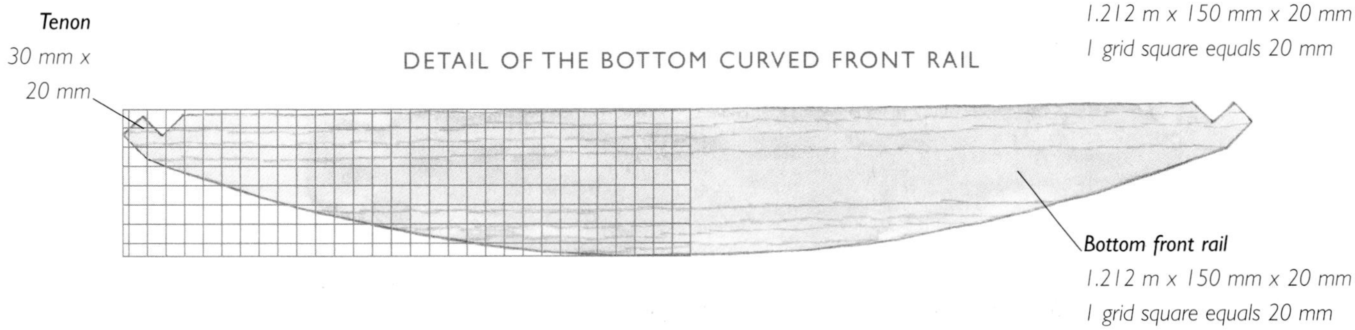

Bottom front rail
1.212 m x 150 mm x 20 mm
1 grid square equals 20 mm

Step-by-step: **Making the corner patio planter**

Marking the curve
Bend the rule to mark out one
half of the curve at a time

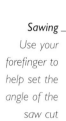
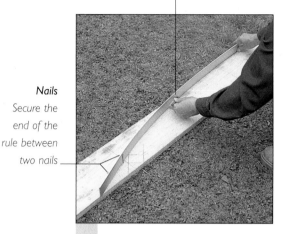

Nails
Secure the
end of the
rule between
two nails

1 Set out the design of the curved
front rails on the 150 mm-wide
board. Use the metal rule to achieve the
shape of the curve. Fret out the profile
with the jigsaw.

Cutting the tenon
Cut down the grain of the wood
to the waste side of the line

Sawing
Use your
forefinger to
help set the
angle of the
saw cut

2 Set out the ends of the straight back
rails with tenons 30 mm long and
20 mm wide, the waste piece measuring
30 mm long and 15 mm wide. Cut the
joint with the crosscut and tenon saws and
tidy up with the chisel.

Chisel
Square the back of the
chisel with the line

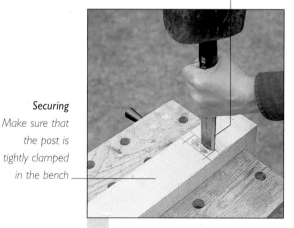

Securing
Make sure that
the post is
tightly clamped
in the bench

3 Cut the three main posts to length
and set out the position of the
mortises. Clear the bulk of the mortise
waste with the drill and then cut back to
the line with the mallet and chisel.

Bottom board
The wide
board goes at
the bottom

Screwing
Run a screw
through the
mortise and
tenon joint

4 Assemble the frame, knock the joints
home and clench them with screws.
The bottom board is positioned so that
the generous straight edge becomes a
support for the floorboards.

Notched board
Cut the first board so that
it fits around the post

Board ends
Save time
by leaving
the board
ends square

5 Cut the waste lengths of board to make floorboards that fit inside the base, spacing them about 20 mm apart, and fix with screws. The floorboards can be left square-cut where they fit the front rail, but the longest board needs to be notched to fit around the back post.

Helpful hint

If you have plenty of wood to spare and you want to make the finish of the base neater, the ends of the floorboards can be cut to fit the shape of the curved front rail piece.

Bottom of
picket
The bottom of
the pickets
should be flush
with the rail

6 Cut semicircular radius curves on top of the front pickets. Screw the pickets in place, so that they are spaced by the thickness of a board, and so that the bottom edge of the picket is flush with the underside of the front rail. Cut three post capitals (100 mm square and 20 mm thick) and screw them in place on top of the posts. Finally, sand the planter, then paint it and coat with preservative.

Spacer
Use a piece of
scrap wood for
a spacer

Potting table

A potting table is a real boon to keen gardeners. No more stooping to dip into massive bags of compost, or fumbling around looking for a level surface to work on. You simply fill the table's side tray with compost, line up flowerpots and plants, and get on with potting. Everything you need is comfortably to hand.

YOU WILL NEED

Materials *for a potting table 1.295 m wide, 662 mm deep and 1.574 m high. (All rough-sawn pine pieces include excess length for wastage.)*

- Pine: 3 pieces, each 3 m long, 90 mm wide, 40 mm thick (front and back legs)
- Pine: 3 pieces, each 3 m long, 100 mm wide, 20 mm thick (end boards, top and bottom horizontal rails, tray pieces, peg board)
- Pine: 1 piece, 1 m long, 30 mm wide, 20 mm thick (tray corner support blocks)
- Pine: 3 pieces, each 3 m long, 150 mm wide and 22 mm thick (tray base, table base, tabletop, decorative back board, brackets, top shelf)

- Dowel: 1 piece, 1 m long and 22 mm in diameter (pegs)
- Waterproof glue
- Zinc-plated, countersunk cross-headed screws: 100 x 38 mm no. 8
- Teak oil

Tools

- Pencil, ruler, tracing paper and square
- Portable workbench
- Crosscut saw
- Cordless electric drill with a cross-point screwdriver bit
- Selection of drill bits
- Electric jigsaw
- Electric sander with a pack of medium-grade sandpaper
- Paintbrush: 40 mm

SIDE VIEW OF THE POTTING TABLE

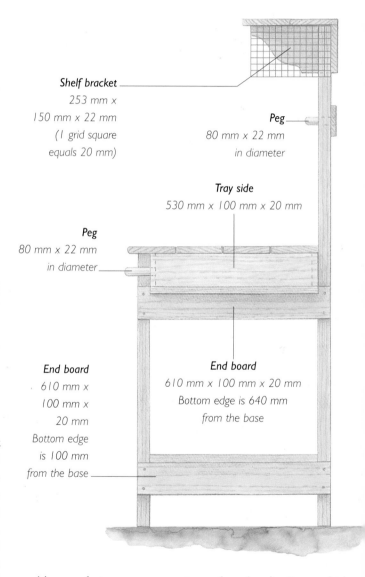

Shelf bracket
253 mm x
150 mm x 22 mm
(1 grid square
equals 20 mm)

Peg
80 mm x 22 mm
in diameter

Tray side
530 mm x 100 mm x 20 mm

Peg
80 mm x 22 mm
in diameter

End board
610 mm x
100 mm x
20 mm
Bottom edge
is 100 mm
from the base

End board
610 mm x 100 mm x 20 mm
Bottom edge is 640 mm
from the base

A POTTING TABLE FOR ALL SEASONS

The total height of the bench is 1.574 m, with the worksurface set at 862 mm high. The top horizontal rails, which link the legs and support the worksurface at back and front, also run through to the right-hand side of the worksurface to form the sides of the compost tray. If you are left-handed, all you do is modify the design so that the rails run through to the other end of the bench. The structure is simple and direct — there are no complicated joints to cut and the horizontal members are butted and screwed to the vertical posts. In use, the tray is filled with compost, small tools are hung on the pegs, seed packets and other items are stored on the top shelf, and of course the base surface is just right for stacking flowerpots and a watering can. Note how the work-surface boards are butted edge to edge, while the base surface boards are spaced to allow for easy cleaning.

It's a perfect no-nonsense piece of garden furniture, which draws inspiration from early nineteenth-century furniture designs in featuring smooth cyma curves on the back board and the brackets. If you are a keen gardener and enjoy taking cuttings and potting on plants, this potting table will contribute something special to your workshop or greenhouse.

Potting table

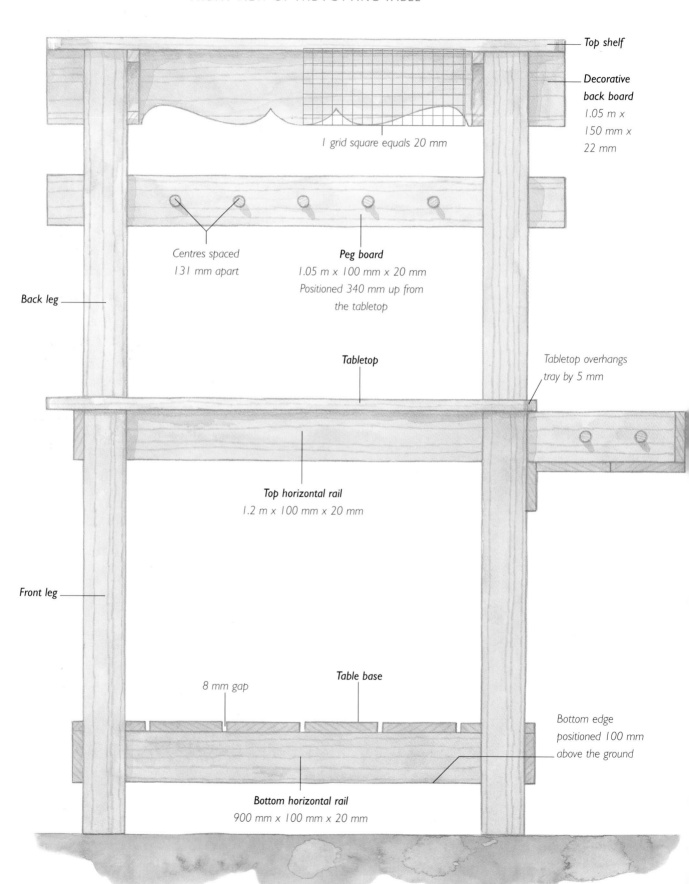

FRONT VIEW OF THE POTTING TABLE

Top shelf

Decorative back board
1.05 m x 150 mm x 22 mm

1 grid square equals 20 mm

Centres spaced 131 mm apart

Peg board 1.05 m x 100 mm x 20 mm Positioned 340 mm up from the tabletop

Back leg

Tabletop

Tabletop overhangs tray by 5 mm

Top horizontal rail 1.2 m x 100 mm x 20 mm

Front leg

8 mm gap

Table base

Bottom edge positioned 100 mm above the ground

Bottom horizontal rail 900 mm x 100 mm x 20 mm

EXPLODED VIEW OF THE POTTING TABLE

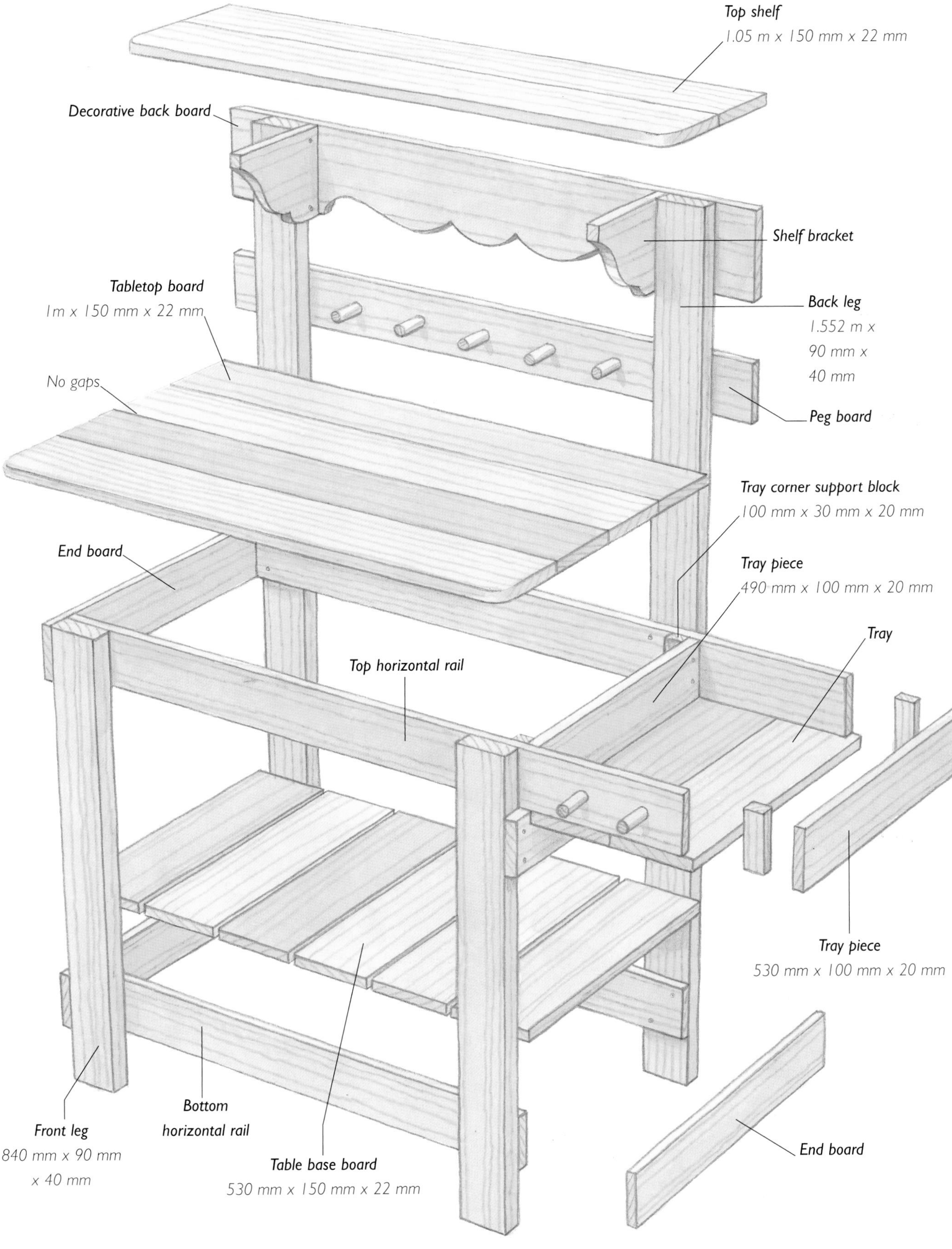

Top shelf
1.05 m x 150 mm x 22 mm

Decorative back board

Shelf bracket

Tabletop board
1m x 150 mm x 22 mm

Back leg
*1.552 m x
90 mm x
40 mm*

No gaps

Peg board

Tray corner support block
100 mm x 30 mm x 20 mm

Tray piece
490 mm x 100 mm x 20 mm

End board

Tray

Top horizontal rail

Tray piece
530 mm x 100 mm x 20 mm

Front leg
*840 mm x 90 mm
x 40 mm*

Bottom
horizontal rail

Table base board
530 mm x 150 mm x 22 mm

End board

Step-by-step: **Making the potting table**

Square
*The horizontal rails must
be square to the legs*

Tray corner support block
*Screw blocks to hold the
tray sides in place*

Parallel
*Make sure that
the two legs
are parallel to
each other*

Leg position
*The leg is on
the outside of
the frame*

Tight fit
*Push the end
board hard
under the top
horizontal rail*

1 Use the crosscut saw to cut all the wood to size. Set out the two 1.552 m-long back legs, linking them with the top and bottom horizontal boards, check for squareness, and then run pilot holes through the boards and fix them with two screws at each intersection.

2 Having built both the front and back units, complete with pegholes in the tray end of the top horizontal rail, link them together with the four 610 mm-long end boards. Screw on the corner support blocks for fitting the two tray pieces.

Board position
*Push the board
hard up against
the back posts*

3 Set the four 1 m-long, 150 mm-wide tabletop boards in position so that they are butted hard up against the two back posts. Leave a 5 mm overhang on the right-hand side, so that the surface hangs over the tray. Check for squareness and fix with screws.

Helpful hint

Before you fix the tabletop boards in place, check that the potting table is square. Use a large square or a tape measure to check that the diagonal measurements are identical.

Shelf bracket
*Fit the board at right
angles to the back post*

4 Trace off the cyma curves
of the decorative back
board and shelf brackets, transfer
the lines through to the wood,
and cut the curves with the
jigsaw. Screw the back board and
brackets in place so that their
top edges are flush with the top
of the back posts. Drill and fit
the peg board.

Screwing
*Run two
screws through
the bracket
and into the
back post*

Cyma curve
*Sand the
curve to a
smooth finish*

Screwing
*Fix the planks with two
screws at each end*

Sandpaper
*Make a double fold
of sandpaper*

Screwholes
*Drill a hole for
each screw
that is near the
end of a plank*

Sanding
*Rub the end of
the peg to a
rounded finish*

5 Fix all the other members in place
(the boards for the base of the table,
and the boards on the underside and ends
of the tray). Position the table base boards
flush with the horizontal rails that link the
legs, but spaced by 8 mm.

6 Use the graded sandpapers to round
over the ends of the pegs, and to
generally bring all the edges and corners to
a slightly rounded finish. Finally, give all the
surfaces a coat of teak oil.

Rabbit ark

Children love rabbits, so why not give them a couple of furry friends to play with? The new members of the family will need housing, and that's where our ark comes in. It folds up for easy transport and has handles so that you can move it around the garden (position it in different locations for the rabbits to trim your lawn).

TIME

About sixteen hours for the woodwork, and another three hours for fixing the wire, hinges and latches.

USEFUL TIP

Buy special rabbit wire – the rabbit cannot get its feet through the holes.

EXPLODED VIEW OF THE RABBIT ARK

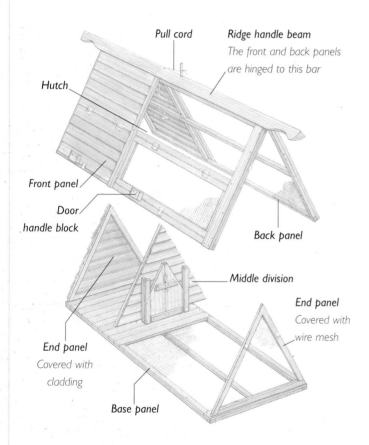

Pull cord

Ridge handle beam
The front and back panels are hinged to this bar

Hutch

Front panel

Door
handle block

Back panel

Middle division

End panel
Covered with wire mesh

End panel
Covered with cladding

Base panel

A-FRAME RABBIT HOME

The clever thing about this rabbit ark is the fact that it folds up for transport and storage. While in essence the ark is made up from seven component parts (a base, two long sides, three triangular divisions and a carrying beam), the ingenious design means that it can be swiftly broken down into three flat-pack units. These are the two sides, which hinge to the handle beam like a book; the base, complete with the two hinged ends; and the middle division.

To put the ark together, set the base flat on the grass, open up the two triangular ends, locate the middle division on its dowels, open the book-like sides and drop them over the ends, and then do up all the latches. When you want to move the ark, ask a friend to help and simply lift it up by the beam handles. To shut the rabbits in for the night, wait until they are safely in the enclosed hutch end, unhitch the pull cord and lower the portcullis door.

YOU WILL NEED

Materials *for a rabbit ark 2.405 m long, 769 mm high and 830 mm wide. (All rough-sawn pine pieces include excess length for wastage.)*
- Pine: 15 pieces, each 3 m long, 35 mm wide and 20 mm thick (for all the frames and corner trim)
- Pine: 4 pieces, each 3 m long, 75 mm wide and 20 mm thick (floorboards)
- Pine: 1 piece, 3 m long, 75 mm triangular section, 100 mm across the hypotenuse (ridge handle beam)
- Pine: 1 piece, 1 m long, 50 mm wide and 34 mm thick (door handle blocks)
- Pine: 1 piece, 2 m long, 75 mm wide and 20 mm thick (end frame trim)
- Pine feather-edged board: 20 pieces, each 3 m long, 100 mm wide and 10 mm thick (for cladding the walls of the hutch end of the ark)
- Pine: 1 piece, 1 m long, 150 mm wide and 22 mm thick (portcullis door)
- Pine dowel: 2 pieces, 300 mm long, one 6 mm in diameter and the other 12 mm (for locating the middle division and making the pull cord)
- Galvanized rabbit wire: 6 m roll, 1 m wide (cage)
- Galvanized staples: 1 kg x 10 mm
- Galvanized butt door hinges: 14 x 60 mm long, 20 mm wide, with screws to fit
- Plated snap-fit case latches: 8 medium size, with screws
- Zinc-plated, countersunk cross-headed screws: 100 x 20 mm no. 8, 100 x 38 mm no. 8, 10 x 50 mm no. 10, 100 x 65 mm no. 10
- Exterior-quality PVA glue
- Nylon cord (for door pull)
- Clear preservative

Tools
- Pencil, ruler, tape measure, marking gauge and square
- Two portable workbenches
- Crosscut saw
- Cordless electric drill with a cross-point screwdriver bit
- Drill bits to match the screw sizes
- Wire snips
- Small hammer
- Electric jigsaw
- Drill bit to match the dowel size
- Electric sander with a pack of medium-grade sandpaper
- Small screwdriver to fit the hinge and latch screws
- Paintbrush: 40 mm

Rabbit ark

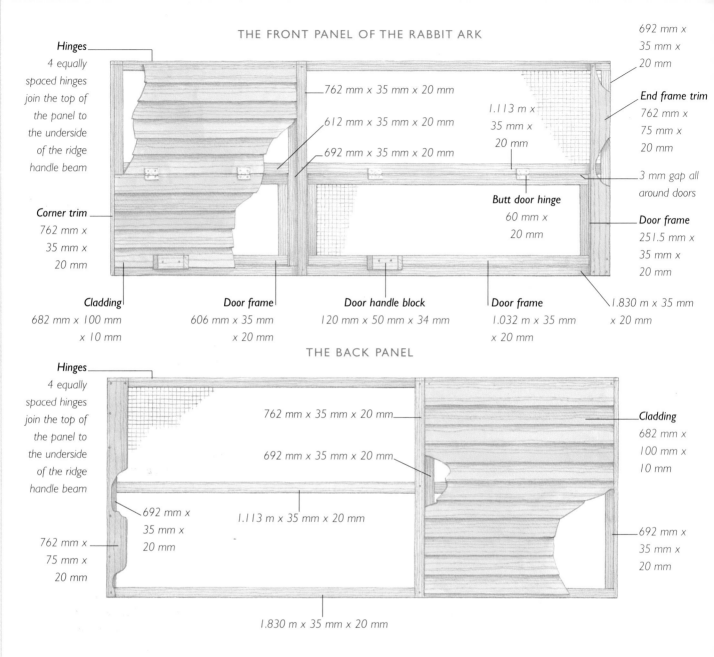

THE FRONT PANEL OF THE RABBIT ARK

692 mm x 35 mm x 20 mm

Hinges
4 equally spaced hinges join the top of the panel to the underside of the ridge handle beam

762 mm x 35 mm x 20 mm

612 mm x 35 mm x 20 mm

692 mm x 35 mm x 20 mm

1.113 m x 35 mm x 20 mm

End frame trim
762 mm x 75 mm x 20 mm

3 mm gap all around doors

Butt door hinge
60 mm x 20 mm

Corner trim
762 mm x 35 mm x 20 mm

Door frame
251.5 mm x 35 mm x 20 mm

Cladding
682 mm x 100 mm x 10 mm

Door frame
606 mm x 35 mm x 20 mm

Door handle block
120 mm x 50 mm x 34 mm

Door frame
1.032 m x 35 mm x 20 mm

1.830 m x 35 mm x 20 mm

THE BACK PANEL

Hinges
4 equally spaced hinges join the top of the panel to the underside of the ridge handle beam

762 mm x 35 mm x 20 mm

692 mm x 35 mm x 20 mm

Cladding
682 mm x 100 mm x 10 mm

692 mm x 35 mm x 20 mm

1.113 m x 35 mm x 20 mm

692 mm x 35 mm x 20 mm

762 mm x 75 mm x 20 mm

1.830 m x 35 mm x 20 mm

THE BASE OF THE RABBIT ARK

1.83 m x 35 mm x 20 mm

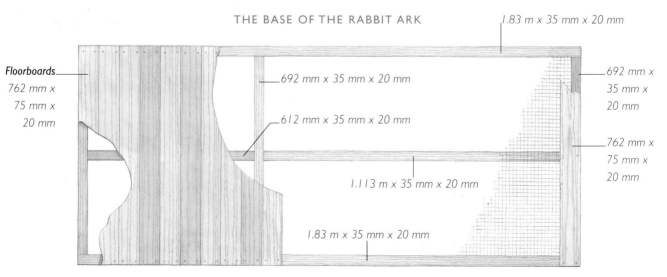

Floorboards
762 mm x 75 mm x 20 mm

692 mm x 35 mm x 20 mm

692 mm x 35 mm x 20 mm

612 mm x 35 mm x 20 mm

1.113 m x 35 mm x 20 mm

762 mm x 75 mm x 20 mm

1.83 m x 35 mm x 20 mm

A TRIANGULAR FRAME (USED FOR THE END PANELS AND THE MIDDLE DIVISION)

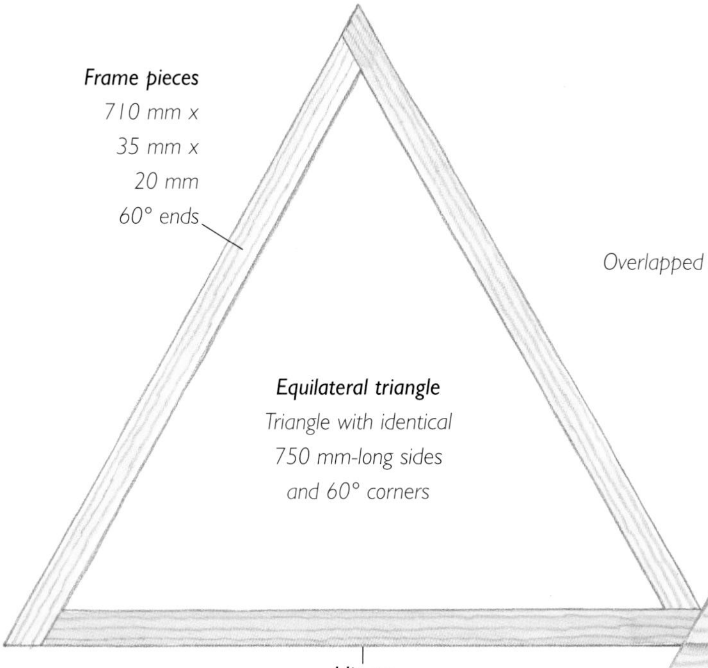

Frame pieces
710 mm x
35 mm x
20 mm
60° ends

Equilateral triangle
Triangle with identical
750 mm-long sides
and 60° corners

Hinges
2 equally spaced hinges join the bottom
of the panel to the edge of the base

AN END PANEL WITH CLADDING

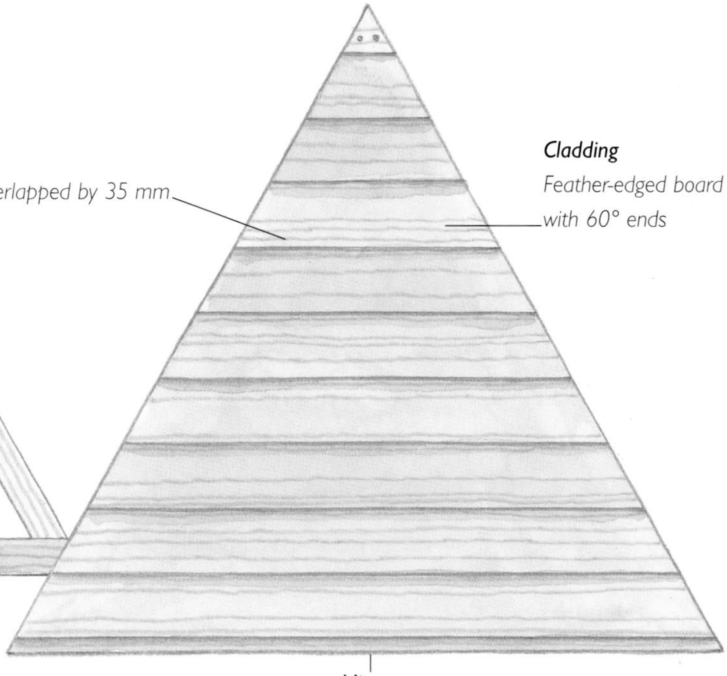

Overlapped by 35 mm

Cladding
Feather-edged board
with 60° ends

Hinges
2 equally spaced hinges join the bottom
of the panel to the edge of the base

MIDDLE DIVISION

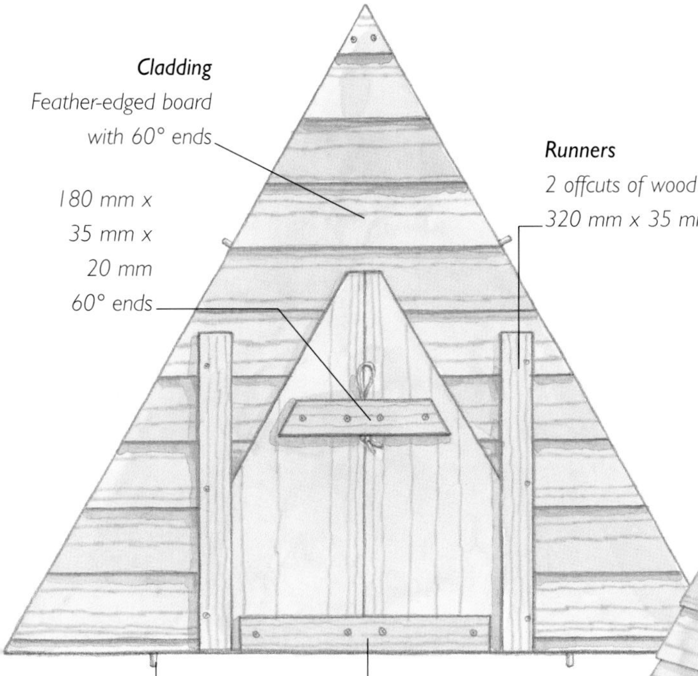

Cladding
Feather-edged board
with 60° ends

180 mm x
35 mm x
20 mm
60° ends

Runners
2 offcuts of wood
320 mm x 35 mm x 20 mm

260 mm x 35 mm x 20 mm

Location dowel

Arched doorway
215 mm high (from bottom
of panel) and 226 mm wide

MIDDLE DIVISION (WITH THE DOOR RAISED)

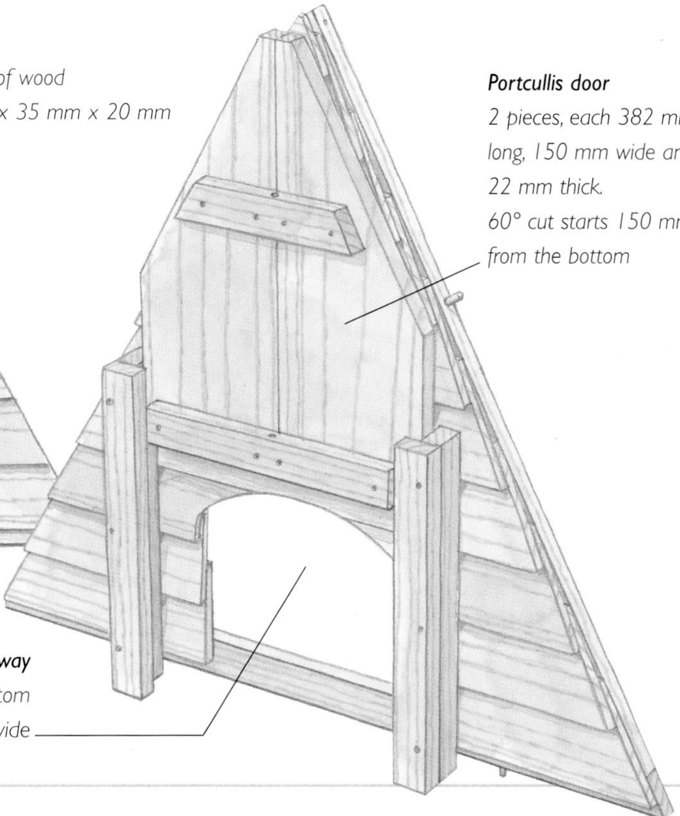

Portcullis door
2 pieces, each 382 mm
long, 150 mm wide and
22 mm thick.
60° cut starts 150 mm
from the bottom

Step-by-step: **Making the rabbit ark**

Screwing
Fix each joint
with two screws

Support boards
Clamp boards
in the
workbench to
support the
frame

1 Cut the lengths of wood that make up the frame, butt joint them together and fix with 65 mm screws. Build all eight frames: the base, the front panel, the back panel, the two doors in the front panel, and the three triangles that make up the end panels and middle division. Screw the door handle blocks in place on the doors with 50 mm screws.

Rabbit wire
Cut the wire about 10 mm
smaller than the frame all around

Cutting
It may help to
bend the wire
out of the way
of the snips as
you cut

Supports
Rest the frame
on a couple of
spare boards

2 Set the base down flat on a couple of spare pieces of wood, and use the wire snips to cut the rabbit wire to fit. Cut the large pieces first. Hammer in staples at about 50 mm intervals. Screw the corner trim in place on the front panel using 38 mm screws (see working drawing).

Screwholes
Drill holes through the feather-edged
board to take the screws

Jig
Use a simple
jig to help you
space the
boards equally

3 Clad the frames with feather-edged board. When you are doing this, use a little scrap of wood, marked off at 65 mm, to ensure that the board overlap is always constant at about 35 mm. Screw the boards in place with 20 mm screws.

Cord loop
Tie a loop for attaching
the pull cord

Door runners
The door
should be a
loose fit within
the runners

Bevel
Saw a bevel on
the underside
of the top of
the door

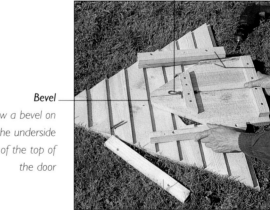

4 Cut out the door hole in the middle division with the jigsaw and build the two door-slide runners from lengths of 35 mm-wide, 20 mm-thick offcuts. Make the door from two lengths of 150 mm-wide board and trim it to fit.

Door pull cord
The door pull cord, complete with the 12 mm dowel handle, runs down through a hole in the ridge handle beam to link up with a looped cord on the top of the sliding door

Location dowels
Spread glue inside the hole and then tap the dowel in place

Alignment
Double-check that the dowels locate in the holes in the floor panel

5 Drill and glue-fit two lengths of 6 mm dowel into the underside edge of the middle division. Set the partition upright on the floor to establish its position, and drill matching location holes in the floor beam.

Helpful hint

If you make a mistake while positioning the location holes for the dowels, leave the location dowel where it is, and plug the location hole with a piece of dowel. Wait for the glue to dry, then sand the plugged dowel flush. Drill another hole.

Fixing hinges
Screw the hinges to the frame first and then to the handle beam

Alignment
Before you fit the latches, ensure the end panel is flush with the sides

Prop the sides
Ask a friend to hold the side panels at the angle shown here

Latches
Have a trial run for fitting a latch so that you know how far apart the two pieces should be

Screwing
Drill pilot holes for the screws and use the correct size of screwdriver

6 Saw and sand the ends of the triangular-section ridge handle beam to make comfortable handles, and screw hinges in place, centring the two sides on the beam's 100 mm hypotenuse.

7 Use 38 mm screws to fit the two 75 mm-wide pieces of end frame trim, to strengthen the end of the cage, and then screw the snap-fit latches in place at a point about two-thirds of the way up the sides of the triangle. Thread and fit the door-pull cord. Paint with preservative.

Classic pergola

If you want to create an instant feature in your garden, which establishes a focal

point and invites visitors to wander under it, consider the merits of a pergola. It

provides a place to sit in the shade, a spot for children to play, somewhere to snooze

on a summer's day and a structure that will host a vine or flowering climbers.

YOU WILL NEED

Materials *for a pergola
2.55 m high and 3.59 m
square. (All rough-sawn pine
pieces include excess length
for wastage.)*

- Pine: 4 pieces, each 3 m long
  and 75 mm square (main
  posts, and the 12 short
  linking posts that laminate
  and link the boat beams and
  top boards)
- Pine: 14 pieces, each 4 m
  long, 150 mm wide and
  20 mm thick (top boards,
  boat beams, support boards)
- Pine: 4 pieces, each 2 m long,
  50 mm wide and 30 mm
  thick (brackets)
- Pine: 6 pieces, each 4 m
  long, 30 mm wide and
  20 mm thick (various
  temporary battens)

- Zinc-plated, countersunk
  cross-headed screws:
  100 x 48 mm no. 8,
  10 x 65 mm no. 10
- Brown preservative

Tools

- Pencil, ruler, tape measure,
  compass, bevel gauge
  and square
- Two portable workbenches
- Crosscut saw
- Electric jigsaw
- Large clamps: 4 clamps
- Cordless electric drill and
  cross-point screwdriver bit
- Drill bits to match screws
- Spirit level
- Electric sander with a pack of
  medium-grade sandpaper
- Paintbrush: 40 mm

COOL CANOPY

This project is made up from four posts set square to each other, with the top of the posts linked by two laminated "boat" beams on paired support boards, and six top boards crossing the boat beams at right angles. The boat beams are made by sandwiching the 300 mm-long linking posts between boards in such a way that the posts protrude at the top of the beam by 150 mm, providing link-up points for the topmost boards.

The structure is held square and prevented from wracking by eight brackets. We have allowed a good amount of extra length for the bracket pieces so that you can mitre the ends at 45° without worrying about cutting them too short. The ends of all the top boards are decorated with a classic cyma curve (an S-shaped detail), which can be cut easily with the jigsaw. The crossover of the boards at the corner posts, plus the addition of the top boards, results in a generous, bold structure which is really eye-catching. We purchased the wood ready-treated, and used the preservative to touch up the cut edges.

CORNER DETAIL OF THE CLASSIC PERGOLA

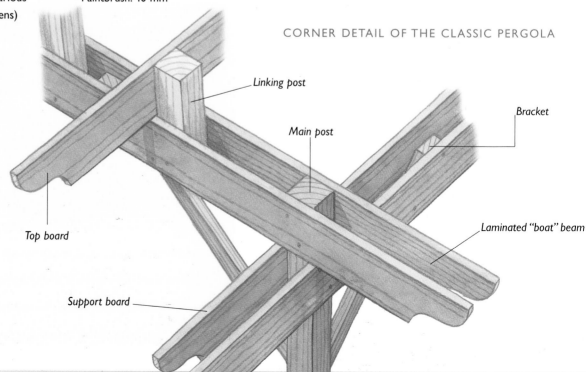

Linking post

Main post

Bracket

Top board

Laminated "boat" beam

Support board

Classic pergola

FRONT VIEW OF THE CLASSIC PERGOLA

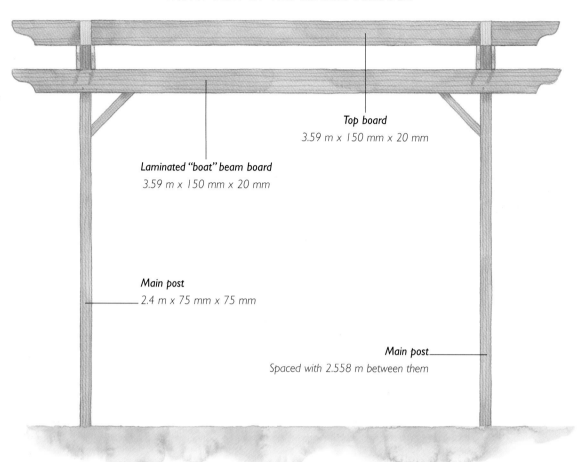

Top board
3.59 m x 150 mm x 20 mm

Laminated "boat" beam board
3.59 m x 150 mm x 20 mm

Main post
2.4 m x 75 mm x 75 mm

Main post
Spaced with 2.558 m between them

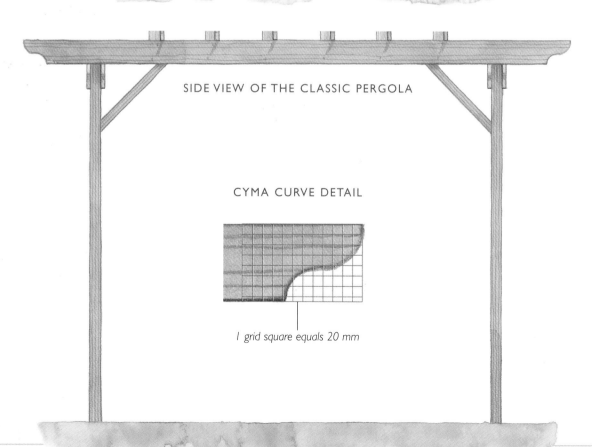

SIDE VIEW OF THE CLASSIC PERGOLA

CYMA CURVE DETAIL

I grid square equals 20 mm

EXPLODED VIEW OF THE CLASSIC PERGOLA

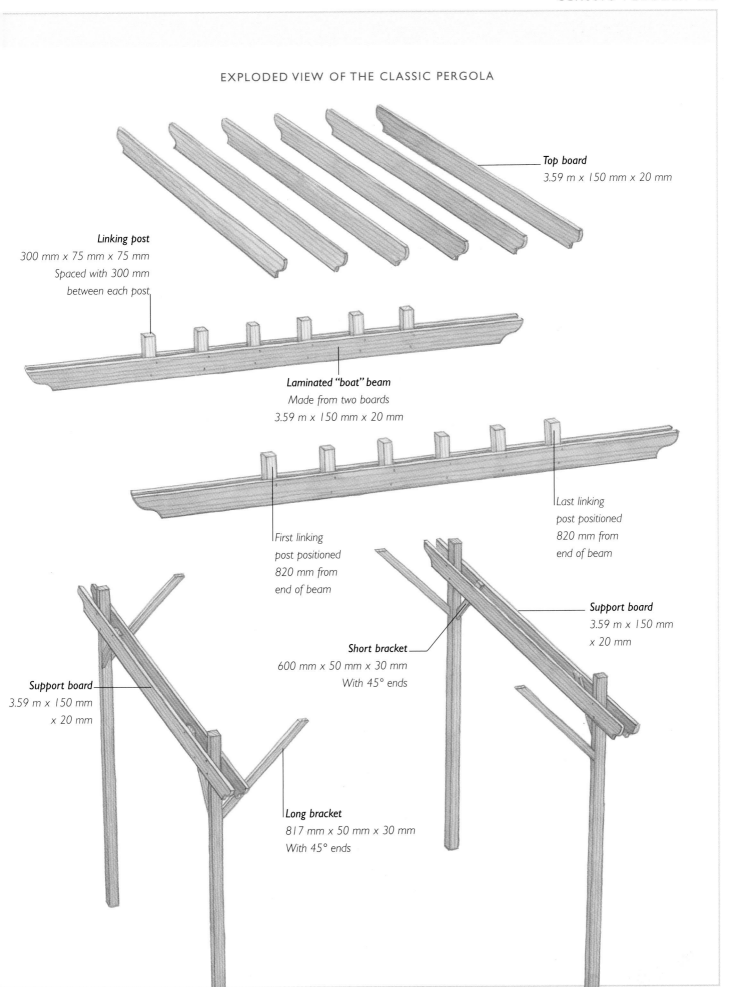

Top board
3.59 m x 150 mm x 20 mm

Linking post
300 mm x 75 mm x 75 mm
Spaced with 300 mm
between each post

Laminated "boat" beam
Made from two boards
3.59 m x 150 mm x 20 mm

Last linking
post positioned
820 mm from
end of beam

First linking
post positioned
820 mm from
end of beam

Support board
3.59 m x 150 mm
x 20 mm

Short bracket
600 mm x 50 mm x 30 mm
With 45° ends

Support board
3.59 m x 150 mm
x 20 mm

Long bracket
817 mm x 50 mm x 30 mm
With 45° ends

Step-by-step: **Making the classic pergola**

Jigsaw
Fit the jigsaw with a new blade

Fixing
Run screws through from both boards

Template
Use the waste bit as a template for drawing the other shapes

Workboard
Use a spare piece of 150 mm-wide wood as a workboard

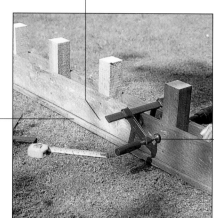

Clamp
Secure the post with a clamp and then screw it into position

1 Use the crosscut saw to cut all the wood to size. Draw the cyma curve on the end of one of the fourteen top, boat and support boards, and fret out with the jigsaw. Use the waste as a pattern for the shape of all the other board ends.

2 Sandwich six of the 300 mm-long linking posts between two shaped boards to make a boat beam. Establish the position of the linking posts and clamp them in place. Run 48 mm screws through the boards and into the posts. Re-run the procedure to build the other boat beam.

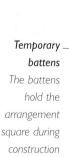

Temporary battens
The battens hold the arrangement square during construction

3 Set the boat beam on the ground and screw the two main posts in place, using one 48 mm screw for each post. Link the bottom of the posts with a batten. Set a batten across the diagonal, make adjustments until the two diagonal measurements are identical, and screw it in position with 48 mm screws.

Helpful hint

Don't remove the temporary supporting battens until the main posts are securely in the ground, and the beams are braced with the brackets.

Assistance
You may need one or two people
to help you at this stage

4 Set the two-post boat-
beam structure upright and
use battens to prop it in place.
Check the vertical with a spirit
level. Make adjustments by
altering the position of the struts.

Spirit level
Check the
frame to
ensure that it
is upright
and square

Batten
supports
Use battens to
create tripod-
like supports

Clamp
Clamp the boards in place if you
have trouble holding them

5 When you have mounted both boat-
beam structures square with each
other, so they are well placed and upright,
link them with the two pairs of support
boards that run underneath the boat
beams. Screw the four support boards to
the main posts with 48 mm screws.

Support boards
The paired
boards provide
extra support

Top boards
Butt each
board hard up
against the
linking post

6 Fix the six top boards with 48 mm
screws. Cut the brackets to shape
(45° ends) and fix between the posts and
cross beams. Use 65 mm screws where
the brackets join the posts and 48 mm
screws where they join the beams. Sand
the pergola and paint it with preservative.

Inspirations: **Pergolas**

The visual impact of a structure clothed in flowers can be absolutely stunning. Perennials such as wisteria, roses, honeysuckle, clematis, passion flower, jasmine and climbing hydrangeas can be relied on to delight you every year. Annuals such as morning glory, sweet peas and nasturtiums can be grown to provide extra colour, or used to create a pergola that changes its coat each season.

ABOVE **A pergola can be a frame for climbing plants, a focal point in a rose garden or a place for a swing. This rustic green wood pergola, with its decorative balustrades, makes an attractive addition to any garden.**

RIGHT **As well as supporting flowers, a pergola is perfect for grapevines or for creating a tapestry of exciting leaf effects, weaving the blazing reds of Virginia creeper, or various colours and shapes of ivy.**

FAR RIGHT **A pergola with brick pillars creates a traditional walkway, hosting plants such as wisteria, which has blooms that droop attractively through the beams. Scented roses make for an equally pleasant experience.**

Victorian tool shed

This beautiful shed draws inspiration from a Victorian earth closet that I loved when I was a child. The proportions of the design make a garden shed that is just right for storing your lawnmower and tools. If you would like to build an attractive and practical tool shed that will impress your neighbours, have a go at this one.

TIME

A weekend (about twelve hours for the woodwork, and another four hours or so for fixing the hinges and latch, and getting it painted).

USEFUL TIP

We recommend that you buy a strong padlock for the door: tool sheds are a target for burglars.

YOU WILL NEED

Materials *for a tool shed 2.546 m high, 1.259 m wide and 1.230 m deep. (All rough-sawn pine pieces include excess length for wastage.)*

- Pine: 35 pieces, each 3 m long, 35 mm wide and 20 mm thick (frames for front, side, back, door and roof; braces for side and back panels; corner trim; doorway battens; roof support blocks; roof ridge boards; roof location bar)
- Pine: 6 pieces, each 3 m long, 150 mm wide and 20 mm thick (decorative barge boards, front feature boards, finial and floorboards)
- Pine: 2 pieces, each 2 m long, 50 mm wide and 30 mm thick (floor joists)
- Pine: 2 pieces, each 3 m long, 65 mm wide and 20 mm thick (ledge and brace details for the door)
- Pine feather-edged board: 60 pieces, each 3 m long, 100 mm wide and 13 mm thick (for cladding frames)
- Galvanized T-strap hinges: 3 hinges, about 250 mm long

- Galvanized sliding gate latch, complete with screws and coach bolts to fit
- Zinc-plated, countersunk cross-headed screws: 200 x 38 mm no. 8, 100 x 50 mm no. 8
- Galvanized nails: 2 kg x 40 mm x 2.65 mm
- Roof felt: 1.2 m x 300 mm
- Acrylic paint, colours to suit
- Clear preservative

Tools

- Pencil, ruler, tape measure, marking gauge and square
- Two portable workbenches
- Crosscut saw
- Cordless electric drill with a cross-point screwdriver bit
- Drill bits to match the screw, nail, dowel and vent hole sizes
- Small hammer
- Coping saw
- Electric jigsaw
- Small screwdriver
- Electric sander with a pack of medium-grade sandpaper
- Paintbrush: 40 mm

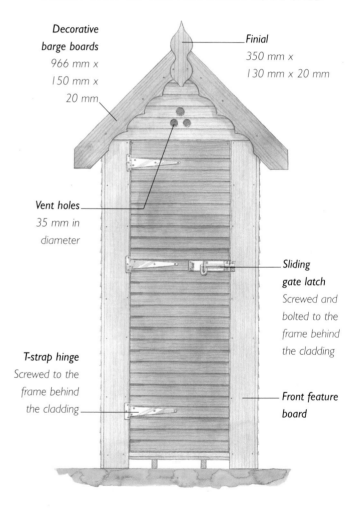

FRONT VIEW OF THE VICTORIAN TOOL SHED

Decorative barge boards
966 mm x 150 mm x 20 mm

Finial
350 mm x 130 mm x 20 mm

Vent holes
35 mm in diameter

Sliding gate latch
Screwed and bolted to the frame behind the cladding

T-strap hinge
Screwed to the frame behind the cladding

Front feature board

PRETTY AND PRACTICAL

The tool shed comprises four primary frames (the front, back and two sides), which are all made from 35 mm x 20 mm sections covered in feather-edged board. It has a steeply pitched roof sloping down at each side, a narrow door and airholes in the gable. The decorative details are made from 150 mm-wide boards. The floor is built directly on small-section joists, the idea being

you can mount the shed on blocks, a concrete base or slabs. The structure is designed so that two people can easily move the component parts to the site. The interior has been left plain, so that you can customize it to suit your own requirements. We are planning to fit an 150 mm-wide board for screwhooks and pegs to store the spade, fork, rake and so on. There will be an extra-strong hook for the mower, and a shelf at gable level for small items.

Victorian tool shed

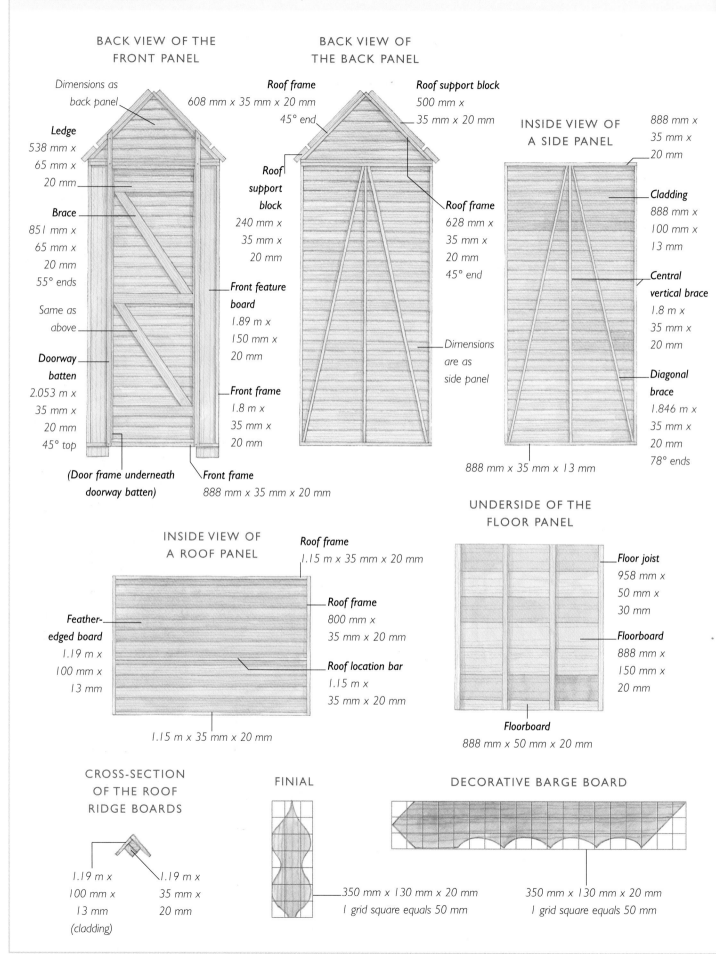

BACK VIEW OF THE FRONT PANEL

Dimensions as back panel

Ledge
538 mm x 65 mm x 20 mm

Brace
851 mm x 65 mm x 20 mm 55° ends

Same as above

Doorway batten
2.053 m x 35 mm x 20 mm 45° top

(Door frame underneath doorway batten)

Front feature board
1.89 m x 150 mm x 20 mm

Front frame
1.8 m x 35 mm x 20 mm

Front frame
888 mm x 35 mm x 20 mm

BACK VIEW OF THE BACK PANEL

Roof frame
608 mm x 35 mm x 20 mm 45° end

Roof support block
500 mm x 35 mm x 20 mm

Roof support block
240 mm x 35 mm x 20 mm

Roof frame
628 mm x 35 mm x 20 mm 45° end

Dimensions are as side panel

INSIDE VIEW OF A SIDE PANEL

888 mm x 35 mm x 20 mm

Cladding
888 mm x 100 mm x 13 mm

Central vertical brace
1.8 m x 35 mm x 20 mm

Diagonal brace
1.846 m x 35 mm x 20 mm 78° ends

888 mm x 35 mm x 13 mm

INSIDE VIEW OF A ROOF PANEL

Roof frame
1.15 m x 35 mm x 20 mm

Roof frame
800 mm x 35 mm x 20 mm

Roof location bar
1.15 m x 35 mm x 20 mm

Feather-edged board
1.19 m x 100 mm x 13 mm

1.15 m x 35 mm x 20 mm

UNDERSIDE OF THE FLOOR PANEL

Floor joist
958 mm x 50 mm x 30 mm

Floorboard
888 mm x 150 mm x 20 mm

Floorboard
888 mm x 50 mm x 20 mm

CROSS-SECTION OF THE ROOF RIDGE BOARDS

1.19 m x 100 mm x 13 mm (cladding)

1.19 m x 35 mm x 20 mm

FINIAL

350 mm x 130 mm x 20 mm
1 grid square equals 50 mm

DECORATIVE BARGE BOARD

350 mm x 130 mm x 20 mm
1 grid square equals 50 mm

EXPLODED VIEW OF THE VICTORIAN TOOL SHED

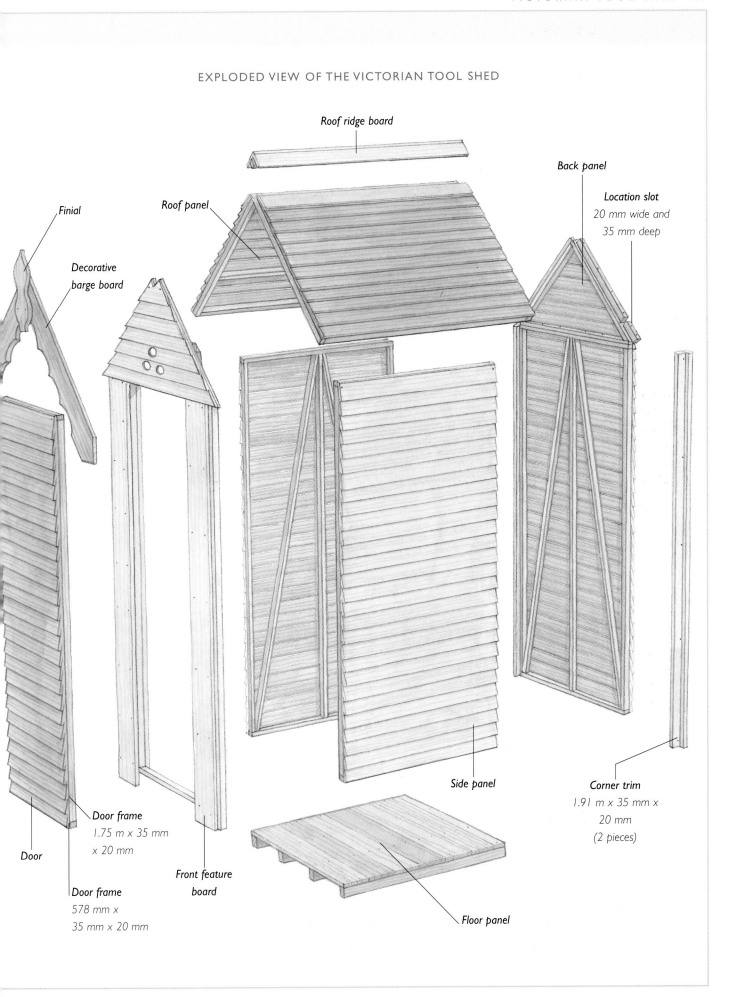

Roof ridge board

Finial

Back panel

Location slot
20 mm wide and
35 mm deep

Decorative
barge board

Roof panel

Door

Door frame
1.75 m x 35 mm
x 20 mm

Door frame
578 mm x
35 mm x 20 mm

Front feature
board

Side panel

Floor panel

Corner trim
1.91 m x 35 mm x
20 mm
(2 pieces)

Step-by-step: **Making the Victorian tool shed**

Knot-free wood
*Make sure that the door frames
are free from knots*

Uprights
*Set the front
frame and door
frame pieces
(for supporting
the front
feature board)
150 mm
apart at the
outside edges*

1 Cut the wood to size. Take the lengths of wood that make the front panel, and butt joint them with 38 mm screws. Set the two 150 mm-wide front feature boards in place on the front of the frame (at either side of the door) and fix with 38 mm screws. Adjust for squareness. Screw the doorway battens on the back of the frame with 38 mm screws.

Screwholes
*Drill holes to
take the screws*

Squareness
*Set the frame
square by
checking that
the diagonal
measurements
are identical*

Tight fit
*The braces
should be cut
to fit perfectly
within the
squared frame*

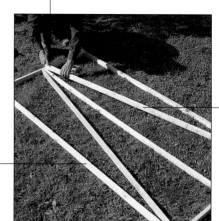

2 Build the back frame in much the same way as already described, only this time, fit a central vertical flanked by two diagonal braces. Aim to make the braces fit tightly into the frame. Build two identical side panel frames complete with central, vertical and diagonal braces, as described for the back frame.

Roof location bar
*Set 500 mm from the
ridge side of the frame*

Screws
*Have two screws
at each joint*

Roof frame
*Choose an
extra good bit
of wood for
the eaves*

3 Build the door frame with the two sections of wood, using 38 mm screws, and 50 mm screws for fixing the diagonal brace pieces. Make two identical roof frames, each including a roof location bar, using two 38 mm screws at each joint.

Check angles
*Make sure the frame is
a right-angled triangle*

*Roof
support block*
*Fix each block
with two
38 mm screws*

Location slot
*Use an offcut
of wood to
ensure that the
location slot
will take the
roof panel*

4 Make two identical triangular gable frames with roof support blocks positioned to make location points for the roof frames. An offcut is used to ensure that the location slot is the correct size.

Cladding
The cladding needs to be level
with the top of the plate

Jig
Use a simple jig to help you
space the cladding properly

Coping saw
Cut the
cladding clear
of the roof
location slot

Nail holes
Drill holes
before nailing,
to avoid
splitting the
wood

Parallel
Check with a
tape measure
occasionally to
make sure that
the boards are
still parallel

5 When you have covered the gable frames by nailing on the feather-edged boards (a technique for positioning the boards is described in the Rabbit Ark project on page 96), use the coping saw to cut through the cladding to make a roof location slot, 20 mm wide and 35 mm deep, on the two elevated sides of the gable triangle.

6 Clad the other frames with feather-edged board. Use a simple jig to ensure that the overlap of the boards is constant. Drill holes for the nails, making sure that the nail doesn't pass through an underlying feather-edged strip. Use the jigsaw to make the decorative barge boards. Sand all the panels and paint them on the outside.

Fixing panels
Run screws
down through
the side panel
and floorboards
and into the
floor joists

7 Set the wall panels on the base and fix with 50 mm screws running into the floor joists. Locate the roof panels and screw in place with 50 mm screws. Wrap felt over the join between the two roof panels and fix with nails. Use 38 mm screws to fix the ridge board on top of the felt. Screw the decorative barge boards to the front edges of the panels, and the finials to the barge boards, with 38 mm screws. Drill three vent holes in the front gable. Fit the hinge and latch. Give all surfaces a coat of preservative. The floor panel should have an extra coat of preservative on the underside and on the ends of the joists.

Treehouse

Children love climbing trees, and will be absolutely delighted with this hideaway. In their imagination it may become anything from a hilltop castle to a pirate ship on the high seas, or a magic carpet gliding over cities and deserts. It also makes a perfect retreat for adults to escape the world! Select a sturdy, established tree.

FRONT VIEW OF THE TREEHOUSE

Panels
The roof and wall panels are constructed from 64 x 32 mm sections and then covered with feather-edged board

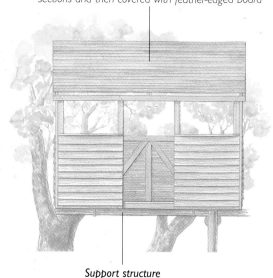

Support structure
This is constructed to suit the shape of the tree

A BIRD'S-EYE VIEW

The treehouse is made up from seven primary frames – two for the front, one for the back, one for each side, one for the base, and one for the roof. They are all made from 64 mm x 32 mm sections covered in feather-edged board. The roof slopes down towards the front, so that the overhang protects the inside of the house from wind and rain. The base is supported directly on beams that are fixed to the tree with coach screws if required. We were able to create a stable support structure with just three horizontal beams and two vertical poles, but you will need to build a support arrangement to suit the shape of your chosen tree. The whole structure is designed so that the frames can be built on the ground and then moved up into the tree.

The actual business of getting the structure into the tree is not only tricky, but also potentially very dangerous. You will need at least four strong people to help, plus a pair of ladders and lots of thick rope. You must all wear gloves and stout boots, and you should elect one person to lead operations. In the interests of safety, children and pets must be kept at a distance.

YOU WILL NEED

Materials *for a treehouse 2.267 m wide, 1.918 m deep and 1.910 m high. (All rough-sawn pine pieces include excess length for wastage.)*
- Pine: 25 pieces, 3 m long, 64 mm wide and 32 mm thick (long members for the frames for the walls, roof and floor)
- Pine: 20 pieces, 3 m long, 76 mm wide and 16 mm thick (floorboards)
- Pine feather-edged board: 30 pieces, 3 m long, 100 mm wide and 13 mm thick (wall cladding)
- Pine feather-edged board: 17 pieces, 3 m long, 200 mm wide and 13 mm thick (roof cladding)
- Pine: 2 pieces, 764 mm long, 100 mm wide and 13 mm thick (sills)
- Rope: 20 m, 10 mm in diameter (for lashing the floor panel to the support frame)
- Galvanized square-headed coach screws: 150 mm long, quantity as necessary (optional)

- Zinc-plated, countersunk cross-headed screws: 200 x 50 mm no 8, 200 x 65 mm no. 8
- Galvanized nails: 1 kg pack of 50 mm x 2.65 mm

Tools
- Pencil, ruler, tape measure, marking gauge, square and spirit level
- Two portable workbenches
- Ladder (length to suit site)
- Bolt wrench (if using coach screws)
- Crosscut saw
- Hammer
- Electric drill
- Cordless electric drill with a cross-point screwdriver bit
- Countersink drill bit to match the screw sizes
- Drill bit to match the size of the nails
- Drill bit to match the diameter of the rope
- Electric sander with a pack of medium-grade sandpaper
- Pair of clamps

Treehouse

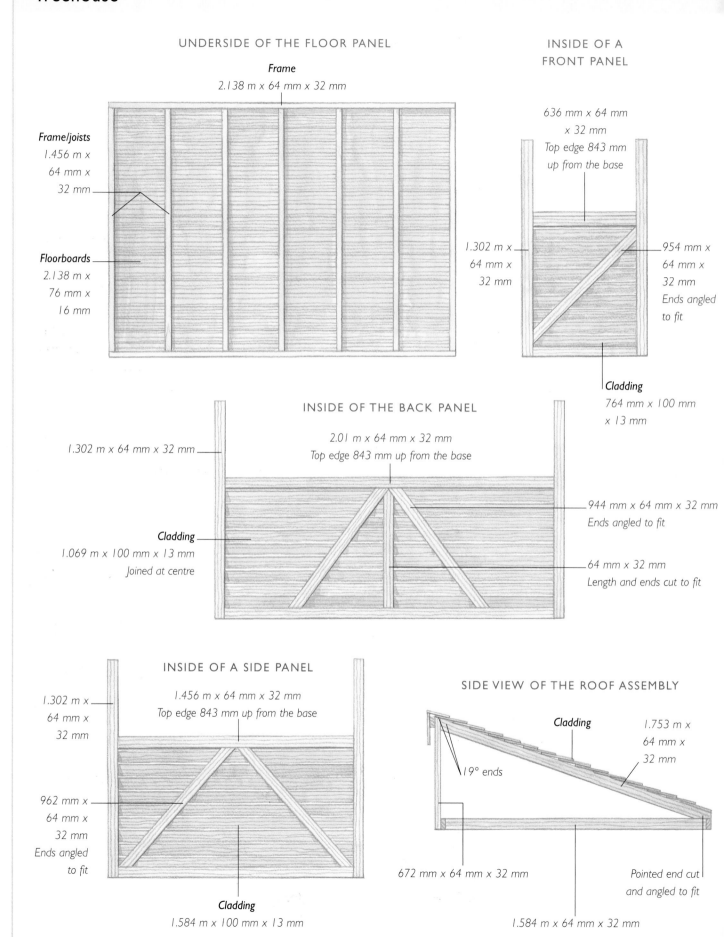

UNDERSIDE OF THE FLOOR PANEL

Frame
2.138 m x 64 mm x 32 mm

Frame/joists
1.456 m x
64 mm x
32 mm

Floorboards
2.138 m x
76 mm x
16 mm

INSIDE OF A
FRONT PANEL

636 mm x 64 mm
x 32 mm
Top edge 843 mm
up from the base

1.302 m x
64 mm x
32 mm

954 mm x
64 mm x
32 mm
Ends angled
to fit

Cladding
764 mm x 100 mm
x 13 mm

INSIDE OF THE BACK PANEL

2.01 m x 64 mm x 32 mm
Top edge 843 mm up from the base

1.302 m x 64 mm x 32 mm

Cladding
1.069 m x 100 mm x 13 mm
Joined at centre

944 mm x 64 mm x 32 mm
Ends angled to fit

64 mm x 32 mm
Length and ends cut to fit

INSIDE OF A SIDE PANEL

1.456 m x 64 mm x 32 mm
Top edge 843 mm up from the base

1.302 m x
64 mm x
32 mm

962 mm x
64 mm x
32 mm
Ends angled
to fit

Cladding
1.584 m x 100 mm x 13 mm

SIDE VIEW OF THE ROOF ASSEMBLY

Cladding

1.753 m x
64 mm x
32 mm

19° ends

672 mm x 64 mm x 32 mm

Pointed end cut
and angled to fit

1.584 m x 64 mm x 32 mm

EXPLODED VIEW OF THE TREEHOUSE

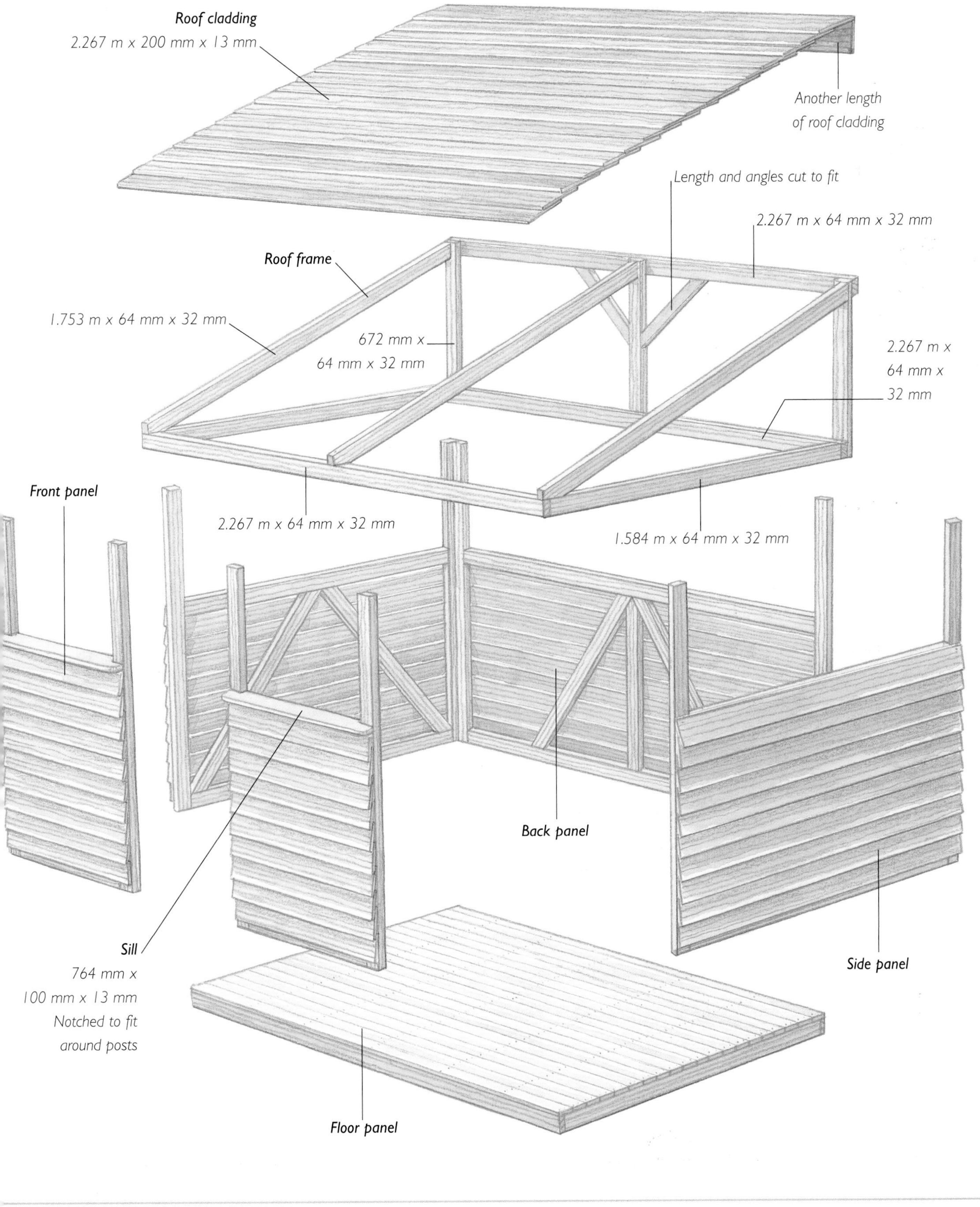

Roof cladding
2.267 m x 200 mm x 13 mm

Another length
of roof cladding

Length and angles cut to fit

2.267 m x 64 mm x 32 mm

Roof frame

1.753 m x 64 mm x 32 mm

672 mm x
64 mm x 32 mm

2.267 m x
64 mm x
32 mm

2.267 m x 64 mm x 32 mm

1.584 m x 64 mm x 32 mm

Front panel

Back panel

Side panel

Sill

764 mm x
100 mm x 13 mm
Notched to fit
around posts

Floor panel

Step-by-step: **Making the treehouse**

Support poles
Fix three or more poles to the tree to make a horizontal platform

Rope-fixing points
Drill holes through the floor joists at points for roping the floor to the tree

Branches
Trim off branches that will be in the way

Square frame
Check the frame is square by comparing the diagonal measurements

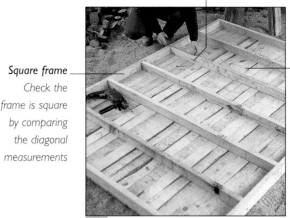

Floorboards
All the boards need to be screwed to the joists — one 50 mm screw at each intersection

 Choose a strong, established tree with suitable branches. Prepare the site (the area within the tree) by cutting back branches if necessary. Build a sturdy support frame to make a platform for the treehouse. Wedge it between the branches or fix to the tree with coach screws if needed. Check that the supports are level.

2 To make the floor panel, first build a frame about 2.138 m long and 1.520 m wide, complete with secondary joists, using 65 mm screws. Screw on the 76 mm-wide floorboards with 50 mm screws. Drill rope-fixing holes through the joists at points where they will be useful for lashing the floor to the support frame.

Bracing
The diagonal struts reinforce the frame and hold it square

Corner joints
Fix the frame together using two screws at each corner

Nailing
Nail the cladding to the frame at every intersection

Cladding
Keep the boards evenly spaced and parallel (overlap the boards by at least 20 mm)

Pilot holes
Drill holes for nails (especially those that occur near the end of a piece of wood)

3 Using 65 mm screws, build the back wall frame, making it 2.138 m wide and 1.302 m in total height. Brace the bottom of the frame with two diagonals that centre on the underside of the top of the frame at sill level (no sill on back).

4 Fix the 100 mm-wide feather-edged board on the back wall frame. Working from the bottom upwards, and stopping short of the level of the sill, drill pilot holes through the boards and nail them to the frame with 50 mm nails.

Diagonals
Measure the diagonals to determine
whether the frame is square

Brace
Fit a diagonal
brace to hold
the frame
square

Levelling
If necessary, add wedges under
the base to make it level

Fixing
Thread rope
through the
holes in the
joists and
around the
support beams

Additional
support
We added
vertical posts
for extra
strength

5 Build the frames for the other walls and roof in much the same way as already described, all the while double-checking that the measurements tally and the frames are square. Cut and fit two sills to the front frames with 65 mm screws.

6 Heave the base up into the tree and lash it in place with rope. The rope allows the structure to flex in the wind without either the treehouse or the tree coming under too much stress.

Joining the panels
Screw the uprights to each other
near the top, middle and bottom

Fixing to
the base
Drive screws
through the
wall panel
frames and
into the
base frame

Temporary stays
Remove stays after the
roof is secured

Safety
Make sure that
the ladder is
positioned
safely and ask
a friend to help
hold it in place

Fixing the roof
Screw the roof
frame to the
top corners of
the wall frames

7 Lift the two side wall frames up into the tree, clamp them to the base, and screw them in position with 65 mm screws. Remove the clamps. Repeat the procedure with the back wall frame.

8 When the back and the two side frames are securely in place, hoist the roof frame into position and screw it to the corner uprights of the wall frames. Finally, screw the two front frames to the side walls and to the roof. Use 65 mm screws throughout.

Children's playhouse

This playhouse has wonderful decorative details, making it look as though it is straight out of *Grimm's Fairy Tales*, and is therefore guaranteed to stimulate children's imaginations. If you have children or grandchildren aged up to about twelve, they will find the playhouse great fun, and you will get much enjoyment from the project.

TIME

Two long weekends (one weekend for building the frames, about twelve hours for building the door and window, and the rest of the time for finishing).

USEFUL TIP

For safety reasons, plastic is used for the window "glass".

YOU WILL NEED

Materials *for a playhouse 1.91 m high, 1.844 m wide and 1.635 mm deep. (All rough-sawn pine pieces include excess length for wastage.)*

- Pine: 40 pieces, each 2 m long, 35 mm wide and 20 mm thick (frames, small trimmers, roof location bar, roof support blocks)
- Pine tongue-and-groove: 5 pieces, each 2 m long, 90 mm wide and 8 mm thick (stable door, decorative shutters, offcuts for glazing beading to fix the window)
- Pine: 12 pieces, each 2 m long, 150 mm wide and 22 mm thick (floorboards, decorative barge boards, decorative trim, back finial; offcuts for exterior glazing strip, window sill, door handle and door surround)
- Pine: 4 pieces, each 2 m long, 65 mm wide and 30 mm thick (floor joists, front finial)
- Pine: 4 pieces, each 2 m long, 65 mm wide and 35 mm thick (for covering the corners)
- Pine: 1 piece, 2 m long, 75 mm x 75 mm triangular section (roof ridge board)
- Pine feather-edged board: 100 pieces, each 2 m long, 100 mm wide and 10 mm thick (cladding; wall plates)

- Zinc-plated, countersunk cross-headed screws: 200 x 38 mm no. 8, 100 x 50 mm no. 8, 100 x 65 mm no. 10
- Galvanized nails: 4 kg x 40 mm x 2.65 mm
- Galvanized flat-headed 10 mm roof tacks: handful (to fix felt)
- Polycarbonate sheet: 330 mm x 345 mm (window)
- Piano hinges: 512 mm and 672 mm long, with screws to fit
- Water-based, exterior paint: matt white and blue
- Roof felt: 2 m long and 300 mm wide (for fixing under the roof ridge board)

Tools
- Pencil, ruler, tape measure, marking gauge and square
- Two portable workbenches
- Crosscut saw
- Cordless electric drill with a cross-point screwdriver bit
- Drill bits to match the screw and nail sizes
- Coping saw
- Electric compound mitre saw
- Hammer
- Electric sander with a pack of medium-grade sandpaper
- Paintbrush: 40 mm
- Pair of clamps

FRONT VIEW OF THE PLAYHOUSE

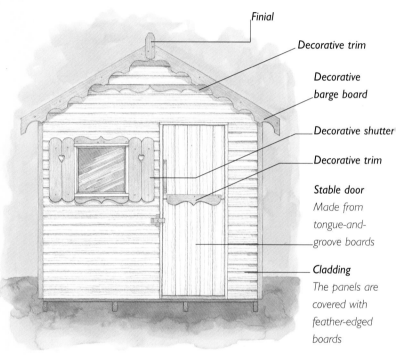

Finial

Decorative trim

Decorative barge board

Decorative shutter

Decorative trim

Stable door
Made from tongue-and-groove boards

Cladding
The panels are covered with feather-edged boards

A MINI HOUSE FOR MINORS

If you want to delight your children or grandchildren, you will happily spend a couple of weekends building this project. This is the playhouse that children dream about. It is high enough to stand upright in, the stable door can be shut from the inside, it has a proper weather-tight window, and there is plenty of space. The floor base measures 1.525 m x 1.255 m, so there is enough room for three or four children to spread out their sleeping bags. We have detailed the playhouse to suit children aged four to eight – with lots of fairy-tale trim and soft colours – but, for older children, the details can be changed and stronger colours used.

We have envisaged that you will make the frames outside your garage or garden workshop, and then move them to the site. We have fitted piano hinges because they close the gap between the door and the frame, preventing children from serious accidents to their fingers. Children can close the stable doors from the inside, but you can also open the playhouse from the outside.

Children's playhouse

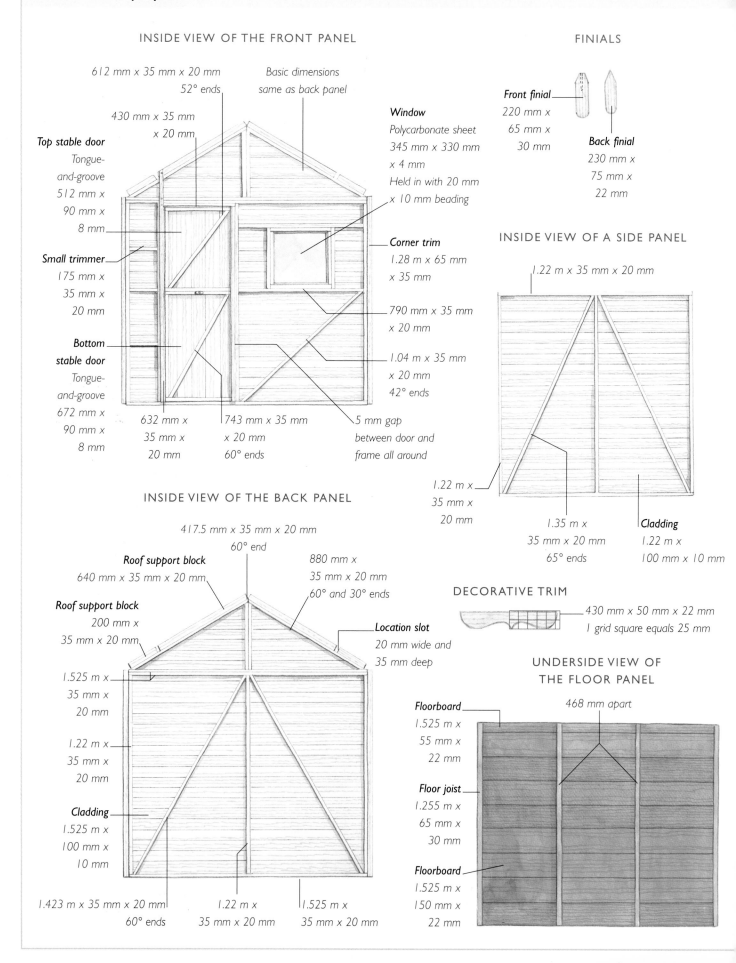

INSIDE VIEW OF THE FRONT PANEL

612 mm x 35 mm x 20 mm
52° ends

Basic dimensions
same as back panel

430 mm x 35 mm
x 20 mm

Top stable door
Tongue-
and-groove
512 mm x
90 mm x
8 mm

Window
Polycarbonate sheet
345 mm x 330 mm
x 4 mm
Held in with 20 mm
x 10 mm beading

Small trimmer
175 mm x
35 mm x
20 mm

Corner trim
1.28 m x 65 mm
x 35 mm

790 mm x 35 mm
x 20 mm

**Bottom
stable door**
Tongue-
and-groove
672 mm x
90 mm x
8 mm

1.04 m x 35 mm
x 20 mm
42° ends

632 mm x
35 mm x
20 mm

743 mm x 35 mm
x 20 mm
60° ends

5 mm gap
between door and
frame all around

INSIDE VIEW OF THE BACK PANEL

417.5 mm x 35 mm x 20 mm
60° end

880 mm x
35 mm x 20 mm
60° and 30° ends

Roof support block
640 mm x 35 mm x 20 mm

Roof support block
200 mm x
35 mm x 20 mm

Location slot
20 mm wide and
35 mm deep

1.525 m x
35 mm x
20 mm

1.22 m x
35 mm x
20 mm

Cladding
1.525 m x
100 mm x
10 mm

1.423 m x 35 mm x 20 mm
60° ends

1.22 m x
35 mm x 20 mm

1.525 m x
35 mm x 20 mm

FINIALS

Front finial
220 mm x
65 mm x
30 mm

Back finial
230 mm x
75 mm x
22 mm

INSIDE VIEW OF A SIDE PANEL

1.22 m x 35 mm x 20 mm

1.22 m x
35 mm x
20 mm

1.35 m x
35 mm x 20 mm
65° ends

Cladding
1.22 m x
100 mm x 10 mm

DECORATIVE TRIM

430 mm x 50 mm x 22 mm
1 grid square equals 25 mm

UNDERSIDE VIEW OF
THE FLOOR PANEL

468 mm apart

Floorboard
1.525 m x
55 mm x
22 mm

Floor joist
1.255 m x
65 mm x
30 mm

Floorboard
1.525 m x
150 mm x
22 mm

INSIDE VIEW OF A ROOF PANEL

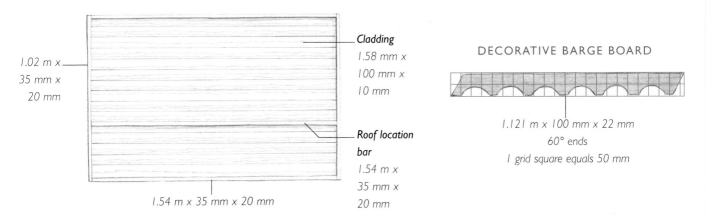

Cladding
1.58 mm x
100 mm x
10 mm

1.02 m x
35 mm x
20 mm

Roof location
bar
1.54 m x
35 mm x
20 mm

1.54 m x 35 mm x 20 mm

DECORATIVE BARGE BOARD

1.121 m x 100 mm x 22 mm
60° ends
1 grid square equals 50 mm

EXPLODED VIEW OF THE CHILDREN'S PLAYHOUSE

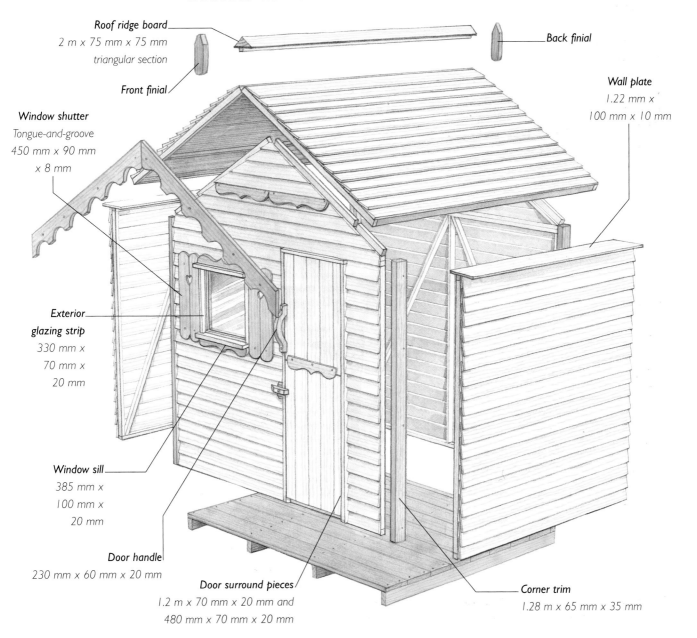

Roof ridge board
2 m x 75 mm x 75 mm
triangular section

Front finial

Back finial

Wall plate
1.22 mm x
100 mm x 10 mm

Window shutter
Tongue-and-groove
450 mm x 90 mm
x 8 mm

Exterior
glazing strip
330 mm x
70 mm x
20 mm

Window sill
385 mm x
100 mm x
20 mm

Door handle
230 mm x 60 mm x 20 mm

Door surround pieces
1.2 m x 70 mm x 20 mm and
480 mm x 70 mm x 20 mm

Corner trim
1.28 m x 65 mm x 35 mm

Step-by-step: **Making the children's playhouse**

Working area
Find an area of level ground to work on

Wood selection
Make sure that the pieces that make the door frame are perfectly straight

Screwholes
Drill holes at the ends of the boards to take the screws

Joints
Use two screws at the joints where possible

Reinforcement
Use lengths of spare wood to strengthen the hinge side of the frame

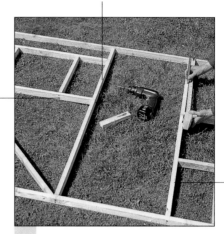

1 Use the crosscut saw to cut all the wood to size. First, make the floor. Set the four floor joists about 468 mm apart and screw the 150 mm-wide floorboards in place with 50 mm screws so that you finish up with a base that measures 1.525 m across and 1.255 m from front to back.

2 Set out the overall size of the front frame and then divide it up, first with the two verticals for the door, then the two horizontals for the window, and so on. Finish with the diagonal braces and the small trimmers at the side of the door. Fix everything with 38 mm screws.

Verticals
Double up the verticals for strength

Overhang
The roof should mostly overhang at the front and only a little at the back

Roof support blocks
The blocks are for locating the roof panel and need to be placed accurately

Location slot
The roof panel should drop into position and not need to be forced

3 Build the gable triangles, complete with the roof support blocks (use 50 mm screws) for locating the roof frames. For the verticals, have two thicknesses of wood set back to back, in order to strengthen the frame and prevent it from twisting.

4 Screw the wall frames together with 38 mm screws and build the roof frame to fit. Locate the roof frame in the location slots that you have created on top of the gable frames. Dismantle the frames and lay them on the ground in readiness for cladding with feather-edged board.

Window frame
Cut the frame from
150 mm-wide offcuts

Turnbuckle
Make a turnbuckle from
a piece of spare wood

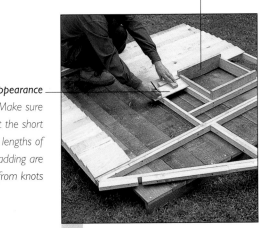

Appearance
Make sure
that the short
lengths of
cladding are
free from knots

Hinges
Put screws in
all the holes of
the hinges, as
they need to
be firmly fixed

Gap
Maintain a
5 mm gap
between the
two doors

5 First frame the window with exterior glazing strips cut from the 150 mm-wide offcuts, and then set to work covering the frame with feather-edged board, nailing it on with 40 mm nails. Clad the rest of the frames as described in other projects (a technique for positioning the boards is described in the Rabbit Ark project on page 96).

6 Build the frames for the doors (using 38 mm screws) complete with the diagonal braces, and cover them with the tongue-and-groove boarding. Fix the doors with the piano hinges and make the stops and turnbuckles from offcuts of 150 mm-wide wood (size and design to suit).

Heart detail
Push the two pieces together to
make the heart shape

Painting
Sand and paint all the panels
inside and out before assembling

Screwholes
Drill holes for
38 mm screws
through the
cladding and
into the
frame behind

Placing
Make sure that
you align the
framework of
the panels
(rather than
the cladding)
with the base

Floor fixing
Screw down
through the
panel frame,
through the
floorboard
and into the
floor joist

7 Make the window shutters. Cut the heart detail (65 mm long and 50 mm wide) on the edges of the boards prior to assembly, using the coping saw. Cut the polycarbonate for the window "glass" to size and fix it with glazing beading strips taken from the tongue-and-groove.

8 Set the floor on site. Clamp and screw the walls in place with 65 mm screws. Position the roof frames, with the roof support blocks in the location slots. Screw on the wall plates with 38 mm screws. Nail the felt over the ridge and screw on the ridge board (50 mm screws).

Stone

Introduction

When we first saw the stone walls that formed the garden boundary of our Cornish quayside cottage, we were amazed. They were beautiful! Ranging in height from a metre to well over three metres, the walls were massively thick and built from course upon course of uncut limestone. And so it was with all the walls in the village. We were brought to a standstill not only by the sheer size of the structures, but also by their physical presence and the fact that every single stone was set in place without mortar.

From then on, we were hooked. We began to scour the countryside for examples of interesting stonework. Over the next few years, we saw stone steps that disappeared into the sea, massive stonework railway arches built by Isambard Kingdom Brunel, tin mine towers, stone cellars, and so on. After years of looking and touching, exploring and drawing, we wanted to have a go at stonework ourselves. We began to search for some good "how-to" books, but soon discovered that although there were plenty of books that described stone structures, there was nothing much that actually told you how to mix the mortar and set one stone upon another. We came to the conclusion that if we wanted to do

stonework, we simply had to get on with it. As a result, we have worked on all manner of garden stonework projects – everything from walls and pillars, paths and rockeries, through to Japanese gardens and gateposts – and enjoyed it immensely.

Stonework is an amazingly vigorous and dynamic craft. The forms are large and bold, the techniques are adventurous and expressive, and the end results are truly monumental and last forever. We invite you to roll up your sleeves, take up the challenge, and build something that you will be very proud of!

Alan & Gill

HEALTH AND SAFETY

Many stoneworking procedures are potentially dangerous, so before starting work on the projects, check through the following list:

- Make sure that you are fit and strong enough for the task ahead. If you have doubts, ask your doctor for specific advice.
- When you are lifting large lumps of stone from ground level, minimize back strain by bending your knees, hugging the stone close to your body, and keeping the spine upright.

- If a slab of stone looks too heavy to lift on your own, ask others to help.
- Wear gloves, a dust-mask and goggles when you are handling cement and lime, cutting stone with a hammer and chisel, or when using the angle grinder.
- Never operate a machine such as a grinder or drill, or attempt a difficult lifting or manoeuvring task, if you are overtired.
- Follow the manufacturer's instructions when using the angle grinder.

Part 1: **Techniques**

Designing and planning

The secret of building a successful stonework feature lies in the detail. It does not matter whether you are young or old, what is more important is enthusiasm and a willingness to spend time designing and planning the whole operation – from choosing the individual stones, through to organizing the delivery, mixing the mortar, and cleaning your tools. Stonework will enhance any garden, whether it is large or small.

FIRST CONSIDERATIONS

- Do you live in an area where the predominant building material is stone? Are there stone quarries within a radius of 20 kilometres?
- If most of the houses near you are built from brick and wood (therefore the chances are that there are no stone quarries in your area), are there any other sources of supply, such as builder's merchants or architectural salvage companies?
- Will local companies deliver small quantities of mixed stone?
- Is there adequate access to your garden – a road clear of traffic, a wide gateway, and a good drive?
- If the stone is unloaded in your driveway, or at your gate, will it cause any problems of access for you or your car? Will it damage the surface of the drive? Will it pose a danger to children or passers-by?
- How are you going to move the stone from the gate to the site? Are you going to move it yourself with a wheelbarrow and a sack barrow? Or are you going to ask friends to help, then move it with the aid of levers and rollers?
- Is your garden reasonably level, with paths wide enough for a wheelbarrow? Or does it have a lot of lawn and few pathways – if so, how will you move the materials?

Choosing a suitable project

When you have found satisfactory solutions to sourcing the stone and have worked out how and when it is going to be delivered, you can start to consider the ergonomics of the projects in the context of your specific needs: this boils down to working out how you are going to move the stone around the garden. In most instances, we have specifically designed the projects so that they are made up from small, easy-to-lift stones (albeit the sum total weight of all the stones might be considerable), but one or two of the projects do use single, monolithic stones. For example, if you have chosen to make the Pedestal Table (page 244), you have to work out how you are going to lift the table slab into position. There are a couple of ways to deal with it: you can build the pedestal before you take delivery of the table slab, then ask the stone supplier to lift the slab straight into position, or you can call on your friends and family to help you. The only thing you mustn't do is back down from building the project!

Planning the project

Whoever said that stonework is made up in equal parts of inspiration, perspiration, and planning, was right. Miscalculations can result in many hours of wasted time and effort. For example, when we failed to remember that a three-tonne delivery of gravel was arriving one day, it was simply tipped in our gateway. It was a good thing the sun was shining, because we spent about eighteen hours moving it in a wheelbarrow – just so we could use the car!

Plan your projects in as much detail as possible. It makes sense to schedule the building for a time of year when the weather is likely to be reasonable, so that the concrete will dry quickly and easily, and does not need to be protected from frost. When you have taken delivery of the sand, cement and stone, you need to consider the finer points of the operation. Is the structure going to get in the way of other activities? Is the ground so boggy, bumpy or rocky that you need to rethink the foundation? Are you building over an existing underground electricity cable? Is the structure going to cause water to collect? Are all the comings and goings with wheelbarrow and water going to damage the lawn? Are neighbours going to object? And so on. When all these questions have been answered, move all the materials to the site and cover them so that they are shielded from the weather.

Buying the right tools and materials

When you are starting to do stonework, buy yourself a basic, inexpensive tool kit appropriate for the project that you intend to make. But in the long run, expensive, high-quality tools are the best option, because they will last for years.

It is sensible for beginners to buy their materials one bag at a time; however, it is far cheaper to order sand, gravel, cement and rock in bulk. For example, twenty 50 kg bags of gravel purchased one at a time from the local builder's merchant cost the same as a 4-tonne lorry-load of loose gravel ordered from a quarry. Much the same goes for all the other materials. So, buy materials in bulk if possible to cut costs to the minimum.

The general rule of thumb is the more you want to buy, the lower the cost per unit, and most specialist suppliers are more than happy to haggle over the price. So, phone up at least three suppliers, specify your needs, and see who gives you the lowest quote. Then ask the other two suppliers if they want to better that price. Once you have agreed the price over the phone, ask the supplier to confirm your order in writing, setting out the product quantities, the total cost, and the delivery date and time.

STONEWORK DESIGNS FOR THE GARDEN

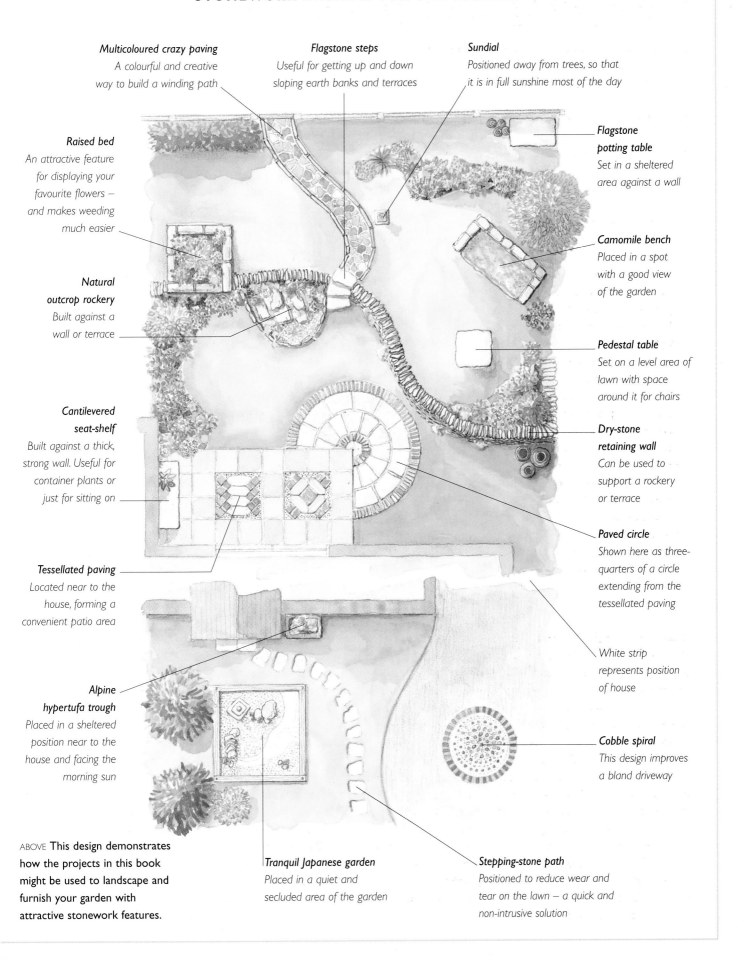

Multicoloured crazy paving
A colourful and creative way to build a winding path

Flagstone steps
Useful for getting up and down sloping earth banks and terraces

Sundial
Positioned away from trees, so that it is in full sunshine most of the day

Flagstone potting table
Set in a sheltered area against a wall

Raised bed
An attractive feature for displaying your favourite flowers – and makes weeding much easier

Camomile bench
Placed in a spot with a good view of the garden

Natural outcrop rockery
Built against a wall or terrace

Pedestal table
Set on a level area of lawn with space around it for chairs

Cantilevered seat-shelf
Built against a thick, strong wall. Useful for container plants or just for sitting on

Dry-stone retaining wall
Can be used to support a rockery or terrace

Paved circle
Shown here as three-quarters of a circle extending from the tessellated paving

Tessellated paving
Located near to the house, forming a convenient patio area

White strip represents position of house

Alpine hypertufa trough
Placed in a sheltered position near to the house and facing the morning sun

Cobble spiral
This design improves a bland driveway

ABOVE **This design demonstrates how the projects in this book might be used to landscape and furnish your garden with attractive stonework features.**

Tranquil Japanese garden
Placed in a quiet and secluded area of the garden

Stepping-stone path
Positioned to reduce wear and tear on the lawn – a quick and non-intrusive solution

Tools

The secret of tackling the projects successfully is using the correct tools for the job. A top-quality tool will make a huge difference to the ease with which a task can be accomplished. It is altogether more comfortable to hold, longer lasting, and ensures that tasks are completed in as short a time as possible.

TOOLS FOR HANDLING STONE

Sack barrow

Gloves

Bucket

Wheelbarrow

Protecting your feet and hands

Wear solid leather workboots, preferably with reinforced steel toecaps, to prevent your feet from getting squashed by a stray dropped stone, and work-gloves to save your hands from getting cut, abraded and otherwise damaged. The gloves might take a while to get used to, but they will protect your hands from the relentless wear and tear that is involved in working with a hammer and chisel, lifting stones and mixing sand and cement.

Making the work easier

Of all the tools you can buy, it is the wheelbarrow, sack barrow and bucket that make life easier when tackling stonework. By the time you get to the end of a project you will have formed a deep and loving relationship with both your wheelbarrow and sack barrow! A good wheelbarrow will save your back from a huge amount of stress and strain. If you buy one with a large inflated rubber tyre, and a tip-stop bar that protrudes in front, you will be able to bounce your way up steps and over rocks, and just as

easily be able to stop and tip out the load from the barrow. The wheelbarrow is used primarily for transporting wet and dry granular materials such as loose earth, sand, gravel and concrete.

A sack barrow is used for moving single, heavy items such as bags of cement, flagstones or large chunks of stone. It works on the lever principle, enabling you to lift and move weights that would otherwise be completely unmanageable. To use it, you nudge the platform under the item to be moved, pull back on the handles so that the weight is sitting over the wheels (over the fulcrum), then go on your way. A good, strong sack barrow will, depending upon the mass of the object, allow you to move anything up to 150–200 kg in weight with ease.

Finally, you need three or four plastic buckets. Don't bother about buying good-quality items, because buckets are more or less disposable – just buy the cheapest that you can find and use them until they fall apart. Some suppliers will cut the price if you purchase in multiples. Buckets are used for a variety of tasks, including transporting water for mixing into mortar and concrete.

TOOLS FOR MEASURING AND MARKING

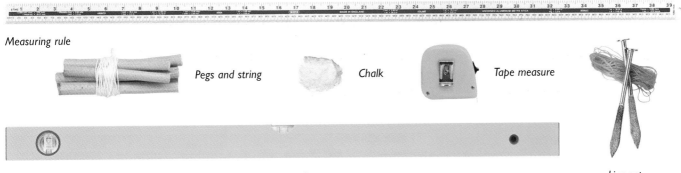

Measuring rule

Pegs and string

Chalk

Tape measure

Spirit level

Line set

Measuring

Ideally, you need two measuring tools – a flexible tape measure for setting out the site plan, and a rule for measuring individual rocks and blocks within the project. Make sure that both tools are marked out in metric and imperial, so that you can deal with products that are described in either system. If possible, buy a waterproof, fibreglass tape measure, as this will stand up better to the damp and dirt involved in stoneworking.

Marking out

The main tools are pegs and string for setting out the foundation on the ground, chalk for drawing a plan on a concrete base, and a spirit level for checking the horizontal and vertical levels within the structure. Buy one with a strong aluminium body. You may also wish to use a line set for guiding the courses of stone and estimating the course heights. The pegs are stuck into the ground (or a course), and the line stretched between them.

TOOLS FOR PREPARING A SITE

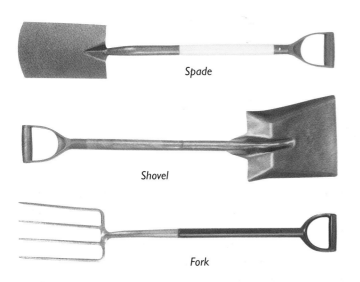

Spade

Shovel

Fork

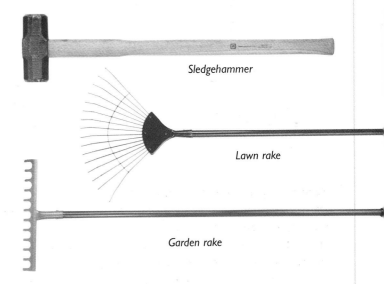

Sledgehammer

Lawn rake

Garden rake

Removing turf and digging earth

A spade is used to prepare the site. Having marked out the size of the foundation, take the spade, cut down through the thickness of the turf, and slice it into easy-to-manage squares. Scoop it straight into the wheelbarrow and remove it from the site. Finally, dig out the earth to the required depth and clean out to a flat base.

Compacting hardcore and raking

A sledgehammer will make short work of compacting hardcore. The smaller the stones, the easier it is to compact – builder's rubble requires a lot of effort, while crushed stone more or less puts itself into place. The procedure is simple: spread a thin layer

over the foundation area and pound it into place, walking backwards and forwards over it from time to time.

The tool used for raking depends upon the material in question. It is best to use a fork for moving and breaking up clumps of earth, a garden rake for spreading gravel and shingle, and a lawn rake for spreading sand and for tidying up.

Mixing cement and moving gravel

The simplest way of mixing cement and moving gravel is to use a carefully chosen, good-quality shovel. Wash the shovel after mixing cement. Never try shovelling with a spade, or digging with a shovel – both exercises are a back-breaking waste of time!

TOOLS FOR SHAPING STONE

Mason's hammer

Angle grinder

Cold chisel

Bolster chisel

Club hammer

Breaking stone

One of the most direct ways of shaping or truing up stone (meaning to tap off a corner or shape an edge) is to use a mason's hammer, sometimes known as a brick hammer. The hammer is used on its own, without a chisel of any description. Cradle the stone (in your hand, on soft ground, or on a pad) and strike it repeatedly, working in a line. Flip it over and repeat the procedure on the other side, until the waste piece falls away.

To trim an edge back to a drawn line, the mason's hammer can again be used alone. Hold the stone with the edge to be worked nearest to you, and then hit it with a series of rapid pecks, so that the waste falls away as chips. If you find that you enjoy working with stone, and decide that you are going to try lots of the projects, it would be a good idea to get yourself a stout leather bib apron, as added protection from flying slivers of stone.

Cutting stone

While breaking stone with a mason's hammer is relatively approximate, cutting stone is a more accurate procedure that involves using a club hammer with a bolster chisel or a cold chisel.

The bolster chisel is used for hefty tasks such as chopping a stone in half. To cut a stone down the run of the grain – in much the same way as splitting a log – you simply set the chisel on the end grain and work backwards and forwards until you see the stone begin to fracture. You

then work away at a crack until the stone splits into two pieces. To break a large stone across the run of the grain – like cutting a long log into two lengths – draw a line with chalk, and hit it with the club hammer and bolster chisel. Repeatedly work around all the faces until the stone falls into two.

A cold chisel is appropriate for more delicate tasks, such as trimming an edge, or other fine adjustments.

Sawing stone

In the context of this book, sawing stone involves using an electric angle grinder to cut flagstone slabs. The grinder is first fitted with a stone-cutting disc, as described by the manufacturer. You must wear a dust-mask, a pair of goggles, gloves and stout workboots. The grinder is connected up to an 110 volt power supply by means of a yellow-box transformer. The disc is placed on the drawn line and the tool is run forward to make the cut. As the angle grinder creates an enormous amount of dust, it is best to work outside, setting the stone down flat on the grass and holding it with your foot (keeping it well away from the line of cut). It does not matter if the disc slips off at the end of the line, because it simply cuts into the grass and no damage is done. If you feel at all unhappy about the prospect of using an angle grinder, ask a knowledgeable friend to show you how to do it. Never use a grinder if you are tired or in any way under stress.

CAUTION

It is vital to wear goggles for all stone-breaking and cutting operations, to protect your eyes from dust, chips of stone and fragments of metal. Wear a dust-mask when using the angle grinder.

TOOLS FOR CONCRETE AND MORTAR

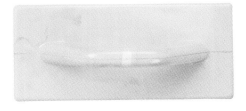

Mortar float

Bricklayer's trowel

Pointing trowel

Spreading concrete and mortar

If you want to achieve a smooth finish once the concrete or mortar has been tipped into place, you have to use a mortar float or plasterer's trowel. Made from steel, wood or plastic, the float is used with an even, side to side smoothing action – in much the same way as you use a bricklayer's trowel. If you want the water to rise to the surface (to create an ultra-smooth finish), use a steel float, otherwise one made from plastic or wood will suffice. Always clean the float under running water after use, especially on the underside and around the handle.

Handling mortar

The bricklayer's trowel is designed for transferring large slaps of mortar. The pointing trowel is shaped for pointing, and for raking out some of the mortar from between the courses for decorative effect. Many beginners find it easier to use the smaller pointing trowel for both tasks. Use the tool that you feel comfortable with and change over if and when you feel the need. Many people find that although the large trowel certainly gets the mortar shifted quickly, its weight puts a strain on the wrist. Make sure that your chosen trowel has a well-shaped handle, which feels good to hold.

TOOLS FOR FINISHING A PROJECT

Electric drill

Masonry drill bit

Claw hammer

Rubber mallet

Flat screwdriver

Wire brush

Broom

Cross-point screwdriver

Gardening trowel

Holes and fixings

Stonework also involves drilling holes, banging in nails, and driving in screws. It is best to use an electric drill in conjunction with a masonry drill bit for boring holes into rock, a carpenter's claw hammer for nailing foundation frames, and both flat and cross-point screwdrivers for pushing home the screws. If a giant-size electric drill is required, rent it by the day from a hire shop.

Levelling and cleaning

You may find a rubber mallet useful for nudging individual stones into place. A wire brush is excellent for cleaning stray blobs of mortar from the stone when the mortaring process is finished. At the end of a long day's work, a good, stiff-bristled bass broom makes it much easier to get through the tedious task of tidying up. Wash the broom after use to remove grit and grime from the head and handle, and store it with the head uppermost, so the bristles have a chance to dry out.

Planting

A gardening trowel is needed for planting a selection of plants in projects such as the Natural Outcrop Rockery (page 166) and the Raised Bed (page 176). It is also a handy little tool for scooping up small amounts of sand and cement. Buy a couple of them and use them for the various tasks.

Materials

We are not concerned about the geological make-up of the various materials – apart from identification, it does not contribute anything to the projects to know whether a rock is igneous or metamorphic. We have concentrated on the common names and the working characteristics of the rocks.

NATURAL STONE

York stone

Flagstone

Rockery stone

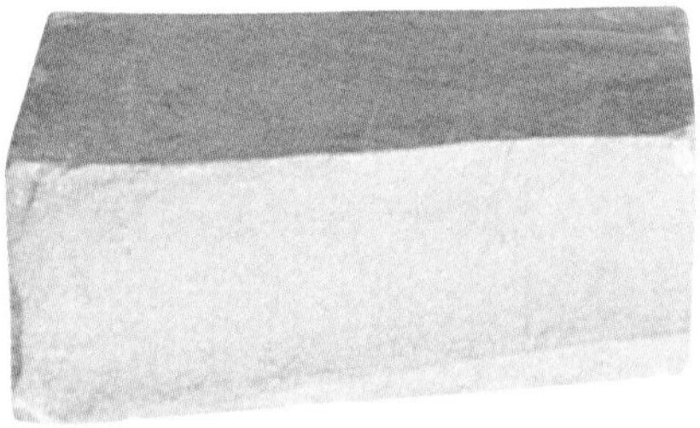

Limestone

Pink limestone

Wall limestone

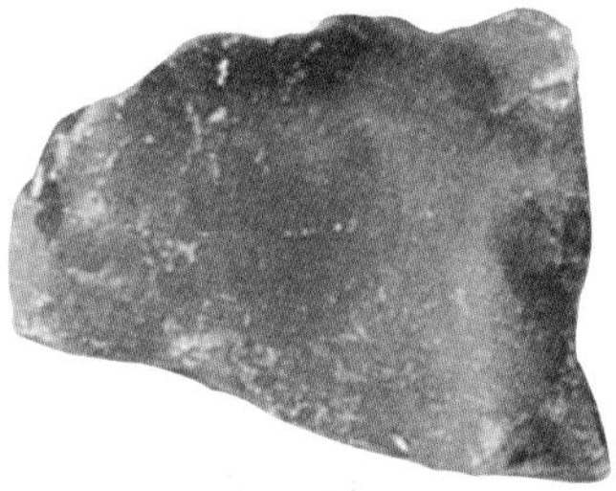

Reclaimed slate

Cobbles

Paddle stone

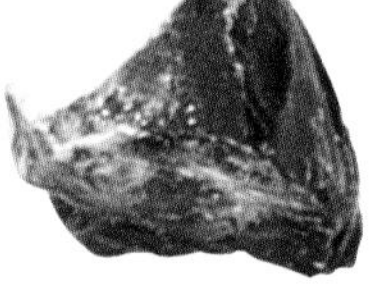

Napped flint

Roof slate

Limestone

Limestone was once very popular as a building stone, because it is easy to shape, in any direction, to make steps, slabs and blocks. However, there are now so many reconstituted stone look-alike "limestone" blocks on the market, that the genuine item has fallen from favour. While it is prohibitively expensive to use new sawn and faced limestone, salvaged architectural limestone is reasonably priced. When we needed cut blocks of white stone to make the Japanese lantern for the Tranquil Japanese Garden (page 206), we found salvaged limestone to be by far the best option, because it had the most attractive appearance.

Always identify the direction of the grain prior to laying the blocks, making sure that the layers within the grain sit horizontally rather than vertically. If you are not sure which way the grain runs, look very closely at the salvaged stone to see how the various faces were arranged in their previous setting, and then simply copy the arrangement in your project.

Sandstone

Sandstone and limestone are both formed by deposition – meaning that the stone is created from layers of material put under enormous pressure. Limestone is made up of organic remains such as shell and bones, and sandstone is particles of quartz or sand. Sandstone ranges in colour from pinky-red and brown through to black, green and blue-grey. Some stones are so hard that they ring when struck, while others are so soft and crumbly that they can be broken like dry biscuits. Depending upon the variety, sandstone is good for dry-stone walling, stepping stones and flagstones. Always avoid stone that flakes when touched, as it is likely to have been damaged by frost.

Slate

The geological formation of slate is the result of the heating of clay deposits under pressure. Slate is characterized by its blue, black or green colour, and smooth, shiny surface. It can be split into thin sheets, which are mainly used for roofing.

In this book, slate is used in the form of small pucks of "paddle" stone sold by quarries, and as broken roof stone sold by architectural salvage companies. While slate does not easily blend in with limestone and sandstone, so it cannot be used in large lumps in equal partnership, small pieces make an effective colour contrast. For example, the Flagstone Potting Table (page 232) uses thin layers of slate with deeply raked joints to contrast with the rather severe blocks of limestone. Be aware, when you are choosing your stone, that the terms "slate" and "roofing stone" are commonly interchanged and used to describe all manner of stone types that can be broken into thin sheets.

Granite

While there is no denying that granite is immensely strong and attractive in both colour and texture – ranging from dark green-blue through to a pinkish grey – it is also so hard that it is almost impossible to work. Certainly you can just about make headway with a grinder, and sometimes you can be lucky with a hammer and bolster chisel, but mostly it is too difficult to cut. If you really want to use granite, search out pieces in the stoneyard that suit your needs as they stand. For example, you could use salvaged road blocks and kerbstones to build the lantern in the Tranquil Japanese Garden (page 206), setts to edge the Paved Circle (page 194), massive pieces of quarry stone as feature stones in the Natural Outcrop Rockery (page 166), or even large salvaged field posts as guardians or sentinels. Be very wary about obtaining pieces of granite that are bigger than you need, because they are usually so impossible to work that the task is not worth the wear and tear on your tools. One of the best ways of using granite is in its crushed state, as a decorative spread.

RECONSTITUTED STONE

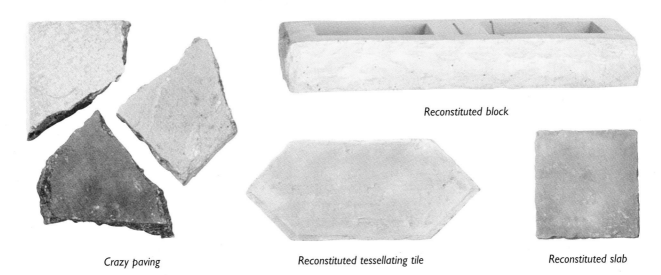

Reconstituted block

Crazy paving

Reconstituted tessellating tile

Reconstituted slab

Reconstituted blocks

Reconstituted stone blocks are concrete blocks – sometimes made with an aggregate containing the stone that they seek to imitate – that are made to look like natural stone. There are double-sided blocks that imitate rough-tooled limestone, blocks that look like fieldstone, blocks that resemble sawn limestone, and so on. In many instances, you can cut costs by collecting the blocks direct from the manufacturer.

You may wish to substitute reconstituted blocks in the projects to save money, but they are usually not as beautiful as the real thing. The best way to regard them is as a little taster that will lead you into the more exciting adventure of using natural stone.

Reconstituted slabs

While reconstituted blocks can look quite crude, reconstituted slabs, on the other hand, are a great idea. Made in much the same way as the blocks, often with an aggregate containing the stone that they are masquerading as, many reconstituted slabs are so convincing that at first sight they cannot be distinguished from the real thing. Such slabs come in all sorts of shapes, sizes, colours and textures: tessellating shapes that look like red quarry tiles, sand-stone paving slabs, on-edge stone and brick slabs, limestone and sandstone flagstones, and many other forms and designs. If you want to cut costs, they can be substituted when a project calls for thin layers of stone. Pick slabs that are described as "colour-fast".

CHIPS, GRAVEL, GRIT, CEMENT AND LIME

Limestone chips

Smooth gravel

Pink gravel

Medium gravel

Pea gravel

Oyster shell

Sharp sand

Sand and gravel

Soft sand

Cement

Lime

CAUTION

Cement and lime are corrosive and can seriously burn the skin. Always wear goggles and gloves, and wash your hands and face after working with them.

Soft sand

Soft sand, sometimes called builder's sand, is used for making smooth-textured mortar. Sold by the bag or lorry-load, the colour and texture of the soft sand on offer will usually relate to the colour of the stone in your area. If you are building with local stone, it is best to use local soft sand. However, builder's suppliers purchase some sand from far-distant quarries, so you do have to check the colour of your intended purchase to make sure it is suitable. If you are looking for good colour and low cost, your best option is to order your sand in bulk from a local pit.

Always make sure that the sand has been well washed and is free from salt and particles of clay. Salt damages mortar and concrete. If the sand smells rank, or contains animal or vegetable matter, or looks in any way contaminated, go to another supplier.

Sharp sand

Sharp sand is nearly always used for making concrete, and is also added to soft sand to make a coarse, bulky mortar. In terms of colour and cost, much the same can be said for sharp sand as for soft. Whether the sand comes from a pit, quarry or river, or is a mixture of naturally occurring sand and crushed stone, it is vital that it is free from clay, loam and organic matter.

Check it if you have any doubts: clean sand will not stain your fingers, and if you put it in a glass of water, shake it up and leave it to stand, you should end up with just a thin film of silt on top of the sand, and clear water. If there is a layer of scum floating on the water and a salty smell – a bit like a beach at low tide – then the chances are that it is unwashed sea sand, which is totally unsuitable for making mortar and concrete.

Cement

Cement powder – sold in 25 kg and 50 kg bags, and described generically as "Portland cement" – is one of the chief ingredients of mortar and concrete. Though it is undoubtedly true to say that you can save money by ordering a large number of 50 kg bags, this is the one instance where it is much better to buy just enough for the job in hand. Not only are 50 kg bags difficult to handle, but they are also flimsy and liable to tear, the cement powder is susceptible to damp, and loose powder is highly corrosive and very bad for the skin, eyes and lungs.

Lime

Lime is used together with cement and sand to make mortar. Though a "cement mortar" can be made without lime (undoubtedly harder and stronger than lime and cement mortar), it is also so hard that it stains the stone and pulls it apart. As with cement powder, it is best to order lime in small quantities and to store it in a dry place. Lime is highly corrosive, to the extent that you should wear goggles and a mask when mixing, and gloves for general handling. If you are mixing on a windy day, when the lime is blowing about, wash your face and hands afterwards.

Aggregates

Concrete consists of Portland cement, and a mixture of sand and stone known as an aggregate. The shape and size of the particles of sand and stone within the aggregate decide the character of the concrete – meaning its strength, hardness, durability and porosity.

Commonly, aggregate is made up from graded 2–3 mm sand, broken stone and various types of crushed and graded gravel. For the projects in this book, choose an average mix made up from small-sized gravel and sand. If you want to make a very coarse concrete, for a thin levelling slab, you can bulk out your mix by adding a small amount of crushed brick or broken stone – just break it up with a hammer, damp it down, and add it to the mix.

Gravel, limestone chips or oyster shell may also be laid down as a decorative surface. Choose a fine gravel such as pea gravel for a delicate appearance; limestone chips provide a chunkier effect. Gravel colour depends on the stone it is made from.

OTHER MATERIALS

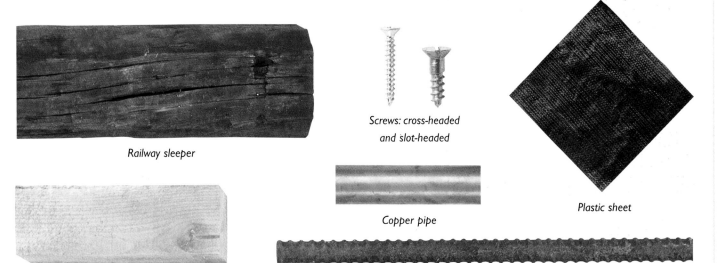

Railway sleeper

Screws: cross-headed and slot-headed

Plastic sheet

Rough-sawn pine section

Copper pipe

Iron reinforcing bar

Wood and fixings

Foundation frames should be made up from rough-sawn softwood, as sold by most garden centres. Do not worry too much about the quality of the wood or the length of time it has been seasoned – other than to see that it is reasonably strong along its length. To fix these temporary frames, you can use a mixture of screws and nails, or whatever comes to hand. It's a good idea to use high-quality, pressure-treated wood to make the frame for the Tranquil Japanese Garden (page 206).

The lengths of railway sleeper used under the Alpine Hypertufa Trough (page 186), and for bending the copper pipe in the Cantilevered Seat-Shelf (page 220), can be obtained as small offcuts. Avoid railway sleepers that ooze tar or creosote – they will ruin the tools and stain your hands and clothes.

Metal and plastics

The iron bar and copper pipe used for the Cantilevered Seat-Shelf (page 220) can be obtained from a builder's merchant as inexpensive offcuts. The iron bar is sold as reinforcement bar or "rebar", while the copper tube is used for plumbing. The plastic sheet used under the Tranquil Japanese Garden (page 206) is available from builder's merchants, plastics suppliers or garden centres.

If you are keen to cut down on costs, visit the nearest building site and see if the site manager can spare you any scraps. If you are successful in your quest, before you take your haul away it's a good idea to ask the site manager to sign a note to the effect that the materials have been given to you, just in case you are questioned by the site security guards. Scrap metal merchants may also be willing to let you have small items free of charge.

Mixing mortar and concrete

Stonework involves the frequent mixing of mortar (for laying stone) and concrete (for foundations). If you can achieve a mix with a good texture, colour and working consistency, the construction process will go smoothly. Follow the old adage that says, "Mixing a little not a lot, gets the job done in half the time".

MIXING A SMALL AMOUNT OF MORTAR IN A WHEELBARROW

Mixing procedure

1 Use a shovel to carefully measure the dry ingredients into the wheelbarrow – first the sand, then the Portland cement and the lime. Continue until the barrow is about half-full. Turn the ingredients over several times until they are thoroughly mixed.

2 Pour about one-third of a bucket of water into one end of the wheelbarrow, then drag small amounts of the dry mix into the water. Repeat the process until all the water has been soaked up by the dry mix.

3 Turn over the whole heap several times, all the while adding small amounts of water, until you can chop it into clean, wet slices.

Mixing
Drag the dry mix into the water

MIXING A COARSE LIME AND CEMENT MORTAR

This mortar is made up of a 50/50 mixture of soft sand and sharp sand, Portland cement and lime. Because it is coarse, it is good for filling large gaps and wide courses. Measure the dry ingredients on to a board with a shovel – first the sand, then the cement and lime. Mix it up, dig a hole in the centre, and pour in about half a bucket of water. Work round the heap, dragging small amounts of the dry mix into the water. If the water threatens to break over the rim, swiftly pull in more of the dry mix to stem the flow. When the water has been soaked up, add more until the mortar is the correct consistency. The finished mixture should form crisp, firm slices that stand up under their own weight without crumbling.

MIXING CONCRETE FOR FOUNDATION FOOTINGS

A concrete suitable for foundations contains cement, sharp sand and aggregate. With a shovel, measure the sand and the Portland cement on to the board. Turn over the mixture thoroughly, until it is well blended. Dig a hole in the centre of the mound, pour in about half a bucket of water, and then gradually drag the dry mix into the water. Continue until you achieve a wet, sloppy mixture. Finally, measure in the aggregate. Carry on turning it over and adding small amounts of water until a shovelful of the mixture holds its shape when it is formed into a ridge.

ABOVE It is often convenient to use a wheelbarrow for mixing mortar – bear in mind that you will need to give it a good clean afterwards.

MORTAR AND CONCRETE MIXES

Smooth lime and cement mortar
Lime and cement mortar, suitable for fine- to medium-course stonework, is made up from 2 parts Portland cement, 1 part lime and 9 parts soft sand. The sand should be chosen to complement the colour of the stone.

Coarse lime and cement mortar
A coarse lime and cement mortar, appropriate for bulking out wide courses, can be constructed from 2 parts cement, 1 part lime, 4 parts soft sand and 4 parts sharp sand. The proportion of sharp sand to soft sand should be modified to suit the texture of your chosen stone.

Concrete for foundations
A good, general-purpose concrete, suitable for small footings and foundations, is made of 1 part Portland cement, 2 parts sharp sand and 3 parts aggregate. (The aggregate is made up from gravel graded to pass through a 25 mm sieve.)

Moving stone

Even though we live in an age of cranes and hoists, you will almost certainly have to physically move the stone by hand from the driveway, where it has been delivered, to the site in the garden. This section shows you how to do it with ease. But if you suspect that a stone is too heavy, ask a friend to help rather than risking injury.

MOVING HEAVY SLABS

Moving the slab
Rock the slab on to one corner and pivot it round

Use rough board to protect lawns

Moving procedure

1 Slabs weigh about 150–200 kg, so ask a friend to help you. First, use a sledgehammer to bang a couple of wooden wedges under one edge of the slab to lift it about 70 mm off the ground. Put two wooden boards on the ground in the spot where the slab will be. Leave a small gap between them.

2 Together, grip the jacked-up edge of the stone (the stronger person being ready to push, and the other person ready to pull and steady). Heave the stone upright until it is standing on edge.

3 Rock the slab on to one of the bottom corners and pivot it so that the raised corner is pointing in the direction of the site. Lower this corner, then swing the other corner around, "walking" the slab across the garden. Keep stopping to rest along the way.

4 When you have reached the new location, lower the stone on to the wooden boards (these maintain a gap between the stone and the ground, preventing your hands from getting trapped). Lift an edge and ease the boards out.

MOVING HEAVY ROCKERY STONES

Moving procedure

1 Having asked a friend to help, take a solid metal wheelbarrow (one with a large pneumatic tyre) and wheel it up to the stone. Lie it on its side with one edge alongside the stone.

2 Place a pad of old carpet between the stone and the wheelbarrow, then manoeuvre the stone into the wheelbarrow. One of you eases the stone and the other holds the wheelbarrow.

3 When the stone is in the wheelbarrow, push and pull the wheelbarrow into an upright position, working together. Ease the stone to lie over the wheel. Always be ready to steady the wheelbarrow during its journey.

RIGHT Roll heavy stones if possible, rather than lifting them. To protect your back when you have to lift a heavy weight, keep your knees bent, with your spine upright, and your weight balanced over your feet.

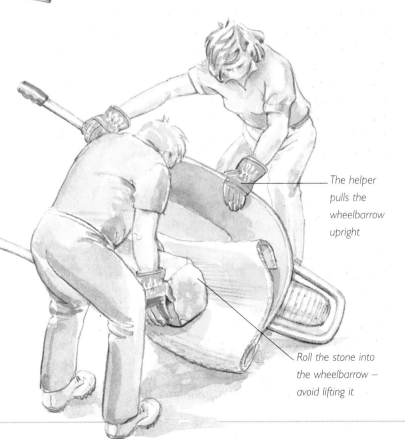

The helper pulls the wheelbarrow upright

Roll the stone into the wheelbarrow – avoid lifting it

Cutting stone

In many ways, the art and craft of good stonework is concerned with fitting and using stone as you find it, but when there is no option other than to make a cut, the main part of the challenge is getting it right. Today, much cutting is done with an electric angle grinder but traditional chisels are still required for some tasks.

CUTTING STONE USING AN ANGLE GRINDER

Choosing the correct angle grinder

Angle grinders are deceptively easy to use, but it is important to choose the correct grinder for your needs. While it is generally much easier to use a heavy-duty 230 mm-diameter grinder than it is to use a lightweight 115 mm-diameter model, most beginners are not going to get much use out of a large grinder. It is best to hire various grinders to start with, and see how you get on.

Pay great attention to the serious business of safety. You need goggles to guard your eyes against fragments of stone, metal and dust, a dust-mask to protect your lungs from stone dust, ear defenders to shield your ears from noise, gloves to ward off splinters, and stout boots to armour your feet.

When you are ready to make a cut, switch on the power and move the machine forwards, all the time remaining ready to resist kickback.

Choosing and fitting the cutting disc

Select a stone-cutting disc to fit your grinder. Disconnect the power cable, turn the spindle over by hand, and press in the lock button until the spindle stays put. Unscrew the clamping ring, slide on the correct disc, replace the ring and use the special wrench to tighten up. Release the lock button and turn over the disc by hand to ensure it does not wobble or scrape. When you are happy that everything is correctly and safely assembled, you are ready to turn on the power and make the cut.

The correct working set-up

When using an angle grinder, it is a good idea to ask a helper to be present in case of any problems. First, establish a working area on the lawn, and ban children and pets.

Set the slab to be worked on the ground. Make sure that none of your helpers is standing in front of the line of cut. Keep your feet well away from the cutting line. On no account kneel in line with the cutter, in case it slips. Never try to force the pace of the machine, and never twist the disc. If the cutting wheel looks in any way chipped, cracked, or warped, change to a new disc.

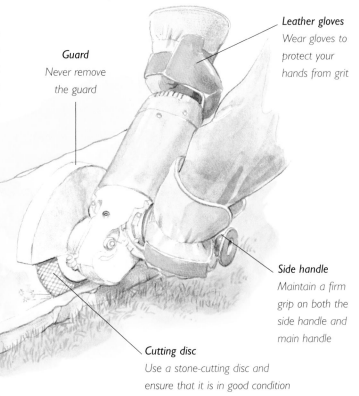

Guard
Never remove the guard

Leather gloves
Wear gloves to protect your hands from grit

Side handle
Maintain a firm grip on both the side handle and main handle

Cutting disc
Use a stone-cutting disc and ensure that it is in good condition

ABOVE Take the utmost care when using an angle grinder: it is a potentially dangerous tool. Follow safety procedures carefully.

Cutting procedure

1 Set the slab down flat on the grass and draw out the line of cut with a tape measure, chalk and straight-edge. Check that the grinder is in good working order, and kit yourself out with goggles, a dust-mask, thick leather gloves and stout boots. It is advisable to wear ear defenders too.

2 Hold the grinder so that the wheel is at right angles to the slab. Brace yourself, and, keeping your feet well out of the way, switch on the power. Hold the spinning disc to the chalk line and carefully make a light, scoring cut.

3 Make several runs to deepen the line of cut, then switch off the power and flip the slab over on the grass. Switch the power back on and re-run the whole procedure on the other side. Continue repeating the process until the slab breaks into two.

CUTTING STONE USING CHISELS

Using the bolster chisel

Bolster chisels are used for breaking and cutting stone. Purchase the best chisel that you can find – ideally one that has been drop-forged, hardened and tempered, and fitted with a one-piece moulded plastic protective grip. Take the club hammer and a piece of stone, and experiment with various cuts and blows. The first thing you will observe is that the angle of the chisel, in relation to the weight of the blow, is critical to the cut. For example, a light, tentative tap with the chisel held at right angles to the stone will result in a chip, while a heavy, decisive blow will result in a fracture. If you want to trim an edge, you angle the chisel towards the edge, lower it slightly, and then make the blow. The edge will break away, leaving a peak on the edge face. By adjusting the angle of the chisel, it is possible to change the shape of the edge peak.

Using the cold chisel

Cold chisels are used for more delicate cutting tasks than bolster chisels. Purchase a top-quality 25 mm-wide chisel – choose one that has been drop-forged, hardened and tempered. Support a slab of stone on a pad and use the club hammer to try out various cuts. To trim an edge, hold the chisel at a very low angle to the stone, with the cutting edge looking to the edge of the stone, then make a light blow so that the waste breaks away as a chip rather than a chunk. Experiment with various angles and the weight of strike, until you can, to some extent, predict the outcome.

Sharpening chisels

Drag and roll the end of the chisel against the grindstone until the ragged edge has been ground to a mitred bevel. Grind the cutting edge back to the original angle of about 60 degrees, continually dipping the tool into water to prevent the steel from overheating.

Cutting a stone in two

1 Chalk the line of cut on both sides of the stone, and put the stone on something soft to help absorb the shock – such as a pad of old carpet, a pile of sand, or the lawn. Make sure that you are wearing goggles and strong leather gloves.

2 Take a bolster chisel in one hand and a club hammer in the other, and make a series of light passes to score the line. Do this three times, all the while increasing the power of the blows.

3 Repeat the procedure on the other side of the stone, and then after about three passes, strike the chisel with maximum force until the stone breaks along the line.

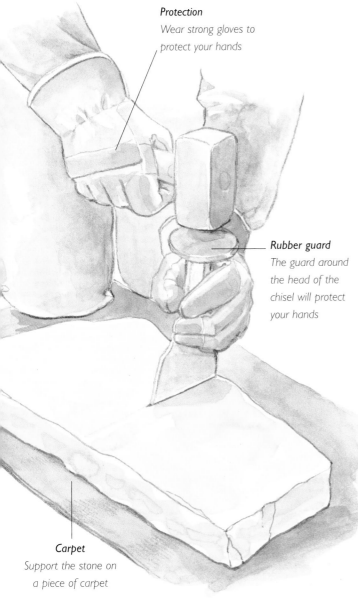

Protection
Wear strong gloves to protect your hands

Rubber guard
The guard around the head of the chisel will protect your hands

Carpet
Support the stone on a piece of carpet

ABOVE **Cutting stone using a bolster chisel and club hammer.**
Hold the chisel firmly on the mark and deliver a well-aimed blow.

HOW TO AVOID TOO MUCH CUTTING

Fitting is better than cutting
The secret of good stonework is, as far as possible, to use the stone as you find it. Choose your stone with great care, spending a long time selecting pieces for the best possible fit. If you work in this way, all you will have to do is to slightly modify edges and corners so that the pieces fit snugly alongside one another. Always try to fit rather than cut.

Striking blows
When you have decided on the position of the cutting line, set the edge of the chisel on the mark and strike it with a club hammer. Repeat this procedure until the cut has been made. A single, well-aimed blow with the hammer is many times more effective than lots of little misaligned taps.

Working with the grain
Study the stone carefully and identify the grain, or strata lines. Try, as far as possible, to align your cuts with the run of the grain. This ensures the stone cuts cleanly.

Making foundations

Every stone structure starts with a foundation ranging from gravel through to crushed stone, compacted hardcore and concrete. This section shows you how to select the option that suits your needs. It is important not to skimp on quantities. If in doubt, make a foundation bigger rather than smaller.

TYPES OF GROUND AND FOUNDATION REQUIREMENTS

Inspecting the site

Have a good look at the site. Dig a small hole to see what it is like under the topsoil. Is it hard and rocky, or is it soft and squashy? Is there a lot of rock and rubble on site? Is it well drained or boggy? In the light of your survey, and in the knowledge that the options for a foundation range from a trench filled with gravel, through to a trench with compacted hardcore and layer of stone, or a trench with compacted hardcore and a layer of concrete, or various combinations of these, spend time considering your needs.

For example, if you wanted to build the Camomile Bench on page 238, and you have a dry, rocky site, you could get away with an 80 mm slab of concrete and a shallow layer of concrete. But on a wet site, you would need to dig a trench about 300 mm deep, half-fill it with gravel for drainage, and then top it off with a generous layer of concrete.

If you are unsure what sort of drainage your site has, dig a trial hole, fill it with water, and see how long it takes to drain away.

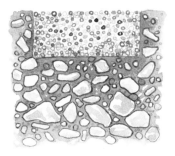

LEFT A gravel footpath needs no foundation if it is set in a well-drained, compacted soil. The gravel is adequately contained.

LEFT A compacted hardcore foundation for a concrete footpath. This is suitable for soil with moderate drainage.

CONSTRUCTING A CONCRETE SLAB FOUNDATION

Building procedure

1 Carefully measure the site, bang in wooden pegs to mark the limits of the foundation, and run a string around the pegs. Remove the turf and dig down to a depth of about 250 mm. Clean the trench out to a level base. Move all the turf and the loose soil from the site.

2 Bang two wooden pegs into the trench base, positioned away from the sides as shown, so that they stand proud by about 200 mm (they are about 50 mm below the turf level). Bridge the pegs with a spirit level and make adjustments until they are at the same level. Try not to destroy the top of the pegs when hammering.

3 Half-fill the trench with hardcore and, being careful not to knock the pegs, compact it with a sledgehammer. Finally, top up the trench with concrete and tamp it level with a wooden beam. You should just be able to see the top of the pegs.

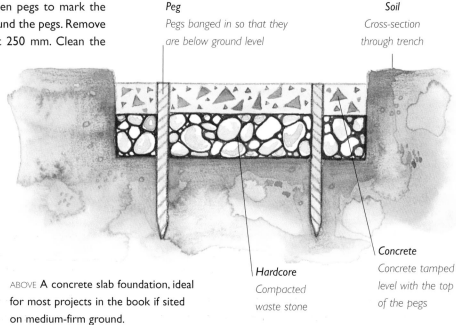

Peg
Pegs banged in so that they are below ground level

Soil
Cross-section through trench

Hardcore
Compacted waste stone

Concrete
Concrete tamped level with the top of the pegs

ABOVE A concrete slab foundation, ideal for most projects in the book if sited on medium-firm ground.

A ROCK AND RUBBLE FOUNDATION

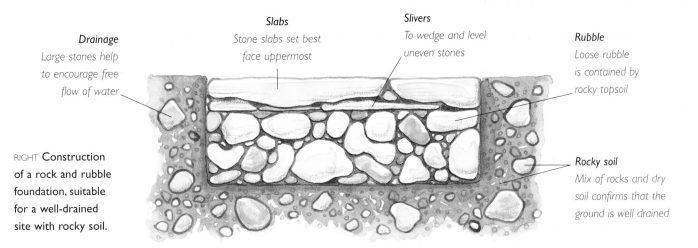

Drainage
Large stones help
to encourage free
flow of water

Slabs
Stone slabs set best
face uppermost

Slivers
To wedge and level
uneven stones

Rubble
Loose rubble
is contained by
rocky topsoil

RIGHT **Construction**
of a rock and rubble
foundation, suitable
for a well-drained
site with rocky soil.

Rocky soil
Mix of rocks and dry
soil confirms that the
ground is well drained

If you have a well-drained, rocky site, with a thin layer of topsoil, and a lot of loose stone and builder's rubble available, and you intend to build a project such as the the Dry-Stone Retaining Wall (page 212), you can easily get away without laying a concrete slab. Dig a trench to a depth of about 300 mm, and then systematically fill it with rock and rubble, all the while pounding it with the sledgehammer. When you get to within about 100 mm of ground level, carefully select large slabs of stone to cover the hardcore. Use small slivers and wedges of stone to adjust the level of the slabs so that they are firm and stable.

OTHER FOUNDATION EXAMPLES

If you have a well-drained site, you can lay a minimal foundation and top it off with a concrete slab. Let's say that you want to build the Pedestal Table on page 244. Dig a hole to a depth of about 400 mm and knock in four side pegs. Nail wooden battens to bridge pairs of pegs, keeping them at the same level, and finishing up with the battens just below turf level. Half-fill the trench with hardcore and fill with concrete, up to the level of the battens. Drag a tamping beam across to skim the concrete level. Be careful not to knock either the pegs or the battens out of alignment.

If you have a boggy site, you need to keep the foundation drained by digging two trenches for the hardcore. These are bridged and topped with a concrete slab.

Wooden batten
The board contains
the rubble and concrete
during construction

Concrete
A slab of concrete is cast
to the level of the pegs

Hardcore
Deep trenches provide
greater stability

Concrete slab

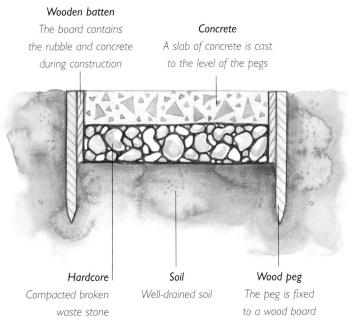

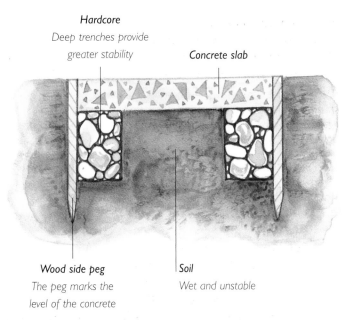

Hardcore
Compacted broken
waste stone

Soil
Well-drained soil

Wood peg
The peg is fixed
to a wood board

Wood side peg
The peg marks the
level of the concrete

Soil
Wet and unstable

ABOVE **Use this foundation construction for well-drained sites. The surrounding soil needs to be reasonably compact and stable.**

ABOVE **This type of construction is suited to soil that is boggy, loose and generally unstable. The hardcore walls provide good drainage.**

Paving and paths

Paving and paths not only enhance the garden in the sense that they are functionally desirable, they can also be visually exciting in terms of materials. Paths lead the eye – a path winding out of sight behind a hedge invites exploration and can impart an air of mystery. If you want to know more, keep reading.

DESIGNS FOR PATHS

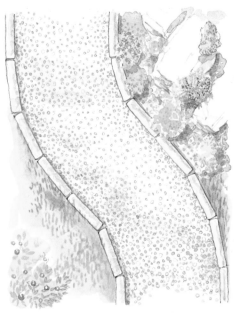

ABOVE **A gravel path edged with concrete "stone" blocks, which are supported by banked earth borders. The length of the kerb blocks defines the shape of the curve.**

ABOVE Reconstituted stones or flagstones framed by rows of bricks set on their edge. There is plenty of design scope with various combinations of materials and patterns.

ABOVE Randomly-shaped stepping stones make an attractive feature, and are less intrusive than a solid path. The spaces between them must be equal.

Functional paths and paving

Have a look at your garden and consider how it might benefit from having one or more functional paths, or perhaps an area of utility paving. Perhaps you have trouble pushing your wheelbarrow down an existing path because it is too narrow? Would the vegetable garden be easier to work if it were divided up by a number of paths? Would it be a good idea to create a path along the shortest route from the back door to the compost heap? Do you want to avoid having to tiptoe across a muddy lawn? Do you wish that a particular area was dry so that children could play on it? Do you want a path wide enough for a wheelchair?

Designer paths and paving

The purpose of a designer path is not necessarily to take the shortest possible route, or even to provide a surface that is smooth and dry, but rather to provide the user with an exciting, dynamic, tactile and visual experience. Ideas such as irregular stepping stones that curve across the lawn and disappear behind a shrub, the feel and sound of gravel underfoot, an area of paving that is decorated with an inset design, a paved circle with a bench seat – all encourage visitors to change pace and appreciate their surroundings. Well thought-out designer paths and areas of paving can enhance the landscape, adding shape, colour, texture and mystery to the composition of the garden.

Think how a path or an area of paving might improve your enjoyment of the garden. A paved circle would allow you to sit outside on a warm summer's evening. Or you could build a crazy paving path to wander around the rockery and on to a camomile bench. Maybe you could design a combined path and paved circle, which could include a stone seat and barbecue. Your challenge may be a path that encircles the house, or a path that wanders off into the woods. The possibilities are endless.

FLAGSTONE PATH CONSTRUCTION

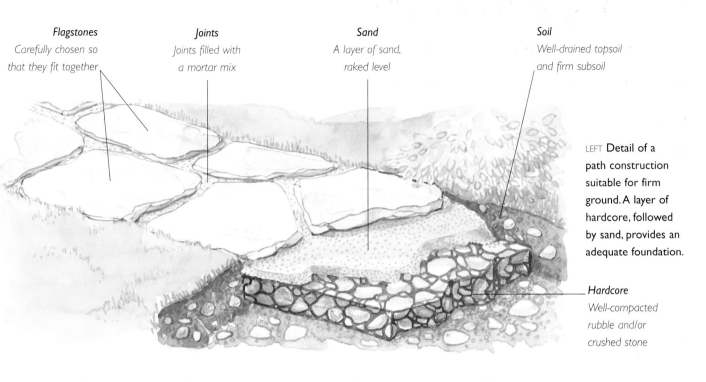

Flagstones
Carefully chosen so
that they fit together

Joints
Joints filled with
a mortar mix

Sand
A layer of sand,
raked level

Soil
Well-drained topsoil
and firm subsoil

LEFT Detail of a
path construction
suitable for firm
ground. A layer of
hardcore, followed
by sand, provides an
adequate foundation.

Hardcore
Well-compacted
rubble and/or
crushed stone

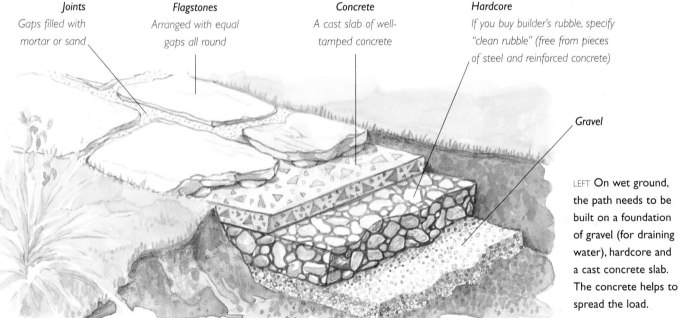

Joints
Gaps filled with
mortar or sand

Flagstones
Arranged with equal
gaps all round

Concrete
A cast slab of well-
tamped concrete

Hardcore
If you buy builder's rubble, specify
"clean rubble" (free from pieces
of steel and reinforced concrete)

Gravel

LEFT On wet ground,
the path needs to be
built on a foundation
of gravel (for draining
water), hardcore and
a cast concrete slab.
The concrete helps to
spread the load.

Flagstone paths on firm ground

If the ground is stony and well drained, and you plan to use good-size flagstones, it is only necessary to build a foundation of hardcore topped off with a layer of sand.

Dig a trench to a depth of about 200 mm and half-fill it with well-compacted builder's rubble or crushed stone, to a thickness of 100 mm. Top this with a 50 mm-thick bed of well-raked, level sand, and then set the stones in place. Brush sand, containing a mixture of grass and flower seeds, between the joints. This will encourage the ingress of plants to bind the stones firmly together.

Flagstone paths on wet ground

When the ground is soft and badly drained, and you want to use flagstones, you need to build a foundation of gravel covered by well-compacted hardcore and concrete.

Dig a trench to a depth of about 250 mm and fill it with gravel to a thickness of 50 mm. Spread builder's rubble or crushed stone over the gravel to a thickness of 100 mm. Finally, top the hardcore with a 50 mm-thick bed of well-tamped concrete, and set the stone in place. Brush sand between the joints. The gravel foundation base will allow water to drain under the path.

Rock gardens

The whole subject of building rock gardens and arranging stone is so subjective that it is difficult to offer advice.

Go and look at other gardens, touch as many stones as you can, take a trip to a rocky beach or a mountain slope

to get inspiration from the natural landscape, and then decide what appeals to you.

ROCKERY DESIGN AND SITING

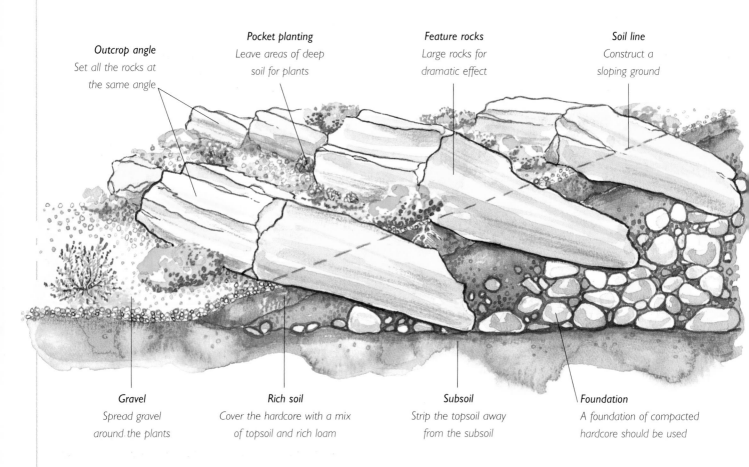

Outcrop angle
Set all the rocks at
the same angle

Pocket planting
Leave areas of deep
soil for plants

Feature rocks
Large rocks for
dramatic effect

Soil line
Construct a
sloping ground

Gravel
Spread gravel
around the plants

Rich soil
Cover the hardcore with a mix
of topsoil and rich loam

Subsoil
Strip the topsoil away
from the subsoil

Foundation
A foundation of compacted
hardcore should be used

Rockery design

A good rockery looks as if it is just the tip of a massive outcrop of stone that is hidden away under the ground. Do not attempt to build a rockery from hand-sized stones, arranging them haphazardly in an unlikely position, such as close to a lush border or round a swimming pool. It is much better to use a small number of large, well-weathered feature rocks, and to site them so that they rear up through an otherwise controlled area, such as a gravel bed or lawn.

Stone groups

Groups of rocks or large stones are sometimes likened to families, and through the centuries, they have often inspired folk tales. When these large rocks are set together in an otherwise rock-free landscape, they seem to invite questions and attention, and

cannot easily be ignored. Try this out for yourself on a slightly smaller scale, by grouping three big stones together on your lawn. Family, friends and neighbours will be sure to comment.

Standing guardians

Many societies have a tradition of erecting lone standing stones, for example the Japanese, the Chinese, and the Celts of ancient Britain. In the form of a monolithic slab set in the ground, such stones are almost invariably thought of as being guardians or sentinels. They are used to represent power, strength, permanence and dignity. If you want something similar in your own garden, the only problem with stones of this size is how to move them into position. If you have not got access to a tractor and hoist, ask a dozen or so friends to help, and move the stones with ropes, planks and rollers, a metal tube A-frame and a car winch.

OTHER TYPES OF ROCK GARDEN

Gravel and stone garden

A gravel and stone garden can be formal, with low walls, a tight pattern of stones, and a bed of gravel to cover the ground. Alternatively, it can be informal, with a natural spread of stones, and graded gravel to suggest a riverbed or scree. Start by planning out the paths, then cover the site with woven plastic sheet (to prevent weeds growing but allow drainage). Arrange a few good-size stones, then spread rivers of graded gravel and grit.

Grass and stone garden

To create a grass and stone garden, set three or four large stones (like islands) in a cropped lawn. Try various groupings for the stones and then, when you are happy with the layout, experiment by leaving selected areas of grass uncut. If there are wild meadow flowers growing in the long grass, and perhaps a sheltered space to sit in, or a flat slab of stone for a table, so much the better.

Pit and stone garden

One of the joys of walking in the country is coming across a secret, quiet place, that nobody else seems to know about. We once found a little dell, with a circle of rocks, several grassy mounds, and a sunken area in between. The dell appeared to be the site of something that had fallen into decay. Perhaps it was once an old house, an ancient village, or a well.

You can achieve a similar effect by digging a shallow hole in the lawn, grassing over the resulting mounds of soil, and grouping a few feature stones around the site.

ABOVE A gravel and stone garden. Spread the gravel so that it flows around the larger stones like a riverbed.

ABOVE Grass and stone garden. Let the grass around the stones grow long and mow a passageway between the mounds.

PLANTING A ROCKERY

Rock plants need a soil made up of one part fine gravel or grit, one part sand, and one part garden loam. Assess your soil to see whether it is alkaline or acidic, and purchase plants accordingly. For lime-loving rockery plants, use this basic soil mix, and scatter handfuls of flaked limestone about the site. Acid-loving plants will appreciate the addition of finely chopped bark instead.

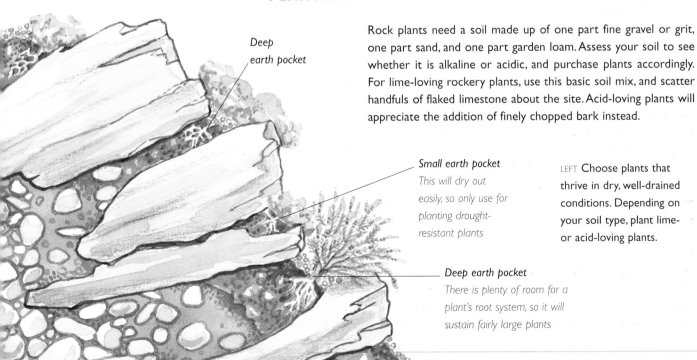

Deep earth pocket

Small earth pocket
This will dry out easily, so only use for planting drought-resistant plants

LEFT Choose plants that thrive in dry, well-drained conditions. Depending on your soil type, plant lime- or acid-loving plants.

Deep earth pocket
There is plenty of room for a plant's root system, so it will sustain fairly large plants

Walls and other structures

An old proverb says, "A wall without a gate is a prison, while a wall with a gate is a paradise". Building a stone wall is a wonderfully creative and fulfilling experience: one moment you have a space and the next you have a structure! It may be a practical wall to keep the children in, or a grand wall to make a statement.

DIFFERENT TYPES OF WALL

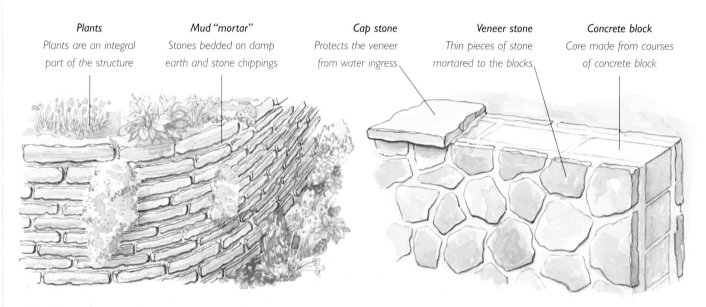

Plants
Plants are an integral part of the structure

Mud "mortar"
Stones bedded on damp earth and stone chippings

Cap stone
Protects the veneer from water ingress

Veneer stone
Thin pieces of stone mortared to the blocks

Concrete block
Core made from courses of concrete block

ABOVE Dry-stone retaining wall. The horizontal courses must be kept in line and the vertical joints staggered. The plants help bond the wall together because the roots run back into the retained soil.

ABOVE Veneered wall. Stones are arranged in a pattern that fits together well, and bedded in mortar. The stones are fixed one line at a time, leaving the mortar to stiffen before the next line is started.

Dry-stone walls

Dry-stone walls are traditionally made from whatever stone happens to be around, such as fieldstone, stone from the local quarry, or stone from a riverbed. Dry-stone walls always look at home in their surroundings for the simple reason that their colour and texture blends with the landscape in which they are found. In cross-section, dry-stone walls always taper in from a wide base, with low walls sitting directly on the ground, and high walls starting in a trench well below frost level. The walls may be topped off with coping stones on edge, stones laid flat, a layer of concrete and cobbles, or even a mix of stones, loose earth and turf.

Retaining walls

A retaining wall is best defined as a low wall that is used to hold back earth. Such walls are usually built on a sloping site where there is a need to step the ground to make a terrace. If you want to terrace a steep slope, it is better to go for a series of low walls rather than one or two high ones. Where the earth is heavy and wet, the

CAUTION

Make sure that all stone structures are strong, stable and adequately reinforced. Until you are experienced, don't attempt to build structures that are higher than head-height.

foundation is created in a deep trench, the wall is made extra wide at the foot, and as much rock spoil as possible is heaped behind the wall to supply extra drainage.

Mortared walls

Mortared walls are usually built on a concrete foundation. The courses are made from "ashlar" (cut and shaped stone) or rubble (uncut fieldstone). However, many mortared walls are made from salvaged cut stone and carefully selected fieldstone. There are four rules for building this type of wall: always rake back the mortar to reveal as much of the stone as possible, use a mortar that contains a good proportion of lime, make sure the mortar is stiff, and always wet the stone just before bonding. If you have any concerns about your wall-building project, such as getting the proportions of the mortar mix right, finding the colour or absorption rate of your chosen stone, deciding on the depth of the courses or the precise siting of the wall in the garden, it is a good idea to start off by building a small trial section of wall.

HOW TO BUILD A STRAIGHT WALL

Building procedure

1 Dig a trench to a depth of between 200–300 mm and lay a foundation of compacted rubble, topped with concrete (see page 148). Use a spirit level at all stages to ensure that everything is level.

2 Lay a course of stones, selecting and cutting stones to achieve best fit, for the whole length of the wall. Do your best to make sure that the stones are all of more or less equal thickness.

3 Put the stones carefully to one side, wet them and spread a generous layer of mortar over the foundation slab. Bed the stones in place on the mortar, and tap them down with the hammer. Make sure that the second course is well staggered against the first.

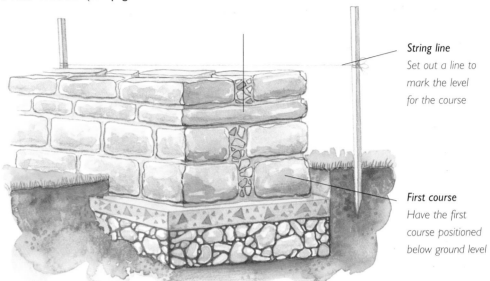

Tie stones
Have a tie stone

String line
Set out a line to mark the level for the course

First course
Have the first course positioned below ground level

PILLARS AND PIERS

Building a pillar

The techniques for building piers, square-section pillars and round-section pillars are similar. Building a round-section pillar, however, is a wonderful, skill-stretching experience that should not be missed. You are forever doing your best to fit the individual stones so that they run as close as possible to the circular section plan. It is best to practise laying a course of stones without mortar first of all (all the stones that fit the edge of the circle, and then all the stones to fill in). Next put them to one side, spread the mortar, and bed the selected and trimmed stones in place. Tap down the whole layer of stones with a trowel or hammer, check the horizontal and vertical truth with a spirit level and make adjustments, then move on to the next course. If the courses bulge, stop building until the mortar has cured.

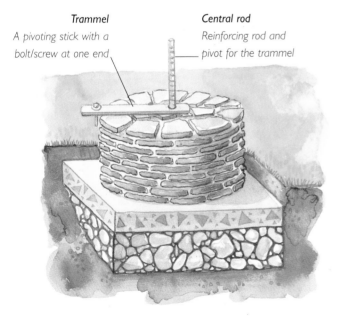

Trammel
A pivoting stick with a bolt/screw at one end

Central rod
Reinforcing rod and pivot for the trammel

ABOVE **This method of building a round pillar uses a central rod and a trammel (a stick that is rotated to check the circumference).**

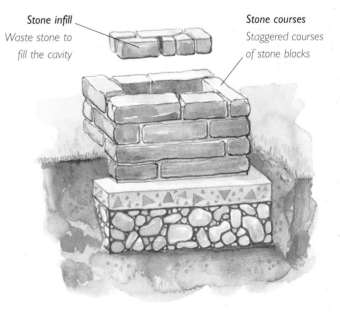

Stone infill
Waste stone to fill the cavity

Stone courses
Staggered courses of stone blocks

ABOVE **A square stone pier. Courses are established and then infilled with waste stone. All the vertical joints are staggered.**

Part 2: **Projects**

Stepping-stone path

Rough-cut stepping stones make a delightful path, which is perfect for light foot traffic, great for children playing jumping games, and also suitable for pushing a wheelbarrow on. The flow of stones meandering across the lawn fulfils a design function too, beautifully leading the eye from one garden feature to another.

TIME

About half a day (for nine medium-size stones).

SAFETY

Setting the stones is a difficult, finger-nipping task, so make sure that you wear thick leather gloves.

YOU WILL NEED

Materials *for a path with nine stepping stones*

• Flagstones: 9 salvaged slate or limestone flags about 500 mm long, 400 mm wide and 50 mm thick
• Soft sand: about 1 bucket of sand per stone

Tools

• Wheelbarrow
• Spade
• Fork
• Bucket
• Wooden tamping beam: about 500 mm long, 60 mm wide and 50 mm thick
• Sledgehammer

SITING THE PATH

Before you decide where to put the path, think about the ebb and flow of traffic in the garden. Work out how many times, during your day-to-day activities, you walk from one point to another. For example, when you empty the kitchen waste on to the compost heap, do you always take the same route? Do you avoid certain routes because the ground is muddy? Are there any worn areas on the lawn, which indicate heavy wear? They will be dusty and bald in summer, muddy and dipped in winter.

When you have considered all the options and variables, map out the best route for the path. Before you calculate the number of stones and their spacing, take into account the length of stride of the people most likely to use the path. Have a trial "stepping out" across the lawn to work out the required spacing. When you come to choosing the stones, it does not matter if they are different sizes and odd shapes, or even if there are great variations in thickness, as long as each stone has one sound, level face.

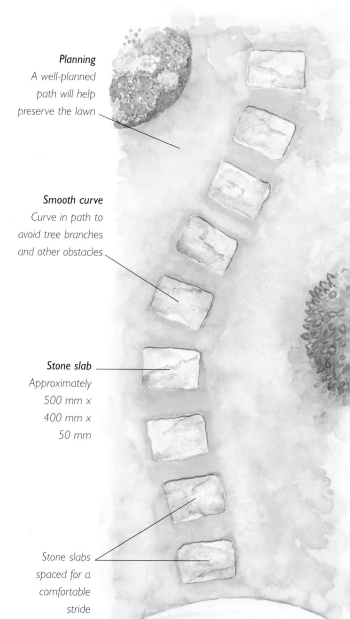

PLAN VIEW OF PATH

Planning
A well-planned path will help preserve the lawn

Smooth curve
Curve in path to avoid tree branches and other obstacles

Stone slab
Approximately 500 mm x 400 mm x 50 mm

Stone slabs spaced for a comfortable stride

Patio area

CROSS-SECTION THROUGH PATH

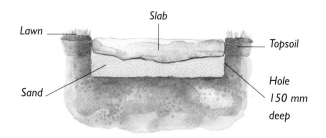

Lawn

Slab

Topsoil

Sand

Hole 150 mm deep

Step-by-step: **Making the stepping-stone path**

Spacing
*Check that the spacing
suits your length of stride*

Best face
*Make sure that
the best face of
the flagstone is
uppermost*

1 Set out the flagstones on the lawn, spacing them to suit the stride of the people who will use the path. Experiment with various alignments – curved, straight, or winding – until you are pleased with the overall effect. Arrange the individual flags so that the best face is uppermost.

Helpful hint

If, when you're putting the stones down, you notice that any are starting to delaminate slightly with handling, it is a sign that the stone is not very stable, and would wear rapidly. Reject it and replace with another.

Alignment
*Adjust the flagstones so that
they are aligned with each other*

Lifting turf
*A round-pronged fork
is good for this*

Depth
*Aim for a
recess about
150 mm deep*

Turf
*Only pick up as
much turf as
you can lift
comfortably*

2 Use a small, clean, sharp spade to cut into the ground around each stone. Hold the spade upright and cut to a depth of about 200 mm, making sure that the cuts cross over at the corners. Repeat this procedure for all the stones in the line.

3 Carefully lift the stone to one side. Quarter the defined turf with the spade, and use the fork to lift the quarters into the wheelbarrow. Take to the compost heap. With the spade, excavate the recess to an overall depth of about 150 mm.

Hole depth
Make adjustments to holes to
suit varying thicknesses of stone

Stone height
The stone needs to be
10 mm lower than the lawn

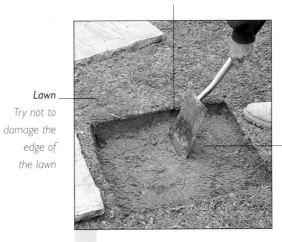

Corners
Clean the
earth from
the corners of
the holes

Lawn
Try not to
damage the
edge of
the lawn

Sand
Spread sand
over the recess

4 Work along the line of flagstones, removing the turf and soil, until you have a line of holes that fit the stones. Pay particular attention to the corners of the holes – they need to be crisp and clean.

5 Gauge the thickness of the stone and the depth of the hole, spread sand to a depth of 80–90 mm, then bed the stone in place. (Lift the stone and adjust the sand until the flagstone is about 10 mm lower than the lawn.)

Sledgehammer
Let the shaft of the hammer
slide through your hands

6 When the flagstone is nicely bedded on the sand, place the wooden beam diagonally across it and use the sledgehammer to gently tamp the stone into place. If the stone tilts or sinks, simply lift one edge and adjust the level of the sand.

Footwork
Hold the beam
secure with
your feet

Depth
If the slab does
not sit level,
remove it and
adjust the sand
underneath

Cobble spiral

Cobbles set in concrete make a great decorative feature, which can be employed to direct the movement of cars on your drive. The spaced cobbles are slightly uncomfortable to drive over, so visitors will instinctively steer round them. If you would like to enhance your drive with a feature that is attractive, hard-wearing and functional, cobbles are wonderfully suitable.

YOU WILL NEED

Materials *for a circle 1.8 m in diameter*
- Hardcore:
  3 wheelbarrow loads broken rubble or stone
- Concrete: 1 part (50 kg) cement, 2 parts (100 kg) sharp sand, 3 parts (150 kg) aggregate
- Cobbles: 50 kg x 80 mm cobbles (allows for choice)
- Shingle: 25 kg x 25 mm shingle (allows for choice)

Tools
- Tape measure and chalk
- Wheelbarrow
- Sledgehammer
- Mason's hammer
- Spade and shovel
- Bucket
- Wooden tamping beam: about 900 mm long, 100 mm wide and 20 mm thick
- Bricklayer's trowel

MARKING AND PLANNING

Decide on the size of the circle according to your drive. Our circle has been made in an old flowerbed with an existing brick edging, but you could make a larger circle with a cobble edging (the radius of the circle should be no larger than you can reach).

Wash the cobbles, grade them from large to small, and have a trial dry-run. With tape measure and chalk, mark out a circle on the drive, pinpointing the centre. Transporting the cobbles in the wheelbarrow, position the biggest and best cobble at the centre. Add further stones to make a spiral, working clockwise, and finishing up with the smallest cobbles. Once the cobbles are in place, use the shingle to run a secondary spiral within the first.

We have increased the overall dynamic effect of the spiral by tamping the concrete to make a pattern that radiates out from the centre. Once the concrete has been mixed, you have to work at speed before it sets. Finally, don't forget to place a barrier around the finished circle so that you don't drive over it by mistake while it is drying.

PLAN VIEW OF THE COBBLE SPIRAL

Driveway
Existing concrete and brick edging

Edge detail
Edge of concrete is bevelled

Brick edging
Bricks arranged face-up around the circle

Concrete
1.8 m in diameter

Cobbles
80 mm cobbles set into concrete

Shingle
25 mm shingle set into concrete

CROSS-SECTION DETAIL

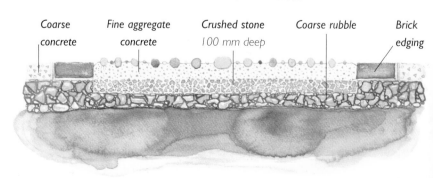

Coarse concrete

Fine aggregate concrete

Crushed stone
100 mm deep

Coarse rubble

Brick edging

Step-by-step: **Making the cobble spiral**

Hardcore
*Pound the hardcore in place
with the sledgehammer*

Tamping
*Work with a rapid
tapping action*

Brick edge
*Be careful not
to damage any
existing edging*

Pivot
*Pivot one
end of the
beam on the
centre point*

Radial pattern
*Tamp the
concrete into a
radial pattern*

1 Having marked out the circle, dig it out to a depth of about 180 mm. (If you need to break up the concrete of the existing drive, use the sledgehammer and mason's hammer to do so.) Shovel in the hardcore and use the sledgehammer to pound it into place. The hardcore layer should be 100 mm deep.

2 Measure out the dry ingredients that go to make the concrete (cement, sharp sand and aggregate). Fill the bucket with water. Mix sufficient water into the dry ingredients to make the correct consistency of concrete. Shovel the concrete into place, then use the beam to bring it to the same level as the brick edging and tamp it into a radial pattern.

Trowel angle
*Angle the trowel into
the brick edge*

Cobbles
*Grade the cobbles
into sizes*

Smooth finish
*Run the trowel
around until
the concrete is
smooth*

Spiral
*Arrange the
stones into
a smooth
spiral shape*

Tapping
*Allow the
weight of the
sledgehammer
to fall on
the cobble*

3 Holding the bricklayer's trowel at a sharp angle, run it around the edge of the concrete. Do this a couple of times, to achieve a smooth, bevelled finish.

4 Select a good cobble for the centre and use the weight of the sledgehammer to tap it very gently into place. Repeat the procedure with a dozen stones, establishing the pattern.

Damaged cobbles
Put damaged cobbles to
one side and avoid using

5 Continue setting out the cobbles, making sure they are aligned and then tamping them into place with the sledgehammer. Stand back periodically to check that the spiral relates evenly to the circle.

Trial placing
Set out about
six cobbles at a
time. Check for
size and fit
before you tap
them into place

Spacing
Try to keep
the spacing
between the
lines consistent

6 When you have placed all the cobbles, use the shingle to run a second spiral within the first. Use the mason's hammer to tap the pebbles into position. Leave the concrete to cure for seven days before driving on it.

Shingle
Run the line
of shingle
between the
big cobbles

Helpful hint

Wash individual stones in water and set out a sequence of six or so stones at a time. Don't strike the stone, but rather let the weight of the hammer do most of the work. Continue gently tapping until the stone is slightly more than half buried in the concrete.

Natural outcrop rockery

A swift and easy way to add a dynamic feature to an otherwise level expanse of lawn

is to build a rockery that looks like a natural outcrop. Rocks breaking through the

ground suggest that there are powerful dynamic forces at work within the garden,

while the well-drained environment allows you to cultivate a broad range of plants

that enjoy these conditions.

TIME

A weekend to build, two days of good weather for arranging the stones and for planting.

SAFETY

Moving large stones is hard, dangerous work – get someone to help you.

YOU WILL NEED

Materials *for a rockery 3 m x 2.4 m x 600 mm*
- Soil: 1 tonne (5 parts good-quality topsoil to 1 part sharp sand)
- Feature rocks: 6 large sandstone rocks (the biggest you are able to move)
- Split sandstone: approximately 1 tonne (for foundation stones and decorative edging)
- Secondary rocks: 6 medium-sized sandstone rocks

- Alpine grit: 25 kg crushed granite
- Oyster shell grit: 25 kg well-washed crushed shell

Tools
- Fork
- Wheelbarrow
- Spade
- Club hammer
- Gardening trowel

A ROCK AND HEATHER MIX

Study the garden and think about the various options for the positioning of the rockery. Do you want to have a rockery island surrounded by a sea of lawn, or are you going to build it as a peninsular feature that divides two areas of lawn? Are you going to buy in the topsoil and build the rockery as a self-contained feature, or are you going to use earth moved from another project? (If you can use earth left over from another project, such as a pond excavation, or the topsoil removed prior to building an extension to the house, you save both time and money.)

The task of moving the rocks and earth is a major part of this project. Ideally, you need to plan the whole operation so that they only have to be shifted a short distance. Use a wheelbarrow and ask a friend to help you manoeuvre heavy rocks (see page 145).

It is preferable to choose a site for the rockery that is well away from formal borders, so that it does not create an imbalance between the various plantings in the garden. When we designed this rockery, we had in mind the sort of natural outcrop that you often see at the bottom of scree slopes, where rock and heather meet green pasture.

PLAN VIEW OF THE ROCKERY

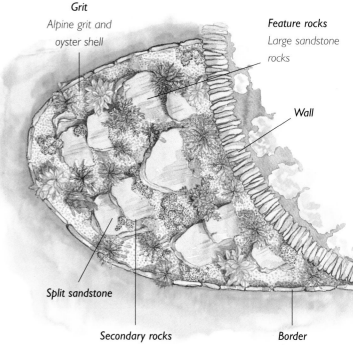

Grit
Alpine grit and oyster shell

Feature rocks
Large sandstone rocks

Wall

Split sandstone

Secondary rocks
Medium-sized sandstone rocks

Border
Pieces of split sandstone

CROSS-SECTION OF THE ROCKERY

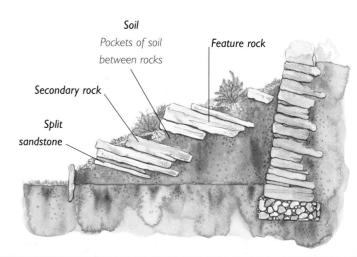

Soil
Pockets of soil between rocks

Feature rock

Secondary rock

Split sandstone

Step-by-step: Making the natural outcrop rockery

Retaining wall
*Use an existing feature
as a retaining wall*

Pocket slope
*Angle the hole so that it
is deepest at the back*

Spreading soil
*Work the earth
with the fork
and your feet*

Pocket
*Dig a pocket
to match the
size of the
stone*

Trial fit
*You may need
several
attempts to get
the stone to fit
the hole*

1 With the fork, work the mound of earth to remove weeds, lumps of clay and unwanted stones. Walk back and forth over the earth to collapse cavities and compact it into shape.

2 Load stones into the wheelbarrow and move them to the site. The large stones are grouped like a series of steps. Dig a pocket towards the bottom of the mound and carefully ease one of the largest feature stones into place.

Earth anchor
*Load earth on the tail
end of the stone*

3 When you are pleased with the overall position and angle of the feature stone, take some pieces of split sandstone and use the club hammer to bang them under the stone. The sandstone will wedge the feature stone firmly in place.

Wedging
*Compact the
earth so the
front of the
stone rears up.
Wedge waste
stone under
the front of
the rock
to preserve
the angle*

Helpful hint

Compact the earth under the leading edge of the stone until the stone is rearing up at the front with the bulk of its weight at the tail end. Add fragments of waste stone (or old bricks, concrete, or hardcore) to the compacted earth.

Secondary stones
Use smaller stones to
complement the arrangement

Soil
Soil incorporates grit
for drainage

Outcrop angle
The stones
should rear
up at the
same angle

Stone angle
Trowel earth
under the
stone to adjust
the angle

Edging
Use stone on
edge to define
the rockery

4 Work up the slope repeating the procedure, until you achieve a series of steps that slope back slightly into the mound. Trowel earth in and around the stones to hold them in place.

5 When you have completed the basic outcrop, with all the stones rearing up at the same angle, dig a trench around the mound and define it with an edging of split sandstone. Plant the rockery.

Plant colour
Choose plants that have
different seasons of interest

6 Finally, when you have completed your planting, scatter handfuls of alpine grit and crushed oyster shell in and around the plants and stones, to cover the earth and help give the impression that the rockery is part of a natural outcrop.

Watering
Water the
plants to settle
the roots

Alpine grit and oyster shell
The spread of grit and
oyster shell helps the earth
to retain moisture

Inspirations: Rockeries

The contrast between large stones and minute plants is uniquely beautiful. However, rockeries come in many shapes and sizes, from the austere sand and rock gardens of Japan, through to the little stone rockeries that characterized English suburban gardens in the 1920s and 1930s. Regardless of size, most rock gardens use stone and plants to suggest or replicate a natural setting. There are rock plants suitable for all situations, from exposed sites to crevices, and both sunny and shady positions.

RIGHT A flight of railway sleeper steps has been transformed into an eye-catching rockery simply by edging the steps with carefully chosen limestone rocks, spreading an infill of crushed stone between the wooden treads, and planting with species that thrive in a well-drained alkaline soil.

ABOVE A water rockery garden of Welsh slate planted with dwarf conifers and alpines. This rockery is reminiscent of high mountain passes, ice-cold springs and tranquillity.

RIGHT A Feng Shui rockery garden designed by Pamela Woods. Large feature rocks, gravel, wooden decking and water create a sublimely peaceful garden space.

Tessellated paving

An exciting and creative way of repairing an existing paved patio is to replace damaged slabs with an infill pattern of tessellated tiles. All you do is remove the slabs, revealing the underlying base, then bed in the tiles with a skim of mortar.

YOU WILL NEED

Materials *for 2 areas of paving 920 mm square*
- Mortar: 2 parts (30 kg) cement, 1 part (15 kg) lime, 9 parts (135 kg) soft sand
- Concrete tiles (imitation terracotta): 8 lozenge tiles (510 x 215 mm), 22 small square tiles (150 x 150 mm), 1 large square tile (300 x 300 mm)
- Shingle: 25 kg washed shingle (15–25 mm)

Tools
- Club hammer
- Wheelbarrow
- Tape measure and piece of chalk
- Bucket
- Spade and shovel
- Wooden tamping beam: about 400 mm long, 60 mm wide and 25 mm thick
- Mortar float
- Bricklayer's trowel

PRETTY AS A PICTURE

In this project, the word "tessellate" refers to the act of grouping tiles so that they fit together like a mosaic or a tiled floor. Identical square tiles tessellate to make a chequer-board pattern, but more dynamic effects can be obtained when two or more different shapes are arranged to create an overall repeat pattern, like the lozenge-shaped and square tiles in our two designs.

We lifted eight concrete slabs to create two identical square recesses. To remove a slab, hit it in the middle with a club hammer and pick the broken pieces out with a trowel. Note how we have used three shapes to fit the frame – a lozenge and two different squares – and then filled in around the tiles with a pattern of shingle. It is best to start with just a few shapes, playing around with various arrangements until you come up with an exciting design, and then to purchase additional tiles to suit your needs.

PLAN VIEW OF THE TESSELLATED PAVING

Shingle
Decorative shingle set in mortar

Small square tile
150 x 150 mm

Paved area
Existing paving slab surround

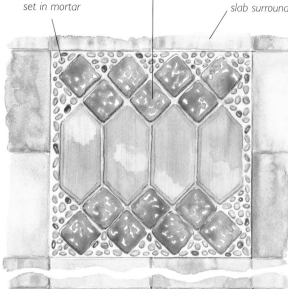

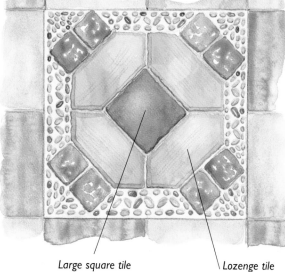

Large square tile
300 x 300 mm

Lozenge tile
510 x 215 mm

CROSS-SECTION OF THE TESSELLATED PAVING

Shingle   Tiles   Mortar

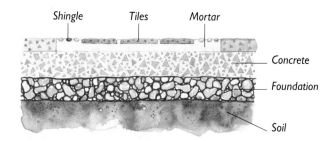

Concrete
Foundation
Soil

Step-by-step: **Making the tessellated paving**

Existing slabs
Make sure existing slabs are stable

Corners
Make sure the mortar gets right into the corners

Tamping
Use a wooden beam to tamp the mortar level

Float
Work the float from side to side

Uniform bed
Aim for a smooth, level finish

1 Use the tape measure and chalk to draw guidelines on the concrete slabs. Sprinkle water over the exposed foundation, shovel the mortar into place, and tamp it level with the beam so that it ends up slightly lower than the slabs.

2 Use the mortar float to skim the mortar into the corners and right to the edges of the recess. Work the float from side to side to achieve a uniform bed with no cavities or bumps.

Centre-line
Make sure the tiles are aligned with the registration marks

3 One at a time, dip the tiles in a bucket of water, shake off the excess and then very carefully set them in position on the wet mortar. When the design is in place, use the handle of the bricklayer's trowel to tap and adjust the individual tiles.

Tapping
Use the handle of the trowel to tap the tile in position

Wet the tiles
In hot weather sprinkle water over the tiles to hold back the drying time of the mortar

Tile level
Keep the tiles level with
the surrounding slabs

Bedding
Move the tile
from side to
side to bed it
in place

4 If, at any point along the way, a tile sinks too deeply or sticks up at an angle, lift it with the point of the trowel, add a little more mortar, and then gently bed it back into place.

Helpful hint

If the day is sunny and the tiles feel hot and dry to the touch, soak the back of each tile in water just prior to bedding it into the mortar. Wiggle the tile rapidly on the spot until you feel it begin to settle.

Shingle patterns
Arrange the
shingle into a
pleasing pattern

5 Finally, when all the tiles are in position, use the shingle to make patterns in the remaining areas of mortar. Set the pebbles in one at a time. Leave for 24 hours before it is dry enough for light traffic, or seven days before it is ready for heavy use.

Cleaning
Use a damp
cloth to clean
the tiles and
remove spots
of mortar

Raised bed

A raised bed gives you the opportunity to add an extra planting area to your garden, and the change in level creates interest. You can build it on an existing patio or area of concrete. The good thing about raised beds is that you do not have to stoop to weed them. This one is built from double-sided reconstituted stone blocks.

TIME

A weekend to build (two full days to build on an existing patio base).

COMMENT

Reconstituted stone blocks are heavy and fragile. Handle the blocks with care, preferably wearing gloves.

YOU WILL NEED

Materials *for a bed 1.10 m square and 510 mm high*
- Mortar: 2 parts (20 kg) cement, 1 part (10 kg) lime, 9 parts (90 kg) soft sand
- Double-sided "York stone" blocks: 48 blocks, 450 mm long, 150 mm wide and 65 mm thick
- Straight "York stone" coping blocks: 8 blocks, 450 mm long, 185 mm wide and 47 mm thick

Tools
- Wheelbarrow
- Tape measure and piece of chalk
- Spirit level and a length of batten
- Shovel
- Bucket
- Bricklayer's trowel
- Mason's hammer
- Pointing trowel
- Stiff brush

A BED ON THE PATIO

If you are looking for a project that involves the minimum of effort and expertise, this is a good one to try. The sizes specified for the wall blocks and coping blocks allow you to build a rectilinear form without the need for cutting. The clever design of the blocks means that all the on-view faces are textured.

This project is designed to be set directly on to a base of existing patio slabs, avoiding the need to build a foundation. The bed can be sited away from walls, so that it can be viewed and approached from all sides, or it can back on to a wall. If you are going to put it near a building, make sure that there is enough space for you to move the blocks into position.

PLAN VIEW OF THE RAISED BED

CROSS-SECTION OF THE RAISED BED

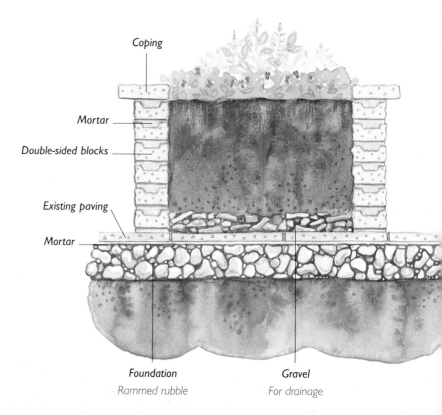

Coping

Mortar

Double-sided blocks

Existing paving

Mortar

Foundation
Rammed rubble

Gravel
For drainage

Peat-based growing medium

Coping block
450 x 185 x 47 mm

SIDE VIEW

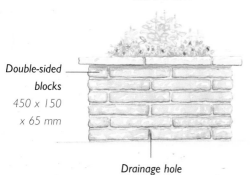

Double-sided blocks
450 x 150 x 65 mm

Drainage hole

Step-by-step: **Making the raised bed**

Chalk lines
Use the chalk to set out guidelines

I Use the tape measure, chalk and spirit level to establish the position of the bed. Take eight wall blocks to form the first course of the bed. Arrange them in position so that each side of the bed shows two long faces of the blocks and one end face.

Spirit level
Check with the spirit level to see if the blocks are sitting level

Drainage
Leave one vertical course open on each side of the first course for a drainage hole

Helpful hint

When you come to testing with the spirit level, be aware that a vertical height difference of, say, 5 mm might be caused by no more than a blob of mortar. Wipe both the spirit level and the top of the blocks before taking a reading.

Buttering
Butter the end of the block with the mortar

Mortar
Do not worry about mortar oozing out inside the bed

Mortar bed
Lay down a generous bed of mortar

Tapping
Use the hammer to tap blocks into line

Staggered courses
Arrange the courses so that the blocks overlap joins

2 Use the bricklayer's trowel to lay down a bed of mortar. Dampen the blocks and patio slabs. Place a block on the mortar, butter the end of the next block with mortar and set it alongside. Continue in the same way for all eight blocks.

3 Check that the blocks are level with the spirit level and the batten. Tap any blocks that stand proud with the mason's hammer. Repeat the procedure for the next course of blocks. Note how the pattern of blocks is staggered.

Sighting
*Look down the wall and
tap blocks into position*

Mortar
*Clean the mortar off the top
before levelling*

Checking
*After each
course, check
that blocks
are level and
aligned*

Levelling
*Make sure that
both the batten
and the spirit
level are free
from blobs of
mortar*

4 Continue laying one course of blocks upon another, all the while checking that they are horizontal with the spirit level and batten, tapping blocks into place with the mason's hammer, and tidying up the mortar with the pointing trowel.

5 When you have built all six courses, rake out some of the mortar with the pointing trowel. Clean up with the stiff brush and check the overall squareness of the structure by setting the spirit level across the corners. If you need to make adjustments, use the batten to tap blocks into place, rather than the spirit level.

Tapping
*Use the trowel handle to tap
the blocks into final position*

6 Finally, lay a bed of mortar on the top course and set the coping stones in place. Their back edge should be level with the inside face of the wall; the front edge forms a nosing or lip around the bed. Before filling the bed with soil, allow two days for the mortar to dry.

Bedding
*Twist the block
slightly back
and forth while
applying light
pressure*

Raking
*Leave the raking
(scraping excess
mortar from
between the
blocks) until the
mortar is half-set*

Flagstone steps

Flagstone steps are not only a practical and functional means of coping with a steep,

sloping garden, but are also a dynamic design feature in their own right. The steps

lead the eye from one level to another, and suggest that there are other exciting

areas of garden still to be explored. This project consists of three steps.

CROSS-SECTION OF THE FLAGSTONE STEPS

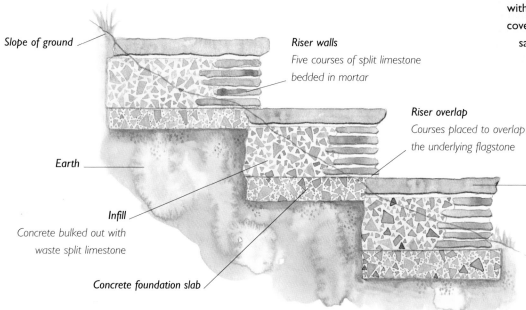

Slope of ground

Riser walls
Five courses of split limestone bedded in mortar

Riser overlap
Courses placed to overlap the underlying flagstone

Earth

Flagstone slab
Limestone or slate salvaged flagstone (best to have the worn side facing uppermost) bedded in mortar

Infill
Concrete bulked out with waste split limestone

Concrete foundation slab

YOU WILL NEED

Materials *For 3 steps, each 600 mm wide, 420 mm deep and 170 mm high*
- Concrete: 1 part (40 kg) cement, 2 parts (80 kg) sharp sand, 3 parts (120 kg) aggregate
- Mortar: 2 parts (24 kg) cement, 1 part (12 kg) lime, 9 parts (108 kg) soft sand
- Slate or limestone flagstones: 3 salvaged flags, about 600 mm long, 420 mm wide and 40 mm thick
- Split limestone: 3 square metres salvaged roof stone, about 15 mm thick

Tools
- Wheelbarrow
- Bucket
- Tape measure and a piece of chalk
- Spade and shovel
- Wooden beam for tamping: about 600 mm long, 80 mm wide and 50 mm thick
- Spirit level
- Mason's hammer
- Bricklayer's trowel
- Club hammer
- Pointing trowel

UP AND DOWN THE GARDEN

Study the site and visualize how the steps will relate to the overall layout of the garden – the slope of the land, other features within the garden, and underground structures, such as foundations and pipes. When the flagstones are in place, the treads measure no less than 420 mm from the edge of the step to the riser. The riser walls are about 125 mm high, to give a total step height of no more than 170 mm. Each step is constructed in four stages – laying the concrete foundation slab, building the riser wall, back-filling behind the riser wall, and setting the flagstone in place.

The concrete foundation slabs are made from a 1-2-3 mix – 1 part cement, 2 parts sharp sand and 3 parts aggregate, and the infill is bulked out with waste stone. The mortar is 2-1-9 mix – 2 parts cement, 1 part lime, and 9 parts soft sand. The riser walls are built from five courses of salvaged roof stone, with the best edges of the stone placed on view. Finally, while we have covered the cut-in ground at the sides of the steps with pieces of flint, you might prefer to use something different, such as gravel, found field-stone, turf, ground-cover plants or crushed bark.

Flagstone steps

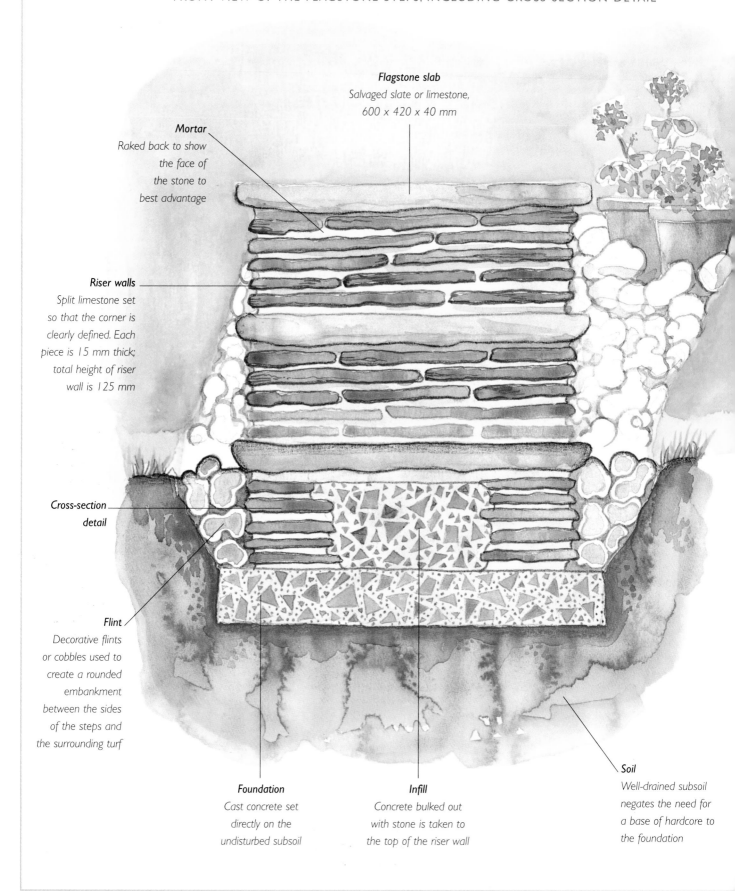

Flagstone slab
Salvaged slate or limestone,
600 x 420 x 40 mm

Mortar
Raked back to show
the face of
the stone to
best advantage

Riser walls
Split limestone set
so that the corner is
clearly defined. Each
piece is 15 mm thick;
total height of riser
wall is 125 mm

Cross-section
detail

Flint
Decorative flints
or cobbles used to
create a rounded
embankment
between the sides
of the steps and
the surrounding turf

Foundation
Cast concrete set
directly on the
undisturbed subsoil

Infill
Concrete bulked out
with stone is taken to
the top of the riser wall

Soil
Well-drained subsoil
negates the need for
a base of hardcore to
the foundation

PLAN VIEW OF THE FLAGSTONE STEPS

Flagstone slab
Slabs arranged to follow curve of the route

Flagstone slab
Slab set so that the weathered face is uppermost

Stone riser
Well bedded in mortar

Mortar
Mortar spread over the infill and trowelled level

Foundation
The foundation slab should extend beyond the riser wall

Infill
Bulked out with whatever rock or rubble waste is available

Front edge
Flagstone positioned so that the front edge overlaps the riser wall

Flagstone edge
Slab arranged so that the side edge overlaps the riser walls

Path
Path is dug so that it is on the same level as the first concrete slab

Step-by-step: **Making the flagstone steps**

Trench
*Cut the trench so that
there is room to work*

Spoil
*Try to minimize the amount
of earth fall at this stage*

Tamping
*Tamp the
concrete level
with the
wooden beam*

Marking
*Draw around
the slab
with chalk*

Alignment
*Angle the
flagstone in the
direction of
the flight*

1 To build the first step, mark out the foundation trench with the tape measure, making it about 900 mm wide and 700 mm from front to back. Dig down to a depth of 100 mm. Fill the trench with concrete and tamp it down with the wooden beam. Check that it is level.

2 Leave the concrete foundation to harden overnight. Next, place a flagstone on the concrete, angling it in the direction of the flight, and mark the position with the chalk. Put the flagstone to one side.

Corners
*Keep the corners crisp
and square*

Trimming
*Trim the stone
for the best fit*

3 Allowing for the flagstone to overhang at the front and side edges by 10–20 mm, select pieces of limestone for the front and side walls of the riser. Trim them to size with the mason's hammer. Pay special attention to the construction of the front and corners of the riser, and make sure they are square.

Helpful hint

The more time that you spend at the dry-run stage – choosing and arranging the stones for best fit, and trimming edges to shape – the easier it will be when you come to bedding the stones on the mortar.

4 Build the box by bedding the five courses of split limestone in mortar, building to a height of 125 mm. Fill the cavity with concrete and waste stone, tamp down level with the beam, and leave to set. Use the bricklayer's trowel to butter a 30 mm-layer of mortar over the top of the step. Some of the mortar will ooze out when the flagstone is positioned.

Filling
Fill the cavity with concrete and waste stone

Levelling
Tamp the courses level with the beam

Positioning
Slowly lower the flagstone on to the bed of mortar

Horizontal check
Check the foundation with the spirit level

Adjustment
When the slab is in place, adjust it so that the front edge slopes down by 10 mm, so rain can run off

Tamping
Use the beam to tamp the concrete level

Concrete
The concrete foundation needs to be level with the flagstone

5 Carefully lower the flagstone into position. Tamp down with the club hammer and check it is level with the spirit level. Adjust the stone so that the front edge slopes down by 10 mm. Use the pointing trowel to tidy up the mortar.

6 To build the next step, dig another foundation cavity (the same size as the first cavity) behind the first step. Fill the cavity, build the riser walls and position the flagstone as previously described. Repeat the procedure for each new step.

Alpine hypertufa trough

In the 1940s, gardeners developed a technique for covering old glazed white kitchen sinks with a mixture of sphagnum moss, sand and cement to make them look like stone. It was called hypertufa, after tufa, the rock it ressembled, and became all the rage. This project takes the technique one step further, in that we cast a whole trough from hypertufa. The project rises up like magic from the ground!

TIME

Two weekends: two days to dig out the mould and for casting (five days for the hypertufa to cure), and two more days for digging out the trough.

SAFETY

This project involves a lot of strenuous digging and heaving – you will need a willing helper.

CROSS-SECTION OF THE TROUGH

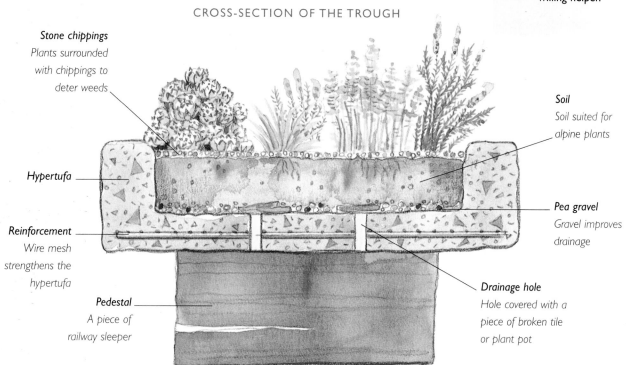

Stone chippings
Plants surrounded with chippings to deter weeds

Soil
Soil suited for alpine plants

Hypertufa

Pea gravel
Gravel improves drainage

Reinforcement
Wire mesh strengthens the hypertufa

Pedestal
A piece of railway sleeper

Drainage hole
Hole covered with a piece of broken tile or plant pot

YOU WILL NEED

Materials *for a trough 600 mm long, 400 mm wide and 130 mm high (not including height of pedestal)*
- Hypertufa mix: 25 kg cement, 25 kg sharp sand, 100 kg sphagnum moss
- Broomstick dowel: 2 x 150 mm long
- Wire grid mesh: 25 mm mesh, 570 mm long, 370 mm wide
- Railway sleeper: 400 mm long, 300 mm wide, 145 mm thick

Tools
- Spade and shovel
- Tape measure
- String line and 8 pegs
- Spirit level
- Sledgehammer
- Gardening trowel
- Mason's hammer
- Wheelbarrow and bucket
- Wooden tamping beam: about 600 mm long, 80 mm wide and 25 mm thick
- Wire clippers
- Pointing trowel
- Stiff brush

BURIED TREASURE

Find an area of rough, uncultivated ground in the garden for casting the trough – perhaps a corner of the vegetable plot, or a flower bed that is going to be grassed over. Ideally, you need an area that is reasonably well drained: a mix of heavy loam and clay (where you can squeeze a handful of the earth into a ball that holds its shape) would be perfect. If you study the working drawings and the photographs, you will see that the trough is cast upside-down, with a sheet of wire mesh used to reinforce the base. The drainage holes are created by the two dowels. The hollows and bumps in the ground are reversed to become bumps and holes in the trough or, to put it another way, the hollow of the trough starts out as a bump in the ground. The finished trough weighs about 150 kg, which might make it difficult to get out of the ground, so enlist the help of friends and family.

Alpine hypertufa trough

FRONT VIEW OF TROUGH

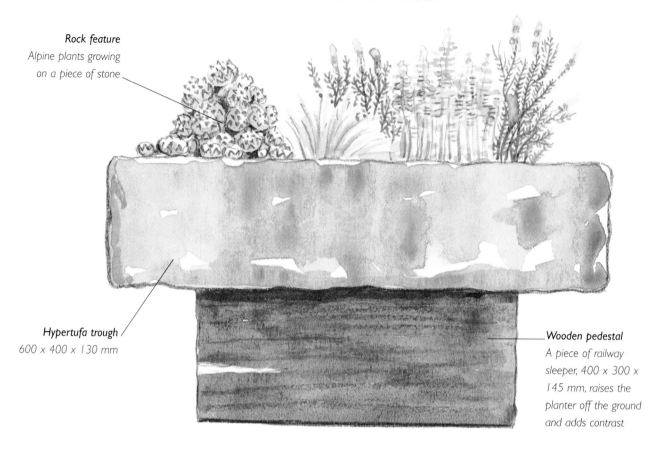

Rock feature
Alpine plants growing
on a piece of stone

Hypertufa trough
600 x 400 x 130 mm

Wooden pedestal
A piece of railway
sleeper, 400 x 300 x
145 mm, raises the
planter off the ground
and adds contrast

PLAN VIEW OF TROUGH

Sides of trough
Casting hypertufa in
earth produces a
rugged, stone-like finish

Strong sides
Sides are at least
70 mm thick

PLAN VIEW OF TROUGH DURING CASTING

Hypertufa
A final layer – smoothed and
levelled – covers the mesh

Reinforcement
Wire mesh is positioned within
the thickness of the base

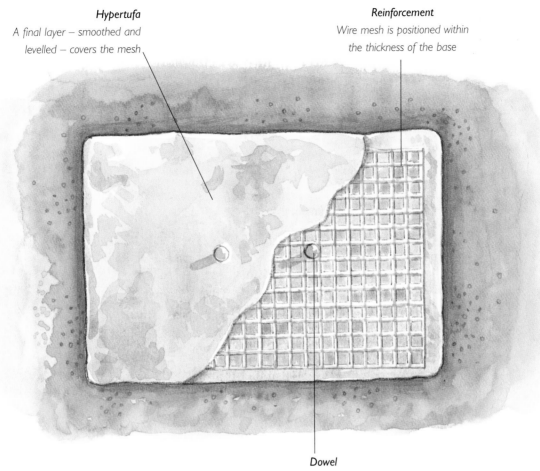

Dowel
Dowel inserted through the mesh and entire
thickness of the base (to create drainage holes)

CROSS-SECTION OF TROUGH DURING EXCAVATION

Excavation
A hole is dug
around the trough

Hypertufa

Dowel

Reinforcing mesh
Set approximately
half-way through
the 50 mm
thickness of the
trough base

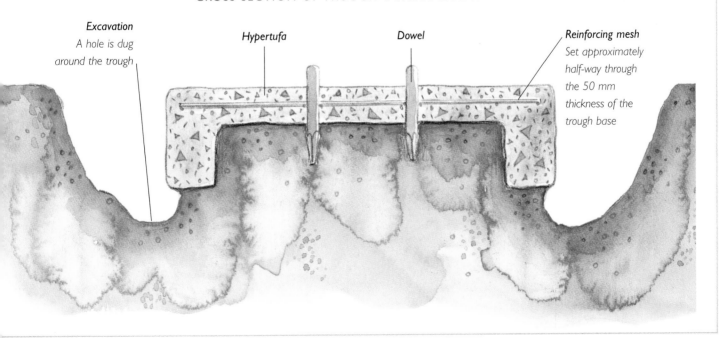

Step-by-step: **Making the alpine hypertufa trough**

Marking out
Set the shape out with pegs and string

Corners
The position of the pegs allows the string to cross over at the corners

1 Clear the ground of weeds and stones, and skim it level with a spade. Use the tape measure, string and pegs to set out a rectangle about 600 mm long and 400 mm wide.

Helpful hint

The traditional method of using two pegs at the corners, with the strings crossing, not only allows you to set out the shape without damaging the earth at the corners, but it also means that you can leave the arrangement in place when you are excavating.

Level
Adjust the level of the earth prior to pounding

Pounding
Pound the earth to a hard, compacted finish

Scoring
Use the point of the trowel to score a guideline

Depth
Clean out the earth to a depth of 50 mm

Digging
Work with small strokes to keep the edges crisp

2 Having pegged out the form and checked the overall level with the spirit level, take the sledgehammer and systematically pound the earth around the strings until it is hard and compact.

3 Following the line of the string, score the rectangle on the ground with the gardening trowel. Remove the pegs and string. Excavate the area to a depth of about 50 mm. Try and keep the sides of the excavation clean and sharp.

Trench width
The trench needs to
be 70 mm wide

Trench depth
Dig out the
trench to a total
depth of
130 mm

4 Measure in 70 mm from
the sides of the hole and
then sink this area a further
80 mm. You should be left with an
upside-down trough shape, with a
total depth of 130 mm. Bang the
two dowels into the central base
with the mason's hammer. Mix up
the hypertufa by adding water to
the cement, sharp sand and moss.
It should resemble porridge.

Dowels
Be careful you do
not break up the
earth when you
hammer in
the dowels

Wire mesh
If necessary, trim the mesh
to fit over the two pegs

Curing
The water improves
the curing process

Tamping
Top up the
hypertufa so it
is level with the
ground and
tamp down

Holes
The drainage
holes run
right through
the base

Cleaning
Scrub off all
traces of earth
using a brush

5 Fill the excavation with hypertufa to
within 25 mm of the surface, and
tamp it level with the beam. Cut the mesh
with the clippers and fit it over the pegs.
Top up the mix to ground level and tamp
down. Smooth off with the pointing trowel.

6 Wait about five days for the
hypertufa to cure, then carefully
excavate the trough. Ease out the two pegs
and use a stiff brush and running water to
remove all traces of loose earth. Sit the
finished trough on the railway sleeper.

Inspirations: Troughs and planters

Nothing beats troughs and planters for versatility in the garden. They can be filled with eye-catching displays at any time of year, giving you the opportunity to make the most of what is in season. Many objects can be used as containers, ranging from a classic lead cistern from a grand house, to a stone drinking trough for animals, an old sink, or a modern reconstituted stone or wooden trough.

ABOVE **A** classic trough hosts a flourish of *Helichrysum petiolare*, pelargoniums and various seedlings. The trough neatly indicates that the door is not in use. The plants have all been left in their pots so that the display can be changed easily.

RIGHT **A** simple stone trough contrasts beautifully with the traditional brickwork of the walls and the bold ceramic pot alongside. The planting themes of the two containers echo each other, visually linking two rather different objects together.

FAR RIGHT **An** ancient stone trough, planted with *Aubretia deltoidea*, mounted on a stone pedestal. It is thought by the owner that both the trough and the base are ecclesiastical – perhaps a font with a piece of broken capital for the base.

Paved circle

The wonderful thing about a paved circle is that it immediately becomes a focus point in the garden. Children enjoy playing hop, skip and jump games on the pattern of stones, it is a good surface for bench seats and tables, and it makes a really great barbecue area. This design is about 2.5 m in diameter, but make it bigger if desired.

CROSS-SECTION OF HALF OF THE PAVED CIRCLE

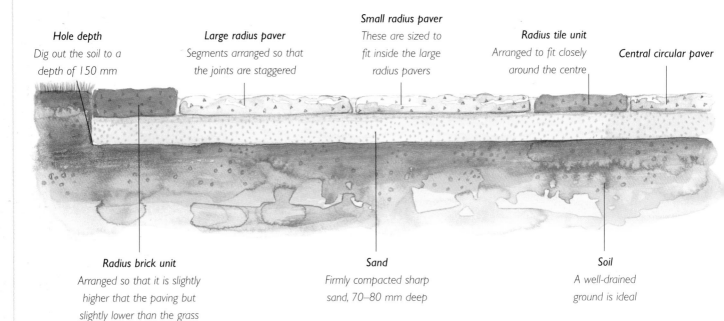

Hole depth
Dig out the soil to a depth of 150 mm

Large radius paver
Segments arranged so that the joints are staggered

Small radius paver
These are sized to fit inside the large radius pavers

Radius tile unit
Arranged to fit closely around the centre

Central circular paver

Radius brick unit
Arranged so that it is slightly higher that the paving but slightly lower than the grass

Sand
Firmly compacted sharp sand, 70–80 mm deep

Soil
A well-drained ground is ideal

YOU WILL NEED

Materials *for a circle 2.54 m in diameter*
- Central circular paver: 450 mm in diameter
- Radius tile units: 4 x 235 mm (inside radius)
- Small radius pavers: 16 x 485 mm (inside radius)
- Large radius pavers: 16 x 675 mm (inside radius)
- Radius brick units: 16 x 1.04 m (inside radius)
- Sharp sand: 50 kg
- Lime: 50 kg

Tools
- Wheelbarrow
- Tape measure
- String line
- Spade
- Fork
- Rake
- Heavy wooden mallet
- Wooden tamping beam: about 500 mm long, 60 mm wide and 50 mm thick
- Spirit level
- Bass broom

MAGIC CIRCLES

Wander around your garden to work out the best place for a circle that is about 2.5 m in diameter. It could be under a tree, which would make a nice shaded area for a bench seat and table, or in a central position to make a feature, perhaps with a sundial. Study the garden in terms of adequate drainage, shade, sun, and flow of traffic, and assess the pros and cons of the options.

When you have decided on a possible site, make sure that the area is free from underground pipes and drain covers. If you have the plans for your property, pipes may be marked; if not, dig very carefully. Use the string line to scribe a circle to size, and then stand back to see how it fits in with the garden. As a further check, to make sure that you like the position of the circle before committing to construction, set out the slabs and leave them in place for a couple of days. Note how the circle relates to the sun and shade throughout the day. When you are satisfied with the position, chop around the circle with the spade, remove the paving slabs to a safe place, and the work can begin.

Paved circle

PLAN VIEW OF HALF OF THE PAVED CIRCLE

Radius brick level
The edging is set
slightly lower than the
surrounding grass

Spacing
Slab spacing adjusted
until the joints look even

Levels
All the radius pavers, radius tile units
and the central paver are set at the
same level, but slightly lower than that
of the radius bricks

Dry-mix mortar
A dry mix of lime and
sand is brushed into
the joints

Radius tile units
235 mm (inside radius)
Segments arranged so that the
radial joints are equally spaced

Central circular paver
450 mm in diameter
Can be shaped, such as a
millstone, or made of bricks

Textured paver surface
*Textured sides set uppermost, and
similar-looking segments are not
placed next to each other*

Radius brick units
1.04 m (inside radius)
*Set so that the joints are offset equally in
relation to the paver joints*

Grass
*The higher level of the
grass allows you to
mow the lawn without
damaging the brick
edging or the
lawnmower*

Inside radius measurement
*The distance from the centre of the circle
to the inner-facing edge of a segment*

Small radius paver
485 mm (inside radius)

Large radius paver
675 mm (inside radius)

Step-by-step: **Making the paved circle**

Earth
Dig out the earth to a
depth of 150 mm

Circle centre
The intersection of the
arcs marks the centre

Stones
Remove any
rubble and
big stones

Raking
Rake the
sand level
and smooth

Compacting
Do not worry
about walking
on the sand

1 Use the spade and fork to remove all the turf and earth from the marked area down to a depth of about 150 mm, and rake the earth level. Cover the area with a layer of sand to a depth of 70–80 mm, and rake it smooth and level.

2 To find the centre of the circle, use the string line. Set it to measure the radius of the circle, then spike the line at a couple of points around the circumference and strike arcs. The intersection of the arcs is the centre of the circle.

Tamping
Hit the beam with the mallet
rather than hitting the slab

3 Put the circular slab at the centre and tamp it in place with the mallet and wooden beam. Check with the spirit level and make corrections until the slab lies absolutely level.

*Horizontal
check*
Make sure the
slab is
positioned
correctly using
the spirit level

Levelling
You might need
to pack sand
under the slab to
adjust the level

Segments
Handle fragile segments with great care

4 Working outwards from the centre, carefully position the other slabs (the circle of radius tile units, the circle of small radius pavers, and so on), all the while checking with the spirit level and correcting any dips and hollows with extra sand.

Packing
A dipped slab needs to be raised with extra sand underneath

Helpful hint

If you experience difficulties when you come to spacing the slabs, finding joints either too wide or too tight, use pieces of hardboard or plywood, 10–15 mm thick, as spacers. Insert them between the slabs to gauge the distance.

Joints
Continue brushing until the joints are filled and level

Staggered joints
Make sure that the segments are centred with adjacent joints

Bass broom
Use a stiff broom to move the mortar mix around

5 Make sure, when you come to fitting the radius brick units, that the joints are staggered with the large radius pavers.

6 Finally, shovel the dry-mix mortar (a mixture of 2 parts sand to 1 part lime) over the slabs. Use the bass broom to spread and sweep it evenly into all the joints. Spray water over the whole circle.

Multicoloured crazy paving path

This path draws its inspiration from the hard colours and cool curves of the 1950s.

It is relatively cheap to make, and will inject retro zing into any garden. You can

choose the colour selection according to your personal artistic vision.

TIME

A weekend (about eight hours to prepare the site and fit the kerbstones, and eight hours to lay the slabs).

SAFETY

Slabs sometimes spit out splinters when being broken, so wear goggles if you have to trim any.

YOU WILL NEED

Materials *for a path*
4.5 m long and 1 m wide
- Concrete "York stone" blocks: 20 blocks, 450 mm long, 150 mm wide and 65 mm thick
- Broken concrete paving slabs: about 5 square metres
- Concrete: 1 part (50 kg) cement, 2 parts (100 kg) sharp sand, 3 parts (150 kg) aggregate
- Shingle: 1 tonne medium-sized shingle (pea gravel)
- Sharp sand: 1 tonne
For the dry-mix mortar:
- Lime: 25 kg
- Cement: 25 kg
- Sand: 100 kg (taken from the tonne of sharp sand)

Tools
- Wooden pegs and string line
- Wheelbarrow
- Spade
- Bricklayer's trowel
- Mason's hammer
- Shovel
- Rake
- Spirit level
- Walking board: about 900 mm long, 300 mm wide and 30 mm thick
- Sledgehammer
- Bass broom

COOL, CRAZY COLOURS

The good thing about a crazy paving path is that it can be as wide and curvy as you like, because it doesn't have to conform to the limitations of a particular size of slab. If you have a fancy for a path that snakes around the beds and borders, crazy paving is a good option. Better still, the pieces of broken concrete slab are cheap, so you get a longer path for your money.

Consider how a path might complement the shape of your garden. Visit manufacturers and builder's merchants to look at the available slabs. Some slabs are smooth on one side and heavily textured on the other, with the colour running through the thickness, while others are smooth on both sides and have only one coloured face. When you have made your selection, play around with the broken pieces to see how they might fit together to create an overall uniformity. Plan out the route of the path and mark the edges with pegs and string. Clear the ground down to a depth of 150 mm, making it 1 m wide. Dig a trench at either side of it, 250 mm wide and with a total depth of 250 mm.

CROSS-SECTION ACROSS THE WIDTH OF THE PATH

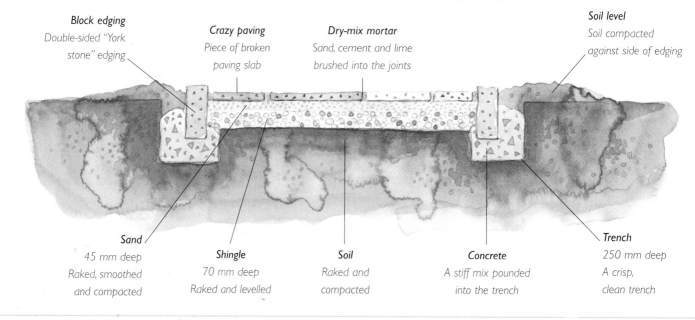

Block edging
Double-sided "York stone" edging

Crazy paving
Piece of broken paving slab

Dry-mix mortar
Sand, cement and lime brushed into the joints

Soil level
Soil compacted against side of edging

Sand
45 mm deep
Raked, smoothed and compacted

Shingle
70 mm deep
Raked and levelled

Soil
Raked and compacted

Concrete
A stiff mix pounded into the trench

Trench
250 mm deep
A crisp, clean trench

Multicoloured crazy paving path

Tight curves
*Blocks broken to
make a smooth curve*

Dry-mix mortar
*Sand, cement
and lime brushed
into the joints
and damped
down with water*

Pavers
*Different colours
distributed evenly*

Edging
*Double-sided "York stone"
blocks, 450 x 150 x 65 mm*

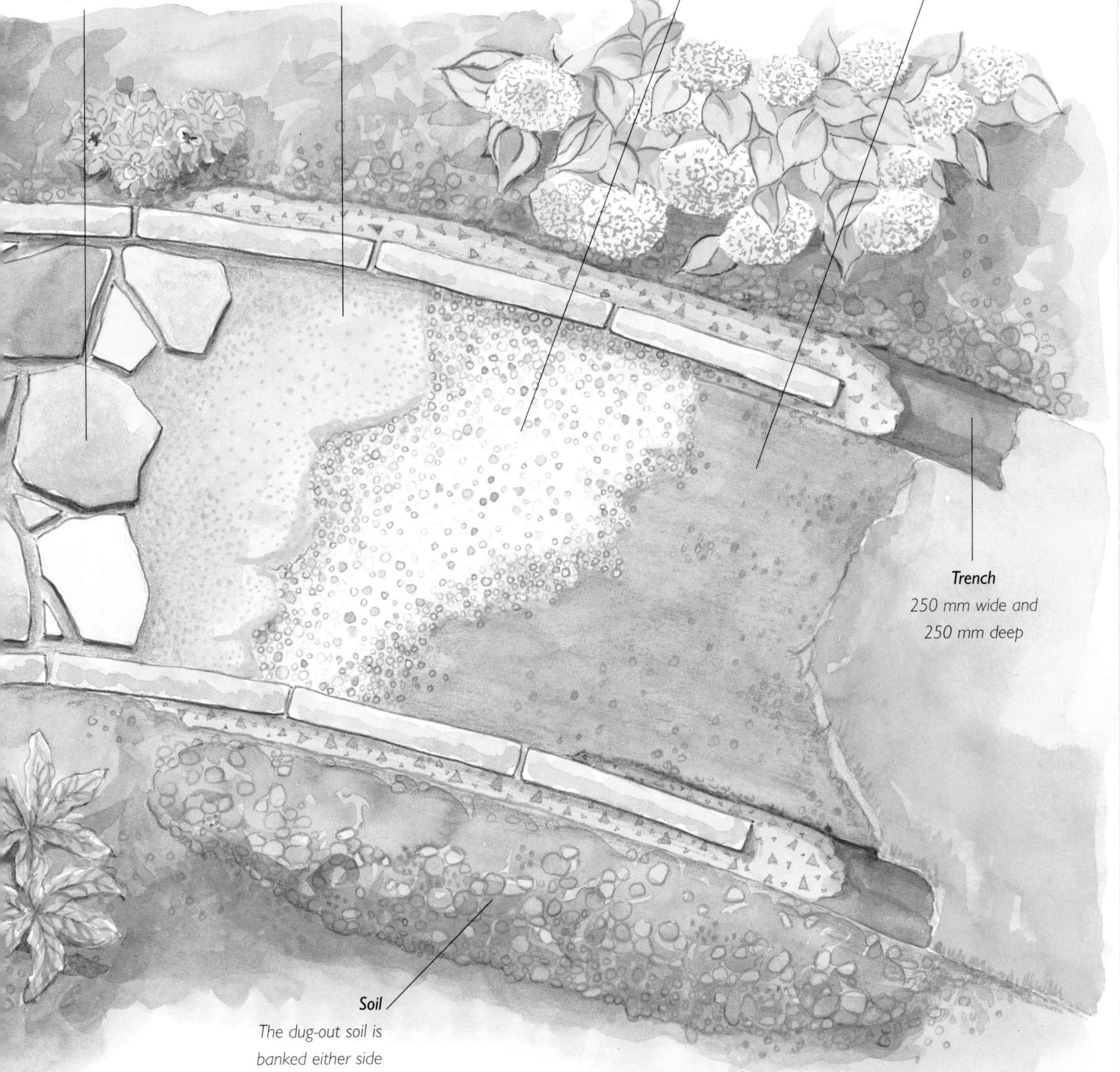

Paver

Pavers arranged so that they fit together

Sand

Clean sand 45 mm deep, raked, compacted and levelled

Shingle

70 mm deep, raked and compacted pea gravel

Soil

Subsoil left undisturbed

Trench

250 mm wide and 250 mm deep

Soil

The dug-out soil is banked either side of the path

CROSS-SECTION ACROSS THE LENGTH OF THE PATH

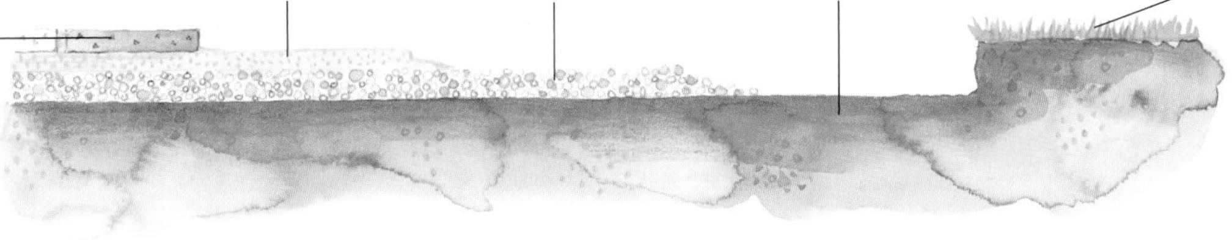

Grass

Removed grass used for composting

Compacted sand

Shingle

Compacted soil

Coloured paving slab

Carefully selected for size, shape and colour, and bedded in sand

Step-by-step: Making the multicoloured crazy paving path

Concrete
Be generous with the amount of concrete

Raking
Rake the shingle to a depth of 70 mm

Cavity
Push the shingle right into the kerb trench

Levelling
Use the trowel handle to nudge the blocks into position

Compacting
Firm up the shingle with your feet

1 Fill the two trenches with concrete, up to the base level of the path. Carefully set the concrete edging blocks in place to make the kerb. With the bricklayer's trowel and mason's hammer, adjust the blocks so that three-quarters of the block rises above the path base.

2 Shovel the shingle over the earth in the path area and rake it to a depth of 70 mm. Push it into the cavity alongside the edging blocks, and generally rake it so that it follows the level of the ground. Use the spirit level to see whether it is true, and even out by raking if necessary.

Sand level
Keep the sand 35 mm below the kerb stones

3 Cover the shingle with a layer of sand to a depth of about 45 mm. Rake it level and stamp it down so that the surface is about 35 mm lower than the top of the kerb. Check that it is level with the spirit level.

Sand depth
Aim for a depth of 45 mm

Helpful hint

It's always a good idea, when ordering sand and shingle, to specify "well washed". This will minimize the chances of the sand and shingle being contaminated with clay or salt. You cannot use salty sand in concrete or mortar mixes, because it will damage it.

Spacing
Leave a gap of 25 mm
between the pavers

4 Set the pieces of broken slab into place on the sand, leaving about 25 mm between them. Try and position the pieces so that there is a good spread of the various colours.

Laying the slabs
Bed the slabs into the sand

Colours
Aim for an even spread of colours

Walking board
Stand on the board so that you do not dislodge the slabs

Levelling
Use the sledgehammer to help level and embed the slabs

5 Put the walking board on the path and use your weight and the sledgehammer to thump the slabs into place, so that they sit firmly in the sand.

Brushing
Move the dry-mix mortar around with a broom

Dry-mix mortar
Make sure the cement, sand and lime are well blended

6 Make a dry-mix mortar of 4 parts sand, 1 part cement and 1 part lime, and sweep it over the path with the bass broom, so that it falls into all the cracks. Spray with water. Leave for 24 hours.

Tranquil Japanese garden

What better way of creating an area of calm, reflection and tranquility, than to build a traditional Japanese garden? It's a beautiful, simple concept that involves gathering a number of basic elements – a traditional lantern, natural rocks and crushed stone – and then carefully arranging them to form a three-dimensional picture.

TIME

Two weekends (about eight hours to build the frame and level the site, sixteen hours to build the lantern, and eight hours to assemble the whole thing).

SAFETY

Building the lantern involves moving a number of back-breaking lumps of stone, so use a sack barrow and get someone to help you.

YOU WILL NEED

Materials *for a garden 2.4 m square*
- Wooden beams: 4 treated posts, 2.4 m long, 100 mm wide and 100 mm thick
- Pegs: 4 pieces of scrap wood, about 25 mm square and 150 mm long
- Woven plastic sheet, 2.4 m square
- Shingle: 500 kg washed shingle
- Boulders: 3 large limestone rocks
- Split sandstone: 4 or 5 large slices of stone
- Mortar: 2 parts (10 kg) cement, 1 part (5 kg) lime, 9 parts (90 kg) soft sand
- Oyster shell grit: 100 kg washed grit
- Lantern base: block of salvaged weathered cut limestone, about 380 mm square and 140 mm thick
- Lantern column: block of salvaged weathered cut limestone, 700 mm long, 300 mm wide and 130 mm thick
- Lantern table: slab of salvaged weathered cut limestone, 300 mm square and 110 mm thick
- Lantern pillars: slab of salvaged weathered cut limestone, 240 mm long, 180 mm wide and 50 mm thick
- Lantern roof: slab of salvaged weathered cut limestone, 300 mm square and 50 mm thick
- Roof finial: slab of salvaged weathered cut limestone, 150 mm square and 50 mm thick
- Finial cobble: a large feature stone, about 100 mm in diameter

Tools
- Tape measure, square and chalk
- Crosscut saw
- Mallet and 25 mm-wide woodworking chisel
- Electric drill fitted with a 25 mm-diameter woodworking drill bit
- Bucket
- Shovel
- Rake
- Fork
- Sack barrow
- Pointing trowel
- Spirit level
- Electric angle grinder with a stone-cutting disc

THE WORLD IN STONE

Think of the items in a Japanese garden as being elements that symbolize our physical and spiritual world – stones are mountains, raked grit is flowing water, large stones are guardians, stone lanterns light our path, and so on. The whole idea is to create a three-dimensional picture of the world. First you build the frame, then "paint" the scene with the stones.

The stone lantern is made from carefully selected pieces of salvaged stone. The four little pillars that support the lantern roof slab are made up of briquettes. These are cut by a simple procedure that involves using an angle grinder to score lines part-way through a limestone slab, first on one side and then on the other, before snapping the slab. The sides of the briquettes reveal a beautiful texture, the result of a machined face and a natural break. The secret of creating a really stunning lantern is to obtain stones with character – visit an architectural salvage company for the best choice, and spend time making your selection.

CROSS-SECTION OF THE JAPANESE GARDEN

Lantern approximately 1.3 m high

Oyster shell Known variously as "turkey grit" or "poultry grit"

Feature stone Chosen for its size, shape and character

Shingle Pea-size, washed and graded

Wooden frame

Plastic sheet

Tranquil Japanese garden

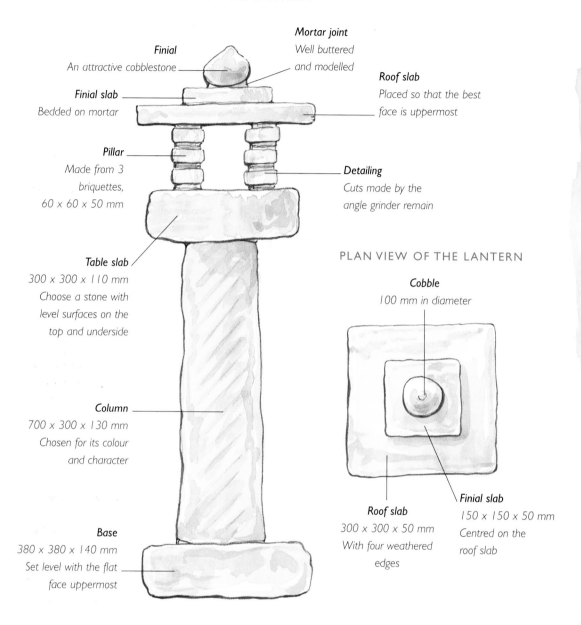

SIDE VIEW OF THE LANTERN

Finial
An attractive cobblestone

Mortar joint
Well buttered
and modelled

Roof slab
Placed so that the best
face is uppermost

Finial slab
Bedded on mortar

Pillar
Made from 3
briquettes,
60 x 60 x 50 mm

Detailing
Cuts made by the
angle grinder remain

Table slab
300 x 300 x 110 mm
Choose a stone with
level surfaces on the
top and underside

Column
700 x 300 x 130 mm
Chosen for its colour
and character

Base
380 x 380 x 140 mm
Set level with the flat
face uppermost

PLAN VIEW OF THE LANTERN

Cobble
100 mm in diameter

Finial slab
150 x 150 x 50 mm
Centred on the
roof slab

Roof slab
300 x 300 x 50 mm
With four weathered
edges

DETAIL OF THE JOINT USED TO MAKE THE WOOD FRAME

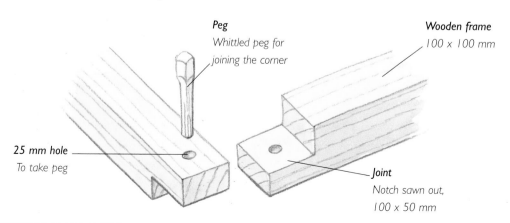

Peg
Whittled peg for
joining the corner

Wooden frame
100 x 100 mm

25 mm hole
To take peg

Joint
Notch sawn out,
100 x 50 mm

PLAN VIEW OF THE GARDEN

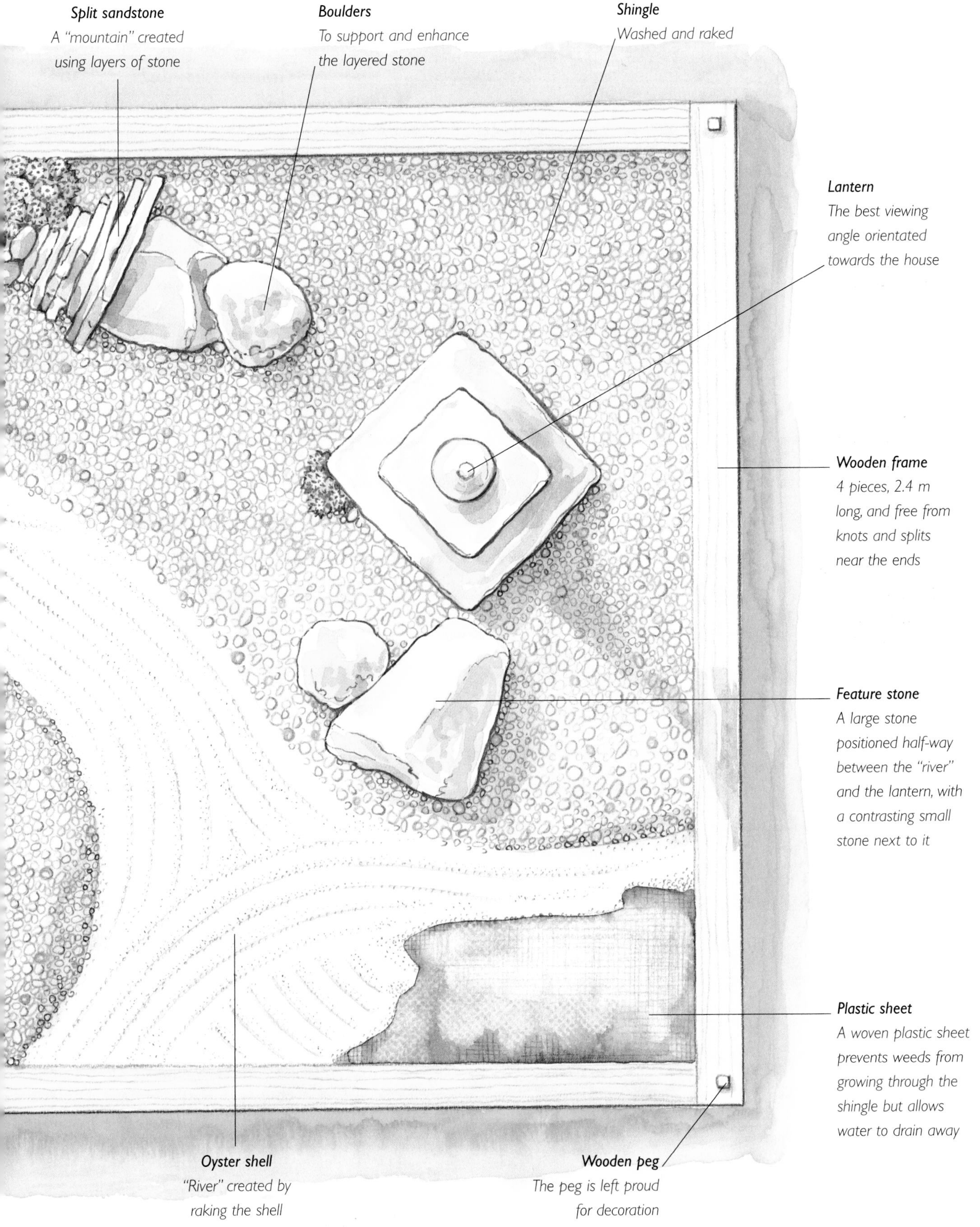

Split sandstone
A "mountain" created
using layers of stone

Boulders
To support and enhance
the layered stone

Shingle
Washed and raked

Lantern
The best viewing
angle orientated
towards the house

Wooden frame
4 pieces, 2.4 m
long, and free from
knots and splits
near the ends

Feature stone
A large stone
positioned half-way
between the "river"
and the lantern, with
a contrasting small
stone next to it

Plastic sheet
A woven plastic sheet
prevents weeds from
growing through the
shingle but allows
water to drain away

Oyster shell
"River" created by
raking the shell

Wooden peg
The peg is left proud
for decoration

Step-by-step: **Making the tranquil Japanese garden**

Shingle
*Make sure
that the
shingle has
been washed
and is free
from salt*

Shovel
*Use the shovel
to spread out
the shingle*

1 Construct the wooden frame. Draw it out using the tape measure, square and chalk. Remove the waste with the crosscut saw, mallet and chisel. Drill holes as shown in the illustration on page 208. Use the chisel to whittle the pegs out of scrap wood, and put the frame together. Position it in the garden. Cover the ground inside it with the plastic sheet, tucking the edges under the frame. Shovel the shingle over it.

Stone
*Use the stones to build a
miniature mountain*

Fork
*A fork is the best tool
for raking the shell*

River
*Leave a
channel
through the
shingle for
making the
"river" feature*

Oyster shell
*Obtained as
grit from
poultry
suppliers*

Making waves
*Drag the fork
to make a
ridge and
furrow pattern*

2 Start placing the symbolic features. Rake the shingle into mounds to make areas of "high ground", then carefully position the boulders and sandstone slabs to create "mountains" and "hills".

3 Decide which area of the garden is to be "water", then spread a thick layer of crushed oyster shell over it. Rake the shell with the prongs of the fork to create "ripples" and "waves".

Column
*Make sure the lantern
column is vertical*

Wedging
*You may need
to use small
pieces of
stone to wedge
the column*

4 Position the base block of
the lantern. Butter the base
of the column stone with mortar,
using the pointing trowel. Set the
column in place. Check that it is
vertical with the spirit level and
then leave until the mortar has
stiffened. Butter the top of the
column with mortar, and lower
the lantern table into position.

Helpful hint

The best you can do when
testing a rugged piece of
stone with a spirit level is
to aim for what was
traditionally known as "best
fit" – meaning you take
readings from all sides and
make a judgement.

Pillars
Tap the blocks straight

Finial slab
*Carefully set the finial
slab in place*

Mortar
*Butter the
blocks with
the mortar*

Mortar
*Butter the
roof slab
with mortar*

Roof slab
*Make sure the
slab is well
bedded on to
the pillars*

5 Set out the dimensions of the
briquettes with the tape measure
and chalk, and use the angle grinder to cut
them out. Butter them with mortar and
build the little pillars. Tap down with the
trowel handle to adjust the levels.

6 Spread mortar on top of the four
pillars. Place the roof slab on the
pillars, and butter it with mortar. Carefully
position the final slab. Set the feature
cobble in place, fixing it with mortar that is
modelled to fit the contours of the stone.

Dry-stone retaining wall

Crisscrossing hill and dale, dry-stone walls are the traditional way of controlling livestock and marking boundaries. The technique evolved over many thousands of years. It does not require cement or mortar – just stone upon stone to create a beautiful structure that is uniquely capable of withstanding the weather.

TIME

A weekend (two days to build a wall about 4.8 m long and 800 mm high).

SPECIAL TIPS

Since carriage costs for transporting stones are so high, it is best to be over-generous when estimating quantities. If in doubt, seek advice from your supplier.

YOU WILL NEED

Materials *for a wall 4.8 m long and 800 mm high*
- Split stone (sandstone or limestone): 1.5 tonnes
- Hardcore for the foundation (either waste stone or builder's rubble): 5 wheelbarrow loads
- Keystone: attractive heavy stone, about 300 mm long, 200 mm wide, 200 mm thick

Tools
- Wheelbarrow
- Spade and shovel
- Tape measure
- String line
- Club hammer
- Bolster chisel
- Piece of old carpet
- Bricklayer's trowel
- Spirit level
- Rake

A PERFECT PATTERN OF STONE

This wall stands about 800 mm high for three-quarters of its length, then runs in a gentle curve down to meet the ground. Study your site and work out the total length of the wall that you intend to build. Reckon on ordering about 1 tonne of stone for every 3-metre length of wall (you will also need about 3 wheelbarrow loads of hardcore). It's a good idea to add on about ten per cent extra for good measure. When you visit the stoneyard, select split stone about 30–100 mm thick, with a flat top and bottom, and a reasonably straight face edge. Choose a firm stone, rather than a stone that crumbles and flakes to the touch. Select rougher, character stones for the coping, such as pieces of weathered stone (maybe even large lumps, rather than slices). Don't forget that you will need hardcore for the foundation trench – this project uses waste stone, but you could also use broken brick, a mixture of gravel and clay, pulverized concrete or whatever else is available.

CROSS-SECTION DETAIL OF THE DRY-STONE WALL

Coping
A line of stones, on edge, to finish the wall

Stone
Split sandstone, limestone or broken pavers

Plants
Plants to reinforce the coping

Earth
The earth is retained by the wall

Tie stones
The occasional use of long stones provides extra stability, tying the wall to the earth

Stone chips
Small pieces of stone used to maintain level

Earth
Firmed up against the base of the wall

Foundation
Compacted rubble

Dry-stone retaining wall

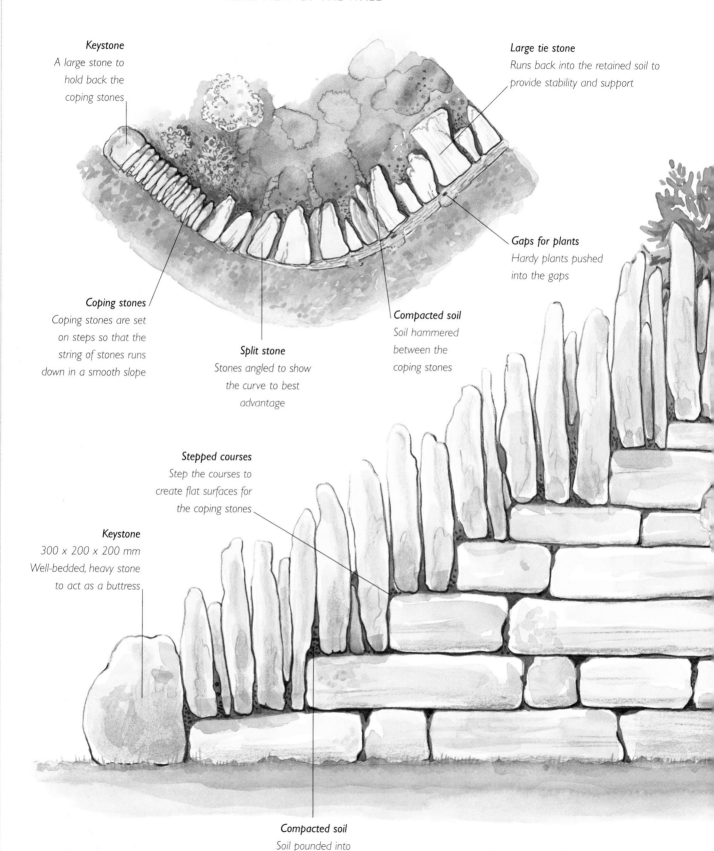

PLAN VIEW OF THE WALL

Keystone
*A large stone to
hold back the
coping stones*

Large tie stone
*Runs back into the retained soil to
provide stability and support*

Gaps for plants
*Hardy plants pushed
into the gaps*

Coping stones
*Coping stones are set
on steps so that the
string of stones runs
down in a smooth slope*

Split stone
*Stones angled to show
the curve to best
advantage*

Compacted soil
*Soil hammered
between the
coping stones*

Stepped courses
*Step the courses to
create flat surfaces for
the coping stones*

Keystone
*300 x 200 x 200 mm
Well-bedded, heavy stone
to act as a buttress*

Compacted soil
*Soil pounded into
the cavities*

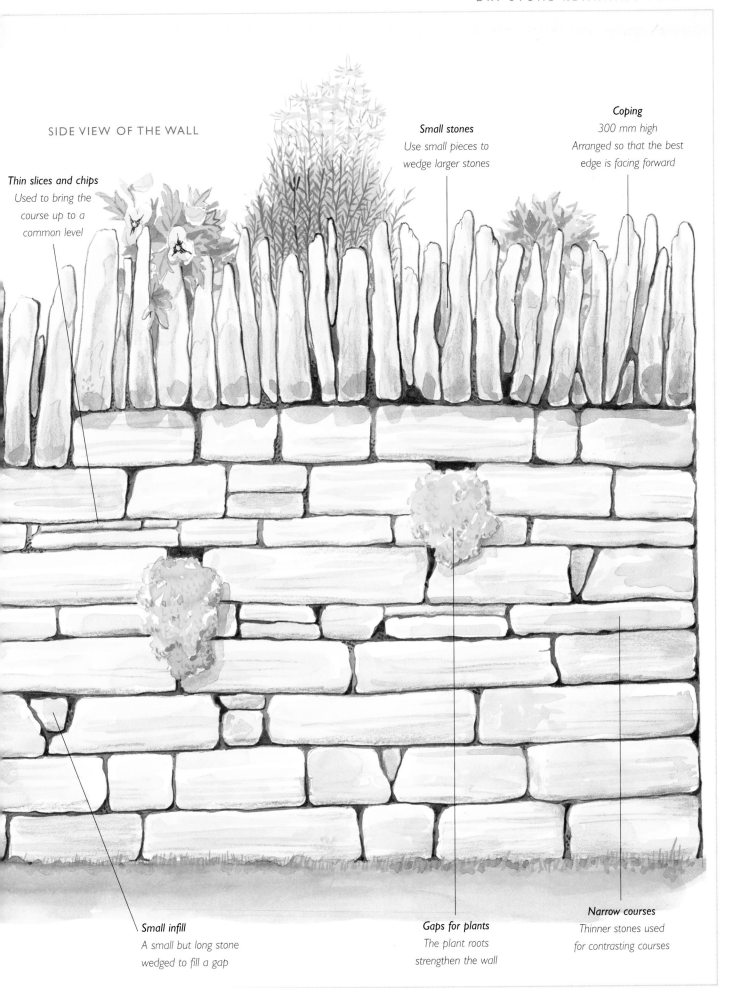

SIDE VIEW OF THE WALL

Small stones
Use small pieces to
wedge larger stones

Coping
300 mm high
Arranged so that the best
edge is facing forward

Thin slices and chips
Used to bring the
course up to a
common level

Small infill
A small but long stone
wedged to fill a gap

Gaps for plants
The plant roots
strengthen the wall

Narrow courses
Thinner stones used
for contrasting courses

Step-by-step: **Making the dry-stone retaining wall**

Earth bank
Slope the bank so it does
not fall into the trench

Club hammer
Use a medium-weight
club hammer

Hardcore
Pound the
hardcore with
the club
hammer to
make a solid
foundation.
Level it off
with earth

Protection
Wear strong
gloves to
protect your
hands

Carpet
Place carpet
underneath
the stone

1 Dig away the earth to reveal the
bank of earth that needs retaining.
Mark out a trench about 300 mm wide and
200 mm deep with the string line and tape
measure, then excavate it and fill it with
compacted hardcore. Level it with earth.

2 Use the club hammer and the
bolster chisel to cut your stock of
stone into reasonably-sized pieces. Support
the stone on the carpet, set the chisel
squarely on top, and then strike the chisel
with a single, well-placed blow.

Tamping
Use the wooden handle
to align the stones

3 Lay the first row of stones
on the levelled foundation,
and use the bricklayer's trowel to
rake earth down from the bank
to support the row. Lay another
row, rake down some more
earth, and so on. Use the club
hammer to compact the
supporting earth and to tamp
individual stones into place. Leave
hand-sized spaces now and again
to form planting pockets.

Bank of earth
Rake the
earth down to
the level of
each stone

Coursing
Adjust the stones so that they are all level

4 At staggered intervals along the rows – say about every metre – carefully select long "tie" stones, and place them so that they run back into the bank. Beat the earth into place around the stones. Check that everything is level with the spirit level.

"Tie" stone
Run the stone into the bank and secure it with earth

Helpful hint

Select the long "tie" stones with care. Go for stones that are slightly broader and thicker at the back end – so that most of the weight is anchored into the bank. This helps to give the wall greater stability.

Wedging
Use small stones to wedge the coping stones

Slivers
Insert slivers of stone to adjust the coursing level

Coping stones
Select character stones for the coping course

Cavities
Gaps between the stones can be filled with turf

Sighting
Look down the wall to spot stones that require tapping into line

5 When you have a good wall, wet the surrounding earth and rake it over the top course. Press a row of vertical coping stones into the mud to top off the wall. Rake earth up and between the coping stones, and pound into place.

6 Sight down the finished wall, bang earth into cavities, and tap misfit stones back into line. Adjust individual stones by banging small slivers of waste stone into the cavities.

Inspirations: Dry stone

While wood and wire fences can be intimidating and visually intrusive, and hedges need a lot of upkeep, dry-stone walls melt into the landscape and require the minimum of maintenance. A well-built dry-stone wall can, at one and the same time, protect, exclude, retain, suggest stability, or simply guide the eye from one part of the garden to another. A dry-stone wall or sculpture speaks of permanence.

ABOVE Slate setts used in a new path. The technique of setting slate on edge is common in Cornwall, England, and seen in cottages, quays and churches.

ABOVE A traditional old dry-stone wall in North Devon, England, made from local fieldstone. Ivy-leaved toadflax has colonized the nooks and crannies. The wall is superbly crafted, and the colour and texture of the stone harmonize perfectly with the location.

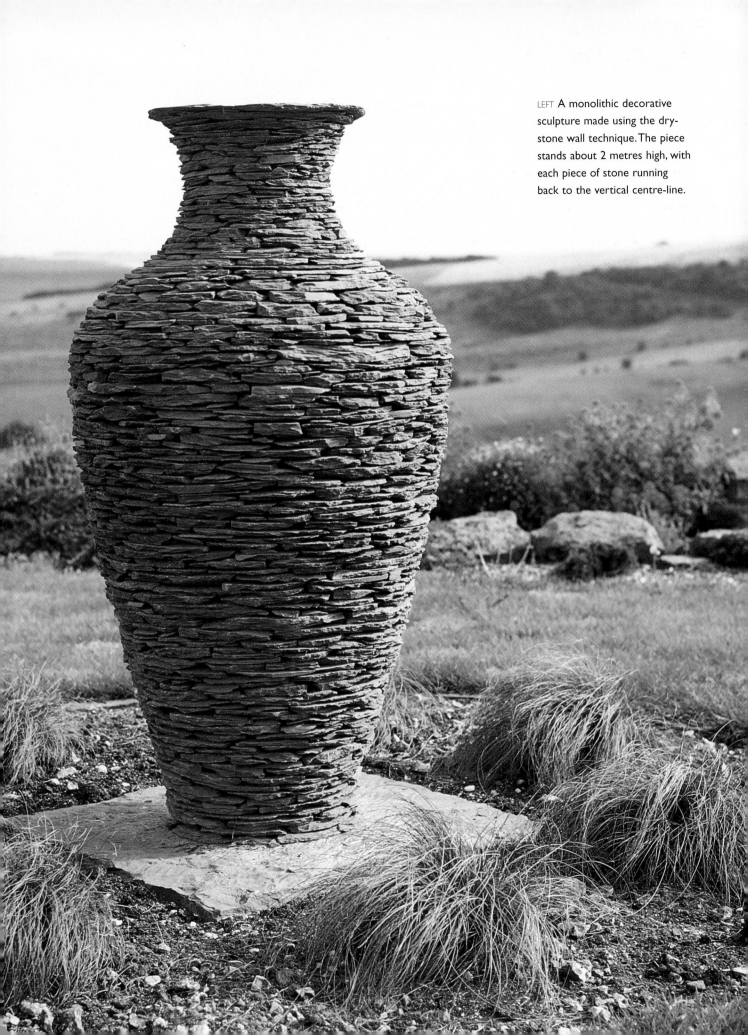

LEFT A monolithic decorative sculpture made using the dry-stone wall technique. The piece stands about 2 metres high, with each piece of stone running back to the vertical centre-line.

Cantilevered seat-shelf

If you would like to build something that uses a massive stone slab and not much

else, and you have a good solid wall in your garden, then a cantilevered seat-shelf is

a really great idea. The seat looks like it is floating on air!

TIME

A weekend to build (eight hours for fixing the iron support bars, and eight hours for shaping the copper sleeves and placing the stone).

SAFETY

Working with the resin capsules is potentially dangerous, so follow the manufacturer's directions very carefully.

YOU WILL NEED

Materials *for a seat-shelf 1.3 m (or up to 2 m) long and 400 mm wide*

- Sill stone: a single salvaged sill stone, 1.3 m to 2 m long, 400 mm wide and 50 mm thick
- Iron reinforcing bar: 2 m long and 20 mm in diameter
- Anchor resin capsules: 3 epoxy acrylate resin capsules, 20 mm in diameter, suitable for fixing metal to stone
- Copper pipe (as used by plumbers): 3 x 550 mm long, 25 mm in diameter

Tools

- Tape measure and piece of chalk
- Large-size angle grinder with cutting discs for metal and stone
- Electric jack-hammer drill fitted with a 25 mm masonry bit (long enough to drill a hole 200 mm deep)
- Mason's hammer
- Spirit level
- A short length of railway sleeper
- Claw hammer

PLAN VIEW OF THE SEAT-SHELF

Wall

Sill stone
Selected for its colour and texture

Anchor resin
A resin capsule is used to fix the bar

Copper pipe
Rolled ends for decorative effect

Iron reinforcing bar
Set 350 mm from the ground

Wall foundation

Hardcore

Brick patio

FLOATING ON AIR

Though this might appear to be a very simple project – no more than a stone slab suspended on cantilevered bars – a lot of work goes into its creation. But if the idea of working with a giant-size drill and a massive angle grinder appeals to you, you will find it fun. The seat-shelf must be sited against a wall at least 250 mm thick, made from solid brick, concrete block, or stone (either the wall of your house, or, better still, a freestanding wall in the garden). The iron reinforcing rods are glued into place by means of anchor resin capsules (sealed glass tubes filled with epoxy resin, a hardener, and granules of stone). The glass tube is eased down the drilled hole, and the iron bar is hammered and twisted into place – the glass breaks, the chemicals mix and cure, and the bar is glued into place. The finished seat-shelf will hold three people, or their equivalent weight in plant pots!

Cantilevered seat-shelf

FRONT VIEW AND PLAN VIEW OF SEAT SHELF

Fixing
*The weight of the sill
stone holds it in place*

Sill stone
*1.3 to 2 m x 400 x
50 mm
Arranged so that the
weathered (textured)
edge faces forwards*

Copper pipe
*Rolled end projects
from under the sill*

Sill stone
*The textured side
faces upwards*

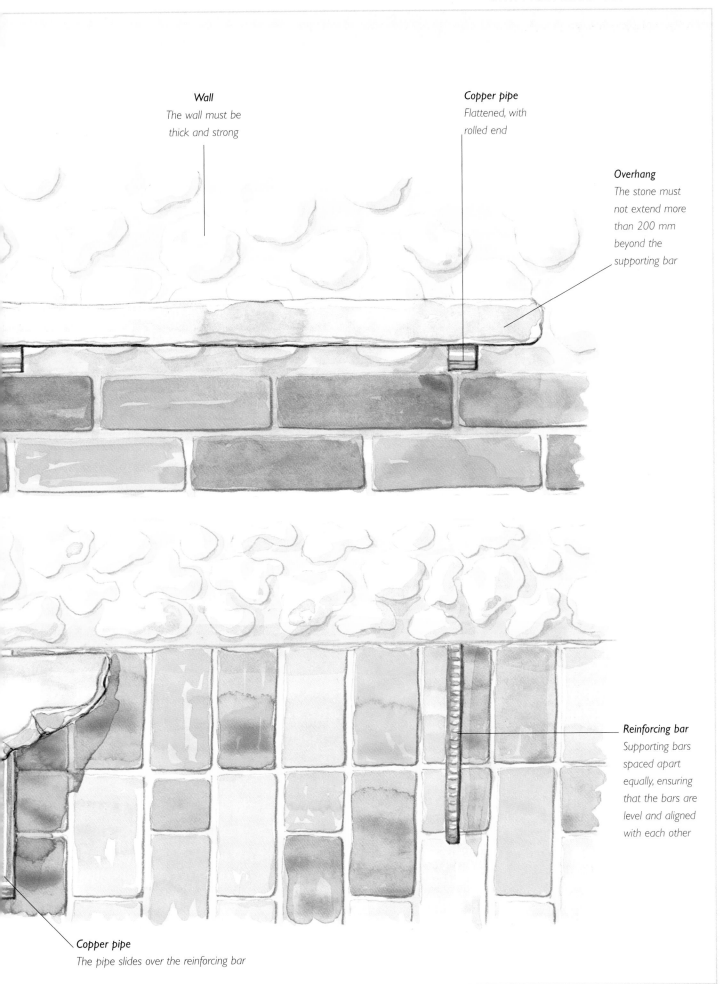

Wall
The wall must be thick and strong

Copper pipe
Flattened, with rolled end

Overhang
The stone must not extend more than 200 mm beyond the supporting bar

Reinforcing bar
Supporting bars spaced apart equally, ensuring that the bars are level and aligned with each other

Copper pipe
The pipe slides over the reinforcing bar

Step-by-step: **Making the cantilevered seat-shelf**

Grinder shield
Always have the shield in place

Protection
Wear gloves, goggles and a dust-mask

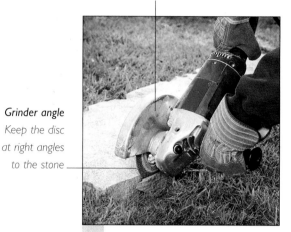

Grinder angle
Keep the disc at right angles to the stone

Metal cutting
Use a disc designed for cutting metal

Iron bar
Stand on the bar so that it stays still

1 Mark out the sill stone to size. Fit the angle grinder with the stone-cutting disc and trim the back edge of the stone slab to a square finish, so that it measures precisely 400 mm wide. Leave the weathered front and side edges intact.

2 Change the disc to the one for cutting metal and cut the iron bar into four lengths – three at 550 mm and one at 350 mm. Make sure your feet are well away from the line of cut.

Hole position
Avoid drilling very hard stones such as granite

3 With the drill, run three holes, 200 mm deep, into the wall. These should be level, 350 mm up from the ground and about 500 mm apart.

Level
All three holes must be level with each other

Drill
Large, powerful drills can be hired from a specialist shop

Loading the hole
Clear out any dust and push the
capsule to the end of the hole

Resin capsules
Handle the
capsules with
great care

4 Slide an anchor capsule into a hole, follow it up with one of the long iron bars, and then hammer the bar with the mason's hammer to break the glass of the capsule. Make sure that the bar is in the correct position and square to the wall, using the spirit level, then leave it until the resin has set.

Helpful hint

Even though you are wearing goggles, make sure, when you come to breaking the glass capsule, that you stand well to one side – so that you are out of the firing line if the resin squirts out of the hole.

Copper pipe
Bang the flattened pipe
end around the iron bar

Railway sleeper
Use the
sleeper to hold
the iron bar

5 Drill a 25 mm hole into the railway sleeper and bang the short length of iron bar into place. One piece at a time, take a length of copper pipe, flatten 150 mm at the end with the claw hammer, and bend the flat section around the iron bar.

Level
Make sure the three bars
are level with each other

Bar
The bar must
be set at
right angles to
the wall

Copper
The cut end of
the pipe should
touch the wall

6 Finally, slide the copper sleeves over the iron bars, check with the spirit level to ensure all is level, and lift the slab into position. Its weight holds it in place.

Sundial

The classic garden sundial must surely be one of the most useful and interesting items to have in the garden. What better way of passing a hot and lazy summer's day than to lounge in the garden and watch as the sundial's shadowy finger slowly but surely marks off the hours? This design fits on an existing patio or other surface.

TIME

A weekend (eight hours to build the base and the column, and eight hours to complete the structure and fit the dial).

SAFETY

Breaking slate is a splintery business, so wear protective goggles.

YOU WILL NEED

Materials *for a sundial 640 mm high and 400 mm square*
- Mortar: 2 parts (20 kg) cement, 1 part (10 kg) lime, 9 parts (90 kg) soft sand
- Flagstone for the base: a salvaged stone about 400 mm square and 80 mm thick
- Flagstone for the table: a salvaged stone about 300 mm square and 60 mm thick
- Split slate: 50 kg of broken pieces
- Split sandstone: 50 kg of broken pieces
- A brass sundial of your choice
- Screws and plugs to fit the holes in the brass plate

Tools
- Wheelbarrow
- Bucket
- Tape measure and piece of chalk
- Pointing trowel
- Spirit level
- Mason's hammer
- Drill fitted with a masonry bit (size to match holes in sundial plate)
- Screwdriver to fit the screws

A SUNNY WAY TO PASS THE TIME

When deciding where to put the sundial, you not only have to consider how the structure relates to the design of the garden, but the position must also be one that gets sufficient sunshine in order for the sundial to work. If your garden is mostly surrounded by tall trees, settle for a position that gets the best of the sunshine when you are most likely to be resting in the garden – maybe after lunch, or late in the afternoon.

The structure is made up of four elements – a flagstone slab for the base, a plinth built up from pieces of sandstone, a cylindrical column constructed from pieces of slate, and another flagstone slab for the table. Mortar holds the whole thing together. In order to successfully align the square brass dial with the square slabs that go to make the base and the table, it is necessary, right from start, to orientate the brass slab towards the sun, so that the dial is showing the correct time. Building can then proceed.

CROSS-SECTION OF THE SUNDIAL

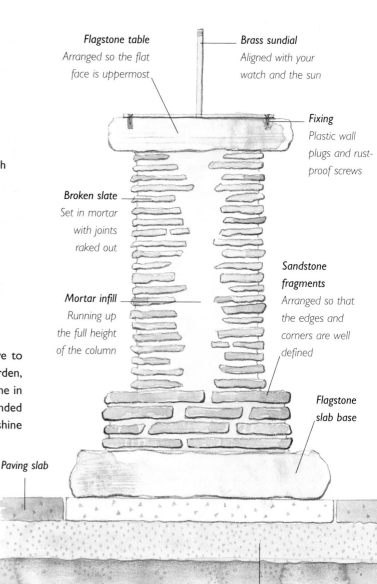

Flagstone table
Arranged so the flat face is uppermost

Brass sundial
Aligned with your watch and the sun

Fixing
Plastic wall plugs and rust-proof screws

Broken slate
Set in mortar with joints raked out

Sandstone fragments
Arranged so that the edges and corners are well defined

Mortar infill
Running up the full height of the column

Flagstone slab base

Paving slab

Soil
Compacted

Sand
Raked level

Sundial

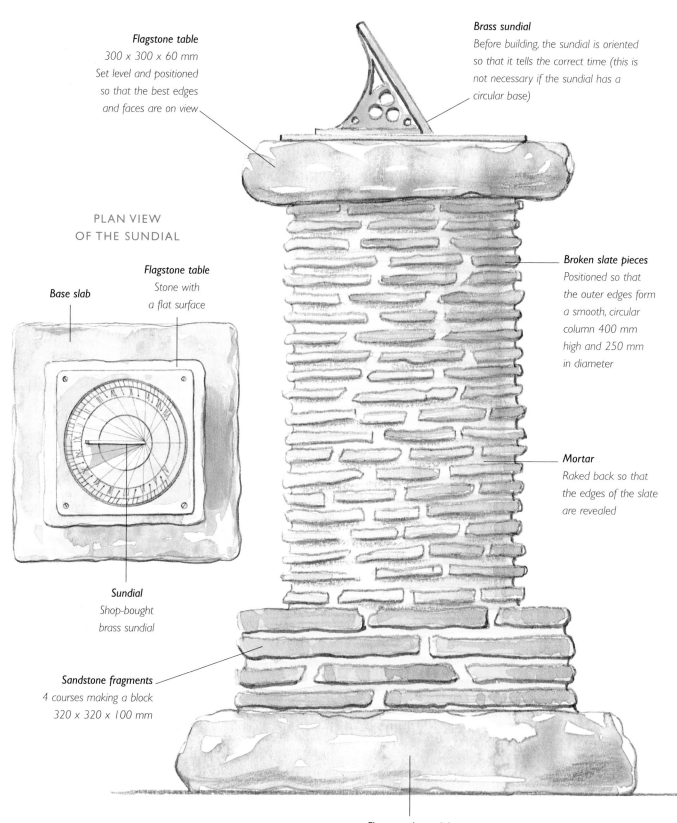

SIDE VIEW OF THE SUNDIAL

Flagstone table
300 x 300 x 60 mm
Set level and positioned
so that the best edges
and faces are on view

Brass sundial
Before building, the sundial is oriented
so that it tells the correct time (this is
not necessary if the sundial has a
circular base)

PLAN VIEW
OF THE SUNDIAL

Flagstone table
Stone with
a flat surface

Base slab

Broken slate pieces
Positioned so that
the outer edges form
a smooth, circular
column 400 mm
high and 250 mm
in diameter

Mortar
Raked back so that
the edges of the slate
are revealed

Sundial
Shop-bought
brass sundial

Sandstone fragments
4 courses making a block
320 x 320 x 100 mm

Flagstone base slab
400 x 400 x 80 mm

EXPLODED VIEW OF THE SUNDIAL

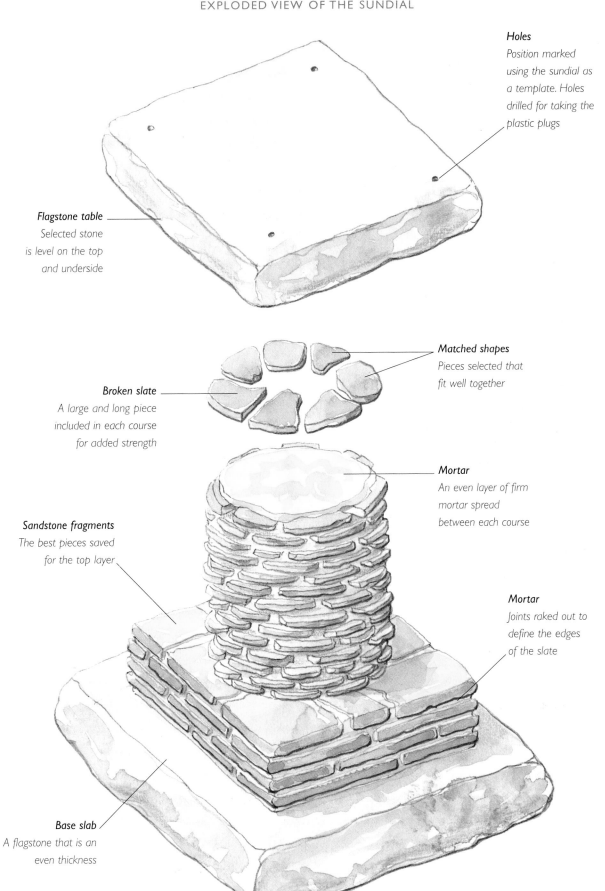

Holes
*Position marked
using the sundial as
a template. Holes
drilled for taking the
plastic plugs*

Flagstone table
*Selected stone
is level on the top
and underside*

Matched shapes
*Pieces selected that
fit well together*

Broken slate
*A large and long piece
included in each course
for added strength*

Mortar
*An even layer of firm
mortar spread
between each course*

Sandstone fragments
*The best pieces saved
for the top layer*

Mortar
*Joints raked out to
define the edges
of the slate*

Base slab
*A flagstone that is an
even thickness*

Step-by-step: **Making the sundial**

Alignment
Rotate the base to match the orientation of the sundial

Levelling
Use slivers of stone to adjust the level if necessary

Bedding
Bed the slab into the mortar

I Put the brass sundial plate on the ground, check the orientation against the sun and your watch, then set the stone base slab on mortar, aligning it with the brass plate.

Trowel work
Tap the stone with the trowel handle until it sits correctly

Plinth
Build the layers up to a height of 100 mm

2 To build the plinth, use the pointing trowel to butter the base with mortar, and arrange the sandstone to make a 320 mm square. Continue until the plinth is about 100 mm high.

Mortar
Lay a bed of mortar

Slate circle
Arrange the slate to make a circle 250 mm in diameter

Bedding
Press the slate into the bed of mortar

3 To build the column, butter mortar on the plinth, and arrange the slate to make a circle 250 mm in diameter. Butter the circle with mortar, add another layer of slate, and so on. Check each layer with the tape measure and spirit level.

Circle circumference
Always aim for a good fit
around the outside edge

Adjusting
Use the mason's
hammer to tap
proud stones
back into line

4 Continue laying circles of slate until the column is about 400 mm high. If the structure looks as though it is going to sag, tap stones into place with the mason's hammer, and stop to allow the mortar to stiffen up before continuing.

Helpful hint

If the day is hot and dry, dip the slate in water prior to bedding it in mortar. This reduces the absorbency of the stone and prevents it drawing all the water out of the mortar. Dip a stone in water, give it a shake and then press it in the mortar.

Screwing
Work carefully to avoid slipping
and damaging the brass

Alignment
Double-check the
orientation of the sundial

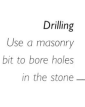

Drilling
Use a masonry
bit to bore holes
in the stone

Bedding
Lower the slab
on to the bed
of mortar

Damping
Wet the
underside of
the stone to
reduce its
absorbency

5 Lay the brass plate on the table slab, and then carefully drill holes, and plug and screw the plate in position. Be very careful that you don't over-tighten the screws and split the stone.

6 Finally, butter the top of the column with mortar and stand the slab and sundial in place. Check the alignment against the sun and your watch.

Flagstone potting table

If you enjoy potting up plants, but are fed up with working on that wobbly bench in the greenhouse, or you simply want to build a beautiful potting table in the nineteenth-century English tradition, this project will prove very satisfactory. The table is perfect for displaying plants when not in use for potting.

TIME

Three days (eight hours to lay the foundation slab, fourteen hours to build the two base piers, and a couple of hours to fit the flagstone).

SAFETY

The flagstone slab is extremely heavy – it needs two strong people to lift it into position.

YOU WILL NEED

Materials *for a table 1 m long, 580 mm wide and 800 mm high*
- Mortar: 2 parts (30 kg) cement, 1 part (15 kg) lime, 9 parts (135 kg) soft sand
- Concrete: 1 part (50 kg) cement, 2 parts (100 kg) sharp sand, 3 parts (150 kg) aggregate
- Slate or limestone flagstone: 1 flagstone about 1 m long, 580 mm wide and 80–90 mm thick
- Split limestone: 1 square metre salvaged roof stone, about 15 mm thick

- Architectural limestone: 8 salvaged cut and faced stones about 250 mm long, 170 mm wide and 130 mm thick

Tools
- Tape measure, straight-edge, piece of chalk
- Spade and shovel
- Wheelbarrow and bucket
- Wooden beam: about 600 mm long, 80 mm wide, and 50 mm thick
- Mortar float
- Bricklayer's trowel
- Mason's hammer
- Pointing trowel
- Spirit level
- Club hammer

CROSS-SECTION OF THE POTTING TABLE

Flagstone table
At least 80 mm thick and set with the weathered surface facing uppermost

Split limestone
Salvaged stone known commonly as "roof stone" or "slate stone"

Cut limestone
Arranged so that the freshly cut face is out of sight

Mortar
Raked back to reveal the edge of the stone

Cast concrete foundation

Hardcore
Compacted waste stone

A TABLE FOR ALL SEASONS

This table needs to be built against a strong brick or stone wall in the garden. It could also be sited against a shed. Ideally, you need an area that is tucked away and oriented so that the wall shields you from the wind, while the sun warms your back.

The decorative effect of the piers is achieved by building alternate courses of cut architectural limestone and layered roof stone. The mortar has been raked out in order to create strong shadow lines that draw the eye to the stone. When you are searching out your materials, opt for salvaged stone – choose large blocks showing a dressed face to all sides, and roof stone with cut edges. Spend time in the stoneyard stacking and arranging the various materials on offer, until you come up with a suitable combination. While all the given measurements are more or less flexible, if you want to vary them, the only proviso is that the pier walls need to be at least 170 mm thick. If, at any point during construction, the walls begin to sag or the mortar oozes from the joints, stop work until the mortar has stiffened up.

Flagstone potting table

FRONT VIEW OF THE POTTING TABLE

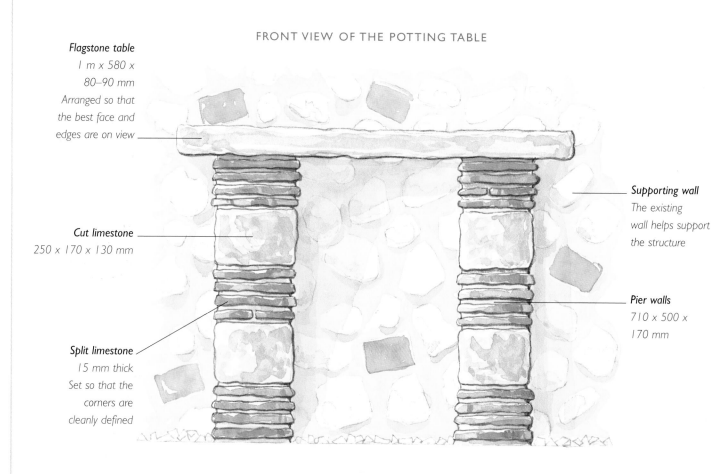

Flagstone table
*1 m x 580 x
80–90 mm
Arranged so that
the best face and
edges are on view*

Cut limestone
250 x 170 x 130 mm

Split limestone
*15 mm thick
Set so that the
corners are
cleanly defined*

Supporting wall
*The existing
wall helps support
the structure*

Pier walls
*710 x 500 x
170 mm*

PLAN VIEW OF THE POTTING TABLE

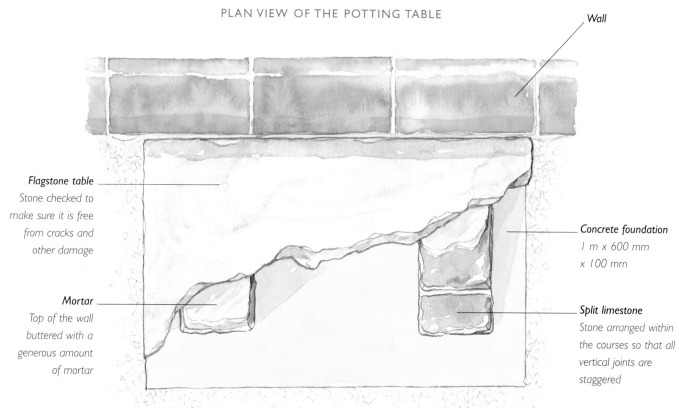

Wall

Flagstone table
*Stone checked to
make sure it is free
from cracks and
other damage*

Mortar
*Top of the wall
buttered with a
generous amount
of mortar*

Concrete foundation
*1 m x 600 mm
x 100 mm*

Split limestone
*Stone arranged within
the courses so that all
vertical joints are
staggered*

CUT-AWAY VIEW OF THE POTTING TABLE

Flagstone table
Slab tilted slightly downwards at the front, so that rain runs off

Smooth surface
Stone chosen that presents a smoothly textured "weathered" surface and good front and side edges

Mortar
Thickness of the mortar adjusted in order to tilt the table

Cut limestone
Arranged so that the best corners are seen from the front

Split limestone
Four courses of stone to equal the height of the cut limestone

Stone chippings
Whole area covered with stone chippings

Concrete foundation
A cast concrete slab positioned slightly below ground level

Hardcore
Clean, well-compacted waste stone

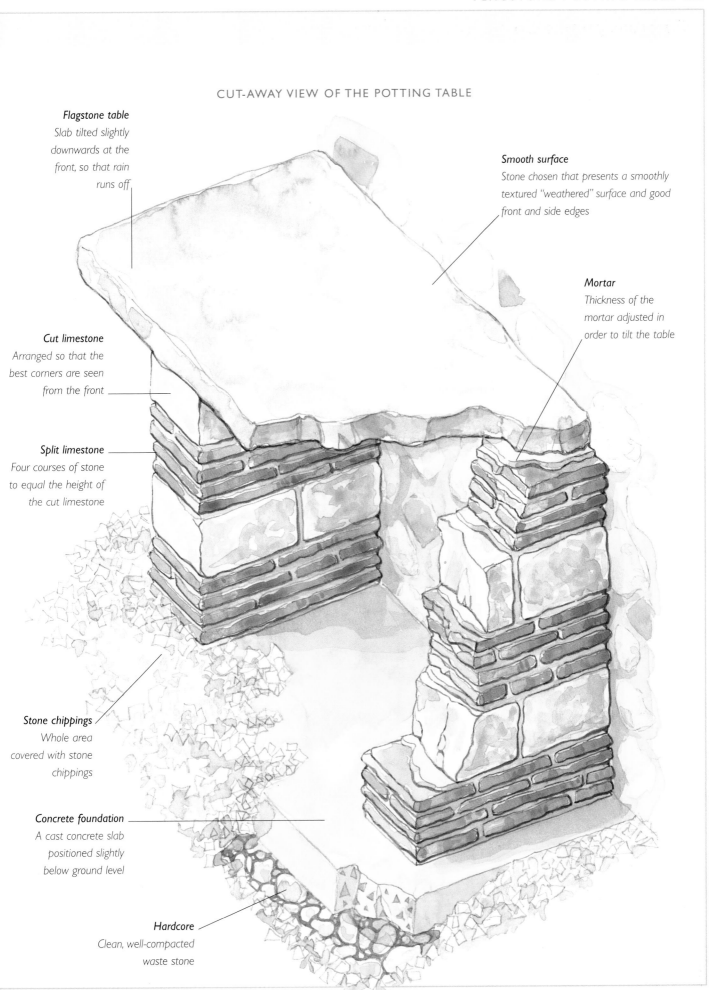

Step-by-step: **Making the flagstone potting table**

Concrete foundation
Aim for a thickness
of 100 mm

Piers
Each pier measures 170 mm
thick and 500 mm wide

Float
Use the float
to bring the
concrete to a
smooth finish

Guidelines
Use chalk to
mark the
positions of
the piers

Spacing
Set the piers
400 mm apart
at the centres

1 Use the spade to clear the foundation area. Make it 1 m wide, 600 mm from front to back, and 200 mm deep. Half-fill it with hardcore, then top it off with a layer of concrete 100 mm thick. Use the wooden beam and mortar float to bring it to a smooth, level finish.

2 Use the tape measure, chalk and straight-edge to draw out the two piers. They should be 215 mm in from each side of the foundation, and 230 mm apart. They measure 170 mm thick, and 500 mm deep from front to back.

Wall
The piers must be built
against a wall

Tapping
Tap the
limestone with
the handle of
the trowel to
bed it in the
mortar

3 Butter mortar on the base slab (within the pier markings) with the bricklayer's trowel, and arrange the first course of split limestone. (Trim it to size with the mason's hammer.) Butter the limestone with mortar, and add another layer. Make sure the corners are as crisp as possible. Insert courses of architectural limestone where appropriate, placing the blocks lengthways to run from front to back of the pier. Continue until the courses reach a total height of 710 mm.

Pier height
The piers are
710 mm high

*Height
adjustment*
The thin layers
of stone allow
for small
adjustments
in height

*Architectural
limestone*

4 Use the pointing trowel
to rake out some of the
mortar from between the various
courses. Do it after about every
three to four courses.

Pointing
Use the point
of the trowel to
clean out the
courses

Helpful hint

When working on a small
project like this, use the
large bricklayer's trowel to
carry and catch the mortar,
and the smaller pointing
trowel to do the pointing.

Checking levels
Use the club
hammer to tap
the slab into
the mortar

5 When you have built both
piers, wait until the mortar
has begun to set. Then butter the
top of the piers with mortar and
bed the table slab in place. Check
that it is horizontal with the spirit
level. If it is not, tap the offending
side of the slab with the hammer.

Finishing
Cover the foundation
slab with your
chosen material

Camomile bench

This simple idea is beautifully effective. The stone bench – a bit like a sofa – has the seat planted out with a mixture of grass and camomile. When you sit down on the camomile, its fragrant scent wafts over you. Buy the non-flowering variety of camomile, *Chamaemelum* 'Treneague', which is used to create camomile lawns.

TIME
Two weekends (eight hours to lay the foundation slab, sixteen hours to build the form, and eight hours for planting the camomile and generally tidying up).

SAFETY
The blocks are heavy, so wear gloves and lift them one at a time.

CROSS-SECTION OF THE BENCH

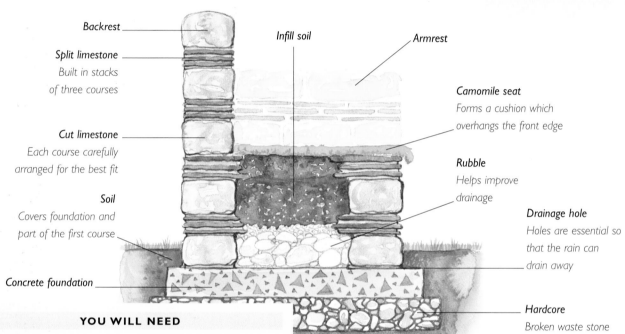

Backrest

Split limestone
*Built in stacks
of three courses*

Cut limestone
*Each course carefully
arranged for the best fit*

Soil
*Covers foundation and
part of the first course*

Concrete foundation

Infill soil

Armrest

Camomile seat
*Forms a cushion which
overhangs the front edge*

Rubble
*Helps improve
drainage*

Drainage hole
*Holes are essential so
that the rain can
drain away*

Hardcore
Broken waste stone

YOU WILL NEED

Materials *for a bench
1.57 m long, 730 mm wide
and 870 mm high*
• Mortar: 2 parts (70 kg)
  cement, 1 part (35 kg)
  lime, 9 parts (315 kg)
  soft sand
• Concrete: 1 part (150 kg)
  cement, 2 parts (300 kg)
  sharp sand, 3 parts
  (450 kg) aggregate
• Split limestone: 2 square
  metres of salvaged roof
  stone, about 15 mm thick
• Architectural limestone:
  about 60 salvaged cut
  and faced stones,
  250 mm long, 150 mm
  wide, 90–100 mm thick
• Hardcore: 1 cubic metre

• Infill topsoil: about
  3 wheelbarrow loads
Tools
• Wheelbarrow and bucket
• Tape measure, straight-
  edge, piece of chalk
• Spade and shovel
• Casting beams: 2 beams
  about 1.6 m long, 80 mm
  wide and 50 mm thick
• Wooden tamping beam:
  1.2 m long, 80 mm wide
  and 50 mm thick
• Bricklayer's trowel
• Pointing trowel
• Mason's hammer
• Spirit level
• Wire brush

A COMFORTABLE FRAGRANCE

If you have ever walked barefoot over a camomile lawn and marvelled at its fragrance and the feel of the soft, lush growth, you can imagine that sitting on a cushion of camomile will also be a very pleasant experience. Everything about this project is a joy – the bench makes a very comfortable and exotic seat, the structure is large and decorative enough for even the grandest garden, and the notion of sitting on the camomile is so novel that the bench becomes a great conversation piece. The structure is made up from courses of cut architectural stone alternating with courses of stacked roof stone. The mix of stone gives an interesting finish; the courses of roof stone are also used to level out the inevitable mismatch and stepping that occurs when using salvaged architectural stone. The overall pattern of the coursing is further enhanced by the raked mortar joints.

Camomile bench

FRONT VIEW OF THE BENCH

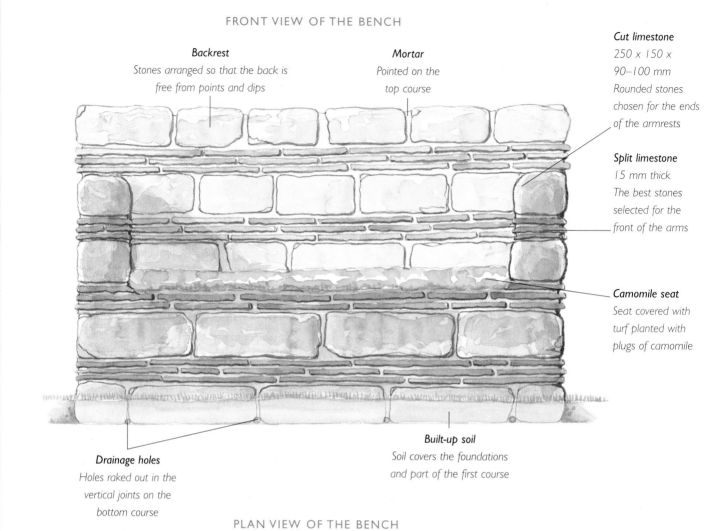

Backrest
*Stones arranged so that the back is
free from points and dips*

Mortar
*Pointed on the
top course*

Cut limestone
*250 x 150 x
90–100 mm
Rounded stones
chosen for the ends
of the armrests*

Split limestone
*15 mm thick
The best stones
selected for the
front of the arms*

Camomile seat
*Seat covered with
turf planted with
plugs of camomile*

Drainage holes
*Holes raked out in the
vertical joints on the
bottom course*

Built-up soil
*Soil covers the foundations
and part of the first course*

PLAN VIEW OF THE BENCH

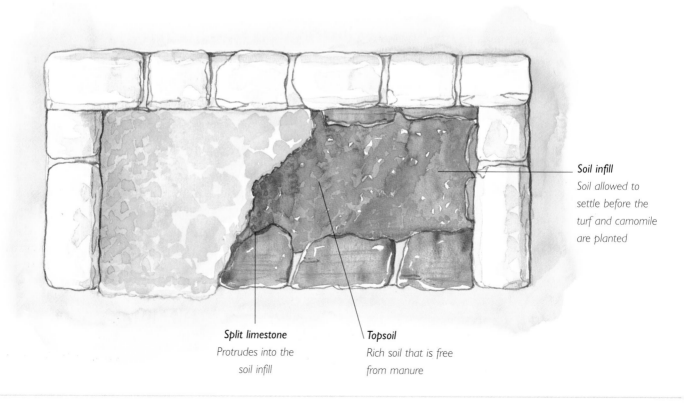

Soil infill
*Soil allowed to
settle before the
turf and camomile
are planted*

Split limestone
*Protrudes into the
soil infill*

Topsoil
*Rich soil that is free
from manure*

CUT-AWAY VIEW OF THE BENCH

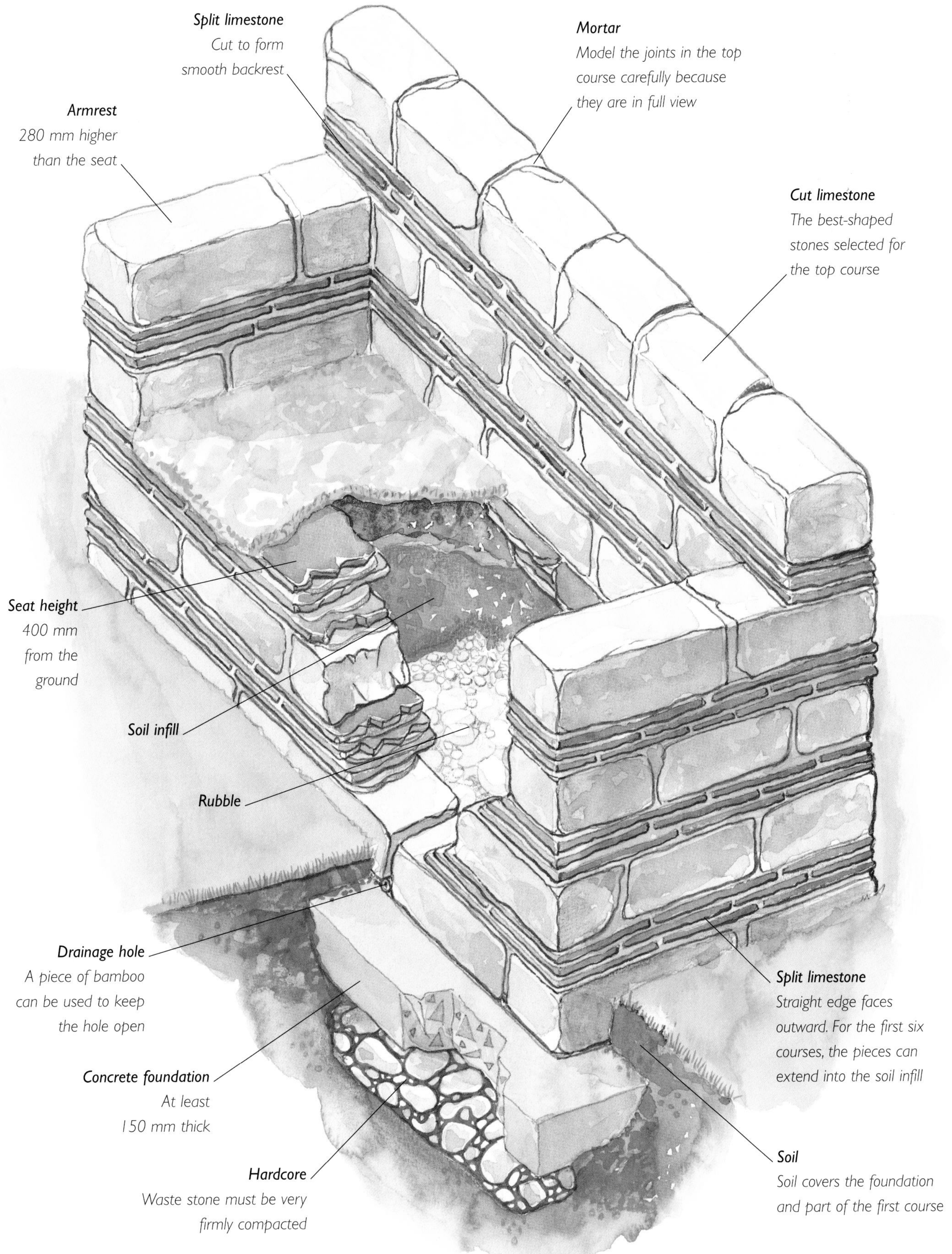

Split limestone
Cut to form
smooth backrest

Mortar
Model the joints in the top
course carefully because
they are in full view

Armrest
280 mm higher
than the seat

Cut limestone
The best-shaped
stones selected for
the top course

Seat height
400 mm
from the
ground

Soil infill

Rubble

Drainage hole
A piece of bamboo
can be used to keep
the hole open

Split limestone
Straight edge faces
outward. For the first six
courses, the pieces can
extend into the soil infill

Concrete foundation
At least
150 mm thick

Hardcore
Waste stone must be very
firmly compacted

Soil
Soil covers the foundation
and part of the first course

Step-by-step: **Making the camomile bench**

Measuring
Use the tape measure to
set out the outline

Foundation
Make the
concrete slab
150 mm thick

Trial fitting
Have a dry fitting
of the stones

Best face
Arrange the
stones so that
the best face
is on view

Best fit
Swap the
stones around
until you have
a well-fitting
arrangement

1 Excavate to a depth of 300 mm and half-fill with compacted hardcore. Position and level the casting beams, 1 m apart, and top them up with concrete. Level with the tamping beam. Use the tape measure, chalk and straight-edge to outline the bench (1.57 m x 730 mm).

2 Arrange the blocks of salvaged architectural stone so that they fit well and the best cut face is looking to the chalk line. Wet the blocks and use the bricklayer's trowel and the pointing trowel to bed them on stiff mortar.

Infill
Pack the bench with top soil

Levelling
Check each
course using a
spirit level

3 To lay the roof stone, spread a bed of mortar, and use the mason's hammer to carefully trim and arrange the pieces of stone. Repeat until you have three courses of roof stone. Lay a layer of architectural stone. Continue laying the alternating courses, and keep checking that it is all level with the spirit level.

Helpful hint

Spend a lot of time choosing the roof stone cornerstones and making sure they are a good fit, and the rest of the course will fall into line more easily.

Cornerstone
Position the architectural cornerstones accurately

Armrest
The armrest course should be tied in with the backrest

Armrest height
Build up to a height of 280 mm above the seat level

Backrest
Build the back using three courses of roof stone and one course of cut limestone

4 When you have built up to the level of the seat (about 430 mm – two courses of architectural stone and six of roof stone), fill the trough with topsoil, and place the stones for the arms of the seat.

5 Build the arms to 280 mm above the level of the seat (two courses of architectural stone and three of roof stone). Continue building the back to a total height of 870 mm above the ground.

Cleaning
Make a special job of cleaning the top of the backrest

6 Finally, when the mortar is well cured, use a wire brush to clean all faces of the structure. Be careful not to blur the crisp finish of the mortar.

Cleaning
Make sure that you clean the mortar from the faces of the cut stone

Wire brushing
Use the brush to define the courses and generally clean up the stonework

Pedestal table

One of the joys of having a garden is being able to sit outside on a summer's evening and slowly sip a long, cool drink, relaxing in a comfortable chair. The picture is completed by the unique pedestal table that holds your drink.

TIME

Two weekends (eight hours to lay the foundation slab, eighteen hours to build the column, and a couple of hours to fit the flagstone).

SAFETY

The flagstone slab is incredibly heavy – it needs at least four strong, fit people to lift it.

YOU WILL NEED

Materials

for a table 900 mm square and 910 mm high

- Mortar: 2 parts (80 kg) cement, 1 part (40 kg) lime, 9 parts (360 kg) soft sand
- Concrete: 1 part (50 kg) cement, 2 parts (100 kg) sharp sand, 3 parts (150 kg) aggregate
- Slate or limestone flagstone for the table: about 900 mm square and 130 mm thick
- Flagstones for the plinth and capital: 2 stones about 570 mm square and 90 mm thick
- Split limestone: 1 cubic metre of salvaged roof stone, about 15 mm thick
- Hardcore: 0.5 cubic metres of rubble or broken stone

Tools

- Wheelbarrow
- Sack barrow
- Bucket
- Tape measure, straight-edge, piece of chalk
- Spade and shovel
- Sledgehammer
- Sawn wood: 4 lengths, about 660 mm long, 80 mm wide and 50 mm thick
- Wooden beam: about 600 mm long, 80 mm wide and 50 mm thick
- Mortar float
- Spirit level
- String and peg
- Bricklayer's trowel
- Mason's hammer
- Pointing trowel

ALL AROUND THE TABLE

In the context of this book, this project is monolithic. There is about one cubic metre of roof stone in the column, and the slab that goes to make the tabletop is so heavy that it takes four strong people to lift it into position. So you must start by assessing how you are going to shift the stone. For example, if you want the table at the end of the garden – over a bridge, the other side of the pond, and behind the border – it presents quite a challenge. You will have to ask family and neighbours to help. We used a wheelbarrow for the roof stone, and a sack barrow for the slabs.

The procedure for building the column is to select and shape pieces of roof stone to fit the circumference of the circle, set them in mortar, fill in the circle with more pieces of slate, and then move on to the next layer of mortar. Every few courses, rake out the mortar to reveal the slate, and make checks with the spirit level to ensure that the stones remain true.

CROSS-SECTION OF THE TABLE

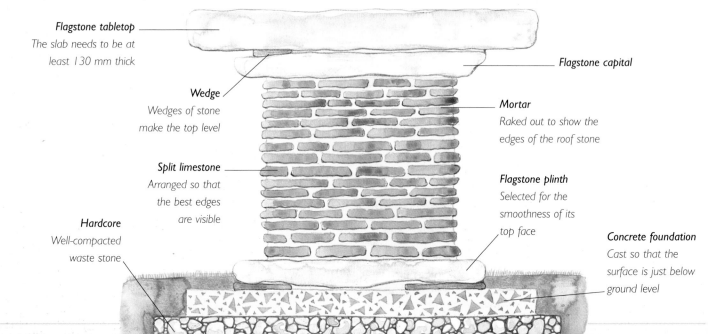

Flagstone tabletop
The slab needs to be at least 130 mm thick

Wedge
Wedges of stone make the top level

Split limestone
Arranged so that the best edges are visible

Hardcore
Well-compacted waste stone

Flagstone capital

Mortar
Raked out to show the edges of the roof stone

Flagstone plinth
Selected for the smoothness of its top face

Concrete foundation
Cast so that the surface is just below ground level

Pedestal table

FRONT VIEW OF THE TABLE

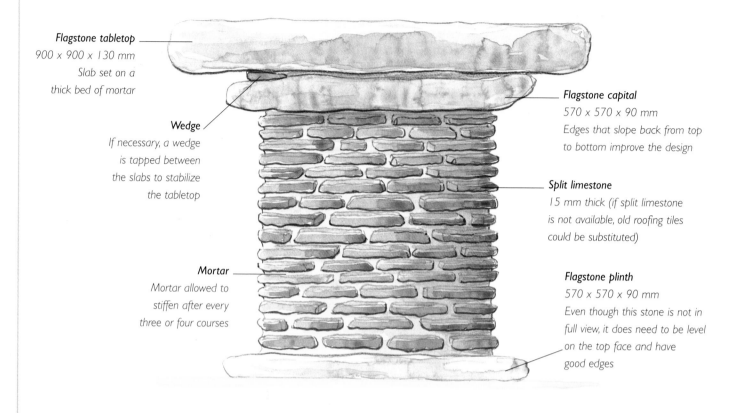

Flagstone tabletop
900 x 900 x 130 mm
Slab set on a
thick bed of mortar

Wedge
If necessary, a wedge
is tapped between
the slabs to stabilize
the tabletop

Mortar
Mortar allowed to
stiffen after every
three or four courses

Flagstone capital
570 x 570 x 90 mm
Edges that slope back from top
to bottom improve the design

Split limestone
15 mm thick (if split limestone
is not available, old roofing tiles
could be substituted)

Flagstone plinth
570 x 570 x 90 mm
Even though this stone is not in
full view, it does need to be level
on the top face and have
good edges

PLAN VIEW OF THE TABLE

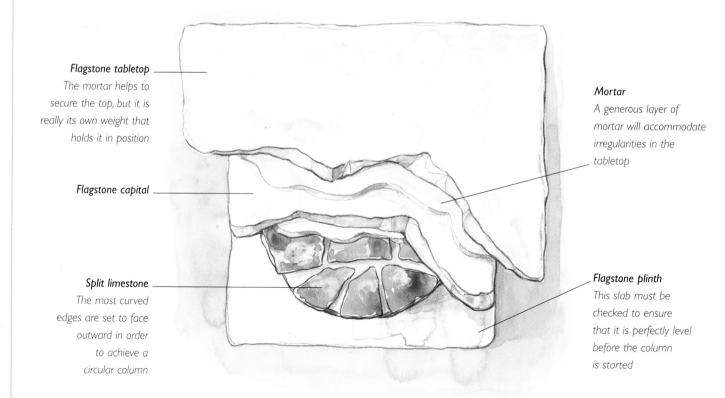

Flagstone tabletop
The mortar helps to
secure the top, but it is
really its own weight that
holds it in position

Flagstone capital

Split limestone
The most curved
edges are set to face
outward in order
to achieve a
circular column

Mortar
A generous layer of
mortar will accommodate
irregularities in the
tabletop

Flagstone plinth
This slab must be
checked to ensure
that it is perfectly level
before the column
is started

EXPLODED VIEW OF THE TABLE

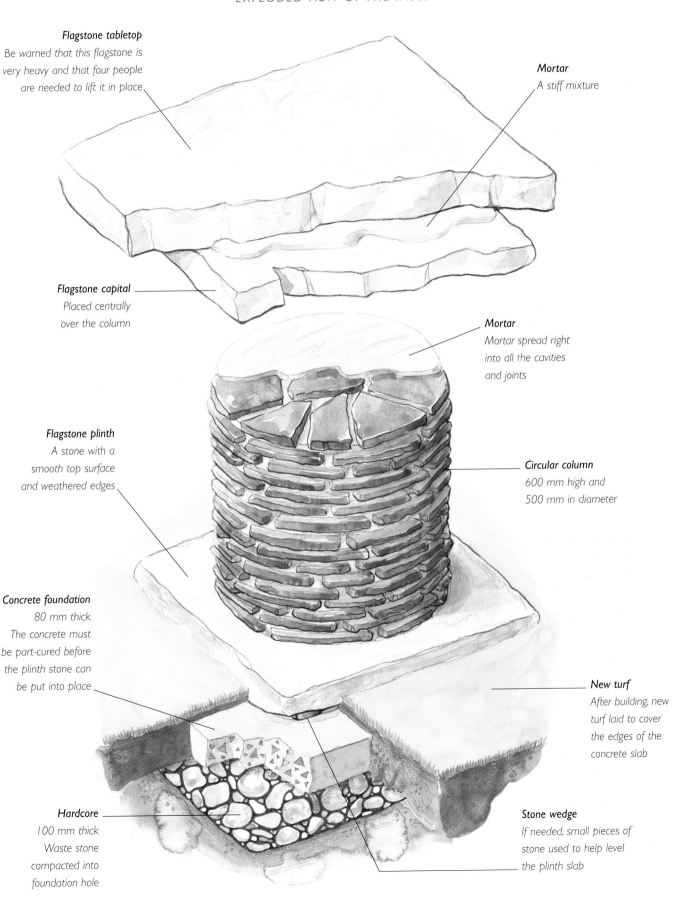

Flagstone tabletop
Be warned that this flagstone is
very heavy and that four people
are needed to lift it in place

Mortar
A stiff mixture

Flagstone capital
Placed centrally
over the column

Mortar
Mortar spread right
into all the cavities
and joints

Flagstone plinth
A stone with a
smooth top surface
and weathered edges

Circular column
600 mm high and
500 mm in diameter

Concrete foundation
80 mm thick
The concrete must
be part-cured before
the plinth stone can
be put into place

New turf
After building, new
turf laid to cover
the edges of the
concrete slab

Hardcore
100 mm thick
Waste stone
compacted into
foundation hole

Stone wedge
If needed, small pieces of
stone used to help level
the plinth slab

Step-by-step: **Making the pedestal table**

Floating
Float the concrete to a smooth finish

Split limestone
Pile up the stone so that it is close to hand

Frame
The frame measures 640 mm square

Levelling
Use the spirit level to check the slab is horizontal

Alignment
Position the plinth stone by using the chalked diagonals

1 Dig out the foundation to a depth of about 200 mm, making it 640 mm square, and half-fill it with hardcore. Ram it down with the sledgehammer. With the lengths of sawn wood, build a rough frame on the hardcore, measuring 640 mm square and 80 mm deep. Fill it up with concrete, and smooth it off with the wooden beam and mortar float.

2 When the concrete has set, remove the frame. Draw diagonals across the base slab to establish the centre, then set the plinth stone in place. Check that it is level with the spirit level. If it is not, insert slivers of stone until it lies horizontal.

Circle of stone
Bed the split stone in mortar to make a 500 mm-diameter circle

Levelling
Check the level after every five courses

Pointing
Pack the mortar under the edges of the plinth stone

Hammering
Tap individual stones to achieve an overall level surface

Trimming
Trim the edges of the stone for the best fit

3 Draw diagonals to establish the centre of the plinth stone, then draw a circle 500 mm in diameter using the string and peg. Use the bricklayer's trowel to butter the circle with mortar and place split limestone around the circumference.

4 Build up about five layers of limestone, then go round with the mason's hammer tapping individual stones into line. Make repeated checks with the spirit level. Continue building until the column is 600 mm high.

Adjusting
Tap proud stones
back into line

Bedding
Butter the top of the column
with a generous layer of mortar

Filling
Fill the
cavities with
mortar and
stone waste

Coursing
Rake out
the mortar to
reveal the
edges of
the stone

Column height
Aim for a
height of
600 mm

5 Walk around the column, checking that the sides are vertical, and use the mason's hammer to tap stones that are standing proud back into line.

6 Use the pointing trowel to butter the top of the finished column with a generous layer of mortar and carefully set the capital stone in place. Make sure that it is aligned with the plinth stone.

Mortar bedding
Butter the top of the capital
slab with a thick bed of mortar

7 Butter the capital slab with a thick layer of mortar, and then call on your helpers to lift the table slab into place. Check that it is level with the spirit level. If necessary, put slices of waste stone underneath to adjust the level until it lies horizontal.

Wedging
Use slices of
waste stone
underneath the
slab to maintain
the level

Helpful hint

Note the sack barrow in the background of this photo. If you intend doing heavy stonework – moving slabs or bags of cement, or even if you want to take some of the effort out of gardening, a traditional sack barrow is ideal.

Water

Introduction

We both enjoy working with water. When we were first married and living in a country cottage, we always liked using the well and messing about with various hand- and wind-driven pumps. Later on, when we began working with wood, stone and garden design, we soon came to realize that water is a uniquely beguiling element. We discovered that building, stocking and maintaining small ponds, from digging the hole to fitting the liner, choosing plants, and getting the pump working, is great fun.

The ambition of this book is to share with you all the pure "playtime" pleasures of working with wood, brick, earth and stone to create water features in the garden. Each project progresses through design considerations to instructions on how to use the tools and materials, how to fit pumps and fountains, and ideas on modifying the projects to suit your individual needs. Colour-wash illustrations show how the structures are put together, and step-by-step photographs illustrate the procedures involved – providing a complete tour through all the stages of designing, making, constructing and finishing. And after the pleasure of building a water feature, you can "soak up" the calming effect of water.

Making water features does not require complex tools or a profound knowledge of earth and pump mechanics, only that you become involved in the exciting and therapeutic experience of working with water – our most precious resource, and one of our most tantalizing natural elements. This book is about working with your hands in the garden, and using your mind and body to create uniquely beautiful water features that everyone can enjoy, both for their visual impact and as a relaxing experience.

So – best of luck!

Alan & Gill

HEALTH AND SAFETY

Many of the procedures for making water features are potentially dangerous, so before starting the projects, check through the following list:

• The projects use safe low-voltage water pumps, but we still recommend using a safety electricity circuit breaker (between the power socket and the plug for the pump), and armoured pipe to protect the power cable. If you are unsure about installing the pumps, ask a qualified electrician to fit them for you.

• Some projects are physically demanding and if you have doubts about whether you are up to it, get advice from your doctor. When lifting large weights, minimize back strain by bending your knees, hugging the item close to your body, and keeping the spine straight.

• Have a first-aid kit and telephone within easy reach. If possible, avoid working alone.

• Wear gloves, dust-mask and goggles when you are handling cement and lime.

• We recommend that you do not build a pond in your garden if you have small children. A toddler can drown in less than 10 mm of water. Other water features are safer, but even so, never leave children unsupervised.

Part I: **Techniques**

Designing and planning

Size doesn't matter! Whether you have a town courtyard or a big country garden, a pond, fountain or other water feature can be accommodated in any size of garden. The secret of building a successful water feature is to spend time carefully designing and planning the whole operation, from walking around the garden and choosing the site, to tidying up when the job is done. This attention to detail guarantees that the end results will be impressive.

FIRST CONSIDERATIONS

- Do you want to involve yourself in a lot of earth-moving, or would you prefer to minimize the digging and build a feature that sits on the ground?
- Do you want a low-cost water feature with a short life, or would it be better to build something that is more expensive but is going to be around for the next 25 years?
- Do small children and pets use your garden?
- Do you want lots of movement and sound – perhaps a small pool with a gushing fountain? Or would you prefer a large, natural pond with abundant plants and wildlife?
- Where and how are you going to hide the water feed and the power cable? Where is the nearest power source?
- Do you want a water feature with minimum maintenance? Or can you cope with lots of work, such as raking leaves out of a pond, adjusting the pumps, and stocking it with plants and fish?
- Are you going to start work in the summer when the ground is dry? If so, can you put up with the upheaval at a time when you are most likely to want to sit out in the garden? Or are you going to work in winter, so that you can appreciate the water feature at the start of the gardening year in the spring?

Choosing the right project

When you have worked through the First Considerations, decide precisely what you want to build, and where in the garden you are going to put it. This involves looking at the land and thinking about the implications of the operations. Let's say, for example, that you want to build the Natural Pond (page 364). The garden is big enough, and you are not put off by all the digging, but where are you going to put the excavated earth? Of course you could pay to have it removed, but why not leave the mound of earth alongside the pond and build a waterfall cascade, or a rockery. If the excavated earth is going to be a problem, it may be better to opt for another project such as the Woodland Grotto (page 334), or perhaps a fountain. You have to assess each project according to your own requirements. You also need to consider how a project affects other members of the household, including safety considerations for young children, and whether it will be a nuisance to neighbours in any way.

Planning the project

The whole project now has to be planned out in the context of your garden. Decide where you want the water feature to be placed in relation to existing garden features, and measure out the distances for the various cables and pipes.

Next, you have to think about the delivery of materials for the project, and the way the movement of those materials is going to affect the everyday use of the garden. For example, if you are going to order a tonne of sand, and you need to dig a trench across the lawn and under a path, you have to consider all the implications. Where can the sand be unloaded? How is an open trench going to affect your passage across the garden? Sit down and write out the order of operations, and work out the details.

Measure your garden and do a rough sketch showing the position and size of the envisaged project. This will give you a good idea of how it relates to other features. Before you start digging up the garden and ordering materials, it's a good idea to do a final check to make sure that the scale of the project is just right. The best way to do this is to set out the dimensions of the project on the ground with pegs and string, and then to cover the site with a large tarpaulin. Live with this object for a few days, and if, at the end of that time, the size is just too much, or you reckon that the intended pond could be a bit larger, or you have spotted a problem concerning the pipework, you can make changes.

Last but not least, you need to draw up a schedule of work, to see if things such as local events and holidays affect your dates. For example, it is no good planning to do a project over a public holiday, if this is when you want suppliers to deliver materials.

Buying the right tools and materials

Though the tools and materials will depend upon your chosen project, there are two guiding principles: it is always wise to purchase the best tools that you can afford, and it is always less expensive to buy materials in bulk. Of course, you could trim costs slightly by making do with your spade for shovelling sand and gravel, rather than getting a shovel, and you can cut down on the thickness of sand under a plastic liner, but consider the implications. Is the wear and tear on your back worth the saving on the shovel? Is the meagre saving on sand going to result in the expensive pond liner being pierced? Do not cut costs at the expense of the success of your project. Consider hiring items such as angle grinders and large drills, rather than buying them.

WATER FEATURE DESIGNS FOR THE GARDEN

Weeping hypertufa boulder
A unique and intriguing water feature that is best placed in a quiet area of the garden

Rocky cascade
Positioned in a secluded corner so that the sight and sound of falling water can be appreciated

Wall mask waterspout
Built against a wall, this is the perfect feature for an old house and garden

Japanese deer scarer
Placed next to a natural pond

Natural pond
The perfect habitat for natural fauna: fish, frogs and newts

Glass waterfall
A chance to get high-tech – also a great feature for courtyard gardens

Romantic fountain
Positioned so that it can be seen from a seating area

Container bog garden
A quick and easy way to bring the garden closer to the house

Copper cascade
Set beside a pond – a beautiful feature using contrasting materials

Mini marble fountain
A perfect feature for a sun lounge

French millstone bell fountain
For best effect, set this fountain in an area of flat lawn

Still pond
Built close to the house so it can be seen from indoors as the rain falls

Perpetual water tap
A water feature that will entertain children and friends

Copper spiral spray
Set in a courtyard, the copper spiral catches the breeze as well as the trickling water

Wine bottle spray fountain
Positioned near a patio seating area so that family and friends can admire it

Woodland grotto
Turns the bottom of your garden into an enchanted wonderland – and a favourite spot for toads

ABOVE The sight and sound of water is truly uplifting. Building a water feature, and then sitting back and looking at your handiwork, are both equally enjoyable experiences. The garden design above demonstrates how the projects in this book might be arranged.

Tools

Using the correct tools makes all the difference to the ease and speed with which you can complete a project. If a tool is too short or the wrong weight, you may get backache, but if it is the right length and well designed, you get the job done more quickly and with less stress. A well-chosen, quality tool is a worthwhile investment.

TOOLS FOR MOVING MATERIALS

Wheelbarrow

Gloves

Bucket

Protecting your feet and hands

You must wear solid workboots, preferably with steel toecaps, to prevent your feet from getting crushed. Gloves might feel a little unmanageable in the first instance, but they will stop your hands getting abraded and otherwise damaged. Digging, lifting buckets, heaving concrete slabs, and mixing sand and cement are all hard on the hands. It's a good idea to have several pairs of gloves: leather for the general work, and rubber for the watery tasks.

Making the work easier

Of all the lifting and carrying tools, it is the wheelbarrow and the bucket that make life easier. The best type of wheelbarrow is one with a large inflated rubber tyre that allows you to bounce your way up slopes and over steps, and a tip-stop bar in front of the wheel that enables you to bring the barrow to a halt and tip out the load. You also need three or four plastic buckets. Get the cheapest you can find and use them until they fall to bits.

TOOLS FOR MEASURING AND MARKING

Measuring

Ideally, you need two measuring tools – a flexible tape measure for setting out the site plan, and a measuring rule for smaller measuring tasks within the project. Make sure that both tools are marked out in metric and imperial, so that you can deal with products that are described in either system. It is also a good idea to get a fibreglass tape measure, which is unaffected by water, whereas a metal tape soon rusts if it gets wet. When you are measuring, follow the old adage "measure twice and cut once" – meaning (in this context) it is much better to double-check at the measuring stage, before you start doing clever things such as digging incorrectly-sized holes in the wrong position.

Spirit level

Tape measure

Marking out

You need four marking-out tools – wooden pegs and string, a thick rope, a piece of chalk and a spirit level. The wooden pegs and string are used for marking boundaries and for scribing circles. The rope maps out large, irregular shapes, such as the Natural Pond (page 364). Buy a type that resists tangling. The chalk is used for drawing on concrete and wood when you need a broad, general mark, rather than for making a precise measurement. Lastly, you need a spirit level for checking horizontal and vertical levels. Buy the best that you can afford, preferably one with a strong aluminum body and shock-proof spirit phials. Look after your spirit level, and try not to drop it.

TOOLS FOR PREPARING A SITE

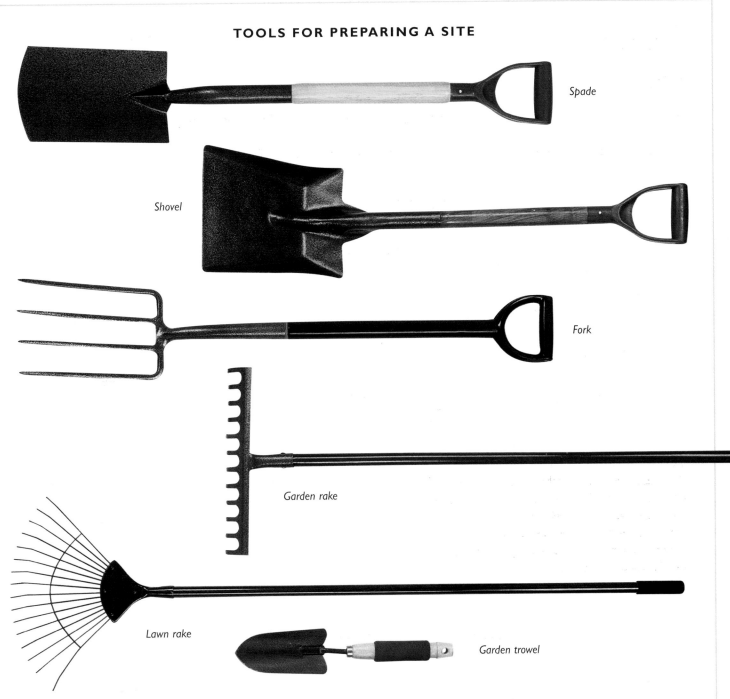

Spade

Shovel

Fork

Garden rake

Lawn rake

Garden trowel

Removing turf and digging earth

A spade and shovel deal with the tasks of removing turf and digging earth. Mark out the size of the pond or water feature, take the spade and cut down through the thickness of the turf. Slice it into easy-to-manage squares, lift these into a wheelbarrow, and unload them off-site. Finally, use both the spade and the shovel to excavate the earth to the required depth.

Compacting hardcore and raking

A club hammer makes short work of compacting hardcore. The smaller the stones of the hardcore, the easier it is to compact. Builder's rubble requires a lot of effort, while gravel settles under its own weight. Avoid rubble that contains lumps of concrete, as they are very difficult to break up. Spread your chosen material over the area and pound it into place with a club hammer.

Use a fork for moving clumps of earth, a garden rake for spreading earth and shingle, a lawn rake for spreading sand and for tidying up and a garden trowel for small excavations. Try to choose tool sizes that match your body size.

Mixing cement and moving gravel

The simplest way of mixing loose material – such as cement, sand and gravel – is to use a carefully chosen shovel. Ideally, you need a tool of a weight and handle length to suit your height and strength. If you are not sure which to buy, always select the shovel with the longest handle. Wash the shovel after mixing cement. Never try shovelling with a spade or digging with a shovel – both exercises are a back-breaking waste of time! Use a wheelbarrow if you need to move the material from one part of the garden to another, even if it's only a few strides away.

MASONRY TOOLS

Mason's hammer

Club hammer

Cold chisel

Cutting concrete, stone, brick and mortar

At various times, you will need to cut a piece of stone or a concrete slab, rake out an existing mortar joint, or generally cut and break hard materials. A club hammer and cold chisel are good for chopping stone to size and for cutting holes in brickwork, while a mason's hammer (also known as a brick hammer) can be used for everything from nipping stone to shape, to banging in wooden pegs, and generally excavating holes in hard and rocky earth. The quality of the tools you buy should depend on whether or not you want them to last for many years or not. For example, an inexpensive chisel will soon lose its edge, but you might well decide that it only needs to last the length of the project. But if a "bargain" tool is going to make life difficult, you do have to consider the wear and tear on your patience.

CUTTING WOOD, PLASTIC AND METAL

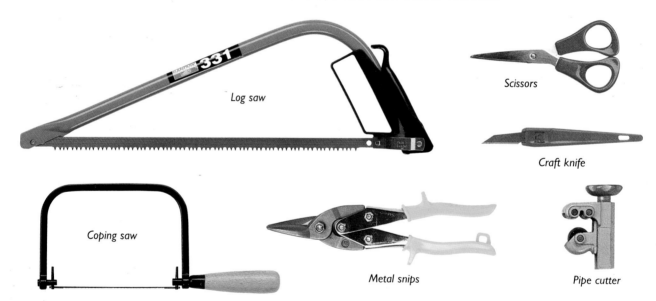

Log saw

Scissors

Craft knife

Coping saw

Metal snips

Pipe cutter

Wood

Generally, most projects can be managed with the log saw, which is perfect for cutting railway sleepers and large-section sawn wood. However, a coping saw is necessary for making the Japanese Deer Scarer featured on page 314. Make sure that both saws have spare blades, so the project will not be held up if a blade breaks.

Plastic

You will need a strong pair of scissors for cutting plastic sheet and the various soft plastic pipes, and a knife for all manner of cutting and whittling tasks. However, you can use the log saw for cutting plastic rainwater pipe and wire snips for some of the water delivery hoses. Some suppliers will cut plastics to specific sizes.

Metal

Metal snips can be used for just about everything from cutting metal and mesh through to cutting some of the tougher plastics, and one or two other tasks besides. Another very useful tool is the pipe cutter, which is a plumbing tool. It is wonderfully easy to use: you simply hook it on the copper pipe, tighten up the single turn-screw, and spin the tool around the pipe until the three wheels cut through the copper. This beautifully designed and inexpensive tool makes a perfect cut every time, without making ragged edges or deforming the pipe. It gives a crisp, cut edge that is set at right angles to the run of the pipe. When you buy the pipe cutter, make sure that it comes with a couple of spare cutting wheels, a mini screwdriver, and instructions for use.

TOOLS FOR CONCRETE, MORTAR AND HYPERTUFA

Bricklayer's trowel

Pointing trowel

Mortar float

Spreading concrete and mortar

If you want to spread concrete or mortar to a smooth finish, you need to use a tool called a mortar float. Made from steel, wood or plastic, the tool is used with an even, side-to-side skimming and smoothing action – in much the same way as you use a bricklayer's trowel. After use, it is vital to wash the float to remove all traces of cement. Never wash your tools at the kitchen sink, as the fine sludge will block up pipes and drains.

Handling mortar

The bricklayer's trowel is designed specifically for transferring large slaps of mortar from where it is mixed to the workpiece. The pointing trowel is for pointing brickwork and more detailed work, but many beginners prefer to use the smaller pointing trowel for all tasks. If you are a novice, use whichever tool you prefer. It is best to avoid the all-plastic trowels and spatulas that are coming on to the market, because they are not as strong.

OTHER ESSENTIAL TOOLS

Drill bit for wood and metal

Flat screwdriver

Electric drill

Adjustable spanner

Cross-point screwdriver

Claw hammer

Paintbrush

Drilling holes

Many of the projects require you to drill holes. Use an electric drill fitted with the appropriate twist bit for drilling holes in sheet metal, plastic, wood and concrete. Always fit an electricity circuit breaker if you are using an electric drill out in the garden, especially when you are working near water. For drilling very small holes that need to be very accurately placed, use a hand drill. For drilling holes through railway sleepers, we prefer to use a carpenter's brace, fitted with a long auger bit.

Tightening up screws and bolts

Many different screw and bolt fixings are used on water features, such as slot-headed and cross-headed wood screws, screw-bolts on hose fittings, slot-headed machine screws in the pumps, and all manner of hex nuts and bolts. Ideally, you need a whole range of screwdrivers and a single top-quality adjustable spanner or

wrench to deal with all these. Many of the hose clips and pumps have fixings that need to be tightened up with a key, but such tools are usually supplied with the product. If you are a beginner – meaning you are starting without a tool kit – it is best to buy the materials first and then get the appropriate tools to fit.

Back-up tools

You will need a whole range of non-specific back-up tools, such as a claw hammer for driving in nails, brushes and various electricity circuit breakers. As such tools can be used generally about the house and garden, it is a good idea to get the best-quality tools that you can afford. As a general rule of thumb, we think it fair to say that tools made by long-established British, American, Swedish and German firms – especially forged metal tools, such as hammers and drills – are many times better than those made in developing countries. Be warned – there are no bargains!

Materials

The materials come from four main sources: a general builder's merchant for items such as sand and cement, a specialist supplier for bulk items such as shingle and topsoil, a garden centre for concrete slabs and plants, and a water garden specialist for plastic sheet, pumps and fountains. Always shop around for the best prices.

SUMPS, PIPES, INSULATION AND LINERS

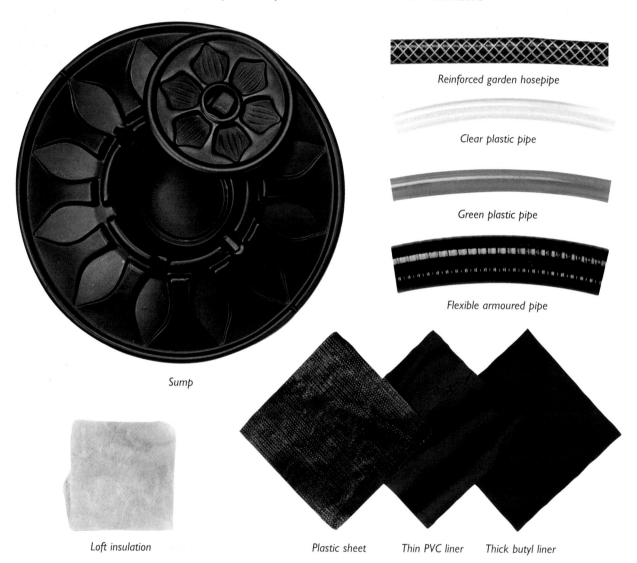

Sump

Reinforced garden hosepipe

Clear plastic pipe

Green plastic pipe

Flexible armoured pipe

Loft insulation

Plastic sheet   *Thin PVC liner*   *Thick butyl liner*

Sumps

A sump, sometimes known as a sump reservoir, or even just a reservoir, is a smallish, bucket-sized container which is sunk into the ground, where it is used to hold just enough water to feed a pump. The pump sits in the sump, pushing water up and out, which then falls to be channelled back into the sump, and so on.

Such an arrangement is ideal when you want to create a feature with moving water, without going to the trouble of building a pool. You can either opt for a self-contained, purpose-built plastic sump that comes complete with its own drainage brim and lid, or you can simply set a plastic bucket in the ground and cover it with a large sheet of plastic (with a slit in it) that directs all the water back into the bucket. If you do decide to use a bucket, remove the handle so that it will not pierce the plastic sheet.

Plastic pipes

Plastic pipes are used to conduct water and protect electric cables. We use large-diameter ribbed pipe, also called armoured pipe, for large-flow delivery, such as for running water from a pond to the top of a cascade. Other gauges of plastic pipe are employed for general pump-to-pipe linkage and for cable protection. All the projects in this book use low-voltage pumps in conjunction with an electricity circuit breaker, and we protect the electric cables variously with best-quality armoured pipe and offcuts of ribbed water delivery hose. When you are working with plastic pipe, using it for water delivery or for linking a pump, be careful not to kink the pipe because it will reduce or cut off the water flow. Try to arrange it in broad, smooth curves.

Lining material

Pond liners are generally made either from black PVC or black butyl rubber. The quality and thickness of the liner relates directly to its durability, so the thicker the liner, the longer it is going to last. At one end of the price scale there is inexpensive, thin PVC sheet that lasts approximately five years, through to very expensive, thick butyl sheet that is guaranteed to last at least 25 years. The thicker, more expensive liners are less prone to sunlight deterioration, accidental tearing and puncturing. Always

protect your chosen liner by bedding it on a layer of sand, fibre-glass loft insulation or special polyester matting. As a general rule, you should avoid walking over a pond liner. That said, if you do have to walk over the liner, make sure that you wear smooth, soft-soled shoes, so that you don't make holes.

Calculating the size of the liner

There are various formulas for calculating the size of the pond liner needed for a project, but we generally work it out by adding three times the depth of the pond to both its finished length and width. For example, if the pond is 3 metres long, 2 metres wide and 1 metre deep, you would add 3 metres to both the length and width, giving a measurement of 6 metres long by 5 metres wide. However, the simplest way to calculate liner size is to dig the hole and run a tape measure from one end down into the hole, and up out of the other side, to calculate the length (and the same for the width). Add about 30 mm to each measurement for an overlap. If in doubt, it is better to buy too big, rather than too small.

COPPER PIPE AND SHEET, PIPE JOINTS AND FIXINGS

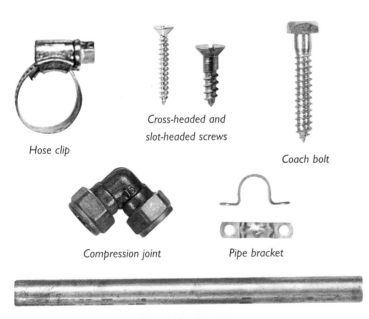

Hose clip

Cross-headed and slot-headed screws

Coach bolt

Compression joint

Pipe bracket

Copper plumbing pipe

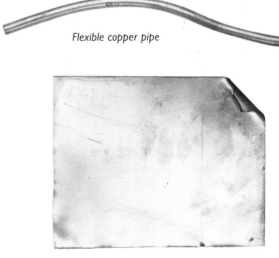

Flexible copper pipe

Copper sheet

Copper pipe and sheet

If you want to have metal on show in the garden, copper is a good choice. Not only is it relatively easy to cut and bend, but it weathers to an attractive blue-green verdigris finish.

We use hard copper pipe (15 mm in diameter) in conjunction with compression joints and pipe brackets for runs from straight to right angle, flexible copper pipe (10 mm in diameter) for bending into more complex curves, and copper sheet for simple constructions. Copper can be softened and coloured simply by using a blowlamp to heat it until it turns cherry red, then dunking it in cold water – at which point it becomes soft enough to bend, and a beautiful dappled bronze colour.

Fixings and pipe joints

The projects all use a range of basic DIY fixings – everything from screws and nails through to coach bolts and patent hose clips. Hose clips are particularly useful when it comes to joining various sizes of pipe to the pump. It is best to purchase a mixed bag of different-sized hose clips, and then pick them to suit the project.

The simplest method of joining two lengths of copper pipe is to use an item known as a compression joint. You simply cut the pipes to length, push the ends in your chosen joint (which can be straight, right-angled, or T-junction) and then tighten them up with a spanner. Such joints can be clenched quite easily – it takes no more effort than turning off a stiff tap.

STONE, BRICKS AND PAVING SLABS, SAND, CEMENT AND LIME

Roofing slate

Paving slab

Rockery stone

Reclaimed roof stone

Brick

Cobbles

Pink gravel

Pea gravel

Oyster shell

Soft sand

Cement

Lime

CAUTION

Cement and lime are very corrosive. Wear goggles, gloves and a dust-mask, and be sure to wash your face and hands after working with these materials.

Stone

The projects feature roofing slate, reclaimed roof stone, rockery stone in the form of limestone and split sandstone, cobbles and different types and grades of shingle and gravel. Slate and sandstone provide sheet material, limestone is good when you want rugged lumps and boulders, and cobbles and gravel are suitable for spreading over large areas. Although the projects describe specific stones, you can buy the type that most closely matches these recommendations, according to what is available in your area. If you only need a relatively small quantity of something – say a couple of bags – then it is simplest to buy it from a builder's merchant. For large amounts (as with the stone used for the Rocky Cascade on page 358), the most economical option is to order the stone directly from a specialist supplier. Prior to placing an order, it is a good idea to phone around several suppliers for options and prices. Make sure the quote includes delivery costs.

Bricks and paving slabs

Bricks and concrete slabs are particularly useful for the projects. We use clay building bricks for edging sumps, and reconstituted concrete slabs for areas of paving. Many reconstituted slabs look so convincing that they cannot be distinguished from the real thing. They are available in all sorts of shapes, sizes, colours and textures, such as tessellating shapes that look like red quarry tiles, sandstone paving slabs, stone on edge, brick slabs and limestone and sandstone flagstones. You can even buy slabs that look as if they have been carved with a picture – these include horse portraits, cottages, Wild West scenes and historical figures such as Horatio Nelson, Buffalo Bill and Sitting Bull.

Sand, cement and lime

Soft sand, sometimes called builder's sand, is used for making smooth-textured mortar, while sharp sand is used for making concrete and coarse mortars. Sold by the bag or lorry-load, the colour and texture of the sand usually relates to the local stone. If you are looking for good colour and low cost, it would be best to order your sand in bulk from a local pit.

Cement powder – sold in 25 kg and 50 kg bags, and described generically as "Portland cement" – is one of the chief ingredients of mortar and concrete. Though it is undoubtedly true to say that you can save money by ordering large numbers of 50 kg bags, this is the one instance where it is much better to buy only a few small bags for the job in hand. Not only are 50 kg bags difficult to handle, but they are also flimsy and liable to tear, the cement powder is susceptible to damp and loose powder is highly corrosive and very bad for skin, eyes and lungs.

Lime is used together with cement and sand to make mortar. Although a "cement mortar" can be made without lime (which is undoubtedly harder and stronger than lime and cement mortar), it is also so hard that it stains the stone and pulls it apart. As with cement powder, it is best to order lime in small quantities and to be sure to store it in a dry place. Lime is highly corrosive, to the extent that you should wear goggles and a dust-mask when mixing, and gloves for general handling. If cement or lime powder blows in your face when you are mixing, swiftly wash your face and then reposition yourself so that you are working out of the wind. Keep lime away from children and pets.

WOOD MATERIALS

Log roll

Rough-sawn pine section

Railway sleeper

Railway sleepers

Several projects use railway sleepers. Second-hand sleepers can be obtained in various lengths and grades at a whole range of prices, from all manner of sources. However, experience has shown us that it is vital to go to the supplier yourself and carefully select individual sleepers, and pay for them as seen. The alternative is to buy them over the phone, and risk receiving a delivery of poor-quality sleepers. You need to specify that the sleepers are "best quality", meaning straight and sound along their length, with no warping or splits, or rusty iron clamps. A good way of checking them is to tap them along their length with a mallet. If they sound

like a drum they are hollow and rotten, and if they ring they are sound. Be wary about cutting sleepers with a power saw, just in case the teeth hit a hidden piece of iron and the saw kicks back. However, if you do want to risk it, be sure to wear gloves and goggles, and follow the manufacturer's safety guidelines.

Log rolls and rough-sawn pine

Log rolls (split round sections mounted on wire) and general rough-sawn sections are best sourced from your local forestry or garden centre. Make sure that the wood is crisp and dry, and avoid anything that looks mouldy or has loose knots or splits.

Ponds

A pond breathes life into a garden. An informal natural pond in a secluded corner, or a formal raised pond in a high-profile position by the patio, gives a garden atmosphere, sound and movement. It adds a wildlife dimension too – not only can you stock it with fish, but it will also attract dragonflies, frogs and birds.

BUYING TIPS

- For a rigid pond liner, fibreglass is more expensive than plastic, but is stronger and lasts longer.
- There are various grades of flexible liner – everything from inexpensive polythene liners that last for about five years, through to butyl liners that are guaranteed for over 25 years (see page 263). All grades last longer if they are bedded on a layer of sand, fibreglass loft insulation or special fabric.
- To calculate the size of the required liner, add three times the depth of the pond to both the finished length and width.
- Peg out the measurements of the pond in the garden several weeks prior to buying materials. This will help you discover the implications of the size and the siting.

TYPES OF POND

Basically, there are two types of pond – a formal pond with a hard landscaped edge (brick, stone or tile), and an informal pond designed to blend in with nature. Both types can be built using either a preformed rigid liner, or a flexible plastic liner. Where the formal pond unit sits above ground level, it is generally easier to use a long-lasting preformed rigid liner of fibreglass or plastic.

A pond is going to be there for a long time, so take into account all the constructional, aesthetic and horticultural considerations. For example, are you strong enough to handle the task? Can you afford the materials and equipment? Is your proposed site big enough and correctly orientated? Whatever the type of pond, choose a site that gets at least six hours of sunlight a day, is well away from trees, and has plenty of room for planting.

HOW TO DESIGN AND MAKE A FORMAL POND

Design notes

This formal pond uses a rigid fibreglass pool unit set at ground level, and the edge of the unit is covered with concrete slabs. We levelled up the site prior to excavation in order to avoid the problems associated with having one of the edges of the pool unit exposed. When you are buying the unit, look for one that has a generous lip, and check that the entire length of the lip is free from thin areas and cracks, and is generally in a good, sound condition. If the lip is in any way faulty, reject the unit.

Making a formal pond

1 Place the unit upside-down on the site and mark the limits with wooden pegs banged into the ground. Measure the depth of the unit and excavate the whole area to that depth, plus 50 mm. Remove the spoil from the site. (Excavated earth may come in handy for another project, such as a cascade or rockery.)

2 Level the base of the hole with a 50 mm layer of soft sand. Sit the unit in the hole and use a batten and spirit level to check the level across the rim. Gradually backfill between the unit and the earth with soft sand, and compact it with a batten.

3 Dig a trench around the rim of the pool (300 mm deep and the width of the edging slabs). Fill it with well-compacted hardcore. Space the slabs and bed them on a generous layer of mortar.

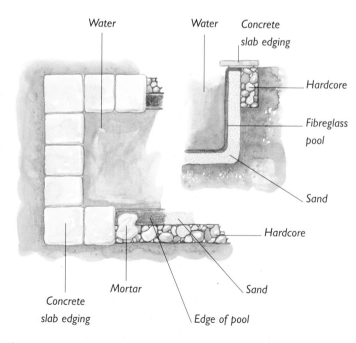

Water   Water   Concrete slab edging

Hardcore

Fibreglass pool

Sand

Hardcore

Sand

Mortar

Concrete slab edging   Edge of pool

ABOVE Plan and cross-section of a straightforward rectangular formal pond made with a preformed fibreglass pool unit, and edged with reconstituted concrete slabs bedded on mortar.

INFORMAL PONDS

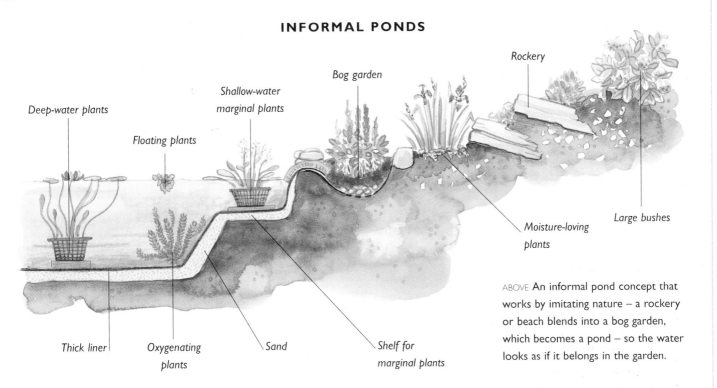

Deep-water plants

Floating plants

Shallow-water marginal plants

Bog garden

Rockery

Large bushes

Moisture-loving plants

Thick liner

Oxygenating plants

Sand

Shelf for marginal plants

ABOVE An informal pond concept that works by imitating nature – a rockery or beach blends into a bog garden, which becomes a pond – so the water looks as if it belongs in the garden.

Design notes

This pond is made with a flexible liner, allowing for maximum informality. The edges of the pond may incorporate features such as a rockery, bog garden or beach. When you are planning out the pond, allow plenty of space for grading the planting to create a seamless transition between the edge of the water and the far reaches of the surrounding slope. View the pond and its surrounds as a series of terraces, with each step providing a different planting opportunity. So, from the depths of the pond to the heights of the terrace, you might have deep-water plants, shallow-water marginals, plants that enjoy boggy earth, and so on up the slope, ending with plants that are not generally associated with ponds. Site the bog garden in a lined gully around one edge. The best way of planting a pond is to set a few plants in place – the deep-water plants, the marginals and possibly the bog plants – and then slowly add to the planting over one or more seasons. By working gradually, you can achieve a better balance of planting effects. For more details, refer to the Natural Pond project on page 364.

CONTAINER PONDS

Some gardens are so small that there is not enough space to build a pond, but it is nevertheless possible to create a fully functioning miniature pond. Plastic waterbutts, sunken barrels, tanks, cisterns, troughs or concrete tubs all make water gardens for unlikely and unpromising places such as conservatories, balconies, verandahs and rooftop terraces. The walls of the container need to be thick enough to ensure a constant water temperature. Avoid antique lead cisterns if you have pets that might drink the water.

It is possible to create a water feature that appears to be much larger than it really is, by clever positioning of additional containers. The trick is to plant up the water container with a few choice water plants, and surround it with a good number of containers holding bog plants. Pack other containers, hosting a variety of plants, around these. In this way, it is possible to achieve a planting that seems to range from deep-water plants through to marginals and those that grow on dry banks.

FISH, FROGS, NEWTS AND OTHER FAUNA

Ponds are much more than a delightful addition to a garden. They also provide a wonderful opportunity to attract water-loving wildlife, which you can enjoy watching. As soon as you have created an area of water – sometimes within hours of finishing the planting around the pond – you will begin to see incredibly beautiful creatures, such as dragonflies and damselflies. Once insects are hovering over the water, they will swiftly be followed by frogs, toads, newts, and all manner of birds and animals.

Many pond lovers are very happy with the wildlife that appears of its own accord, but for others, the main attraction of a pond is that you can have fish in it. The best time for introducing fish is in late spring or early summer, when the water is a suitable temperature. If you decide to stock your pond with fish, you must be prepared to protect the fish from predators such as herons and cats. Hold back from introducing the fish until the pond and its plants have had a chance to get established.

Pumps and filters

Pumps are used in conjunction with filters to circulate water. They are powered by electricity, so safety considerations are very important. The pump, by means of an impeller, draws water in one end and pushes it out through the other (at which point it is attached to a water feature such as a cascade or fountain).

HOW TO CHOOSE THE RIGHT PUMP FOR THE JOB

While there are two main types of pump – low-voltage submersible, and high-voltage surface-mounted – this book only uses the former. We chose these because modern, low-voltage submersible pumps are so safe that they can (via an electricity circuit breaker) be plugged directly into an existing socket. You do not have to build a special shed to hold the pump, as it is just placed in the pond. The circuit breaker eliminates the danger of electrocution. If the cable were damaged, the water could be electrified, but a circuit breaker cuts off the power instantly.

The easiest way to calculate the size of pump required is to simply measure the height from the surface of the water to the top of the fountainhead or cascade, and then to purchase a pump with that capacity. Basically, there are four sizes of submersible pump available: a miniature pump designed for mini water features on the patio, a small pump intended for little fountains, a medium-size pump suitable for an average fountain, and a large pump that is big enough to create a cascade. If in doubt about what to buy, describe the project to the supplier and ask for advice, and then get the biggest pump that you can afford – it is then at least possible to cut back on the water flow if necessary.

BUYING A PUMP

Questions to answer before you visit the water garden specialist:

• What is the vertical distance from the surface of the water to the fountainhead nozzle, or the top of the cascade? (This is known as the head height.)
• What is the distance from the pump to the electricity socket?
• How high above the surface of the fountainhead nozzle do you want the water to reach?
• (For a cascade.) What is the horizontal distance between the pump position and the top of the cascade?
• Do you envisage running two or more projects off the same pump in the future? If so, you will need a dual-outlet pump.
• Do you need a separate filtration unit? Most submersible pumps have built-in filters which cope with small volumes of water (a pond that is less than 2 m in diameter for example), but for larger ponds it is better to connect the pump to a filtration unit. A filtration unit at the side of the pond (not in the water) is easier to clean than a submersible pump.

HOW TO SET UP YOUR PUMP

The position of the pump depends on whether it is going to feed a feature direct, or whether there is a surface filter. The general rule is that if you want it to feed direct, the distance between the pump and the outlet should be as short as possible. If you are fitting a surface filter, the pump must be set up as far away as is practicable from the point at which the water is being returned to the pond.

I Decide on the position of the pump in the pond, mark out a route for the cables and pipes, and dig a trench leading to the pond. Cover the power cables with a protective sheath, such as

Buried delivery pipe

Surface filter

Circuit breaker

Buried (protected) power cable

Submerged pump

flexible armoured plastic pipe, and set the pipes and cables in the trench.
2 Position the pump in the water (on a slab or a few bricks to keep it away from the sludge), fit the outlet delivery pipes, put the electricity circuit breaker in place, and switch on the power.
3 When you are satisfied with the flow, fill the trench, and make sure that all the pipes and cables are hidden from view.

LEFT An ideal pump and filter arrangement for pond features (such as a cascade) that accumulate dirt and debris in the water.

LARGE PUMPS

Fountainhead
*Some are adjustable,
like the nozzle on a
garden hosepipe*

Screw
*Make sure
that the
connector fits
your chosen
fountainhead*

Telescopic outlet pipe
*Extends telescopically
to suit different depths*

*Push-fit
connector*
*Check that
this is
suitable for
your set-up*

*Screw-fit
connector*
*Ensures
secure joints*

Integral adjuster
*Rotates to
restrict flow*

T-junction
*Facility for a tap and
a second outlet pipe*

*Pump and
filter housing*

*Power
selector*

Fixing plates

Large submersible pumps are designed to deliver a good flow of water to one or more outlets, for example a fountain and a water filter. They are able to handle a small amount of mud and sludge without the impeller clogging and grinding to a halt. Such pumps are usually fitted with an integral adjuster that allows you to govern the rate of flow, and a tap that allows you to cut off one of the two outlets. The pump should be cleaned out at least once a week during the running season. Although it needs regular attention to stay in good working order, it is inexpensive and will last for a long time. Assume that the manufacturer's rating of a pump's performance relates to perfect conditions (or is over-optimistic) and buy a pump that appears to exceed your requirements.

MEDIUM PUMPS

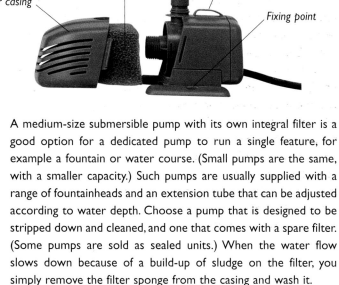

Alternative spray nozzle
*Designed to fit into the
nozzle adapter*

*Fountainhead
spray nozzle*
Produces a fine spray

Nozzle adapter

*Alternative
fountainhead*
*The spray
pattern is
shaped by the
size and position
of the holes*

*Telescopic
outlet pipe*

Filter block
Filter casing

Lifting handle

Fixing point

A medium-size submersible pump with its own integral filter is a good option for a dedicated pump to run a single feature, for example a fountain or water course. (Small pumps are the same, with a smaller capacity.) Such pumps are usually supplied with a range of fountainheads and an extension tube that can be adjusted according to water depth. Choose a pump that is designed to be stripped down and cleaned, and one that comes with a spare filter. (Some pumps are sold as sealed units.) When the water flow slows down because of a build-up of sludge on the filter, you simply remove the filter sponge from the casing and wash it.

MINIATURE PUMPS

Outlet pipe
*A length of pipe
or a connector
fits on to this*

Sucker foot
*Fixes the pump to
base of container*

Miniature pumps are designed specifically for container water features, when you want a pump that is small enough to tuck away under gravel or rocks. They are only capable of powering a small dribble fountain, but are maintenance-free and run silently. It is still essential to plug in this type of pump via an electricity circuit breaker. For safety, if you have children, always buy a pump that the manufacturer describes as "child friendly".

Fountains

Fountains are magical! The moment you install a pump complete with a statuette

and spray, or a pump with a fountainhead that just breaks the surface of the water

in a pond, you create a wonderfully dynamic effect. Fountains are also supremely

practical, in that the movement enriches the water with oxygen.

DECORATIVE AND PRACTICAL USES OF FOUNTAINS

Ornamental fountains

A standard fountain pump comes complete with an extension pipe and a selection of fountainhead spray nozzles. You can either mount the unit directly in the water and simply adjust your chosen nozzle for best effect, or you can fit the pump under a decorative statuette. Connecting the unit directly produces the largest possible spray height above the surface of the water. When the unit is mounted under a statuette, you have to take the height of the statuette into account when you are working out the total height of the spray that can be achieved. For example, if the pump gives a spray height of 500 mm above the water, and it is run through a statuette that is 250 mm high, then it follows that the spray will only push 250 mm above the top of the statuette. So if you want a statuette fountain with a dramatic spray, it is best to buy the statuette first, and then choose a pump size that relates to the height of the statuette. Visit garden centres and specialist suppliers to see the various fountains and sprays in action. Take notes, keep the brochures and generally research the whole project before you make a purchase.

Oxygenating fountains

Oxygen is necessary for the fish and wildlife of a pond. If a fountain's primary function is to oxygenate the water, select the largest pump that you can afford and fit it directly to the fountainhead nozzle, setting the nozzle to produce the most complex spray formation. The greater the turbulence in the water, the greater the amount of oxygen produced: a geyser fountain with a dense, foaming plume will generate more oxygen than a bell jet.

TYPES OF FOUNTAIN PATTERN

ABOVE Geyser fountain: exciting and slightly erratic, and a good choice for an open, breezy site.

ABOVE Bell jet fountain: gives a structured effect that is good for a small, formal pond.

ABOVE Single spray nozzle: a good choice when you want to create a bold, dynamic effect.

ABOVE Fountain jet: a simple no-fuss fountain that is low-cost and looks good in any pond.

Flow control

The vertical distance between the surface of the water and the top of the fountainhead nozzle is called the head height of the water. Maximum head height can be achieved by a pump if the fountain is fitted with a narrow-gauge delivery pipe and the water is clean, but if the delivery pipe is wide and badly fitted, and there is lots of mud in the water, the head height will be much reduced. Check that all the fittings are tight and the pump is working efficiently, push your chosen nozzle on the extension pipe, check that the flow adjuster is set for maximum pressure and minimum flow, and then switch on the power. Finally, fine-tune your chosen nozzle according to the manufacturer's instructions.

When experimenting with the pump, make sure that your hands and the water are clean, because grit will affect the flow of the water. Check that the nozzle size relates to the size of the chosen pump, or you may be disappointed by the effect.

SETTING UP A SIMPLE FOUNTAIN

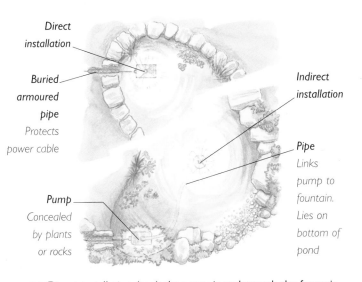

Direct installation

Buried armoured pipe
Protects power cable

Pump
Concealed by plants or rocks

Indirect installation

Pipe
Links pump to fountain. Lies on bottom of pond

ABOVE Direct installation (top): the pump is underneath the fountain. Indirect installation (bottom): the pump is by the side of the pond.

Direct installation

Fountains can be installed directly or indirectly. When a fountain is directly installed, the fountainhead nozzle leads straight off a submersible pump via a vertical extension tube, with the pump sitting on a plinth of bricks or concrete slabs at the bottom of the pond. The very simplest type of set-up has the pump positioned as near as possible to the edge of the pond (for easy access), and no attempt is made to conceal it. This arrangement looks a bit basic, but its advantage is that the pump works at maximum efficiency.

Indirect installation

With an indirect or remote installation, the submersible pump feeds the fountainhead via a flexible tube that runs horizontally across the bottom of the pond. In this arrangement, the pump can be concealed just about anywhere in the pond, and the fountainhead is remote from the pump. The pump is easily accessible, but the reduced efficiency cuts down the height of the spray.

ORNAMENTAL FOUNTAINS

Design notes

It is best to choose an ornamental statuette first, and then select a pump that is powerful enough to force water through the ornament and to at least the same height again. A direct installation, as described below (and on page 294), is the easiest and cheapest method of setting it up, and therefore ideal for the beginner.

Procedure for setting up an ornamental fountain

1 Position the submersible pump on a plinth (a concrete slab, or a few bricks) in the pond and arrange the electric cable so that it is hidden from view. Place the housing over the pump and switch on the power to check the water flow.

2 Fit a flexible extension hose to the pump and secure it with a hose clip. Join the other end of the extension hose to the pipe on the underside of the ornamental statuette, and fix with a hose clip. Put the statuette in position on the housing.

3 Fit the fountainhead nozzle on the statuette. Having put the electricity circuit breaker in place and made sure that it is operational, switch on the power and test the flow and the shape of the spray. Adjust the rate of flow and the nozzle accordingly.

RIGHT A cross-section through a typical ornamental statuette fountain. The statuette is an immediate eye-catcher and perfect for enhancing a small garden pond.

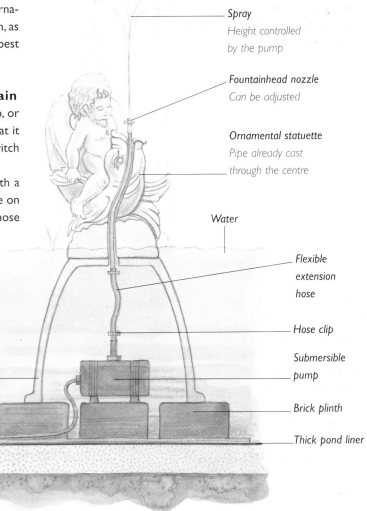

Spray
Height controlled by the pump

Fountainhead nozzle
Can be adjusted

Ornamental statuette
Pipe already cast through the centre

Water

Flexible extension hose

Hose clip

Submersible pump

Brick plinth

Thick pond liner

Housing to support statue

Hidden power cable

Sand

Soil

Cascades, canals and bogs

A basic pond is not just an attractive feature in its own right. It can also be used as a reservoir for feeding other

garden water features such as a cascade waterfall (which could also extend into a water rockery), a formal patio

or courtyard canal, or a bog garden. The moment the pond is in place, you can start planning.

DESIGNING AND MAKING CASCADES

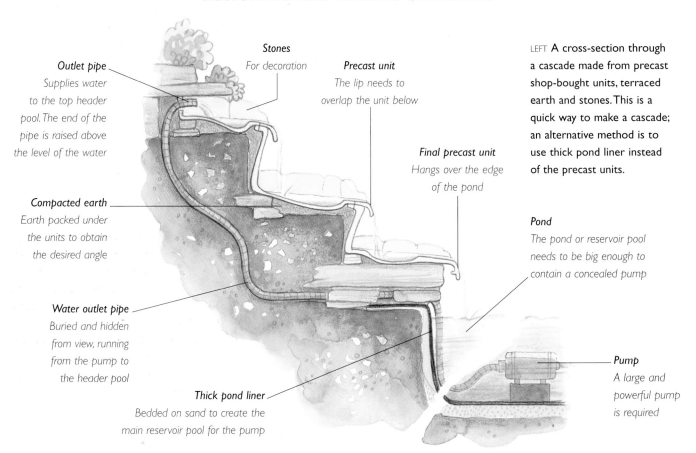

Outlet pipe
Supplies water to the top header pool. The end of the pipe is raised above the level of the water

Stones
For decoration

Precast unit
The lip needs to overlap the unit below

Final precast unit
Hangs over the edge of the pond

Compacted earth
Earth packed under the units to obtain the desired angle

Water outlet pipe
Buried and hidden from view, running from the pump to the header pool

Thick pond liner
Bedded on sand to create the main reservoir pool for the pump

Pond
The pond or reservoir pool needs to be big enough to contain a concealed pump

Pump
A large and powerful pump is required

LEFT A cross-section through a cascade made from precast shop-bought units, terraced earth and stones. This is a quick way to make a cascade; an alternative method is to use thick pond liner instead of the precast units.

Design notes

In essence, a cascade is a series of stepped pools, with a header pool at the top end and a reservoir at the bottom. The first problem you have to sort out is how to achieve the actual slope of the cascade. If your garden is on a slope and you want to build a big cascade, you do not need to do any landscaping; otherwise you have to import earth to make a little hillock.

If you are limited to a patio or roof garden, you can still have a cascade, although on a smaller scale – think in terms of a pot or container cascade. For a swift, easy answer, there are lots of kits for container cascades on the market, which contain the pump, container, and everything you need.

Building a cascade from precast units

Having excavated and built your pond, heaping the spoil to the side, take the first precast unit and bed it at the bottom of the mound of earth, so that it is hanging just over the edge of the pond. Fill the unit with water and adjust it (by packing earth underneath it) so that the water begins to run over the lip and into the pond. Take the second unit and lap it over the first, compacting the earth beneath it beforehand. Fill it with water and adjust its level (again by packing earth underneath it) so that the water overflows into the first unit and back into the pond. Continue lapping one unit over another until you get to the top of the slope. When you are pleased with the way the water flows, bolt or clip the units together.

Sit the pump in the pond, and run the water outlet pipe from the pond back up the slope of earth to the topmost unit. Bury the cables and pipes, landscape the whole mound much as you would a rockery, and plant out the area. Watch the performance of the cascade over several days to make sure it is working correctly. Check the water level when it is all switched off. If it is too low, there may be leaks in the system (tighten the hose clips), or you may need to adjust the way the plastic units lap over each other.

DESIGNING AND MAKING CANALS

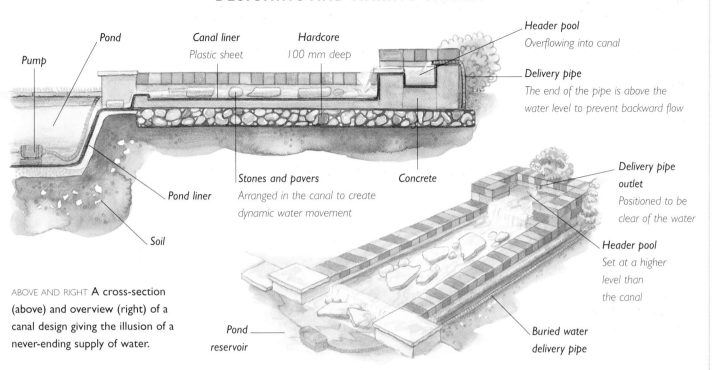

Pump

Pond

Canal liner
Plastic sheet

Hardcore
100 mm deep

Header pool
Overflowing into canal

Delivery pipe
*The end of the pipe is above the
water level to prevent backward flow*

Pond liner

Stones and pavers
*Arranged in the canal to create
dynamic water movement*

Concrete

Soil

Delivery pipe
outlet
*Positioned to be
clear of the water*

Header pool
*Set at a higher
level than
the canal*

Buried water
delivery pipe

Pond
reservoir

ABOVE AND RIGHT **A cross-section
(above) and overview (right) of a
canal design giving the illusion of a
never-ending supply of water.**

Design notes

To construct a canal, water is pumped into a header pool that
overflows into a straight channel, then into a pond. This is similar
to a cascade – water is pumped from a pond to a header pool,
where it then flows back to the pond. The good thing about a
canal is that it can be built with little or no gradient, so if you are
limited by a level site, but want some moving water, a canal is a
good compromise. Dramatic designs may channel water across a
paved area or even a lawn – the proviso being that the water must
be contained and not drain away. The size of the pump governs the
amount of water overflowing from the header pool.

Building a canal

Dig a shallow trench for the canal. One end should run into the
pond. Check with a spirit level that it is just about level, or at least
only sloping slightly (towards the pond). Fill the trench with
100 mm hardcore, and top with concrete. Line with plastic sheet,
and edge the canal with concrete slabs and bricks. Set the pump
in the pond and bury the delivery pipe alongside the trench, with
the outlet overhanging the top end of the canal. Cover the outlet
pipe with a slab. Scatter a few flat slates, broken pavers and small
stones along the canal bed to create interesting water movement.
Finally, fit an electricity circuit breaker.

MAKING A BOG GARDEN

Bog gardens – made by planting up shallow boggy areas around
the margins of a pond – can be used not only to enhance a pond
and make it appear much larger than it is, but also to provide an
environment for water-loving plants and wildlife.

Dig a gully (about 500 mm deep) around the edge of the pond.
Line it with inexpensive plastic sheet, piercing a few drainage
holes, and cover with a shallow layer of shingle. Mix the excavated
soil with lots of well-rotted organic matter, and put it back in the
gully. When it rains, the flow-off from the pond will help keep the
gully damp, making an area that is ideally suited to water-loving
plants. Once the plants are in place, insects, birds, and amphibious
creatures such as frogs, toads and newts will make an appearance.

RIGHT **A cross-section through the edge of a pond and bog
area. Note that the pond liner encompasses the bog area,
at which point it is pierced to allow a degree of drainage.**

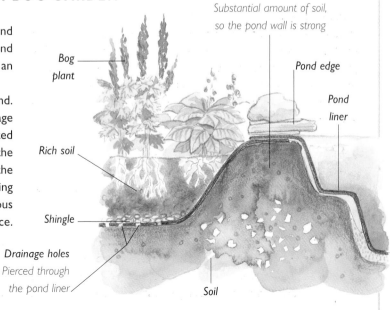

Soil
*Substantial amount of soil,
so the pond wall is strong*

Bog
plant

Pond edge

Pond
liner

Rich soil

Shingle

Drainage holes
*Pierced through
the pond liner*

Soil

Plants for water features

One of the chief pleasures of a water feature is that it provides an exciting environment for planting. One moment you have a lawn and a patio, and borders filled with the usual annuals and perennials, and the next you have the opportunity to extend your planting range with a vast assortment of water- and moisture-loving plants.

THE ROLE OF PLANTS FOR WATER FEATURES

Keeping the water healthy

While a pump, filter and fountain can be used to keep water clear, the whole task can be achieved more efficiently by choosing the right plants. You need submerged oxygenating plants to release oxygen into the water – good for fish and wildlife – and floating broad-leaf plants to use up some of the excess nutriments. The trick is getting the balance right. If there are too few plants, the water soon gets slimy and green, too many broad-leaf plants make the water get clogged up with debris, too few broad-leaf plants allow the sunlight to penetrate the water and overstimulate the growth of green algae. Be prepared to remove plants that start to dominate, or plants that fail.

Food for all

Water plants maintain the oxygen levels of the water in the pond, but they are also needed to maintain the overall cycle of life in the pond. The chain of events in the pond cycle is as follows: the plants produce oxygen and use up carbon dioxide; insects and animals eat the plants, use oxygen and produce carbon dioxide, and eat each other; the waste from animals and insects produces mineral salts, which plants need for healthy growth; plant debris is eaten by water snails and other creatures.

If you notice that one of the elements is beginning to dominate – too much algae, too many snails or whatever – it means that there is an imbalance in the pond that needs to be corrected.

DEEP-WATER PLANTS

Plant choice

Some deep-water plants live with their roots in deep water and have foliage growing both below and on the surface of the water, others are floating plants that drift around the pond, and certain plants grow totally below the surface of the water. Many people are keen to try water-lilies because they are so attractive, but the variety has to be carefully chosen to suit the size of the pond and the depth of water. In ideal conditions, most deep-water plants are fast-growing, so much so that they need to be regularly thinned.

Planting

While plants such as water-lilies need to be planted with their roots in a container on the floor of the pond, the floaters and the underwater oxygenators can simply be tossed into the water. The best way of planting bare-rooted plants such as water-lilies, is to remove all damaged foliage, cut away straggly roots, wash off all traces of algae, and insert the root system in a plastic planting basket filled with aquatic compost. The basket is positioned (on a stack of bricks if necessary) at the bottom of the pond.

RIGHT A detail showing plants in basket containers sited on the bottom of the deepest part of the pond. The leaves of the water-lily check the growth of algae, and the submerged plant pumps oxygen into the water.

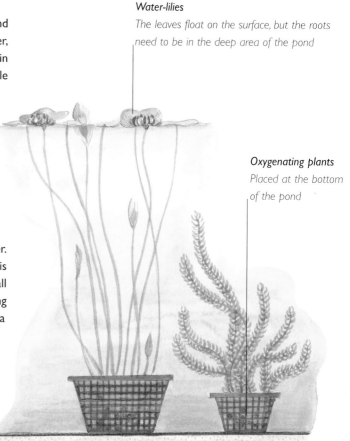

Water-lilies
The leaves float on the surface, but the roots need to be in the deep area of the pond

Oxygenating plants
Placed at the bottom of the pond

MARGINAL PLANTS

Plant choice

Marginal plants thrive in the shallow water around the edge or margins of a pond. Characteristically, marginal plants have strong vertical top growth, and relatively shallow root systems. While most marginals are at their best when their roots are actually in the water, many varieties are just as happy in the soil at the water's edge. Bog plants are suitable for this area. Some marginals produce strong, spiky roots that are capable of piercing plastic pond liners, so choose the varieties with care.

Planting

A planting scheme has to be planned to take into account both the idiosyncracies of the plants and their visual effect. Preferred water depths range from 300 mm through to 20 mm, some plants thrive in mud rather than water, and foliage height varies enormously. It's a good idea to have the plants with the lowest foliage on the shelved edge of the pond, and more vigorous plants in the mud at the water's edge. Experiment with various placings before you actually finalize their position on bank, shelf or underwater.

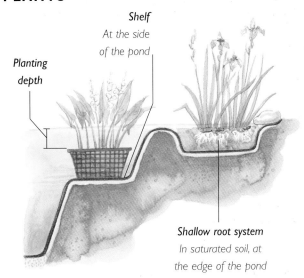

Shelf
At the side
of the pond

Planting
depth

Shallow root system
In saturated soil, at
the edge of the pond

ABOVE A marginal plant (left) sited on a shelf in the pond which raises it to an appropriate planting depth. On the right, a bog plant that likes the very damp or wet soil alongside the pond.

MOISTURE-LOVING PLANTS

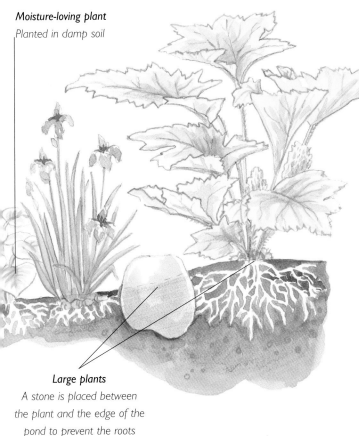

Moisture-loving plant
Planted in damp soil

Large plants
A stone is placed between
the plant and the edge of the
pond to prevent the roots
from damaging the liner

ABOVE Many of your garden plants will benefit by being moved closer to the water's edge. Beware of plants that have strong root systems.

Plant choice

Moisture-loving plants are best defined as plants that thrive in a moist environment – damp earth and a high humidity. They are perfect for linking features such as ponds and cascades to the beds in the rest of the garden. Be careful not to confuse bog plants with moisture-loving plants. The important difference between them is that while some moisture-loving plants will tolerate boggy soil conditions, mostly they prefer damp soil that is well drained and never waterlogged. When you are choosing plants, it is much better to select varieties that will thrive in damp soil, rather than plants that merely tolerate damp conditions. For best performance, you want plants that are totally happy, rather than plants that are making the best of a bad job!

Planting

Prepare the bed with lots of well-rotted organic material, and dig in clay granules if the soil is very sandy. Make sure that the ground remains damp but is not subject to waterlogging. Before buying a plant, find out whether its root depth and foliage height are suitable for the site. Try to grade the foliage height of the planting scheme as it moves away from the pond, so that your eye is gradually led up from the water's edge, and the foliage reaches maximum height with the moisture-loving plants. If you have doubts about the suitability of a plant, buy a small example and plant it to see whether it thrives in the given conditions. It is a good idea to visit all your local garden centres and water garden specialists, where hopefully you will see good examples of planting, and pick up some ideas before making your purchases.

Maintenance

For many people, part of the pleasure of having a pond complete with a pump, fountain, lots of plants, a fish or two, and perhaps a colony of frogs, is the fun involved in keeping the whole set-up in good condition. If you enjoyed playing with water and mud as a child, you'll be in your element.

POND MAINTENANCE

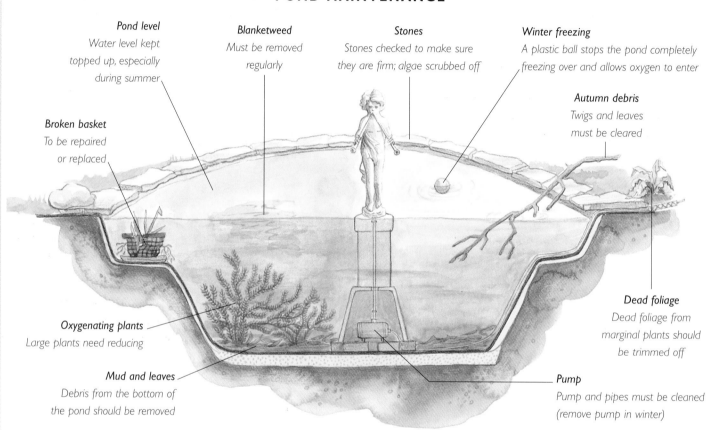

Pond level
Water level kept topped up, especially during summer

Blanketweed
Must be removed regularly

Stones
Stones checked to make sure they are firm; algae scrubbed off

Winter freezing
A plastic ball stops the pond completely freezing over and allows oxygen to enter

Autumn debris
Twigs and leaves must be cleared

Broken basket
To be repaired or replaced

Oxygenating plants
Large plants need reducing

Mud and leaves
Debris from the bottom of the pond should be removed

Dead foliage
Dead foliage from marginal plants should be trimmed off

Pump
Pump and pipes must be cleaned (remove pump in winter)

Cleaning the pond

Clean out the pond in the spring, when the leaf fall of the previous autumn is over and before all the pond plants start into new growth. Use a net on a stick to scoop out dead leaves and twigs. Remove all plants growing in baskets and pull off damaged foliage. Wash the plants and do your best to scrub off all traces of algae. If necessary, repair broken plant baskets with wire and fill them up with fresh soil and grit.

During the cleaning process, be very careful that you do not injure the fish, snails, frogs or anything else living in the mud. Finally, replace all the plants and top up the pond with water. If the pond is so wide that you cannot reach the middle with your net, ask a friend to help. Make a large scoop or drag net (a rectilinear frame of garden wire, with an old net curtain stretched across), and rig it with two long, strong ropes. Working on opposite sides of the pond, take turns pulling the net across.

> ### CAUTION
> During pond maintenance, make sure that you do not damage the liner. Avoid using sharp items such as sticks and garden rakes. Choose rakes with soft plastic prongs and nets with plastic hoops.

Hot and cold weather maintenance

Extreme weather conditions necessitate taking measures to protect the plants and wildlife from damage. In order to maintain the equilibrium of the pond in hot weather, you must check the pond every day and make sure it is topped up with water. If you see the fish gulping for air or notice that the algae is multiplying, then the chances are the pond needs more water and additional oxygenating plants.

In freezing weather, it is a good idea to float a large plastic ball on the water. The movement of the ball will prevent a small area from freezing over, and this clear water not only acts as a vent for toxic gases, but also helps reduce the pressure of the ice on the sides of the pond. Never try to break the ice on a pond with a spike or a hammer. The vibration may have an adverse effect on the fish, you might slip and fall in the pond, and you could drop the tool and damage the liner.

Removing algae

When a build-up of algae or blanketweed (*Spirogyra*) begins to choke the pond, take a couple of bamboo canes and use them to carefully tease the blanketweed away from the various plants. With a cane in each hand, use one cane to support the plant, while poking the other cane into the blanketweed. Roll the weed cane until it takes on a mass of green, and then pull the weed out of the water and wipe it off into a bucket. Continue teasing the weed away from the plants and rolling it on to the cane until the whole mess has been removed from the pond.

Routine plant care

Caring for pond plants is an ongoing procedure that runs right across the year, but spring and summer are the busiest. Spring is the time to clean out the pond, trim decaying leaves from the plants, and remove debris with a scoop net. Do not be tempted to use a lawn rake or fork to remove debris, because if you lose concentration and the tool slips into the pond, you will be left with a punctured pond liner that needs repairing.

You might also need to thin out some of the more rampant oxygenators and divide up clumps of floating plants. Scoop out the plants, divide them up on the bank, and then return small, healthy sections to the pond. Spring is also a good time for reassessing the combination of plants in the pond. You may wish to increase your stock and introduce new plants to the pond. Or if you have too many of a particular plant, now is the time for a cull.

In summer you will need to be constantly trimming off yellowing and dying leaves and shaping up plants, in order to ensure that the pond stays clear of decaying matter and so that plants are encouraged to produce new flowerheads. When you are removing weed and decaying leaves, don't just throw them on the compost heap, but wash them in a bucket of pond water to remove all the small creatures such as water boatmen and snails, and carefully return these to the pond. When you are cleaning out debris, be careful not to let any seed pods fall to the bottom of the pond, or you'll have a crop of unwanted plants.

If you want to introduce new plants and yet you are also worried about introducing unwanted creatures, leave the new plants in a bucket of water for a few days – in a sort of watery quarantine – and wash them prior to putting them into the pond.

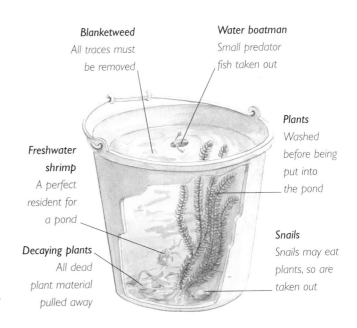

Blanketweed
All traces must be removed

Water boatman
Small predator fish taken out

Plants
Washed before being put into the pond

Freshwater shrimp
A perfect resident for a pond

Snails
Snails may eat plants, so are taken out

Decaying plants
All dead plant material pulled away

ABOVE When you buy new plants, use a quarantine bucket (kept away from your pond) which allows you to select precisely what you do and don't want to introduce into your pond.

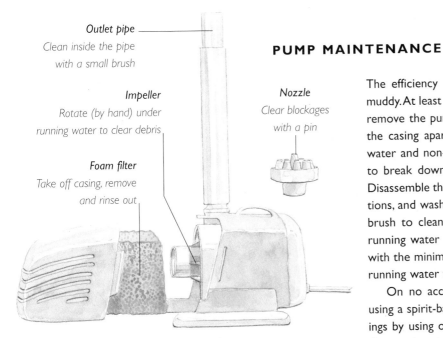

Outlet pipe
Clean inside the pipe with a small brush

Impeller
Rotate (by hand) under running water to clear debris

Nozzle
Clear blockages with a pin

Foam filter
Take off casing, remove and rinse out

ABOVE Clean your pump regularly. If dirt and weed builds up in the filter, the pump will lose power and then grind to a halt. Turn off the power as soon as you notice a pump has stopped working.

PUMP MAINTENANCE

The efficiency of a pump will soon be affected if the water is muddy. At least once a week in high summer, switch off the power, remove the pump from the water, and service it as follows. Ease the casing apart, take out the foam filter and wash it in warm water and non-scented liquid soap. Squeeze the foam repeatedly to break down the compacted mud that collects at its centre. Disassemble the pump and the various fountain pipes and connections, and wash them in warm water and liquid soap. Use a small brush to clean inside the pipes. Turn the impeller round under running water to remove all traces of grit, so that it spins freely with the minimum of friction. Finally, wash the whole pump under running water to remove the soap, and put it back in the water.

On no account try to speed up the cleaning procedure by using a spirit-based solvent, and do not attempt to ease the bearings by using oil. Both these substances will pollute the water in the pond and damage fish and plants. Make sure, when you are testing the pump prior to putting it back into the water feature, that you connect it up via an electricity circuit breaker.

Part 2: **Projects**

Container bog garden

If you would like to have a water garden, but are short of space, or you simply want to try working on something very basic before going on to greater things, a container bog garden is the answer. The waterlogged soil is perfect for a wide range of bog plants. Garden centres often group plants that enjoy wet, well-drained soil together with those that prefer boggy conditions, so make sure that the plant you choose is happy in waterlogged soil, such as one of the water irises.

TIME

One day (two hours to prepare the containers and pot the plant, and the rest of the day for the resin sealant to cure).

SAFETY

If you are allergic to resin, wear protective gloves and follow the manufacturer's advice closely.

YOU WILL NEED

Materials *for a container bog garden 450 mm in diameter and 300 mm high*

- Ceramic outer container: about 450 mm in diameter and 200 mm deep
- Wine bottle corks (to plug the drainage holes in the outer container)
- Resin sealant (for use inside outer container if it is porous): amount to suit the size of your chosen pot

- Washed shingle (small): 1 bucketful
- Ceramic inner container: about 300 mm in diameter and 250 mm deep with drainage holes
- Broken plant pot crocks
- Soil and organic matter mix suitable for plant
- A bog plant

Tools
- Disposable container
- Paintbrush: 30 mm wide

BOG PLANT BEAUTY

Choose two ceramic containers that complement each other in colour or shape. The large outer pot needs to be low and broad, the inner pot relatively tall and slender, and both pots require a strong rim or lip. Ideally, the outer pot needs to be glazed inside and out (or made from non-porous stoneware), and to have no drainage holes. But such pots are very difficult to find, so at the very least make sure that your chosen pot is glazed on the outside. Any drainage holes will be plugged with corks.

Avoid traditional non-glazed earthenware flowerpots, because they are thin-bodied, fragile and porous. To test the porosity of a pot, dab it with a wet finger and see what happens to the moisture. If it sits on the surface like a bead, the pot is non-porous, whereas if it is soaked up, the pot is porous. Before you make your final choice, sit the pots one within the other, make allowances for the depth of the gravel, and see how they look together.

CROSS-SECTION OF THE BOG GARDEN

Bog plant
Ask your local nursery to recommend a species

Inner container
300 mm in diameter and 250 mm deep

Soil
To suit your chosen plant

Outer container
450 mm in diameter and 200 mm deep

Water

Shingle

Step-by-step: **Making the container bog garden**

Porosity
If the pot is glazed on the inside
you can miss out step 2

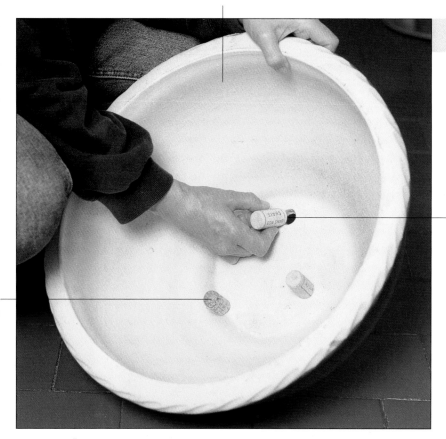

1 Take the outer container, and plug any drainage holes. Dip the corks in the resin sealant and push them into the drainage holes. When you have achieved a tight fit, dribble more sealant around the corks.

Tight fit
Make sure that
the cork plugs
the hole
effectively

Cork
The corks must
be dry when
you put them
in the holes

Sealing
For porous containers. Let the
sealant dry between coats

Compacting
Press the shingle down to
make a firm bed

Coverage
Very porous
ceramic may
need extra
coats of
sealant

2 Pour sealant into the disposable container and thin to a wash with water. Use the paintbrush to brush three or more generous coats of sealant over the inside of the bowl (until you consider it is watertight), and leave it to dry.

Shingle
Use nicely
coloured,
rounded
pebbles

3 Spread shingle inside the container, filling the pot to about half its total depth. Be careful not to dislodge the corks.

Cleaning
Wash out the container
first if it is dirty

4 Take the inner container
and place a layer of broken
crocks over the drainage holes.
Fill it with soil mix, then pot up
your chosen bog plant.

Blocking
the holes
Wash broken
crocks and
lay them to
cover the
drainage holes

Handling
Be careful not
to crack the
containers –
they can be
very fragile

5 Put the inner container in
position, and then very
carefully fill the outer bowl with
water to within 50 mm of the
rim. Check for leakage, wait
awhile for the soil to become
waterlogged, and then adjust the
level of the water.

Helpful hint

Check the water daily and
adjust the level to suit the
needs of your chosen plant.
Get into the routine of
filling the watering can and
leaving it to stand
overnight, so that the water
added to the plant is at a
constant temperature.

Water level
Inspect the
water level
every day and
keep it topped
up to within
50 mm of
the rim

Wall mask waterspout

An enclosed patio or courtyard is wonderfully enhanced by the addition of a classical

mask waterspout. The mask is set into a wall and water gently trickles from it into a

decorative reservoir pool. The sight and sound of the water sparkling as it falls

soothe the senses beautifully – the whole effect is truly magical!

TIME

Two days to prepare the
planter and fix the mask
(allow seven days for the
mortar to cure).

SPECIAL TIP

The electrics must be
protected by an electricity
circuit breaker, which will
instantly cut off the
electricity supply if the pump
or cable is damaged.

YOU WILL NEED

Materials

- Plastic rainwater pipe:
  250 mm long and 60 mm
  in diameter
- Mortar: 1 part (25 kg)
  cement, 3 parts (75 kg)
  sharp sand
- Mask made of cast lead,
  plastic, ceramic or concrete
- Heavy-duty plastic hosepipe:
  3 m long and 20 mm in
  diameter (the type that will
  go around corners without
  deforming)
- Roofing slate: 1 slate
- Submersible pump with cable
- Flexible armoured plastic
  pipe (long enough to
  protect the full length of
  the pump's electric cable)
- Electricity circuit breaker
- Silicone sealant

- Waterproof sealant: 1 litre
- Screws: 4 x 60 mm long
- Hose clips: 2 x 20 mm clips
- Bracket and clips to fix
  hosepipe: 2 x 20 mm clips

Tools

- Tape measure and a piece
  of chalk
- Mason's hammer
- Cold chisel
- Wheelbarrow
- Bucket
- Shovel
- Bricklayer's trowel
- Mortar float
- Electric hammer drill with a
  20 mm masonry bit
- Club hammer
- Pointing trowel
- Paintbrush
- Screwdriver

FALLING WATER

Study the site and decide on the best position for the waterspout,
the type of reservoir you want, and the route for the electricity.
For the reservoir, you can either adapt an existing raised bed as
shown, or use an old sink, stone tub, ceramic bowl or reservoir
kit. Measure the head of water (from the water level in the
reservoir to the mask spout) and purchase a submersible
pump to suit. The pump is set on a brick, with both the electric cable and the hose running through a short length of
plastic rainwater pipe, which protects them from being
crushed by the wall. For extra protection, the cable is passed
through an armoured plastic pipe. Water is pumped from the
reservoir, through the wall, up to the mask, and through the spout.
It drops on to the slate and dribbles back to the reservoir.

CROSS-SECTION OF THE WALL MASK WATERSPOUT

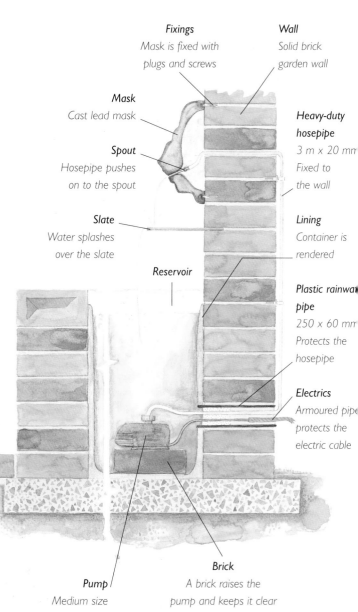

Fixings
*Mask is fixed with
plugs and screws*

Wall
*Solid brick
garden wall*

Mask
Cast lead mask

Spout
*Hosepipe pushes
on to the spout*

**Heavy-duty
hosepipe**
*3 m x 20 mm
Fixed to
the wall*

Slate
*Water splashes
over the slate*

Lining
*Container is
rendered*

Reservoir

**Plastic rainwater
pipe**
*250 x 60 mm
Protects the
hosepipe*

Electrics
*Armoured pipe
protects the
electric cable*

Pump
Medium size

Brick
*A brick raises the
pump and keeps it clear
from sludge build-up*

Step-by-step: **Making the wall mask waterspout**

Cleaning
Remove the earth and plants and wash the area clean

Spout hole
Ensure that you drill at right angles to the wall

Hammer drill
Use a hammer drill and a masonry bit

Render
The reservoir needs to be made waterproof

Mask
Use the mask to establish the position of the spout hole

1 Remove the contents of the raised bed. Using the mason's hammer and cold chisel, chop a hole, 70 mm in diameter, through the bottom part of the wall and into the bed. Slide the plastic rainwater pipe in place and render the interior of the bed with mortar, using the bricklayer's trowel and the mortar float.

2 Holding the mask in place, establish the precise position of the spout hole, and then drill a hole through the thickness of the wall. It must be wide enough for the hosepipe.

Chisel
Use a good-quality cold chisel to chop out the mortar

Gloves
You may slip with the hammer, so wear gloves to protect your hands

3 Ease one end of the hosepipe through the hole in the wall. Establish the position of the slate in relation to your chosen mask, and use the club hammer and cold chisel to chop out the mortar to make a slot to hold the slate. Adjust the slate so that it will interrupt the water flow. Use the pointing trowel to fix it in place with mortar.

Covering
To avoid filling the reservoir with dust and grit, which will block the pump, cover the top with a plastic bag or something similar

Slate
*Interrupts the falling water so the stream
is diffused as it enters the pool*

4 Set the pump in place in the trough and pass the pump's electric cable through the armoured plastic pipe. Fit an electricity circuit breaker. Pull the other end of the hosepipe through into the reservoir, and push it on to the pump outlet. Stop the rainwater pipe with mortar and cap it off with a squirt of silicone sealant.

Hosepipe
*The hosepipe
should fit tightly
on to the pump*

Alignment
*Check that the
mask, slate and
centre of the
reservoir are
in line with
each other*

5 Brush a generous coat of waterproof sealant over the interior of the whole reservoir. With the screwdriver, screw the mask in place, push the hosepipe on to the spout and fix with the hose clips. Fit the hosepipe to the back of the wall with brackets and bracket clips. Wait seven days for the mortar and sealant to cure before turning on the waterspout's water supply.

Helpful hint

If the delivery of water is slow or no more than a dribble, check to make sure that the water hose isn't deformed at the point where it enters the wall.

Inspirations: Wall masks

A classical mask peeping out from behind a curtain of foliage – perhaps the face of an ancient Greek god – is a wonderful, mood-setting feature. It instantly imparts a sense of history to any space. Modern masks can be used to enhance a variety of garden themes. A Japanese mask would complement an austere gravel and stone Japanese garden. Dramatic African or Indian masks would combine well with tropical plants. And masks by artists can be used to inject wit, humour and theatrical effect.

ABOVE **A pottery sun mask, and a** terracotta urn adorned with classical imagery, focus attention on this half-hidden niche at the end of a path. Surrounded by moisture-loving, shade-tolerant plants, this is a beautiful and tranquil corner. The mask spouts a fine stream of water for visual and musical effect.

LEFT The waterspout mask in Heatercombe Gardens in Somerset, England. The perfectly round pool is echoed in the rising sun imagery of the niche. Together with the weathered stone of the walls and pool, and the established vines, the design successfully gives the impression that the pool is ancient – perhaps a Roman well or spring.

ABOVE A modern wall mask with an aged appearance, designed by Claire Whitehouse, at Hampton Court Palace, England. The Greek-style mask trickles water into a stone trough. The pump is placed in the trough and the water delivery pipe runs up the back of the wall.

Mini marble fountain

A fountain gently spouting and overflowing, marbles and pebbles glistening in the water, goldfish shimmering in the sun: this project has all of these. Although the fountain is tiny and the goldfish are made from copper, it is delightful and would be perfect on a patio or as a centrepiece to bring good Feng Shui to a courtyard.

TIME

One day (three hours to prepare the containers and position the pump, and the rest of the day to complete).

SAFETY

Some mini pumps are not suitable for outdoor use, so check before you buy.

PLAN VIEW OF THE MINI MARBLE FOUNTAIN

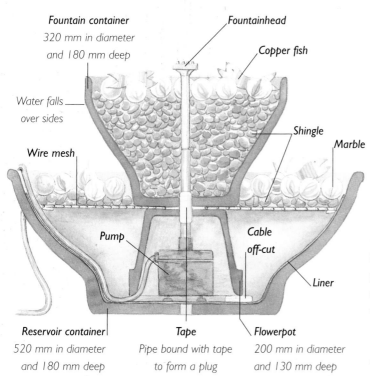

Fountain container
320 mm in diameter and 180 mm deep

Fountainhead

Copper fish

Water falls over sides

Shingle

Marble

Wire mesh

Pump

Cable off-cut

Liner

Reservoir container
520 mm in diameter and 180 mm deep

Tape
Pipe bound with tape to form a plug

Flowerpot
200 mm in diameter and 130 mm deep

DESIGN FOR COPPER FISH

Eye hole
Punched or drilled

Copper
70 mm long, 23 mm wide and 1 mm (or less) thick

(PLAN VIEW)

Copper is bent into this shape

A FOUNTAIN AND A BRIMMING POOL

In essence the project is made up from three ceramic containers – a large, wide pot for the main reservoir, a medium-sized pot for the fountain, and a small flowerpot to contain and conceal the pump and support the fountain pot. The reservoir container can be glazed or unglazed (it will be lined with plastic so it does not matter if it is porous). Wire mesh lies across the top, on to which a layer of marbles is placed. The fountain container is filled with shingle to support the fountainhead and displace the water.

The pump draws water up from the reservoir and pushes it out of the fountainhead, the fountain pot fills and overflows, and the water runs back down to feed the reservoir. When the pump is switched off, the water ceases flowing and gradually trickles back to the reservoir. You may choose any shape of container, as long as the size is such that there is always slightly more water in the reservoir than in the fountain container. The copper goldfish will slowly age to an attractive, irridescent blue-green.

YOU WILL NEED

Materials
for a fountain 520 mm in diameter and 315 mm high
• Ceramic container for main reservoir: about 520 mm in diameter and 180 mm deep
• Plastic pond liner: 900 mm long and 900 mm wide (allows for cutting waste)
• Small submersible pump
• Flexible armoured plastic pipe: long enough to protect the pump cable
• Electricity circuit breaker
• Fountainhead: with extension tube to fit your pump
• Roll of masking tape
• Flowerpot: about 200 mm in diameter and 130 mm deep
• Galvanized 6 mm wire mesh: 600 mm long and 600 mm wide (allows for cutting waste)

• Ceramic container for fountain: about 320 mm in diameter and 180 mm deep with a hole in the bottom
• Shingle (small): half a bucketful of washed shingle
• Copper sheet: 150 mm square and 1 mm thick
• Marbles: 100 glass marbles in assorted colours and sizes

Tools
• Tape measure and a piece of chalk
• Scissors: to cut the plastic
• Knife
• Wire snips
• Pliers
• Scissors: heavy-duty scissors to cut the copper sheet

Step-by-step: Making the mini marble fountain

Liner
If the liner is dirty, wash it before you begin

Size
If you are worried about over-trimming the liner, leave the trimming until the container is full of water

Trimming
Cut off the excess liner 10 mm below the rim

1 Take the reservoir container and use the tape measure, chalk, scissors and knife to trim the pond liner to fit. It should cover the inside of the bowl to within 10 mm of the rim.

Plug
Squeeze the masking tape plug into a cone shape

2 Put the pump in the bottom of the bowl, making sure that the cable is protected by the armoured pipe and the electricity circuit breaker. Fit the fountainhead extension tube to the pump, wrapping masking tape around the tube to make a pliable, cone-shaped plug.

Helpful hint

The cone-shaped plug of masking tape doesn't need to be a watertight fit in the hole, only tight enough to hold the tube in place and to ensure that the top bowl is always topped up – so that the water overflows.

Mesh size
Choose the smallest mesh size that you can find

3 Set the flowerpot upside-down over the pump, pushing the cone-shaped plug of the extension tube through the drainage hole. Use the wire snips and pliers to shape the galvanized mesh into a large disc that fits over the reservoir pot. The fountainhead extension tube pokes through the mesh. The disc should be supported at its centre by the flowerpot, and at its rim by the reservoir pot.

Folded edge
Fold over the edge of the mesh using the pliers

Centre hole
Cut a hole in the mesh so that it fits over the plug

Fountainhead
Pack the shingle tightly around the head

Copper sheet
Choose thin copper that can be cut easily

Shingle
Spread a layer of shingle to completely cover the mesh

Scissors
Use heavy-duty scissors to cut the copper

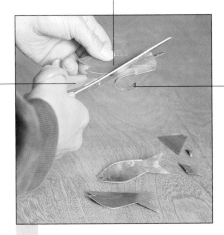

Sharp edges
Be careful not to cut your fingers on the sharp edges

4 Put the fountain container on the upturned flowerpot and wire mesh, fitting the fountainhead on the extension tube, and top up the pot with shingle. Cover the wire mesh with a thin layer of shingle, so the plastic liner cannot be seen.

5 Draw the goldfish on the copper sheet and cut them out with the heavy-duty scissors. Scatter the marbles and fish over the shingle in both of the containers. Fill the reservoir container with water, and switch on the power.

Romantic fountain

There are at least four reasons to install a traditional romantic fountain in your pond: you can appreciate the beauty of the fountain statuette, the sound of the water is delightful, the oxygenated water is good for the pond life and, best of all, the whole thing can be set up in a morning and running by the afternoon.

TIME

One day (a couple of hours to sort out the pump and the fountain, and the rest of the day to complete).

SAFETY

Ask a helper to watch over you while you are bridged over the pond – just in case!

YOU WILL NEED

Materials *for a statuette 430 mm high in a pond 475 mm deep*
- Rubber mat: about 450 mm long and 300 mm wide (or to suit your plinth)
- Bricks: sufficient to bring the top of the plinth level with surface of the water
- Concrete or ceramic pot with a hole in the base to use as a plinth: 400 mm high
- Submersible pump: a large pump to suit the height of your statuette
- Fountainhead: with connections to fit both the statuette and the pump
- Flexible armoured plastic pipe: long enough to protect the full length of the pump cable
- Electricity circuit breaker
- Fountain statuette: 430 mm high, made from concrete, stone or fibreglass

Tools
- Extension ladder: long enough to bridge pond
- Plank: long and narrow enough to fit the ladder
- Steel tape measure

A DELIGHTFUL SPRAY OF WATER

Decide how best to bridge your pond with the ladder (you lie across it in order to install the fountain without getting into the pond yourself) and how to ensure that the ladder is both stable and secure. Calculate the number of bricks needed to bring the plinth up to the surface level of the water. Work out how you are going to site the pump under the plinth, with the power cable running back to the mains, and with the outlet tube of the pump running up through the hole in the plinth to the connection on the underside of your statuette. Plan the route of the cable so that it can be hidden as it exits the pond. Gather the various components together on land and have a dry-run fitting before you go near the water.

CROSS-SECTION OF THE FOUNTAIN

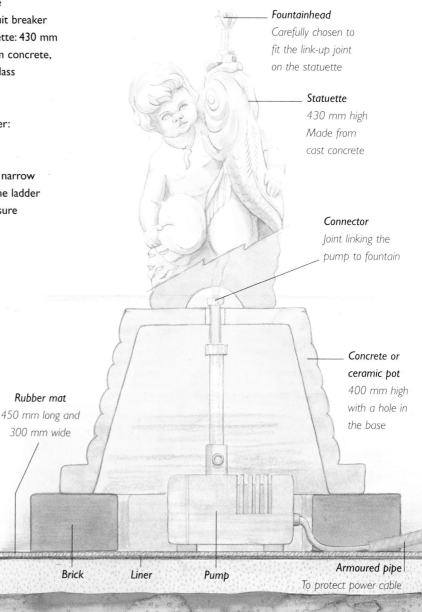

Fountainhead
Carefully chosen to fit the link-up joint on the statuette

Statuette
430 mm high
Made from cast concrete

Connector
Joint linking the pump to fountain

Concrete or ceramic pot
400 mm high with a hole in the base

Rubber mat
450 mm long and 300 mm wide

Brick   Liner   Pump

Armoured pipe
To protect power cable

Step-by-step: **Making the romantic fountain**

Plank
*Use a plank to
distribute your weight*

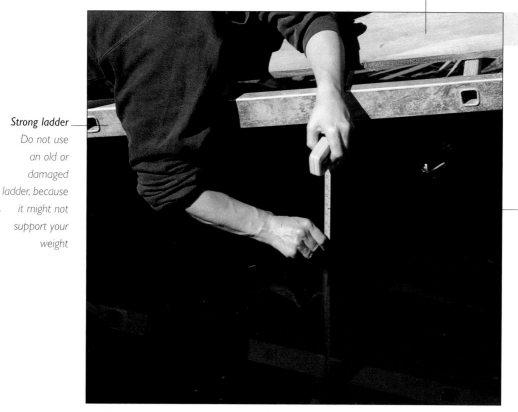

Strong ladder
*Do not use
an old or
damaged
ladder, because
it might not
support your
weight*

1 Bridge the water with the
ladder and the plank, to
allow you to work in reasonable
comfort over the centre of the
pond. Lower the tape measure
into the pond to find out the
depth of the water (the distance
between the pond liner and the
surface of the water).

Tape measure
*For an accurate
reading, keep the
tape measure
vertical*

Height
*Raise the
statuette to
a height
where it sits
on the surface
of the water*

2 Have a trial run to assess
how many bricks will be
required. Spread the rubber mat
on the lawn, and start positioning
the bricks to take the full weight
of the concrete plinth. Build up
the bricks until you raise the top
of the plinth to be level with the
surface of the water.

Helpful hint

The size and weight of the
plinth relate to the size of
the sculpture. If the plinth is
very weighty, you may need
to set up two ladders, so a
friend can help. The plinth
will have to be pushed
across one of the planks.

Be careful
Do not drop the bricks into place,
as they will damage the pond liner

Pump setting
If the pump has flow controls, turn these
to full and adjust later if necessary

Brick
foundation
Arrange the
bricks to make
a broad base
for the plinth

Clean
rubber mat
Wash the
mat before
use to avoid
contaminating
the pond

Safety
Disconnect the
pump while
you are in
contact with
the water

3 When you are satisfied with the trial run, move the whole arrangement into the pond. Start by setting the bricks on the rubber mat, laying them around a space for the pump. Make sure that every brick is stable. You might need small wedges of tile or slate to adjust the height of the bricks. Put the plinth on to check.

4 Put the pump on the mat, encircled by the bricks, and carefully fit the fountainhead connecting tube. Slide the armoured plastic pipe over the electric cable and fit the electricity circuit breaker. Remove your hands from the water, ask a helper to switch on the power, and check that the pump is working.

Pipe position
Ease the pipe up and
through the hole

Ageing
If you like, brush a little milk on the
statuette to encourage algae to form

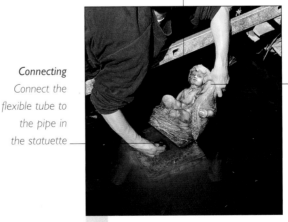

Connecting
Connect the
flexible tube to
the pipe in
the statuette

Be careful
Avoid holding
the statuette at
a fragile point

Plinth
Carefully lower
the plinth over
the pump

5 Switch off the power. Position the plinth so that the pump is fully enclosed, with the extension tube running up through the central hole in the plinth. Repeat the checking procedure.

6 Fit the connecting tube to the statuette, and place the statuette squarely on the plinth, making sure that it is level. Finally, re-run the checking procedure to make sure that you have not dislodged the pump.

French millstone bell fountain

This is a wonderfully tranquil feature to have in a garden. The central French millstone, out of which water wells up into a bell shape, is reminiscent of cobbled courtyards in Provence, bubbling spring waters, and times past. This particular design, which incorporates a surrounding ring of shingle and stones, also draws inspiration from traditional Japanese gardens.

TIME

Half a day (three hours to dig the hole and arrange the bricks and stones, and an hour to bury the power cable and fine-tune the fountain).

SAFETY

The millstone is heavy, so protect your hands with gloves and get help with the lifting.

YOU WILL NEED

Materials *for a millstone fountain 1.25 m in diameter*
- Bricks: about 20 house bricks – enough to edge a circle 1.25 m in diameter
- Sand: a wheelbarrow load
- Sump: a preformed plastic liner about 660 mm in diameter, with a lid to fit
- Small submersible pump
- Fountainhead with a telescopic extension tube
- Flexible armoured plastic pipe: long enough to protect the full length of pump cable
- Electricity circuit breaker
- Millstone: a concrete disc about 400 mm in diameter and 100 mm thick
- Shingle (medium): 50 kg
- Pebbles and cobbles: 25 kg
- Stone: a single carefully chosen "guardian" stone
- Rockery plants

Tools
- Tape measure and string line
- Spade
- Wheelbarrow
- Spirit level

CROSS-SECTION OF THE FRENCH MILLSTONE FOUNTAIN

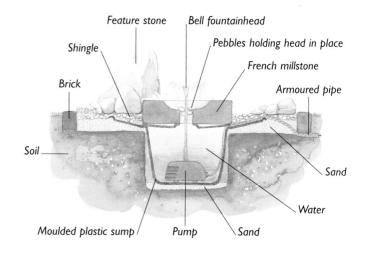

Feature stone Bell fountainhead
Shingle Pebbles holding head in place
Brick French millstone
Armoured pipe
Soil
Sand
Moulded plastic sump Pump Sand Water

PLAN VIEW OF THE FRENCH MILLSTONE FOUNTAIN

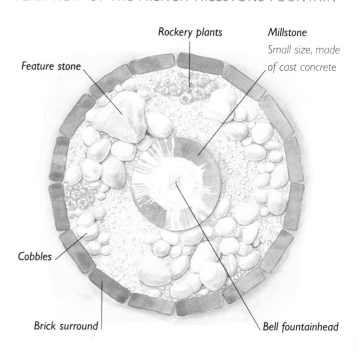

Rockery plants Millstone
Small size, made of cast concrete
Feature stone
Cobbles
Brick surround Bell fountainhead

A BUBBLING FRENCH SPRING

The working action of this fountain is beautifully simple – the pump pushes water up through the fountainhead, it falls in a bell shape on the millstone and the surrounding stones, and then flows back into the sump. The diameter of the sump you purchase must be greater than that of the millstone, and the pump must be powerful enough to push the water up through the thickness of the millstone and on through the fountainhead.

The good thing about this project is that (apart from concealing the power cable) it can be fitted directly into the middle of a lawn without much upset. The telescopic extension tube for the fountainhead is a clever item: you simply adjust the length of the tube to suit the thickness of the millstone and your design features. If you need to create more height with extra cobbles around the fountain, you just lengthen the tube to fit. When selecting the pump, measure the distance between the level of the water in the sump and the top of the millstone, then get a pump that is powerful enough to do the job.

Step-by-step: **Making the French millstone bell fountain**

Structure
The moulded pattern of the surround channels the water into the sump

Sand
Spread an even layer of sand over the earth

Sump brim
Has to catch all the water from the fountain, to channel it back to the pump. The bigger the pump, the more spray is created, and the wider the diameter of the sump brim needs to be

1 Use the tape measure and string line to scribe out a circle 1.25 m in diameter. Dig out the whole area to the depth of the brick edge. Dig a hole in the centre deep enough for the sump, plus 50 mm (for the sand). Edge the circle with bricks. Cover the area between the brick edge and the hole for the sump with a layer of sand 50 mm deep.

Sump lid
Slide the lid over the pump outlet pipe and locate it on the surround

2 Place the sump in the hole and bed the rim in the sand. Arrange the pump (connecting the extension tube and fountainhead), protect the full length of the cable with the armoured pipe, install the electricity circuit breaker and make sure that it is operational.

Helpful hint

If the pump fails to work, or the impeller bearing feels gritty when you turn it round by hand, the water is probably contaminated with sand. Wash the pump under running water, clean out the sump and change the water.

Fountainhead
*Make sure the head
is vertical*

3 After sliding the sump lid in place, so that the pump is protected and concealed, carefully lift the millstone into position. Check with the spirit level that the millstone is true and, if necessary, make adjustments with slivers of rock and sand.

Positioning
*Measure from
the brick
edging to the
edge of the
millstone, to
check the
millstone is
centred*

Levelling
*If necessary, use
small wedges of
stone to level up
the millstone*

4 Spread shingle over the sand and the sump lid, and centre the fountainhead within the millstone by packing it with pebbles. Finally, decorate the area with the guardian stone, cobbles and rockery plants.

Fountainhead
*Pack stone
around the
fountainhead
to centre it in
the millstone*

*Pebbles
and cobbles*
*Use different
sizes of stone to
create contrast*

Weeping hypertufa boulder

Hypertufa emerged in the 1940s in response to a craze for using old stone sinks as plant troughs. Enthusiasts were inspired to disguise glazed white kitchen sinks with a mixture of sphagnum moss, sand and cement – known as hypertufa – to make them look like stone. If you would like to create a weird and wonderful water feature, rather like a friendly alien life-form, a weeping hypertufa boulder is hard to beat!

TIME
Two weekends (two days to cast the boulder, five days for the hypertufa to cure, and two more days for excavating the boulder, digging the sump and fixing the pump).

SAFETY
This project involves a lot of strenuous digging and heaving, so you will need a willing helper.

YOU WILL NEED

Materials *for a boulder 500 mm high and 450 mm in diameter*
- Soft copper pipe: 900 mm long, 10 mm in diameter
- Hypertufa mix: 1 part (25 kg) cement, 1 part (25 kg) sharp sand, 4 parts (100 kg) sphagnum moss
- Sump: a preformed plastic sump about 660 mm in diameter, with a lid to fit
- Medium-size submersible pump
- Flexible armoured plastic pipe: long enough to protect the full length of the pump cable
- Electricity circuit breaker
- Sand: 100 kg (for bedding the slabs)
- Paving slabs: 4 cast concrete slabs about 450 mm square; a single paving slab 300 mm square

- Plastic tube: 500 mm long, 10 mm in diameter, with hose clips to fit (to link the copper pipe to the pump)
- Stone with a hole through to fit your boulder recess
- Cobbles: 25 kg
- Shingle (medium): 50 kg
- Stones: carefully chosen feature stones, size and shape to suit

Tools
- Tape measure and a piece of chalk
- Spade
- Wheelbarrow
- Garden trowel
- Shovel
- Tamping beam: 400 x 80 x 50 mm
- Rope
- Electric drill with a 25 mm masonry bit
- Spirit level
- Screwdriver

WEIRD BOULDER

Find an area of uncultivated ground for casting the boulder. Ideally, it needs to be well drained and made up of a mixture of heavy loam and clay. The boulder is cast upside-down, with the copper tube cast in place, and the "weep" hole is set in a hollow. All the hollows in the surface of the finished boulder start out as bumps on the sides of the hole, therefore the copper tube is inserted into a bump towards the bottom of the hole. The finished boulder weighs something over 150 kg, so it is quite a problem to get it out of the ground. One easy way is to dig a ramp down to the bottom of the cast hole – like a flight of shallow steps – and then loop a rope around the boulder and drag it out in stages.

CROSS-SECTION OF THE WEEPING HYPERTUFA BOULDER

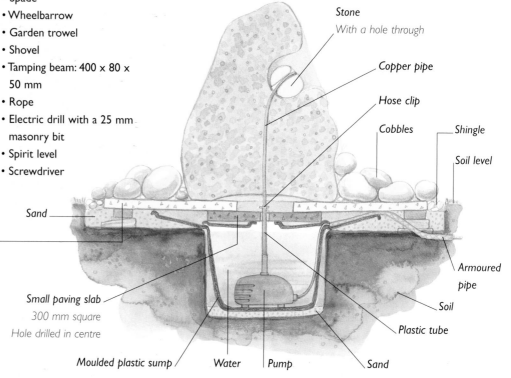

Stone
With a hole through

Copper pipe

Hose clip

Cobbles

Shingle

Soil level

Sand

Large paving slab
450 mm square, bedded on sand and propped with pieces of broken slab to make it slope slightly towards the central small paving slab

Small paving slab
300 mm square
Hole drilled in centre

Moulded plastic sump

Water

Pump

Sand

Plastic tube

Soil

Armoured pipe

Weeping hypertufa boulder

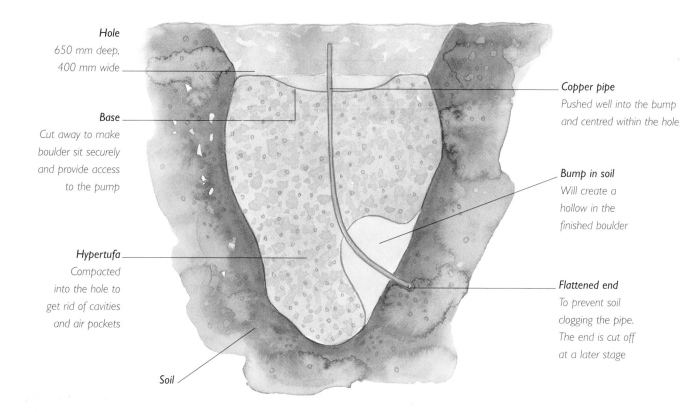

CROSS-SECTION OF THE SOIL MOULD AND BOULDER

Hole
*650 mm deep,
400 mm wide*

Base
*Cut away to make
boulder sit securely
and provide access
to the pump*

Hypertufa
*Compacted
into the hole to
get rid of cavities
and air pockets*

Soil

Copper pipe
*Pushed well into the bump
and centred within the hole*

Bump in soil
*Will create a
hollow in the
finished boulder*

Flattened end
*To prevent soil
clogging the pipe.
The end is cut off
at a later stage*

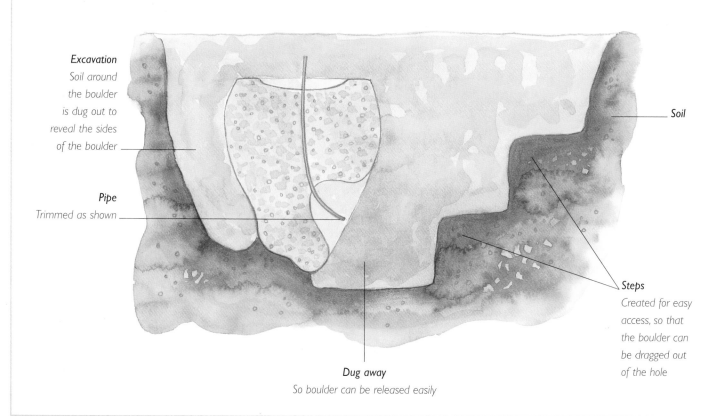

CROSS-SECTION SHOWING EXCAVATION

Excavation
*Soil around
the boulder
is dug out to
reveal the sides
of the boulder*

Pipe
Trimmed as shown

Soil

Steps
*Created for easy
access, so that
the boulder can
be dragged out
of the hole*

Dug away
So boulder can be released easily

SIDE VIEW OF THE BOULDER

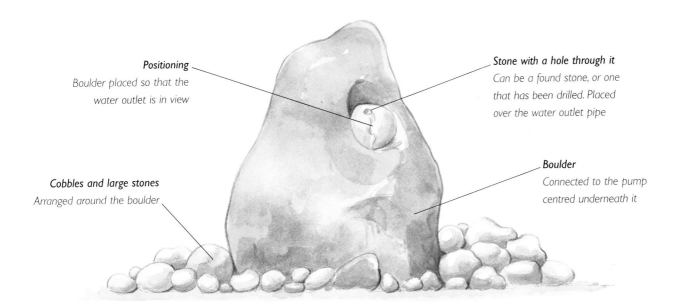

Positioning
Boulder placed so that the water outlet is in view

Stone with a hole through it
Can be a found stone, or one that has been drilled. Placed over the water outlet pipe

Boulder
Connected to the pump centred underneath it

Cobbles and large stones
Arranged around the boulder

PLAN VIEW SHOWING THE ARRANGEMENT OF THE PAVING SLABS

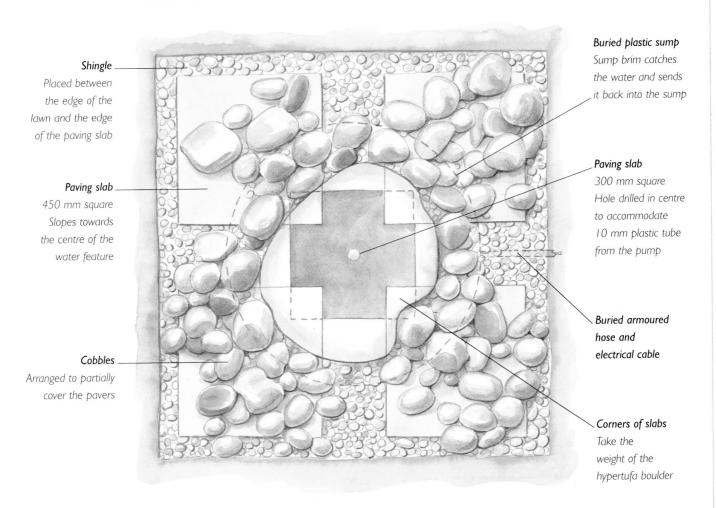

Shingle
Placed between the edge of the lawn and the edge of the paving slab

Paving slab
450 mm square Slopes towards the centre of the water feature

Cobbles
Arranged to partially cover the pavers

Buried plastic sump
Sump brim catches the water and sends it back into the sump

Paving slab
300 mm square Hole drilled in centre to accommodate 10 mm plastic tube from the pump

Buried armoured hose and electrical cable

Corners of slabs
Take the weight of the hypertufa boulder

Step-by-step: **Making the weeping hypertufa boulder**

Rim
Excavate under the rim to create a boulder that narrows at its base

Modelling
The hole starts as a cylindrical space. The rim is then undercut so that the girth of the hole is greater than the rim size. Bumps and indentations on the sides of the hole help the boulder to look more realistic

I Use the spade and garden trowel to carefully excavate the casting hole, making it about 650 mm deep and 450 mm wide. Dig the hole so that it bulges out at the centre and narrows towards the bottom. Model a bump on the side wall, towards the bottom of the hole.

Bump
The size of the bump will equal the size of the pocket in the boulder

Copper tube
Bend the tube so that it hooks into the bump

Tamping
Gently tap the hypertufa mix until water rises to the surface

Bump
The bump will hold its shape better in damp soil or clay soil. If your soil disintegrates, use a plastic container to form the bump

Air pockets
Make sure that you eliminate air pockets and fill all the gaps

2 Flatten one end of the soft copper pipe and push 50 mm of the pipe into the modelled bump (flattened end first). Centre the rest of the pipe within the hole.

3 Add water to the hypertufa ingredients to create a mix with a soft consistency. Shovel the hypertufa, little by little, into the hole, tamping it down with the beam so that it completely fills the hole and there are no air pockets.

Trowel work
Gradually excavate around the boulder

Careful handling
Lower the slab gently to avoid breaking the sump

Sand
Lay a generous bed of sand around the sump

Surrounding slabs
Position each large slab so the corner lies on the centre slab. Check with the spirit level. Prop the outer edge with pieces of broken slab so it slopes slightly towards the centre slab

Steps
Dig a flight of steps to run down to the bottom of the boulder

Centre slab
Place the slab on the sump lid and pull the plastic tube through

4 Wait four or five days for the hypertufa to cure, then use the spade and shovel to dig a flight of steps down to the bottom of the cast. Use the trowel to excavate around the form. Cut a hollow around the copper inlet pipe. With the rope, drag the cast boulder out of the hole and clean off any earth.

5 Set up the sump and pump, with armoured pipe and electricity circuit breaker, as described in step 2 of the French millstone bell fountain project on page 298. Surround with sand. Drill a hole through the centre of the 300 mm slab. Connect the plastic tube to the pump and run it through the drilled slab. Arrange the other four slabs.

Copper inlet pipe
Trim the end of the pipe to leave about 40 mm sticking out of the bottom

Connecting tube
Slide the plastic tube on to the copper inlet pipe

6 Use the hose clips and screwdriver to link the plastic tube to the copper pipe on the underside of the boulder, and then carefully centre the boulder on the slabs. Cut off the flattened portion of the copper pipe protruding from the recess and place the stone with the hole over the end. Decorate the area with shingle and stones.

Helpful hint

Be careful not to break off the delivery end of the copper pipe when moving the boulder. However, if you do, carefully excavate the bottom of the boulder to reveal more pipe.

Wine bottle spray fountain

Moving water and glass are a magical combination. There is something uplifting, almost spiritual, about the way that the water catches the sunlight as it sprays over the glass, and collects in the hollows in the bottles to make tiny pools. Moreover, this project is eco-friendly, because it recycles glass.

TIME

A day (four hours to dig the hole and arrange the bottles, and the rest of the time to bury the power cable and fine-tune the fountain).

SAFETY

The bottle circle is heavy, so handle it with care. Wear goggles when moving it.

YOU WILL NEED

Materials *for a fountain 910 mm in diameter*
- Sump: a sheet of plastic about 1.66 m in diameter (large enough to be pushed down into the hole with a generous overlap all round)
- Small submersible pump
- Flexible armoured plastic pipe: long enough to protect the full length of pump cable
- Electricity circuit breaker
- Pavers: 4 cast concrete slab segments to go around a hole 450 mm in diameter
- Fountainhead: with a telescopic extension tube to fit the pump

- Plastic rainwater pipe: 300 mm long and 80 mm in diameter
- Wine bottles: about 20 with a dimple in the bottom, in various colours
- Strong, waterproof sticky tape): 1 roll
- Bricks: 4 bricks
- Small cobbles and shingle: 12 kg of each
- Plastic carrier bags for infill: 4 bags
- Large cobbles: 25 kg

Tools
- Tape measure
- String line
- Spade

BOTTLE-BOTTOMS UP

This project is unusual because the decorative containment – the area around the fountainhead nozzle – is made from a clutch of upturned traditional wine bottles. The clever thing about gathering together groups of circular-section items of the same diameter, such as pipes, pencils or wine bottles, is that they automatically want to form a circle. However, you do have to begin with a circle of the same size at the centre.

Starting from the centre point, the number of circles or bottles always doubles for each consecutive ring – six in the first ring, twelve in the second ring, 24 in the third, and so on. So if you want to make a much larger arrangement than the one shown here, you just keep collecting bottles and alter the diameter of the circle to suit. The advantage of traditional wine bottles is that the dip in their base, when they are upturned, catches the water. We have used a concrete tile circle to surround the circle of bottles, but you could substitute bricks, cobbles, or whatever you wish.

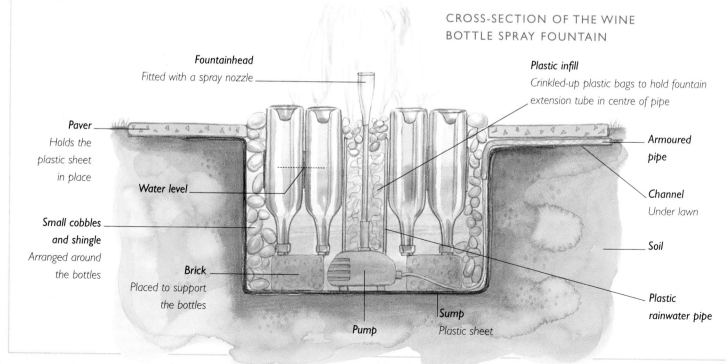

CROSS-SECTION OF THE WINE BOTTLE SPRAY FOUNTAIN

Fountainhead
Fitted with a spray nozzle

Plastic infill
Crinkled-up plastic bags to hold fountain extension tube in centre of pipe

Paver
Holds the plastic sheet in place

Armoured pipe

Channel
Under lawn

Water level

Small cobbles and shingle
Arranged around the bottles

Soil

Brick
Placed to support the bottles

Pump

Sump
Plastic sheet

Plastic rainwater pipe

Wine bottle spray fountain

PLAN VIEW OF THE WINE BOTTLE SPRAY FOUNTAIN

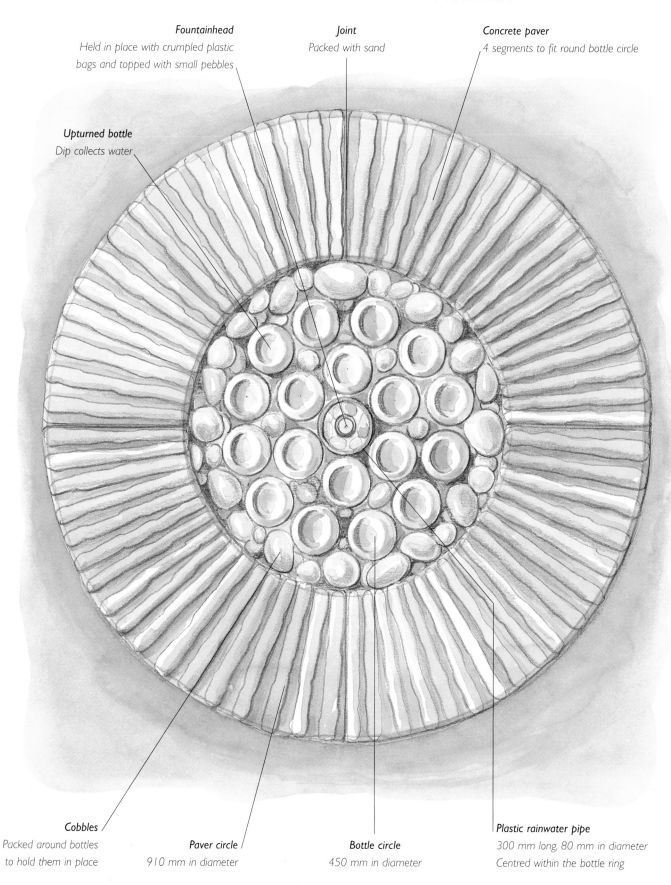

Fountainhead
Held in place with crumpled plastic bags and topped with small pebbles

Joint
Packed with sand

Concrete paver
4 segments to fit round bottle circle

Upturned bottle
Dip collects water

Cobbles
Packed around bottles to hold them in place

Paver circle
910 mm in diameter

Bottle circle
450 mm in diameter

Plastic rainwater pipe
300 mm long, 80 mm in diameter
Centred within the bottle ring

CUT-AWAY VIEW OF THE WINE BOTTLE SPRAY FOUNTAIN

Plastic sheet
Edge of plastic sheet held in place by the paving surround

Tape
Holds bottles together

Fountainhead spray nozzle
Fitted on top of extension tube

Plastic rainwater pipe
Same diameter as the bottles

Plastic infill
Crumpled plastic bags

Paving surround
Made up of 4 concrete pavers

Brick
Supports bottle circle

Pump

Sump
Plastic sheet 1.66 m in diameter

Earth dug away for paving
Grass left at a slightly higher level than pavers

Step-by-step: **Making the wine bottle spray fountain**

Plastic surround
Pull the plastic sheet out and over the edge of the hole to make a drainage apron

Pump
Sit the pump on the bottom of the sump and push on the telescopic extension tube

Testing the pump
Test the pump after every fitting stage, but stand back from the pump and water while the power is on

I Draw out a circle on the ground for the sump hole, using the tape measure and string line. Make it 450 mm in diameter. Cut back the turf and dig out the hole to a depth of 400 mm. Line the hole with the plastic sheet and put in the pump, complete with the fountainhead extension tube. Slide the pump cable down the armoured pipe and dig out a channel to run it below the level of the lawn. Fit the electricity circuit breaker.

Positioning
Set the tile segment in place while keeping the plastic in position

Handling
The tile segments are fragile, so lay them with care

2 Lay the four tile segments so that they encircle the sump hole and hold the plastic sheet securely in place. Connect the fountainhead to the extension tube, and switch on the power to check that everything is working.

Bottle size
Choose bottles of more or less the same diameter

Rainwater pipe
Diameter is 80 mm – similar to that of the bottles

Waterproof tape
Strap the inner ring of bottles with tape

3 Take the length of rainwater pipe, ring it with six wine bottles standing upright, and then bind the whole thing together with the waterproof tape.

Outer ring of bottles
Make sure the bottles fit together well

Be careful
The bottles are heavy, so take care when lifting

Waterproof tape
Strap the tape round the bottles several times until it all feels firm

Testing
Before you turn the bottles over, make sure each bottle is held firmly

Fountainhead
Positioned to go through the rainwater pipe in the centre of the bottle circle

4 Group twelve more wine bottles around the initial six-bottle core, and strap them together with waterproof tape. Continue with the strapping until the whole arrangement is secure.

5 Very carefully, turn the wine bottle arrangement over, and lower it in place over the fountainhead and pump. You might need to put a few bricks in the sump hole to bring the bottles up to the correct height. Fill the spaces around the bottles with small cobbles and shingle.

Cobbles
Use cobbles for decoration and as a way of stopping garden debris from getting into the sump hole

Centring
Use pebbles to centre the fountainhead in the pipe

6 Push plastic bags into the rainwater pipe to centre the fountainhead, and top up with small cobbles. Finally, fill the sump with water and position cobbles around the arrangement. Switch on the pump and adjust the fountainhead for best effect.

Adjusting
Adjust the position of the bottles by wedging pebbles around the edge

Helpful hint

If you want to take the project one step further, you could have the wine bottles set at different heights, with a coloured uplighter lamp installed in the sump to illuminate the bottles and the fountain.

Japanese deer scarer

The Japanese *shishi-odoshi* or deer scarer is amazingly good fun, and very popular with children and dogs alike! Water trickles from a delivery pipe into an upturned spout, a see-saw tips the water back into the pond, the end of the see-saw falls back on the striker stone with a heavy "clunk", and the procedure starts over again.

TIME

A weekend (about twelve hours for the woodwork, and four hours for setting it up and fixing the pump).

SAFETY

Bamboo is very spiky – watch out for razor-sharp edges and splinters.

YOU WILL NEED

Materials *for a deer scarer 1 m in diameter*
- Bamboo: one piece 2 m long and 60 mm in diameter (for see-saw and delivery pipe), and one piece 4 m long and 120 mm in diameter (for main post and support posts)
- Plastic tube: 5 m long and 10 mm in diameter (to link delivery pipe to pump), with hose clips to fit
- Medium-size submersible pump
- Flexible armoured plastic pipe: long enough to protect the full length of the pump cable
- Electricity circuit breaker
- Striker stone

Tools
- Tape measure, pencil and black felt-tip marker
- Coping saw
- Knife: one or more sharp knives
- Electric drill with a 20 mm woodworking bit
- Rod: a length of wooden dowel or metal rod about 900 mm long (to pierce the inner membranes of the bamboo)
- Club hammer
- Spade
- Garden hosepipe

ACHIEVING A BALANCE

The first hurdle in this project is finding a supplier for the bamboo. We discovered two sources – one was the local garden centre, and the other advertised in a specialist garden magazine. When you have obtained the bamboo, walk round your garden and consider the various siting options. For example, are you going to have the deer scarer set up over an existing pond – so that the water routes from the pond, through the bamboo, and then back into the pond? Or are you going to provide the deer scarer with its own self-contained sump?

The water delivery pipe also needs to be arranged so that the input end is hidden from view. That is not a problem if the ground slopes steeply down to the pond, because the input end can easily be hidden away in a convenient shrub or rock, with the rest of the pipe being supported by the two bridge uprights. If, however, your ground is level, one option is to build a pile of rocks or logs, or a little hut, to provide a support and cover for the input.

SIDE VIEW DETAIL OF MAIN POST (CROSS-SECTION)

FRONT VIEW DETAIL OF MAIN POST

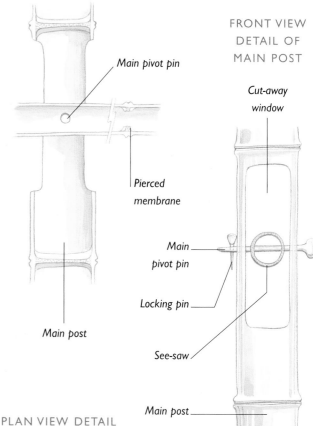

Main pivot pin

Pierced membrane

Main post

Cut-away window

Main pivot pin

Locking pin

See-saw

Main post

PLAN VIEW DETAIL OF MAIN POST

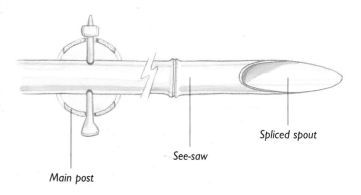

Spliced spout

See-saw

Main post

Japanese deer scarer

CROSS-SECTION OF THE JAPANESE DEER SCARER

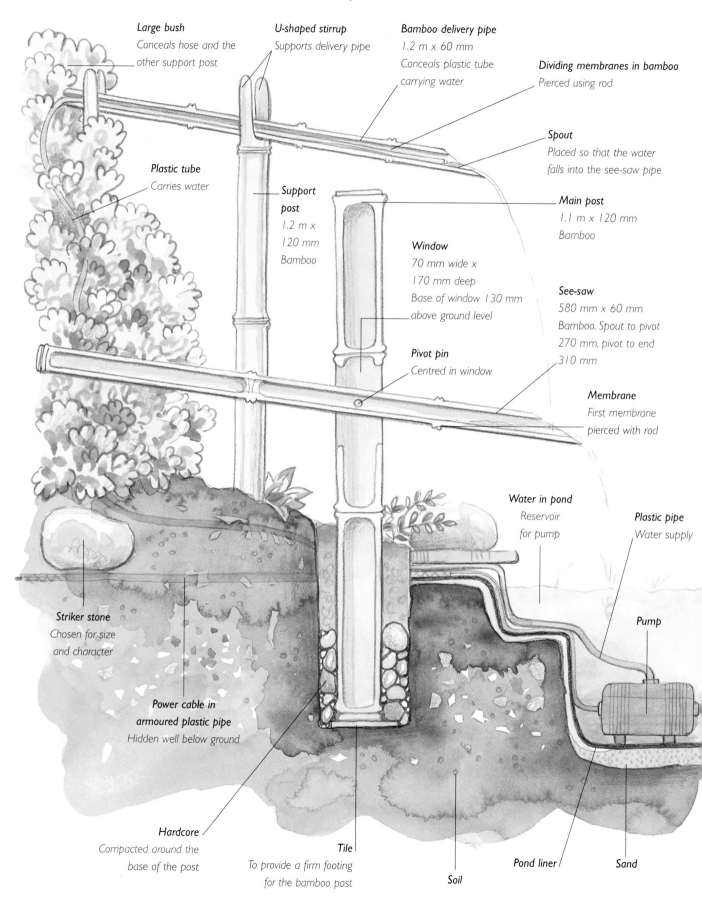

Large bush
Conceals hose and the other support post

U-shaped stirrup
Supports delivery pipe

Bamboo delivery pipe
1.2 m x 60 mm
Conceals plastic tube carrying water

Dividing membranes in bamboo
Pierced using rod

Spout
Placed so that the water falls into the see-saw pipe

Plastic tube
Carries water

Support post
1.2 m x 120 mm
Bamboo

Main post
1.1 m x 120 mm
Bamboo

Window
70 mm wide x 170 mm deep
Base of window 130 mm above ground level

See-saw
580 mm x 60 mm
Bamboo. Spout to pivot 270 mm, pivot to end 310 mm

Pivot pin
Centred in window

Membrane
First membrane pierced with rod

Water in pond
Reservoir for pump

Plastic pipe
Water supply

Striker stone
Chosen for size and character

Pump

Power cable in armoured plastic pipe
Hidden well below ground

Hardcore
Compacted around the base of the post

Tile
To provide a firm footing for the bamboo post

Soil

Pond liner

Sand

PLAN VIEW OF THE JAPANESE DEER SCARER

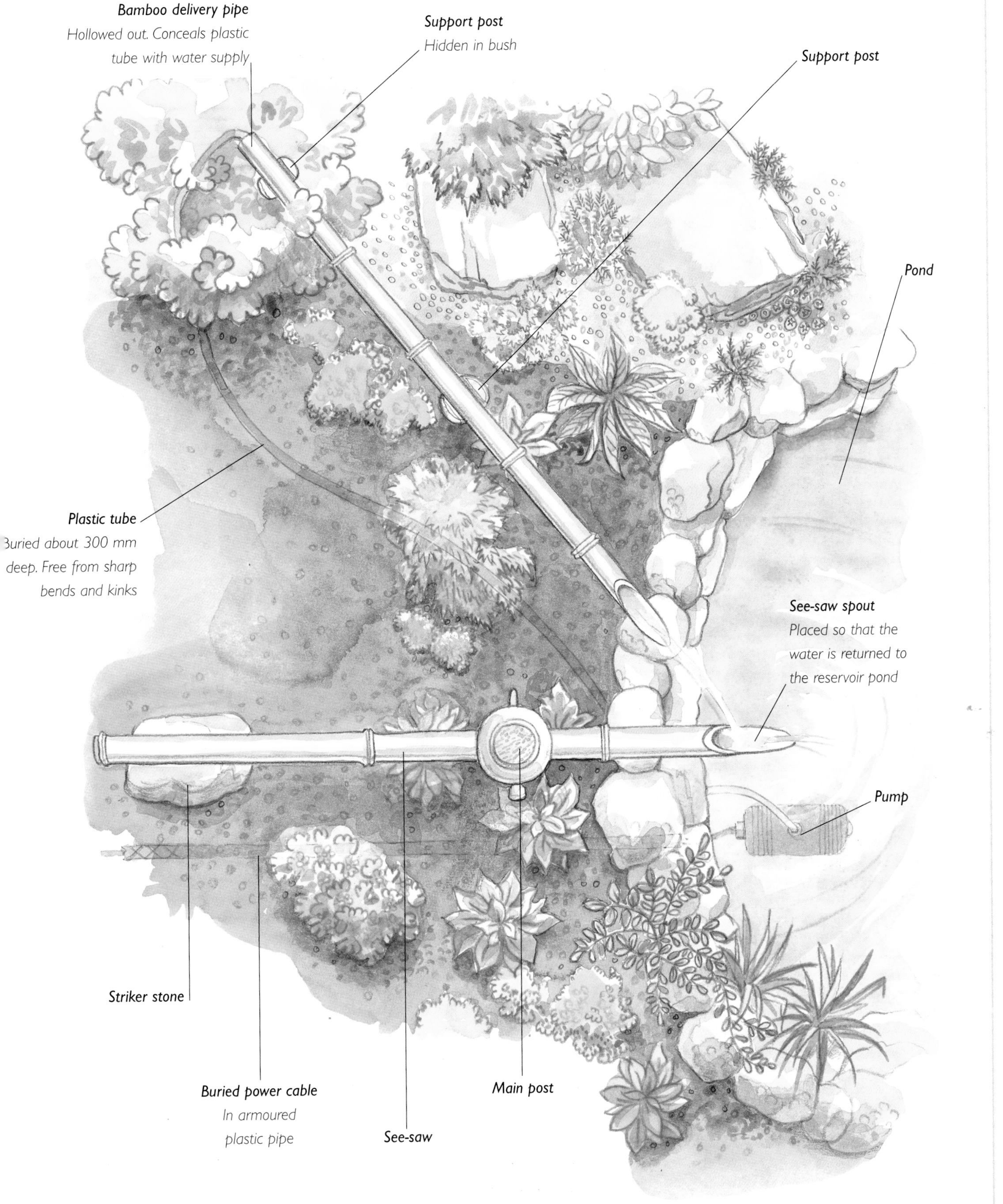

Bamboo delivery pipe
Hollowed out. Conceals plastic
tube with water supply

Support post
Hidden in bush

Support post

Pond

Plastic tube
Buried about 300 mm
deep. Free from sharp
bends and kinks

See-saw spout
Placed so that the
water is returned to
the reservoir pond

Pump

Striker stone

Buried power cable
In armoured
plastic pipe

See-saw

Main post

Step-by-step: Making the Japanese deer scarer

Grip
Hold the bamboo at the top to minimize movement and make sawing easier

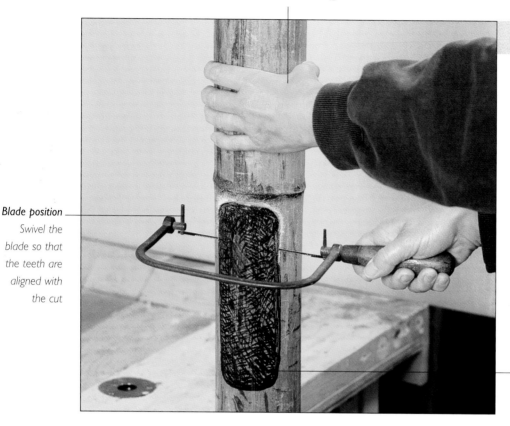

Blade position
Swivel the blade so that the teeth are aligned with the cut

Waste area
Mark the waste to be sawn away

1 Cut a 1.1 m length of 120 mm bamboo for the main post. Use the tape measure, pencil and felt-tip marker to clearly mark the size and position of the two "windows" on the main post for the see-saw – one on each side. The windows are 70 mm wide and 170 mm deep, and the base of each should be about 130 mm above ground level when the post is in position. Carefully cut away the waste with the coping saw. Mark the hole for the pivot pin.

Carving
Carve the pin to make a decorative "knuckle" at the end

Knife control
Brace your thumb against the bamboo so you have greater control over the knife

2 Cut a 580 mm length of the 60 mm bamboo for the see-saw pipe. With the knife, carve a pivot pin out of a bamboo offcut. Make it 200 mm long and 15 mm wide apart from a "knuckle" at one end. Drill a 20 mm hole for the pivot pin through the main post (lining it up with the centre of the window) and 270 mm in from the spout end of the see-saw. Trim the pivot to fit.

Locking pin
The pin needs to be a tight fit in the pivot

Finishing
Use the knife to scrape the edges to a smooth finish

Window
Trim the hole if necessary so that the see-saw can move unhindered

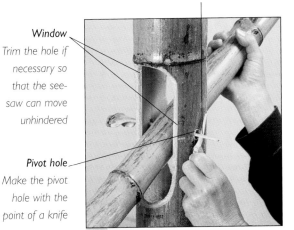

Shaping
Round over all the sharp edges and corners

Added strength
Note that the naturally occurring plate strengthens the joint at the end

Pivot hole
Make the pivot hole with the point of a knife

3 Set the see-saw in the main post, slide the pivot in place, and then cut and whittle a locking pin (from a bamboo offcut) to hold the pivot in position. Use the rod to pierce the membrane in the front end of the see-saw.

4 Cut a 1.2 m length of the 120 mm bamboo and split it down the middle to make the two support posts. Use the coping saw and knife to make the U-shaped stirrup detail at the top of each post. Cut the bamboo delivery pipe to 1.2 m long and use the rod to pierce the membranes in the middle of the bamboo.

Testing
Use the garden hosepipe to test out the best position for the delivery pipe

Mounting
Dig a hole for the main post. Tap hardcore around its base with the club hammer to hold the post firm

5 Mount the main post, then use a garden hosepipe, with water running through it, to help decide where the bamboo delivery pipe should be sited in order for water to pour into the see-saw. Use the plastic tube (where possible, buried 300 mm underground) and the hose clips to link the bamboo water delivery pipe to the pump in the bottom of the pond. Protect the power cable from the pump with armoured pipe (also buried underground) and use an electricity circuit breaker.

Striker stone
Position the striker stone for the loudest and best-sounding "clunk"

Inspirations: Bamboo water features

Japanese gardens are designed to be oases of tranquillity, suitable for reflection and meditation. A deer scarer, filling up with water, gently tilting and pouring, accompanied by the regular beat of bamboo upon stone, seems to represent the inexorable nature of time. There is something truly wonderful about watching the water and the machine working in harmony to produce a rhythm that symbolizes the importance of balance in the natural world.

ABOVE A Japanese deer scarer in action at the Chelsea Flower Show, England. This low-rise version features short bamboo pipes and a large striker stone.

RIGHT If you like the idea of having a Japanese feature, but want something easier to make than a deer scarer, you could build a *tsukubai*. This has a bamboo pipe supplying water to a pot, which overflows and runs into the gravel, where it is channelled and pumped back up through the bamboo spout.

Perpetual water tap

This is a project that will keep people guessing! Water flows from the tap, hour after hour, apparently being allowed to run to waste. Those with a wicked sense of humour will find it great fun to observe visitors' faces when they notice it. The perpetual stream of water is a very successful illusion, and you will find that most people are compelled to turn the tap off, and to berate you for wasting water.

TIME

A weekend (eight hours for the copperwork plumbing, and eight hours for digging the sump and setting up the pump).

SAFETY

Cut copper and clipped wire mesh are both difficult to hold, with lots of splinters of copper and sharp, jagged edges, so be sure to wear goggles and leather gloves.

YOU WILL NEED

Materials *for a perpetual water tap 1 m high and 700 mm in diameter*

- Plastic bucket (for the sump)
- Medium-size submersible pump
- Flexible armoured plastic pipe: long enough to protect the full length of the pump cable
- Electricity circuit breaker
- Natural wooden post: treated with wood preserver, and with bark removed, 1.1 m long
- Tap: brass or copper wall-mounted tap (old or new)
- Copper water pipe: 1.2 m long, 15 mm in diameter
- Compression elbow: 2 copper compression corner joints to fit the pipe
- Copper tap bracket: bracket wall plate with screw thread to fit the tap, a compression joint to fit the pipe, with screw to fix it to the post

- Copper saddle clip: 15 mm with screws to fit
- Hardcore: 1 bucketful
- Slates or tiles (waste pieces)
- Plastic tube: 500 mm long and 15 mm in diameter (to link copper pipe to pump), with hose clips to fit
- Natural border log roll: 2 m long, 300 mm high
- Plastic sheet: a circle about 1 m in diameter
- Galvanized 6 mm wire mesh: 600 mm square (allows for cutting waste)
- Cobbles: 25 kg

Tools
- Wheelbarrow
- Spade
- Tape measure
- Log saw
- Screwdriver
- Pipe cutter: large enough to cut the copper pipe
- Adjustable spanner
- Bucket: for hardcore
- Club hammer
- Scissors
- Wire snips

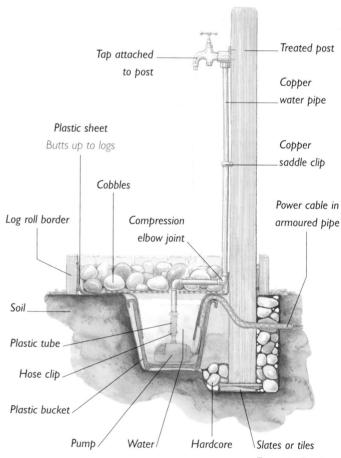

CROSS-SECTION OF THE PERPETUAL WATER TAP

Tap attached to post

Treated post

Copper water pipe

Copper saddle clip

Plastic sheet
Butts up to logs

Cobbles

Compression elbow joint

Power cable in armoured pipe

Log roll border

Soil

Plastic tube

Hose clip

Plastic bucket

Pump

Water

Hardcore

Slates or tiles
To create firm base

WATER ON TAP

The perpetual water tap is an ingenious project: once the pump is running, the tap appears to have been left on. The quaint brass tap, with the understated wooden post and the log roll surrounding fence, suggest that the whole set-up is old. Visit car boot sales and fleamarkets to search out a tap that has character, and that can be wall mounted. Ours dates from the 1920s, and probably comes from an old bath boiler. Clean the tap with metal polish and remove the washer. Because the perpetual water tap is self-contained, with its own integral sump and pump, it can be sited just about anywhere in the garden. However, to consolidate the illusion of a functional tap, choose a spot where you might conceivably want a water supply – perhaps in the corner of an orchard, or by the garden door, or in a courtyard.

Perpetual water tap

PLAN VIEW OF THE PERPETUAL WATER TAP

Copper water pipe
*1.2 m long, 15 mm in diameter
Descends into reservoir*

Tap
*Attached to bracket –
design to suit chosen tap*

Post
*1.1 m long, bark removed and
treated with wood preserver*

Cobbles
*Carefully placed
to hold the plastic
sheet in position*

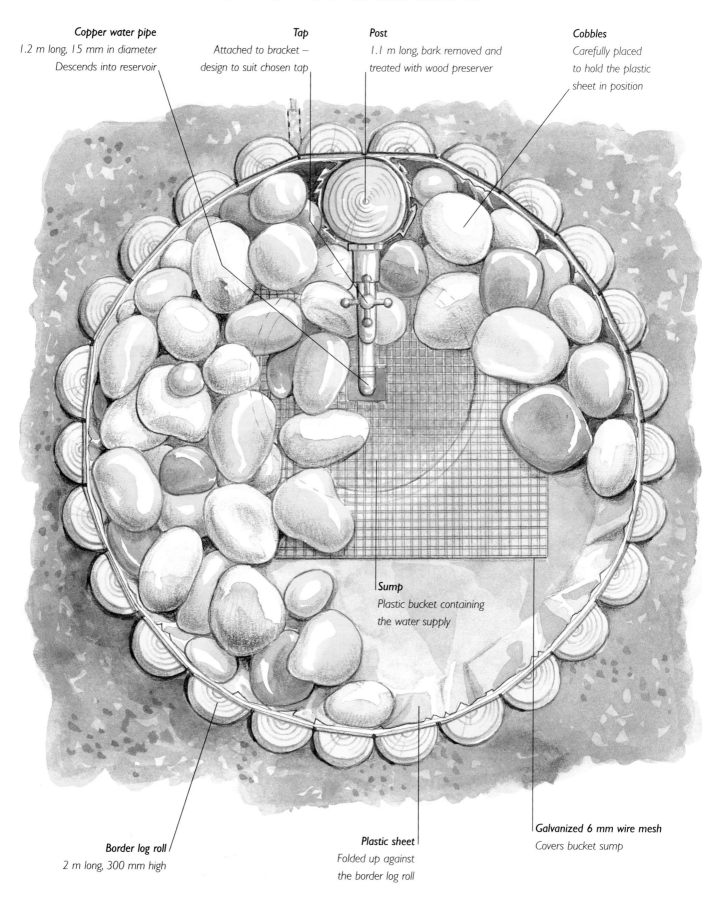

Sump
*Plastic bucket containing
the water supply*

Galvanized 6 mm wire mesh
Covers bucket sump

Border log roll
2 m long, 300 mm high

Plastic sheet
*Folded up against
the border log roll*

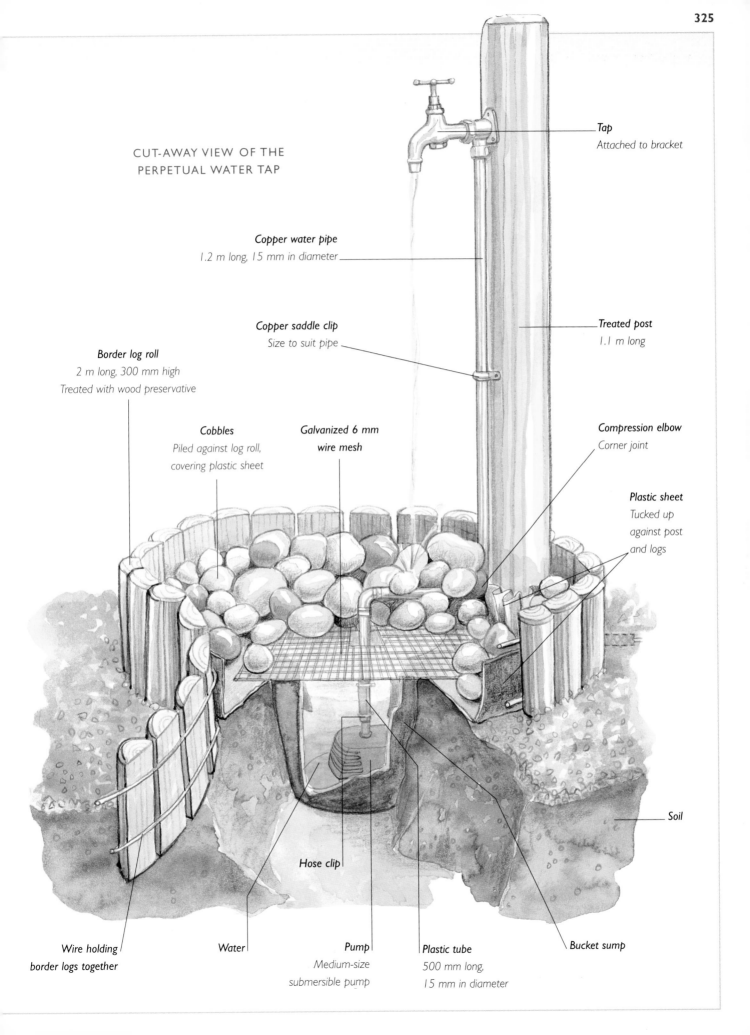

CUT-AWAY VIEW OF THE
PERPETUAL WATER TAP

Tap
Attached to bracket

Copper water pipe
1.2 m long, 15 mm in diameter

Treated post
1.1 m long

Copper saddle clip
Size to suit pipe

Border log roll
2 m long, 300 mm high
Treated with wood preservative

Cobbles
Piled against log roll,
covering plastic sheet

Galvanized 6 mm
wire mesh

Compression elbow
Corner joint

Plastic sheet
Tucked up
against post
and logs

Soil

Wire holding
border logs together

Water

Pump
Medium-size
submersible pump

Plastic tube
500 mm long,
15 mm in diameter

Bucket sump

Hose clip

Step-by-step: Making the perpetual water tap

Spade
Use a small spade for digging clay soil

Stones
Make sure that you remove any sharp stones

1 Use the spade to dig a hole wide and deep enough to hold the plastic bucket. When the bucket is in place, the rim should be flush with the ground. The bucket must not be jammed in place – it should fit easily into the hole. Level the bucket with pieces of stone if necessary.

Pump
Test the pump after every fitting stage

Cable protection
Protect the cable with armoured pipe

Handle
Leave the bucket handle attached until the last moment

2 Clean the bucket and position the pump in it, fitting the cable with armoured pipe and an electricity circuit breaker. Fill the bucket with water. Switch on the power and check that the pump is working. (Pumps can be fickle – keep testing them during construction.)

Copper saddle clip
Bridge over the copper water pipe and screw in place

Bark
Scrape the bark off the post

3 Measure and cut the post to size with the log saw. Use the pipe cutter to cut the pipe lengths, join the pieces of pipe with the compression elbow joints (but do not fully tighten the joints) and fit the tap bracket and tap. Fix the pipe and tap bracket to the post using saddle clips and screws, and tighten the compression joints with the spanner.

Joints
Avoid over-tightening the plumbing joints

Pipe position
Ensure that the pipe is centralized in the bucket

Fixing the post
Bang hardcore around the post until it is firm and stable

4 Set the post in the ground, placing it on tiles to broaden the base of the post and prevent it forcing itself into the ground. The inflow end of the copper pipe goes into the bucket. Put broken hardcore around the post and beat it down with the club hammer. Link the pump to the copper pipe by means of the plastic tube.

Arranging the plastic
Spread out the plastic and ease
it up the side of the log roll

5 Surround the bucket sump with the border log roll, making an enclosed well. Cover the well with the plastic sheet, cutting a cross in the middle so it flaps into the bucket. Cover the plastic with the wire mesh. Trim the plastic (with the scissors) and the mesh (with the snips) so that they fit within the well.

Helpful hint

If you want to have a larger tap and a greater flow of water, you will require a bigger apron of plastic sheet, so that the increased spray of water is directed back into the sump.

Outlet hole
Cut a hole in
the mesh for
the pipe to
slide through

6 Fill the well with cobbles, concealing the plastic and the mesh completely. Finally, fill the bucket with water, switch on the power, and turn on the tap.

Cobble
covering
Pile cobbles
inside the log
surround until
the mesh
is completely
concealed

Post support
The cobbles
around the
post give it
extra support

Copper cascade

This project is ideal if you have a modern garden and want a contemporary water feature to complement it. It is also perfect if you would simply like to try your hand at a copper and wood sculpture. Made from a railway sleeper and copper sheet, water trickles out of a copper tube, into copper cups, and back to the pond.

TIME

A weekend (eight hours for cutting and shaping the copper, four hours for mounting the sleeper, and four hours for connecting the water).

SAFETY

The weight of the sleeper is back-breaking – don't try moving it without help.

YOU WILL NEED

Materials *for a cascade 1.3 m high*
- Copper sheet: 1 x 430 mm long, 260 mm wide, 1 mm thick; 1 x 330 mm long, 250 mm wide, 1 mm thick; and 1 x 230 mm long, 150 mm wide, 1 mm thick
- Railway sleeper: 2 m long, 260 mm wide, 160 mm thick
- Galvanized coach bolts: 3 x 50 mm long and 20 mm in diameter, suitable for fixing field gate hinges
- Soft copper pipe: 2 m long and 10 mm in diameter
- Plastic tube: 500 mm long and 10 mm in diameter (to link the copper pipe to the pump), and hose clips to fit
- Medium-size submersible pump
- Flexible armoured plastic pipe: long enough to protect the full length of the pump cable
- Electricity circuit breaker
- Plastic sheet: about 900 mm long and 400 mm wide

- Cobbles: 25 kg
- Shingle (medium): 50 kg
- Rocks: a selection of feature rocks

Tools
- Thick rope to make handles for moving the sleeper: 4 m
- Blowlamp: plumber's gas blowlamp
- Tape measure and a piece of chalk
- Electric drill with long-reach 20 mm bit
- Metal snips: a pair of metalworker's tin snips large enough to cut the copper sheet
- Claw hammer
- Adjustable spanner
- Spade
- Pipe cutter: a plumber's pipe cutter large enough to cut the 10 mm pipe

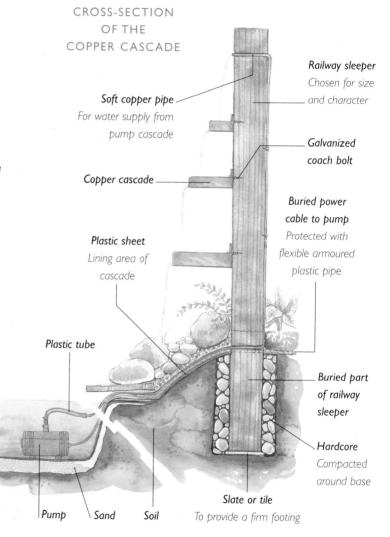

CROSS-SECTION OF THE COPPER CASCADE

Railway sleeper
Chosen for size and character

Soft copper pipe
For water supply from pump cascade

Galvanized coach bolt

Copper cascade

Buried power cable to pump
Protected with flexible armoured plastic pipe

Plastic sheet
Lining area of cascade

Buried part of railway sleeper

Plastic tube

Hardcore
Compacted around base

Pump   *Sand*   *Soil*   *Slate or tile*
To provide a firm footing

RUNNING WATER AND GOLDEN COPPER

The first thing to take into consideration is the weight of the railway sleeper. Though it is undoubtedly heavy – at least 200 kg – we found that we could drag it around the garden with a couple of short lengths of thick rope. With the sleeper set flat on the ground, the lifting procedure is simple. All you do is loop a rope around each end of the sleeper, so that you have two handles, then move it with a lot of very small lifts.

Ideally, the sleeper needs to be positioned over a pond or pool, so that the water flow-off can run back as a little brook. Cutting the copper sheet is hard work, but your supplier may be able to clip it to shape first. The copper needs to be softened before it can be cut. A blowlamp is used to heat the copper until it turns red, then it is plunged into cold water. Next, make your cuts. After a few minutes, you may need to repeat the heating and plunging process, because cutting makes the copper go hard again.

Copper cascade

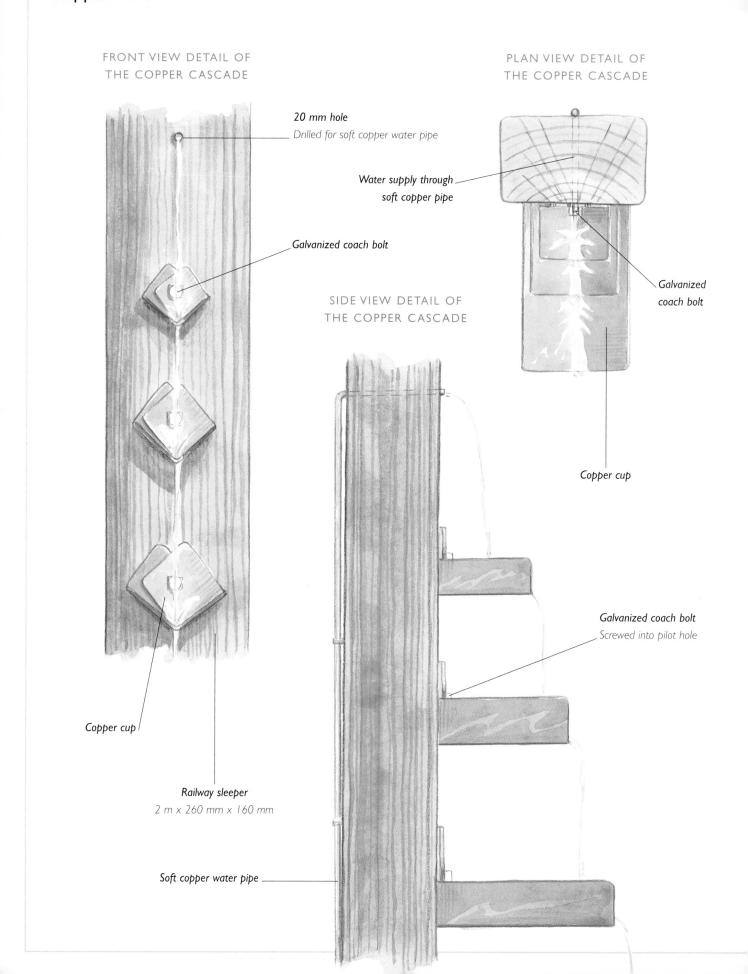

FRONT VIEW DETAIL OF
THE COPPER CASCADE

PLAN VIEW DETAIL OF
THE COPPER CASCADE

20 mm hole
Drilled for soft copper water pipe

Water supply through
soft copper pipe

Galvanized coach bolt

SIDE VIEW DETAIL OF
THE COPPER CASCADE

Galvanized
coach bolt

Copper cup

Copper cup

Galvanized coach bolt
Screwed into pilot hole

Railway sleeper
2 m x 260 mm x 160 mm

Soft copper water pipe

CUTTING PLANS FOR THE COPPER CUPS

Holes
20 mm holes drilled
slightly above centre point

Crossed diagonals
Fix centre point

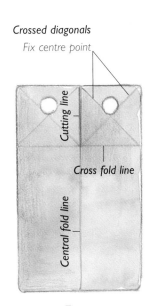

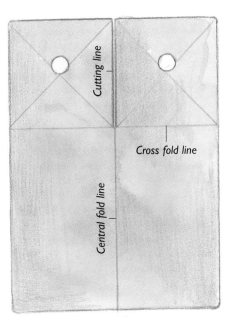

Cutting line

Cross fold line

Central fold line

Top cup
230 x 150 mm

Cutting line

Cross fold line

Central fold line

Middle cup
330 x 250 mm

Cutting line

Cross fold line

Central fold line

Bottom cup
430 x 260 mm

FOLDING STAGES TO MAKE THE COPPER CUPS

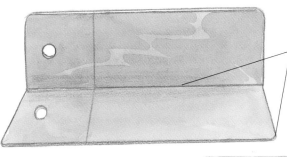

Stage 1
Round off the corners.
Fold over lengthwise to
make a straight gulley

Stage 2
Fold in one flap
until it is at right
angles to the
base of the cup

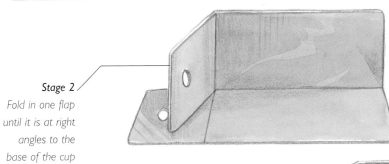

Stage 3
Fold in the other flap so it is
at right angles to the base.
Align the holes for the bolt

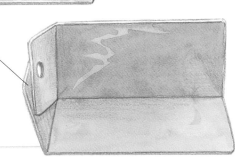

Step-by-step: **Making the copper cascade**

Trimming corners
*Cut off the sharp corners
to make them rounded*

Rounded corners
*Aim for a slightly
rounded corner*

Fold line
*Run the cut
just up to
the chalked
central fold line*

Hardening
*The hammering
will harden the
copper and
it may need to
be reheated*

Hammer work
*Work with
lots of small,
tapping strokes*

1 To make a copper cup, soften the copper sheet with the blowlamp and plunge it into cold water. Use the tape measure and chalk to draw out the design on it. Drill the two 20 mm holes. Use the metal snips to cut down the central fold line to the cross fold line.

2 Bend the copper along the central fold line. Rest it on the railway sleeper – using it like an anvil – and, with the claw hammer, gently tap the copper over the angle. Fold and tap the flaps in the same way, aligning the drilled holes.

Copper colour
*The heat of the blowlamp removes the protective
grease and creates a bronze-like surface*

3 Drill the five 20 mm holes in the railway sleeper – two holes for the water pipe, and the other three holes for the bolts. Use the coach bolts and adjustable spanner to fix the three copper cups in place.

*Fixing the
copper*
*Keep the
copper units
upright as
you tighten
the bolts*

Safety
*Be careful
not to cut
your hands on
the edge of
the copper*

Digging
*Dig a hole just big enough
to take the sleeper*

Bending the copper
*Avoid creating sharp bends, which
will cause the pipe to collapse*

Adjusting
the pipe
*Adjust the pipe
so that the
water falls into
the first cup*

Pipe position
*Shape the
pipe so that it
runs parallel
with the back
of the sleeper*

4 Dig a hole for the sleeper (when the
sleeper is in place at the edge of the
pond, the bottom copper cup should be
about 150 mm clear of the ground). Stand
the sleeper upright in the hole and firm
the earth around it.

5 Run the soft copper pipe from the
pond, through the bottom sleeper
hole, up the back of the sleeper, and then
back through the top of the sleeper. Cut it
to length with the pipe cutter, so that it
exits like a little tap just above the top
copper cup. Avoid sharp bends in the pipe.

Stones
*Reduce soil erosion by putting
stones under the falling water*

6 Run the input end of the
copper pipe into the pond
and link it to the pump with the
plastic tube. Slide the armoured
pipe in place over the cable,
install and check the electricity
circuit breaker. Use the plastic
sheet, cobbles, shingle and rocks
to cover the copper pipe and to
create a stream or dry bed effect.

Stones
and plants
*Arrange plants
and stones to
give the feel
of a natural
stream*

Helpful hint

If you want to swiftly age
the copper and give it a
rich green patina, repeatedly
heat it up with a blowlamp
and brush it with salt,
several weeks before using
it in the project.

Woodland grotto

In many country areas, there are traditional folktales describing the pixies, goblins and sprites who inhabit secret woodland dells, pools and rocky places. If you suspect that there are little people living at the end of your garden, and you would like to build them a mini grotto surrounded by greenery (or you simply want to build a home for your garden's frogs and toads), this is the project for you!

TIME

A weekend (four hours to dig the sump, four hours to set up the base stones, and another eight hours for the rest of the stonework and for fixing the pump).

SAFETY

Make sure that children do not walk on the mesh covering the sump hole, just in case they fall in.

YOU WILL NEED

Materials *for a grotto 900 mm high and 750 mm in diameter*

- Plastic bucket (for sump)
- Medium-size submersible pump to suit height of grotto, with extension pipe
- Flexible armoured plastic pipe: long enough to protect the full length of pump cable
- Electricity circuit breaker
- Plastic sheet: 1 m square
- Galvanized wire mesh: 400 mm square
- Limestone slab: about 600 mm square and 50 mm thick

- Mortar: 2 parts (100 kg) cement, 1 part (50 kg) lime, 9 parts (450 kg) soft sand
- Large limestone boulders: about 25, 200–300 mm in diameter
- Small pieces of broken paving slab for cascade: 2 or 3 pieces
- Shingle (medium to large): 25 kg
- Cobbles: 25 kg (100 mm and bigger)
- Rocks: 7 medium size

Tools
- Wheelbarrow
- Spade
- Scissors
- Pointing trowel

A QUIET PLACE

The inspiration behind this project was a Druid spring that we saw near a village in deepest Somerset, in the south-west of England. It was beautifully situated in a wooded dell well away from the village – a wonderfully quiet and tranquil spot.

The mission of our woodland grotto is the creation of a garden space that is given over to rest and meditation – a sort of coming together of a Japanese water garden, a natural spring, and a clearing in the forest. Once you have studied the designs, think about a possible site. Ideally, it needs to be wooded, with lots of lush green vegetation, and above all, it should be quiet. If you can find a place in dappled shade, which is quite wild, with lots of moss, rotting bark and wood beetles, this would be ideal. The only other thing that needs to be taken into consideration is how to run the water and electricity supplies to the spot.

CROSS-SECTION OF THE WOODLAND GROTTO

Limestone boulders
Mortared together

Water supply pipe from pump

Limestone paving slab

Galvanized wire mesh

Plastic sheet
Cut so the water falls into the bucket

Pump extension pipe
Lies in channel

Buried armoured plastic pipe
Protects the power cable

Bucket
Sump

Pump

Soil

Water

Woodland grotto

PLAN VIEW OF THE WOODLAND GROTTO

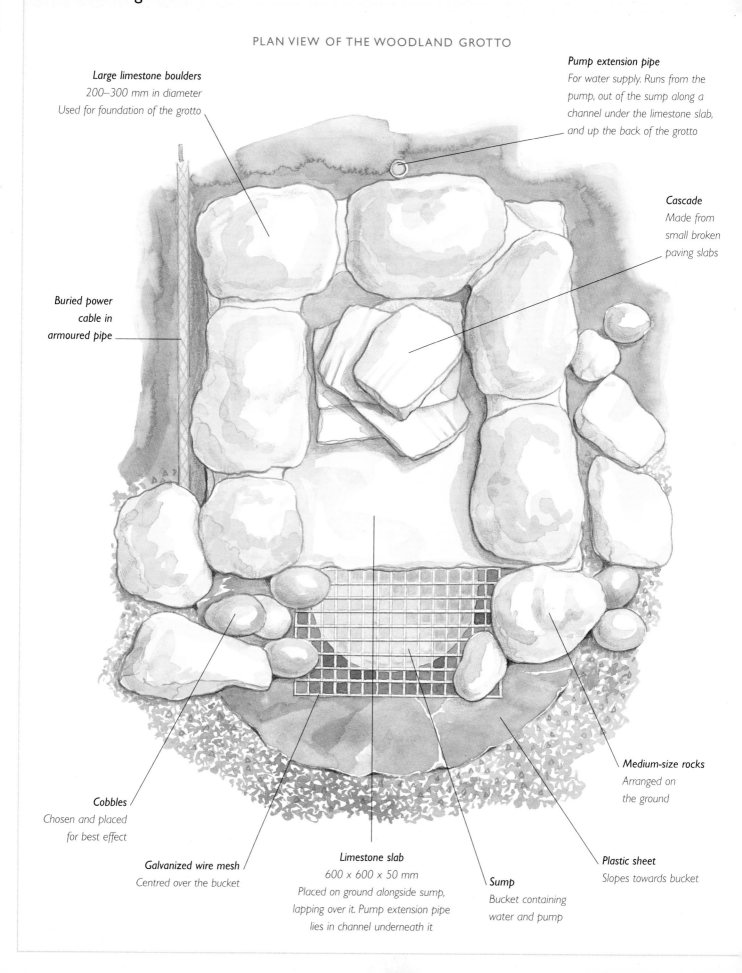

Large limestone boulders
200–300 mm in diameter
Used for foundation of the grotto

Pump extension pipe
*For water supply. Runs from the
pump, out of the sump along a
channel under the limestone slab,
and up the back of the grotto*

Cascade
*Made from
small broken
paving slabs*

**Buried power
cable in
armoured pipe**

Medium-size rocks
*Arranged on
the ground*

Cobbles
*Chosen and placed
for best effect*

Galvanized wire mesh
Centred over the bucket

Limestone slab
600 x 600 x 50 mm
*Placed on ground alongside sump,
lapping over it. Pump extension pipe
lies in channel underneath it*

Sump
*Bucket containing
water and pump*

Plastic sheet
Slopes towards bucket

CUT-AWAY VIEW OF THE WOODLAND GROTTO

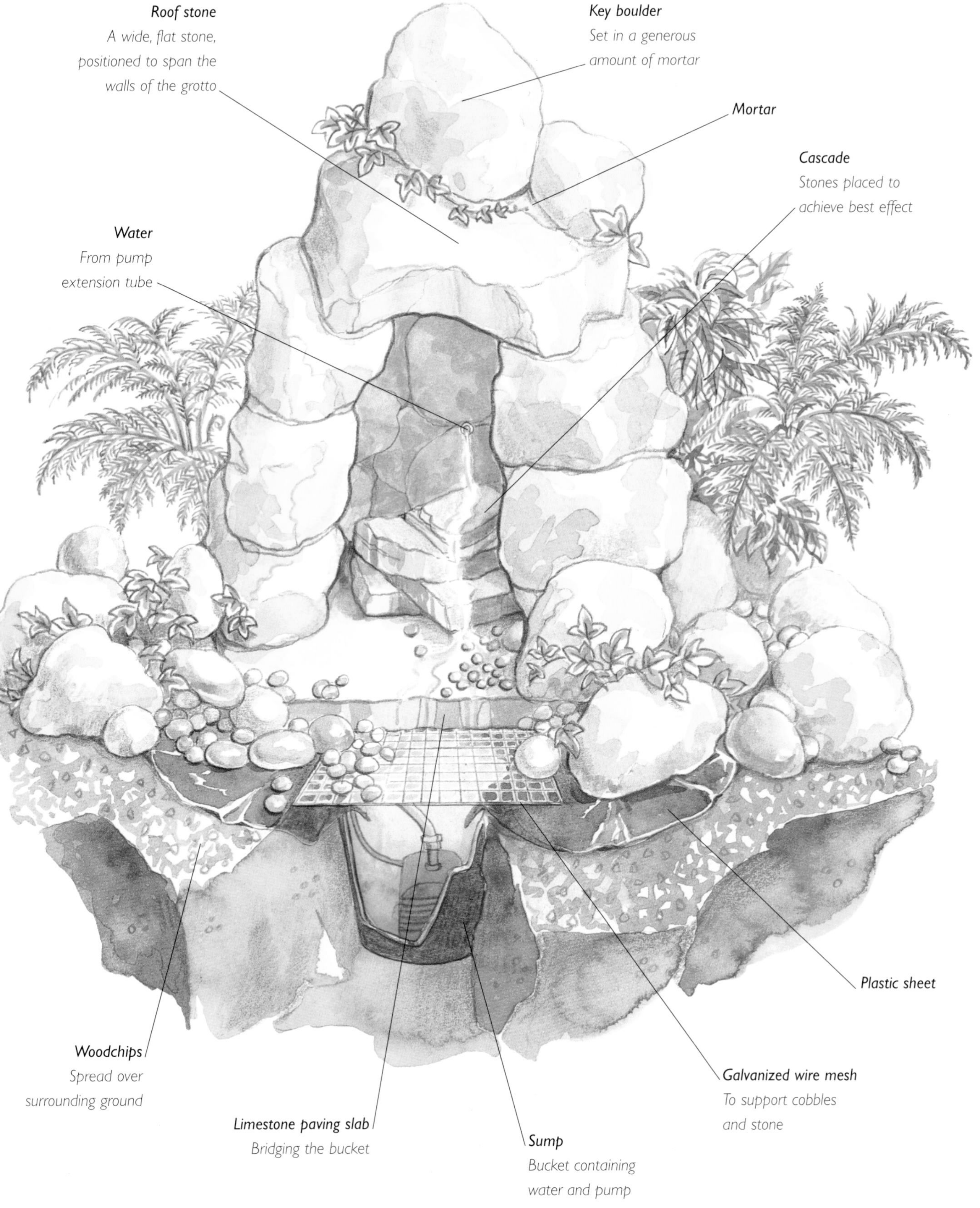

Roof stone
*A wide, flat stone,
positioned to span the
walls of the grotto*

Key boulder
*Set in a generous
amount of mortar*

Mortar

Cascade
*Stones placed to
achieve best effect*

Water
*From pump
extension tube*

Plastic sheet

Woodchips
*Spread over
surrounding ground*

Galvanized wire mesh
*To support cobbles
and stone*

Limestone paving slab
Bridging the bucket

Sump
*Bucket containing
water and pump*

Step-by-step: Making the woodland grotto

Pump extension pipe
Make sure that the extension pipe is set in a channel

Pump
Test the pump after every fitting stage

Handle
Remove the bucket handle prior to spreading the plastic sheet

1 Dig a hole deep enough to hold the plastic bucket for the sump, so that it lies with its rim level with the ground. Set the pump in the bucket, complete with armoured pipe over the cable. Fit the electricity circuit breaker. Fix the extension pipe in the pump, and dig a channel in the ground for it to lie in.

Mortar
Be generous with the mortar around the first ring of boulders

2 Cover the bucket sump with the plastic sheet. Cut a 100 mm slot in the sheet with the scissors, so that all the water from the outlet pipe is bound to flow back into the bucket. Place the limestone slab so that it laps over one end of the sump, and use the mortar and pointing trowel to start building a C-shaped ring of limestone boulders on the slab.

Helpful hint

If the weather is hot and sunny, you will need to spray the boulders with water just prior to bedding them in the mortar.

Extension pipe
Set the pipe so that the water dribbles on to the centre of the slab

Key boulder
Position the top boulder for best effect

Mortar
Build the second ring of boulders when the first layer of mortar has begun to stiffen

Modelling
Use the point of the trowel to clean up and shape the mortar

Extra mortar
If necessary, add mortar to joints that look empty

3 Build a second course of boulders. Run the extension pipe from the back of the grotto and over the ring of boulders to the front, so that the water dribbles on to the centre of the slab. Position the small pieces of broken paving slab to make a cascade.

4 Build two more courses of boulders. Leave until the mortar is part-cured. Sit the final key boulder in place on top of the heap and use the pointing trowel to tidy up the mortar. Add additional smaller boulders as you think fit.

Texturing
Tap the semi-cured mortar with the tip of the trowel to give it a weathered effect

Decorating
Arrange cobbles around the base of the grotto

5 Clean out any grit from inside the sump and cover the top with the mesh. Push the mesh under the front edge of the slab. Finally, cover the plastic sheet and mesh with shingle, and decorate the whole site with cobbles and rocks. You could group stones to resemble a shrine, add personal artefacts, or include plants or driftwood.

Ornament
If you want to, place a brass toad or small concrete statuette inside the grotto

Copper spiral spray

In action, this project is similar to a wind sculpture, where eddies of wind set a wooden spiral in motion. The copper spiral works in much the same way, the only real difference being that water supplies the motive force. The "fun" part of the project, which may test your patience, is adjusting the force and flow of the water.

TIME

A weekend (four hours for shaping the copper, eight hours for building the pool, and the remaining time for completing the project).

SAFETY

The sleepers are awkward to manoeuvre – wear strong boots to protect your feet.

YOU WILL NEED

Materials *for a spiral spray 1.23 m high, 1.3 m long and 880 mm wide*

- Railway sleepers: 260 mm wide and 160 mm thick – 1 x 1.23 m long, 2 x 1.3 m long, 2 x 880 mm long, 2 x 780 mm long, and 2 x 360 mm long
- Woodchips: 8 wheelbarrow loads
- Plastic pond liner: 1.42 m long and 1 m wide (allows for cutting waste)
- Medium-size submersible pump
- Flexible armoured plastic pipe: long enough to protect the full length of pump cable
- Electricity circuit breaker
- Hard copper water pipe (as used by plumbers): 1.8 m long, 15 mm in diameter
- Galvanized nails: 30 flat-headed nails, 60 mm long
- Soft, pliable copper pipe (as used by gas fitters): 1.9 m long and 10 mm in diameter

- Plastic tube: 200 mm long and 10 mm in diameter (to link the soft copper tube to the pump), with hose clips to fit
- Copper sheet: 350 mm square, 0.05 mm thick (soft and thin enough to cut with tin snips)
- Strong nylon fishing line: 500 mm long, with a spinner joint to fit

Tools

- Tape measure and a piece of chalk
- Log saw
- Spade
- Garden trowel
- Spirit level
- Scissors: to cut the plastic
- Claw hammer
- Brace: a carpenter's brace with a 20 mm auger bit
- Pipe cutter: a plumber's pipe cutter large enough to cut the 10 mm pipe
- Metal snips: a pair of metalworker's tin snips large enough to cut the copper sheet

TRICKLING AND TURNING

Part of the fascination of this project is that it is made up from lots of component parts, rather like a large building kit, so putting it together is very satisfying. Watching the spiral spin, and the sight and sound of moving water, are the chief pleasures of the copper spiral spray, so this will affect whereabouts you decide to site it in your garden. Do you want it close by so that you can watch every little ripple as the water plays over the copper? Or would you prefer to view it from a distance?

The actual making procedures are all straightforward, apart from sawing the wood, which requires some effort. It's best to buy a brand new log saw with a pack of blades. To guard your back, make sure that you do the sawing at a height that is comfortable. Do not stoop or overreach. You also need to think about how you are going to manoeuvre the weighty sleepers around the garden.

CROSS-SECTION SIDE VIEW

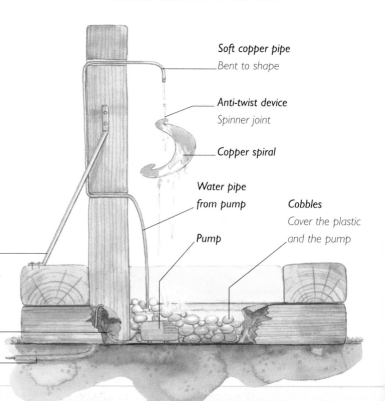

Soft copper pipe
Bent to shape

Anti-twist device
Spinner joint

Copper spiral

Water pipe
from pump

Pump

Cobbles
*Cover the plastic
and the pump*

Support strut
Hard copper pipe fixed with nails

Plastic sheet
*Spread across base and up
against side of the sleepers*

Buried power cable in armoured pipe

Copper spiral spray

PLAN VIEW OF THE COPPER SPIRAL SPRAY

Power cable

Support strut
1.2 m x 15 mm
Hard copper pipe
nailed in place

Cobbles
Conceal the pump
and the plastic sheet

Copper spiral
Tied to copper outlet
pipe so it hangs under
the falling water

Railway sleeper
1.23 m x 260 mm x 160 mm

Hole
20 mm hole drilled 150 mm
down from top of post

Soft copper pipe
Delivers the water

Anti-twist device
Spinner joint from
fishing tackle shop

Copper spiral
Cut from copper sheet

Support strut
1.2 m long
Hard copper pipe

Railway sleepers
Set so that the
rounded, weathered
face is uppermost

Hole
20 mm hole drilled 510 mm
down from top of post

Water pipe from the pump
Soft copper pipe

FRONT VIEW OF THE
COPPER SPIRAL SPRAY

SIDE VIEW OF THE COPPER SPIRAL SPRAY

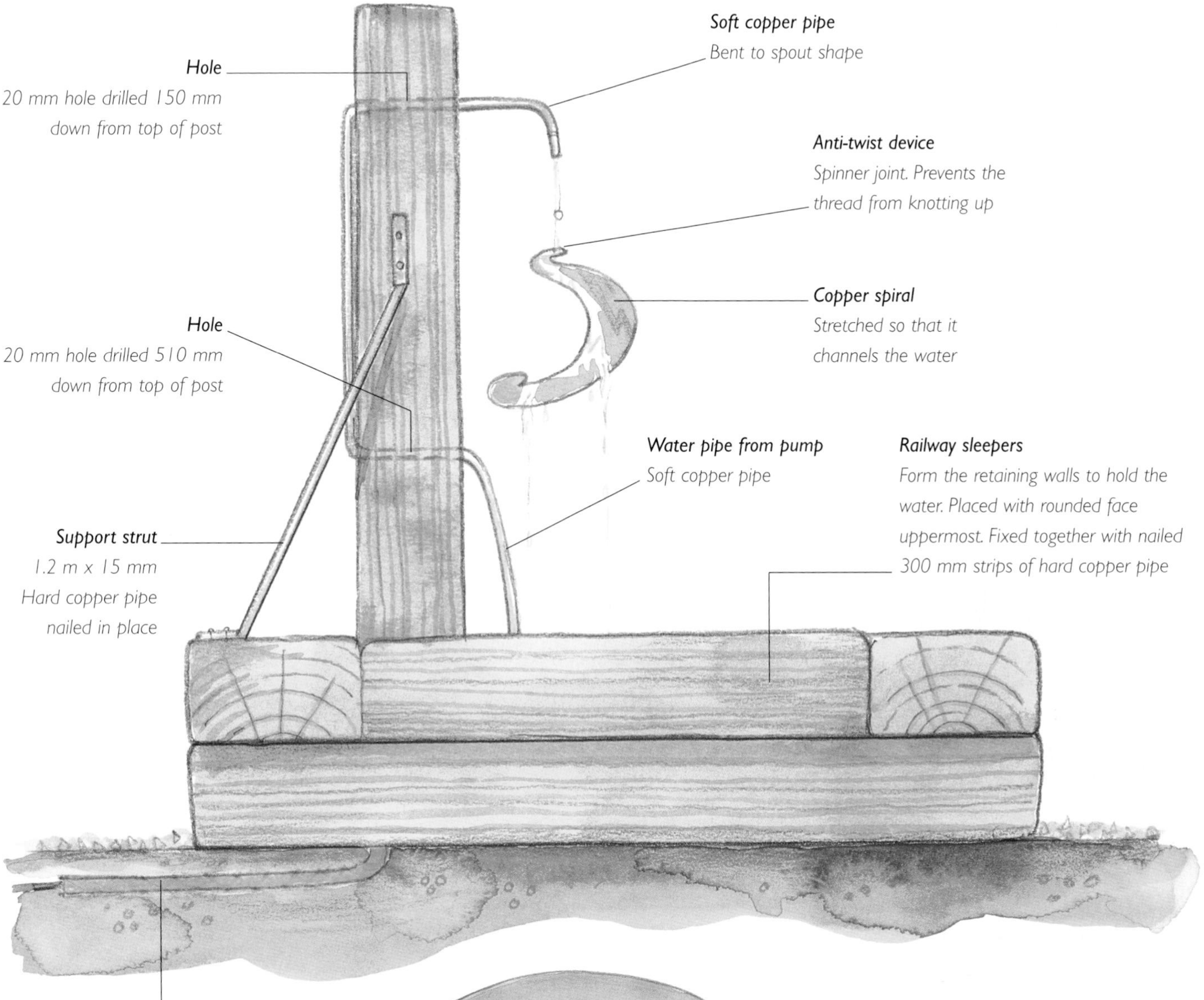

Soft copper pipe
Bent to spout shape

Hole
*20 mm hole drilled 150 mm
down from top of post*

Anti-twist device
*Spinner joint. Prevents the
thread from knotting up*

Copper spiral
*Stretched so that it
channels the water*

Hole
*20 mm hole drilled 510 mm
down from top of post*

Water pipe from pump
Soft copper pipe

Railway sleepers
*Form the retaining walls to hold the
water. Placed with rounded face
uppermost. Fixed together with nailed
300 mm strips of hard copper pipe*

Support strut
*1.2 m x 15 mm
Hard copper pipe
nailed in place*

**Buried power cable
in armoured pipe**

COPPER
SPIRAL DESIGN

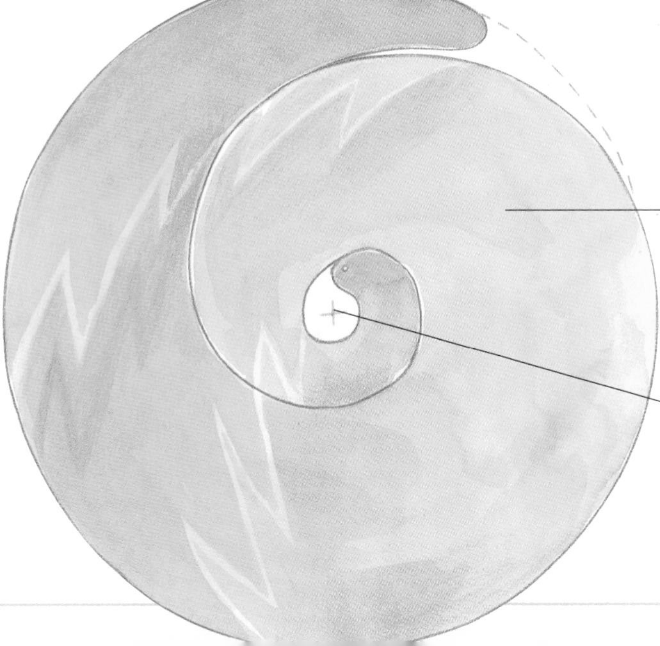

Copper sheet
*350 mm square, 0.05 mm thick
Cut into circle 300 mm in diameter*

Centre point of circle

Step-by-step: Making the copper spiral spray

Corner joint
Butt the sleepers together to make a 90° corner

1 Use the tape measure and chalk to mark out the railway sleepers, then cut them to size with the log saw. Lay out the first course of sleepers on the ground, and use the spade and garden trowel to pack them with earth or woodchips so that they are level. Check with the spirit level.

Levelling
Use the spirit level to check that the sleepers are well placed

Packing out
Lever up the sleepers with a spade and fill any cavities with woodchips

Plastic sheet
Allow a generous overlap of plastic, at least half-way across the sleeper

Corner joint
Set the second layer so that the vertical joints are staggered

Corners
Fold the plastic at the corners to improve the appearance

Copper straps
Sleepers held together with straps fixed with flat-headed galvanized nails

Plastic sheet
Ensure that the plastic sheet is trapped between the sleepers

2 Cover the sleepers with the plastic pond liner, creating a shallow pool. Set the pump in place, together with the armoured pipe to cover the cable. Fit the electricity circuit breaker. Fill the pool with water. Trim the plastic with the scissors.

3 Lay the second course of sleepers on top of the first, sandwiching the plastic sheet and holding it secure. Use the claw hammer to flatten strips of hard copper pipe into straps to lap over the joints and hold the structure together.

Nailing
*Use at least two nails at
each end of the bracket*

Spout
*Make a generously
curved spout*

Vertical post
*Check that the
post is held
straight while
you fix both
brackets*

Bending
*You will need
to bend the
pipe in a wide
curve to get it
through the
second hole*

Pushing angle
*As you push
the pipe
through, keep
it at 90° to
the post*

4 Set the vertical post in position at
one end of the pool, make checks
with the spirit level, and then fix it in place
at the back and sides with lengths of hard
copper pipe. Use as many galvanized nails
as you think necessary.

5 Use the brace and auger bit to drill
two holes, 20 mm in diameter,
through the sleeper. Cut the soft copper
pipe to length with the pipe cutter.
Connect the plastic tube to the copper
pipe and the pump. Slide the copper pipe
into place, running it from the pump,
through and up the sleeper, and out of the
top hole, creating a spout over the pool.

Spinner joint
*The spinner prevents the line
from twisting and breaking*

6 Cut the copper spiral out of
the copper sheet with the
metal snips, and hang it from the
spout by means of the fishing line
and the spinner joint. Position the
spiral so that the falling water
sets it in motion.

Copper spiral
*Adjust the
extension of
the spiral under
a trickle of
water until it
starts to spin
satisfactorily*

Helpful hint

If you want to reduce costs
for this project, you could
use recycled copper to
make the copper spiral. A
salvaged water tank would
be suitable, provided that
the copper is thin enough
to cut easily. Try looking at
your local amenity tip, or
visit a scrap metal dealer.

Glass waterfall

Glass bricks are a winning design feature in their own right, but if you add some decorative copperwork and a waterfall spray, you have something really special. If you live in a townhouse with a small courtyard, and have a passion for minimalism – lots of white walls, glass and flat surfaces – this project will appeal to you.

TIME

Two weekends (eight hours for the copperwork, eight hours for siting the pump, and the remaining time for completion).

SAFETY

The glass bricks need to be protected during transportation.

YOU WILL NEED

Materials *for a glass waterfall 720 mm high and 1.84 m square*

- Sump: a preformed plastic liner about 660 mm in diameter, with a lid to fit
- Plastic sheet: about 1.5 m square
- Medium-size submersible pump
- Flexible armoured plastic pipe: long enough to protect the full length of pump cable
- Electricity circuit breaker
- Concrete slabs: 9 concrete slabs – 1 x 600 mm square, and 8 x 460 mm square
- Waterproof tile cement, as used in bathrooms and swimming pools: 10 kg
- Glass bricks: 6 x 240 mm-square glass bricks, 80 mm thick
- Soft, pliable copper pipe: 1.5 m long and 10 mm in diameter (as used by gas fitters)
- Copper T-junction: pre-soldered junction to fit the 10 mm tube
- Copper sheet: 500 mm long, 160 mm wide, 1 mm thick
- Flexible galvanized wire cable: 5 m long and about 2 mm in diameter (as sold by yacht chandlers)

- Plastic tube: 500 mm long and 10 mm in diameter (to link the copper tube to the pump), with hose clips to fit
- Rafter nail for toggle: 100 mm long
- Oyster shell: 25 kg washed shell
- Woodchips: 5 wheelbarrow loads

Tools
- Wheelbarrow
- Spade
- Scissors
- Straight-edge and chalk
- Electric drill with a 10 mm masonry bit
- Pointing trowel
- Sponge
- Pipe cutter: a plumber's pipe cutter large enough to cut the 10 mm pipe
- Blowlamp: plumber's gas blowlamp
- Claw hammer
- Hand drill with a 2 mm twist bit
- Metal snips: a pair of metalworker's tin snips large enough to cut the copper sheet
- Mallet
- Piece of wood: 500 mm long, 80 mm thick
- Work table with adjustable clamps
- Spirit level

CROSS-SECTION SIDE VIEW OF THE GLASS WATERFALL

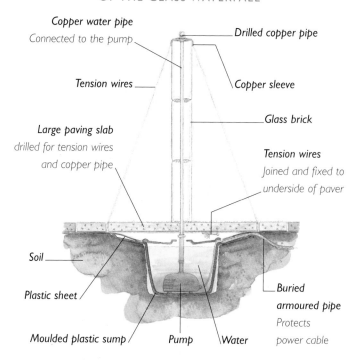

Copper water pipe
Connected to the pump

Tension wires

Large paving slab
drilled for tension wires and copper pipe

Soil

Plastic sheet

Moulded plastic sump

Drilled copper pipe

Copper sleeve

Glass brick

Tension wires
Joined and fixed to underside of paver

Buried armoured pipe
Protects power cable

Pump

Water

THE MAGIC OF GLASS

Glass bricks are actually as strong as house bricks, but glass itself is potentially a very dangerous material. So, if you have boisterous children or pets, or you are in any way worried about safety, it may be better to select another project.

The bricks are cemented together as two three-brick towers, with the bottoms cushioned in cement, the tops clenched by a copper sleeve, and the whole construction triangulated and held taut by yacht rigging cable. The structure is surprisingly strong and flexible – a bit like a mast. While you are putting it together, it is essential to make sure that the bottoms of the glass bricks cannot slide out of alignment on the slab – if you get that right, the rest is comparatively easy. The other thing to bear in mind, when you look at the step-by-step photographs, is that the overall effect will be enhanced when the copper weathers and turns green.

Glass waterfall

PLAN VIEW OF PAVERS

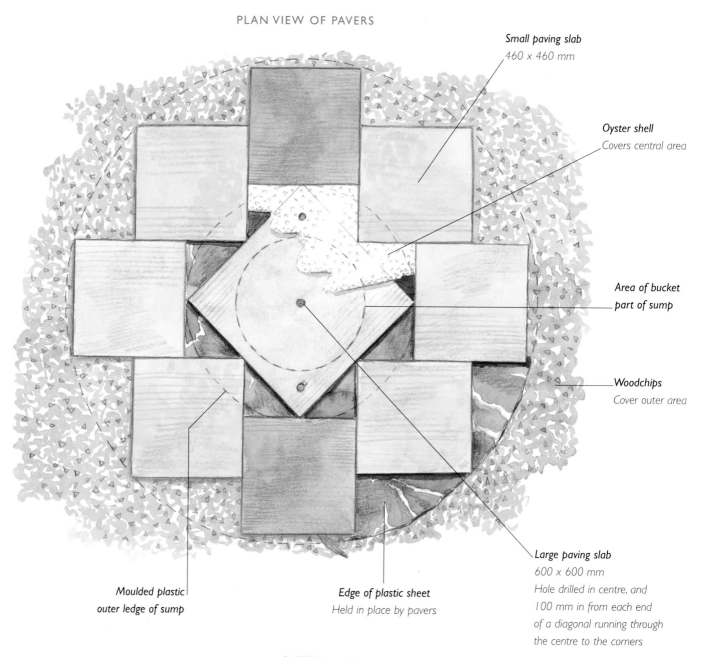

Small paving slab
460 x 460 mm

Oyster shell
Covers central area

Area of bucket
part of sump

Woodchips
Cover outer area

Moulded plastic
outer ledge of sump

Edge of plastic sheet
Held in place by pavers

Large paving slab
600 x 600 mm
Hole drilled in centre, and
100 mm in from each end
of a diagonal running through
the centre to the corners

PATTERN FOR COPPER SLEEVE

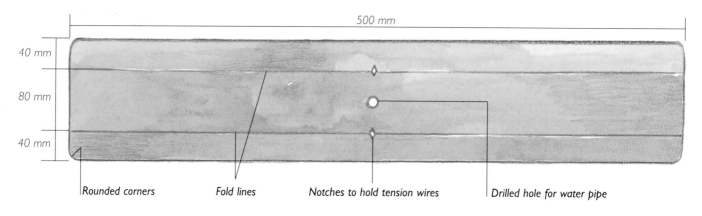

500 mm

40 mm

80 mm

40 mm

Rounded corners   Fold lines   Notches to hold tension wires   Drilled hole for water pipe

FRONT VIEW OF THE GLASS WATERFALL

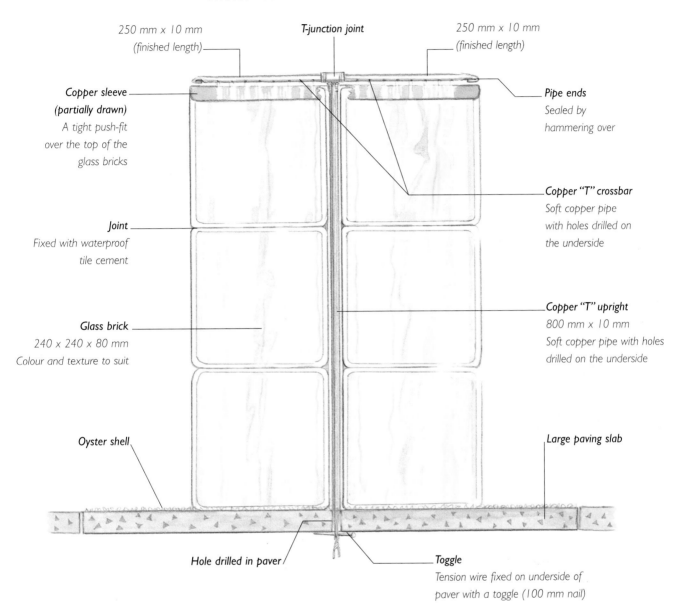

250 mm x 10 mm
(finished length)

T-junction joint

250 mm x 10 mm
(finished length)

Copper sleeve
(partially drawn)
A tight push-fit
over the top of the
glass bricks

Pipe ends
Sealed by
hammering over

Copper "T" crossbar
Soft copper pipe
with holes drilled on
the underside

Joint
Fixed with waterproof
tile cement

Glass brick
240 x 240 x 80 mm
Colour and texture to suit

Copper "T" upright
800 mm x 10 mm
Soft copper pipe with holes
drilled on the underside

Oyster shell

Large paving slab

Hole drilled in paver

Toggle
Tension wire fixed on underside of
paver with a toggle (100 mm nail)

DETAIL OF T-JUNCTION

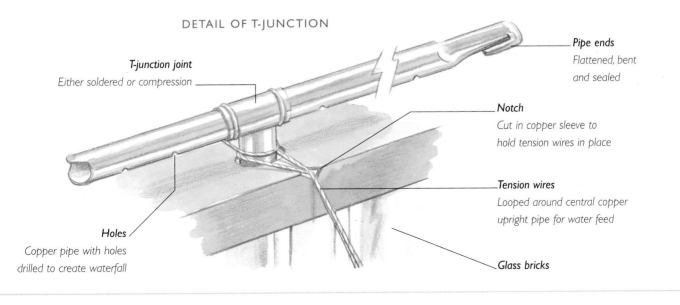

T-junction joint
Either soldered or compression

Pipe ends
Flattened, bent
and sealed

Notch
Cut in copper sleeve to
hold tension wires in place

Tension wires
Looped around central copper
upright pipe for water feed

Holes
Copper pipe with holes
drilled to create waterfall

Glass bricks

Step-by-step: **Making the glass waterfall**

Plastic sheet
Cut the liner so that it covers
the brim of the sump

Drilling holes
Let the drill bit do the work and
do not use excessive force

Pump
Test the pump
after every
fitting stage

Getting started
If your paver
seems extra
tough, it may
be easier to
drill a starter
hole with a
small-diameter
drill bit

Safety
The drilling
creates a lot of
dust, so wear
goggles and a
dust-mask

1 Dig a hole large enough for the
sump. Cover the sump with the
plastic sheet, and cut and shape the sheet
with scissors so that all the water runs
back into the sump. Fit the pump, together
with the armoured cable and electricity
circuit breaker (see page 300, step 2).

2 Find the centre of the large
concrete slab by drawing diagonals
with the chalk and the straight-edge. Use
the electric drill and the 10 mm bit to run
three holes through the slab – one at the
centre, and the other two about 100 mm
in from the corners.

Alignment
Check the bricks are aligned with each
other and each column is vertical

3 Mix the tile cement to a
very firm consistency with
water, then use the pointing
trowel to build the glass bricks
into two towers, three bricks
high. Sponge the excess cement
off the face of the glass.

Cleaning
the joints
Wipe away
the excess
tile cement
to achieve
the best
possible finish

Helpful hint

If you want to take this
project further and build a
larger wall – higher than
three blocks – you will
need to reinforce the wall,
either by enclosing it with a
metal frame, or by building
the glass blocks into a
traditional brick wall.

Drilling
Be careful not to drill
right through the pipe

Mallet
Ideally you need to use
a heavyweight mallet

Sealed ends
Fold the ends
of the pipe
over twice to
make them
watertight

Wood
Use the piece
of wood to
form the
copper shape

Hardening
After shaping,
the copper will
become more
springy, which
will help it grip
the glass bricks

4 To make the copper "T", cut the copper pipe into three pieces with the pipe cutter, slide them into the T-junction, and solder the joint with the blowlamp. Flatten and roll the top ends of the "T" with the claw hammer, and use the hand drill and the 2 mm bit to drill the spray holes on the underside of the arms.

5 To make the copper sleeve, cut the copper sheet to size with the metal snips, soften it with the blowlamp, and use the mallet to fold it round the piece of wood, so that the resulting sleeve is a tight push-fit over the glass bricks.

Tension wire
Adjust the
wire at the
top point so
that the glass
bricks are at
90° to the
concrete slab

6 Cement the two glass towers in place on the slab (they should be almost touching). Sit the arrangement on the work table and run the galvanized cable up from the underside through a corner hole in the slab, feeding it up and around the neck of the copper "T", back down the same corner hole, then across to the other corner hole. Repeat the process from that side. Tighten the wire by twisting the ends together on the underside of the slab, using the nail toggle.

Set the structure in place over the sump, check the level with the spirit level and using the plastic tube, link up with the pump. Decorate the arrangement with the smaller concrete slabs and the oyster shell. Spread woodchips around the perimeter.

Still pond

This pond is reminiscent of Italian courtyards. It can be built with the minimum of effort – there is no digging involved, no cement to mix, and no concrete slabs to cut. Instead it uses various sizes of paving slab, bedded on a layer of raked shingle. The pond is created in a wooden frame. The design of the still pond is such that it can be swiftly remodelled at a later date if you want a change.

TIME

A weekend (eight hours for building the wooden frame and setting it in the bed of shingle, and eight hours for arranging the slabs).

SAFETY

Always keep an eye on children playing near a pond, just in case the slabs tip up and move. If you have very young children, it may be better not to have a pond.

CROSS-SECTION OF THE STILL POND

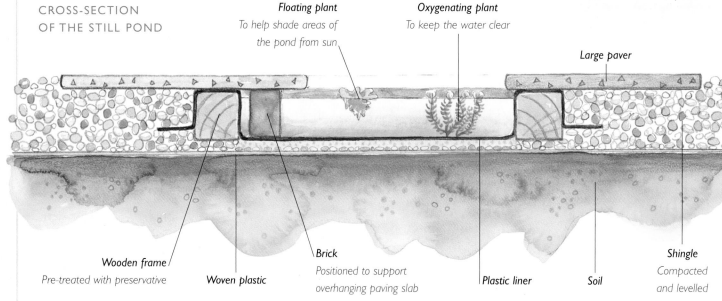

Floating plant
To help shade areas of the pond from sun

Oxygenating plant
To keep the water clear

Large paver

Wooden frame
Pre-treated with preservative

Woven plastic

Brick
Positioned to support overhanging paving slab

Plastic liner

Soil

Shingle
Compacted and levelled

YOU WILL NEED

Materials *for a pond 2.6 m long and 1.4 m wide*
- Weed-stop plastic sheet: as large as your site
- Shingle (medium): 1 tonne washed shingle
- Wood: 3 x 2. 44 m lengths of 100 mm square-section sawn and treated softwood
- Nails: 4 x 150 mm long
- Sand: 2 wheelbarrow loads
- Plastic sheet: 3 m long and 1.8 m wide

- Concrete paving slabs: 20 in various sizes, shapes and colours, ranging from small 300 mm squares through to large 450 mm squares, plus lozenges and rectangles
- Bricks: 8 house bricks

Tools
- Wheelbarrow
- Shovel
- Rake
- Spirit level
- Tape measure and a pencil
- Crosscut saw
- Claw hammer

A RING OF STILL WATER

The clever thing about this project is the fact that it can be completed with just about any shape of slab that comes to hand, without the need to cut to fit. At first sight the pattern of slabs might look a little complicated, but basically there are two lines of slabs, one at each side of the pond. As long as the lines extend a bit further than the length of the pond, the sequence or shape of the slabs is not important. The slabs that extend into the body of the water are supported by little stacks of bricks, rather like mini piers. It is best to avoid walking on the extended slabs, just in case they wobble or break under your weight.

There are two ways of looking at this project. It can either be seen as a temporary eye-catcher – the sort of feature that you build to occupy a space that is waiting for something else to come along and fill it, or you simply enjoy changing the design as and when you feel like it. The unique feature of this design is that you do not need to plan out the arrangement of the slabs – you just start at one end of the pond and finish at the other, working according to materials and inspiration.

Still pond

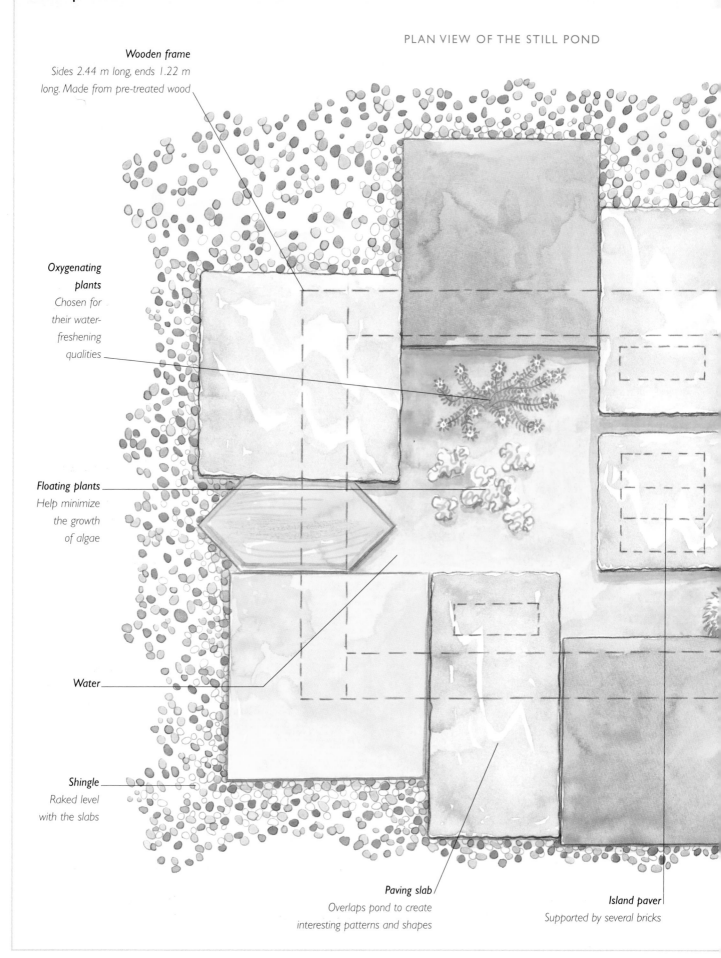

Wooden frame
Sides 2.44 m long, ends 1.22 m
long. Made from pre-treated wood

*Oxygenating
plants*
Chosen for
their water-
freshening
qualities

Floating plants
Help minimize
the growth
of algae

Water

Shingle
Raked level
with the slabs

Paving slab
Overlaps pond to create
interesting patterns and shapes

Island paver
Supported by several bricks

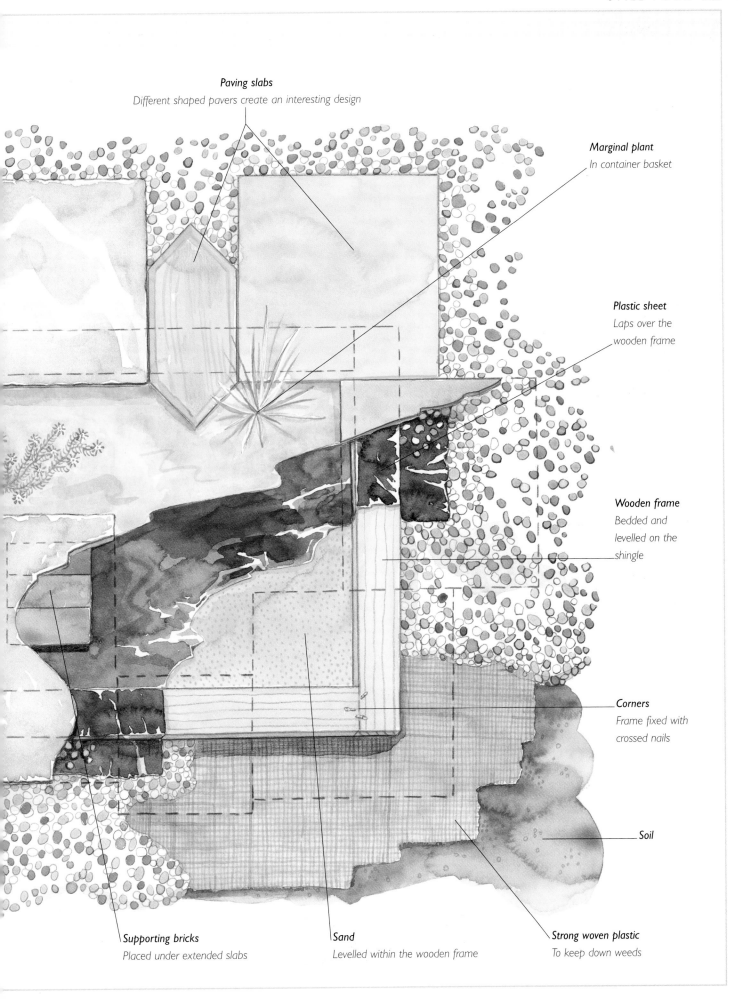

Paving slabs
Different shaped pavers create an interesting design

Marginal plant
In container basket

Plastic sheet
Laps over the wooden frame

Wooden frame
Bedded and levelled on the shingle

Corners
Frame fixed with crossed nails

Soil

Supporting bricks
Placed under extended slabs

Sand
Levelled within the wooden frame

Strong woven plastic
To keep down weeds

Step-by-step: Making the still pond

Shingle
Rake the shingle level

Weed-stop plastic sheet
Use woven plastic sheet to prevent weeds while permitting drainage

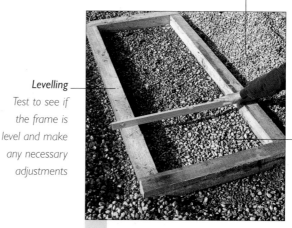

1 Spread the weed-stop plastic sheet over the whole site and cover it with a good layer of raked shingle. Check that all is level with the spirit level.

Shingle
Rake the surrounding shingle level with the top of the frame

Levelling
Test to see if the frame is level and make any necessary adjustments

Sand
After levelling the shingle, spread a layer of sand over it

2 Build the wooden frame with the saw, hammer and nails, and place it on the levelled shingle. Spread a bed of sand inside the frame and rake it over the shingle to a depth of about 80 mm.

Plastic sheet
Spread the edge of the plastic sheet over the top of the wooden frame

Wrinkles
When you have arranged the plastic as best you can, pour in a little water. The weight of the water will indicate any tight or slack areas

3 Spread the plastic sheet over both the frame and the sand, to form the pond liner. Fill the pond with water and cover the edge of the plastic with shingle, so that the top edge of the frame and the surrounding shingle are all at the same level.

Helpful hint

If you want to make this a more permanent structure, simply lay a concrete slab foundation, replace the wooden edging with a mini wall of concrete blocks or bricks bedded in mortar, and then follow on with the sand and the plastic sheet as described.

Handling the slabs
Lower the slabs gently so that
you don't damage the plastic

4 Lay the concrete slabs in place around the pond. Arrange selected slabs so that they extend into the water, supporting them with carefully arranged groups of bricks. Make sure that all the slabs are stable enough to support your weight.

Overlapping
slabs
The slabs that
hang over the
water are
supported by
bricks placed
underneath

Experimentation
Try out different
arrangements of slabs
until you find one that
you prefer

5 Once you have finalized your arrangement of slabs, spend time checking that the overhanging slabs are adequately supported by the bricks – use more bricks if necessary. Sit pots of oxygenating plants in the water and for the finishing touch, place container plants on the slabs and the surrounding shingle.

"Island"
Build a brick
and slab island
in the middle
of the pond

Pond shape
The shape of the
water is as important
as the pattern of
slabs – you may want
both to be regular
and less random

Rocky cascade

The rocky cascade was inspired by a beautiful mountain spring that we saw in the wilds of Wales. Icy water pushed up out of the hillside and cascaded down a series of rocky steps into a huge basin below. The whole vision was one of movement and sound, with water running, flowing, gushing, smashing, trickling and dripping over the stone. This project recreates the scene in miniature.

TIME

Four weekends (two days to dig the terrace, two days to sort out the plastic sheet, fit the pump and build the first wall, and the other four days for finishing the stonework).

SAFETY

This project involves a lot of physical work so, if possible, get someone to help you.

YOU WILL NEED

Materials *for a cascade 1.4 m high, 3 m long and 3 m wide*

- Soil: 3 tonnes soil (this could be the spoil pile dug when building a pond – see the Natural Pond on page 364)
- Submersible pump: largest pump that you can afford
- Flexible armoured plastic pipe: long enough to protect the full length of the pump cable and filter cable
- Electricity circuit breaker
- Filtration system to fit your pump: biggest system you can afford
- Plastic water delivery pipe: 6 m long, 35 mm in diameter (best-quality ribbed pipe with connectors to fit your pump and filtration system)
- Sand: 250 kg soft sand
- Butyl pond liner: best-quality liner, 3.6 m long, 1.8 m wide, 1 mm thick

- Mortar: 2 parts (200 kg) cement, 1 part (100 kg) lime, 9 parts (900 kg) soft sand
- Split sandstone: approximately 3 cubic metres (for the various steps and ledges)
- Secondary rocks: 1 tonne medium-sized sandstone rocks
- Shingle (medium to large): 1 tonne washed shingle
- Alpine grit: 75 kg crushed granite
- Cobbles: 150 kg large cobbles
- Feature rocks: 3 tonnes large sandstone rocks – as large as you can move

Tools
- Wheelbarrow
- Spade
- Shovel
- Spirit level
- Pointing trowel
- Mason's hammer
- Garden hose

A FLIGHT OF WATER

Of all the projects in the book, this is the most stunning, the most expensive, the most time-consuming, and the most rewarding. Earth has to be piled up and sculpted, rocks have to be heaved about the garden, and of course, if you do not already have a pond, you have to build one. (Follow the instructions for the large Natural Pond on page 364, and then simply use the spoil from the hole to create the mound that is the basis of the cascade.)

This project cannot be rushed, so be prepared for it to take up a lot of your time. Also, the only way to move a significant amount of water from the pond to the top of the mound is to invest in a large pump. Despite all these things, the rocky cascade is great to watch in action – well worth all the effort involved!

CROSS-SECTION OF THE ROCKY CASCADE

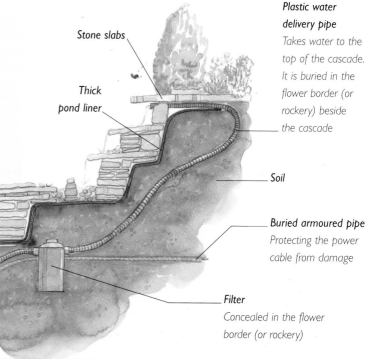

Stone slabs

Thick pond liner

Plastic water delivery pipe
Takes water to the top of the cascade. It is buried in the flower border (or rockery) beside the cascade

Soil

Raised ledge
To allow water to flow underneath

Water

Large pump

Brick support

Buried armoured pipe
Protecting the power cable from damage

Filter
Concealed in the flower border (or rockery)

Rocky cascade

FRONT VIEW OF THE ROCKY CASCADE

Cascade
*Constructed out
of courses of
split sandstone*

Water delivery pipe
*Hidden by large piece
of split sandstone*

Retaining wall
*Forms steps for
the cascade*

Water delivery pipe
Buried in rockery

Shallow pool

Filter
Partly buried

Stone edge of pond
*Lapped over the edge
of the butyl liner*

**Large sandstone feature rocks
and medium-sized secondary rocks**
Placed around the cascade

**Small piece
of split sandstone**
*Placed to divert
water flow*

Large pump
*Sits on bricks to keep
it clear of sludge*

Grass edge to pond
Created with turf

Buried armoured pipe
Protects the power cable

PLAN VIEW OF THE ROCKY CASCADE

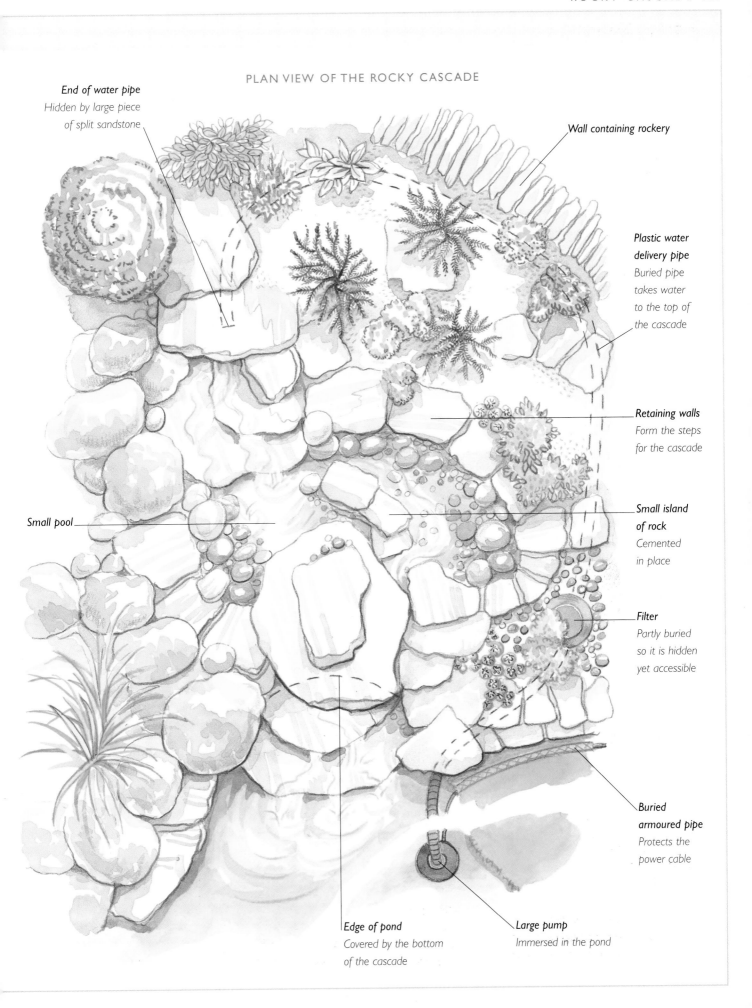

End of water pipe
*Hidden by large piece
of split sandstone*

Wall containing rockery

**Plastic water
delivery pipe**
*Buried pipe
takes water
to the top of
the cascade*

Retaining walls
*Form the steps
for the cascade*

**Small island
of rock**
*Cemented
in place*

Small pool

Filter
*Partly buried
so it is hidden
yet accessible*

**Buried
armoured pipe**
*Protects the
power cable*

Edge of pond
*Covered by the bottom
of the cascade*

Large pump
Immersed in the pond

Step-by-step: **Making the rocky cascade**

Steps
Use the spade to sculpt straight-sided steps in the earth

Water delivery pipe
We specify 35 mm pipe, but choose pipe to suit your pump model

Preserving the edges
Avoid standing on the edges of the steps

Filling in
Push sand and earth around the sides of the filtration unit

Access
Follow the manufacturer's instructions for leaving room for access to the filtration unit, for maintenance

1 Build the mound of earth for the cascade alongside your pond. Use the spade and shovel to cut a series of steps that run from the top of the mound down into the pond. Check that they are horizontal with the spirit level.

2 Set the pump in the water complete with the armoured pipe, electricity circuit breaker and plastic water delivery pipe. Bury all the pipes and the bottom half of the filtration plant.

Following the steps
Let the liner fall into the shape of the steps

3 Cover the whole stepped face of the mound with sand, then carefully lay the butyl liner over it. Using the pointing trowel, build the bottom step with the spilt sandstone and mortar. Lap the lower edge of the liner over the bottom step.

High-quality butyl pond liner
Buy the best thick liner that you can afford

Positioning
Working from all sides, drag the sheet into place

Body weight
Keep your feet well
away from the wall

Water flow
Use a hosepipe to test how
the water will flow

Split
sandstone slab
Choose a
large slab for
the base of
the cascade

Mortar
Force mortar
into all the
joints and
small cavities

Secondary
slabs
Place smaller
slabs to divert
the flow of
the water

4 Build a low wall of split sandstone and mortar at the back of the bottom step, using the pointing trowel and the mason's hammer. This holds the butyl liner in place and forms the riser for the next step. Pack earth and rubble behind the wall.

5 Continue building walls and steps until you reach the top of the mound. At intervals during the process (and when the mortar has begun to set), use a garden hose to check how the water flows from one step to another. If necessary, make adjustments and block gaps with extra stone and mortar.

Water flow
Moving a rock slightly can
change the water flow

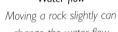

6 Finally, when the mortar has completely cured, use the secondary rocks, shingle, alpine grit and cobbles to fill and embellish selected pools and steps. Place large feature rocks on the steps to create extra runs and eddies.

Rock pools
Pools of water
look good and
improve the
sound of the
cascade

Helpful hint

Within hours of building this project and turning on the pump, we spotted two frogs sitting under one of the overhanging slabs. You too can encourage frogs to take up residence by building little nooks and crannies into the structure.

Natural pond

There is nothing quite so satisfying as a natural pond. The ever-changing character of

the water, the host of plants and, of course, the abundant wildlife – frogs leaping, bugs

scudding across the surface of the water, dragonflies hovering – all come together to

create a uniquely beautiful balance of nature.

TIME

Three weekends
(two days for the digging,
two days for spreading the
sand and fitting the liner, and
two more days to sort out
the edge of the pond and
the planting).

SPECIAL TIP

The levels of the edges are
all-important, so spend extra
time at the excavation stage
making sure they are right.

CROSS-SECTION OF THE NATURAL POND

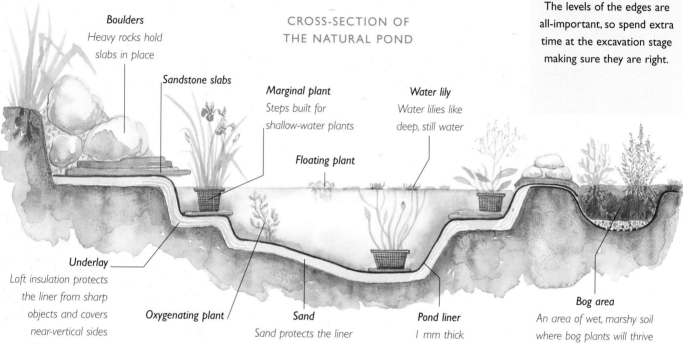

Boulders
Heavy rocks hold slabs in place

Sandstone slabs

Marginal plant
Steps built for shallow-water plants

Water lily
Water lilies like deep, still water

Floating plant

Underlay
Loft insulation protects the liner from sharp objects and covers near-vertical sides

Oxygenating plant

Sand
Sand protects the liner

Pond liner
1 mm thick

Bog area
An area of wet, marshy soil where bog plants will thrive

YOU WILL NEED

Materials *for a pond 5 m long and 1.7 m wide, with a maximum depth of 500 mm*
- Sand: 500 kg soft sand
- Loft insulation: 2 x 9.17 m rolls of glass wool, 600 mm wide and 50 mm thick
- Butyl pond liner: best-quality liner, 9.6 m long, 3.6 m wide, 1 mm thick
- Turf: 4 rolls, 1.5 m long and about 40 mm wide
- Split sandstone: 4 square metres
- Mortar: 2 parts (100 kg) cement, 1 part (50 kg) lime, 9 parts (450 kg) soft sand
- Limestone: 12 basketball-sized boulders
- Grit for base of bog garden: 1 bucketful

Tools
- Wheelbarrow
- Bucket
- Length of rope
- Tape measure
- Spade
- Shovel
- Spirit level
- Batten (wide enough to span your pond)
- Lawn rake
- Heavy-duty scissors
- Club hammer
- Bricklayer's trowel
- Pointing trowel

LIVING WATER

The pond is constructed with steps at various levels. Starting at the edge of the pond, there is a step for the edge of the liner flap, a step for marginal plants, and a gentle slope down to the bottom of the pond. At one side of the pond, the edge of the liner is held down by a mixture of flat slabs of sandstone and limestone boulders, while at the other side it runs under a bank of turf and stones, then on into a slow-draining bog garden ditch.

To protect the butyl liner from being pierced by sharp stones, there is a layer of soft sand over most of the horizontal areas and a layer of glass wool loft insulation over the vertical risers. We opted for a layer of glass wool because our soil is very stony. If your soil is soft and sandy, you could use polyester underlay.

Plan the planting carefully. You need oxygenating plants to keep the water clear, several showy specimen plants for deep-water areas (such as water lilies), marginal plants for the shallow steps around the edges of the pond, and bog plants for the bog areas. If there are bog plants in other parts of the garden, lift, divide and replant them around the pond. If you get the balance of plants right, the water will have cleared about three weeks after planting.

Natural pond

PLAN VIEW OF THE NATURAL POND

Limestone boulders
Mortared on to slabs

Floating plants

Oxygenating plants
Help maintain balance of the pond

Sandstone slabs
Cover liner and hold it in place

Shelf
For marginal plants

Turf
Two layers of turf are used to create grass edges

Butyl liner
Overhangs edge of pond

Small slabs of stone
Disguise the step used for marginal plants

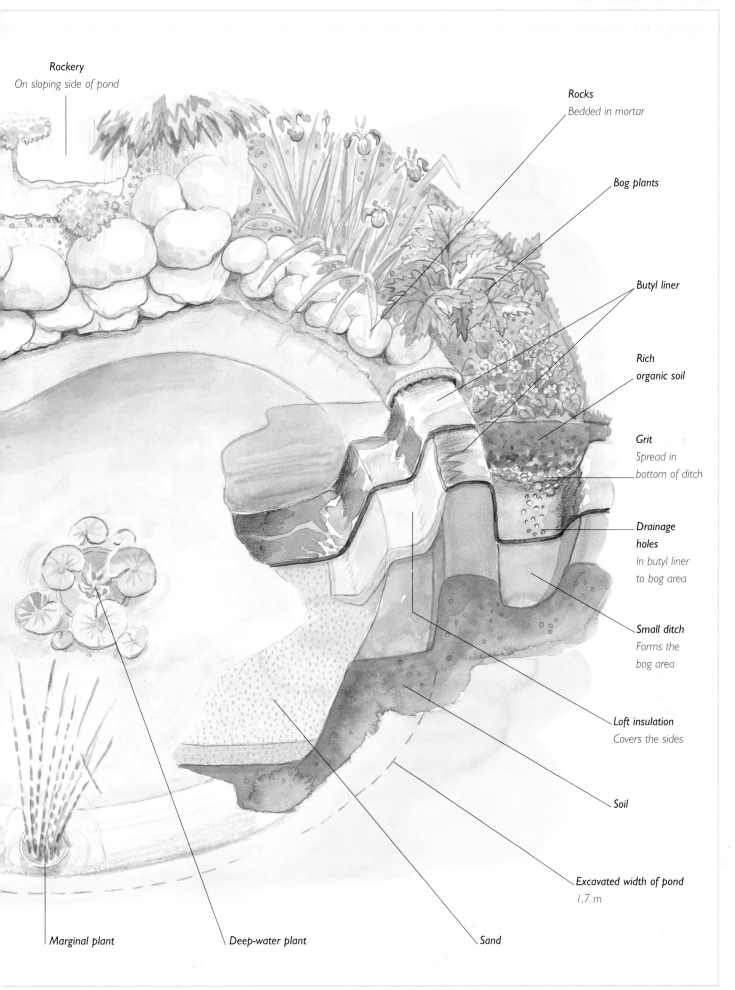

Rockery
On sloping side of pond

Rocks
Bedded in mortar

Bog plants

Butyl liner

Rich organic soil

Grit
Spread in bottom of ditch

Drainage holes
In butyl liner to bog area

Small ditch
Forms the bog area

Loft insulation
Covers the sides

Soil

Excavated width of pond
1.7 m

Marginal plant

Deep-water plant

Sand

Step-by-step: **Making the natural pond**

Earth pile
Push the spoil away so that it doesn't fall back

Edges
Sculpt the edges to a good finish

Levelling
The pond edges need to be perfectly level

Stones
Remove all the sharp stones

Sand
Rake the sand into a smooth layer, removing protruding stones as you work

1 Mark out the overall shape of the pond with rope and the tape measure, and use the spade and the shovel to dig out the earth to the desired depth. With the spirit level and batten, check that the pond edges are all at the same level.

2 Remove all sticks and stones, then spread and rake a bed of soft sand over the entire base of the pond (include all horizontal surfaces). Aim for an overall thickness of no less than 80 mm.

Bank
The bank needs to be sufficiently wide to support the slabs and boulders that make up the edge

Loft insulation
The insulation material can cause skin irritation. Wear gloves and tuck your sleeves into them

3 To prevent stones piercing the liner, cover all vertical surfaces with the loft insulation (cut it to shape with the scissors). Continue adding sand and loft insulation until you are sure all sharp edges are covered to a good depth.

Helpful hint

If the weather is at all windy, the loft insulation may blow about the garden. Do not unroll it until the very last moment (just minutes before laying the plastic sheet). Alternatively, dip it into water so that it is a sodden mass that is unlikely to blow away.

Liner
Take your time arranging the butyl liner, so that you have equal amounts overlapping all round

Arranging the turf
Lay a layer of turf with the earth side up, followed by a layer with the grass side up

Water
Fill the pond with a little water – its weight will indicate where the liner needs rearranging

Watering
Keep the turf well watered until it is established

Water level
Let the edges of the turf trail in the water

4 Being very careful not to dig holes in the sand or dislodge the loft insulation, gently unroll the butyl liner over the whole pond. Slowly fill the pond with water, all the while easing and gently smoothing the rubber to avoid thick folds.

5 Cover selected edges of the pond with sandwiched turf. Lay the first layer of turf with the earth side uppermost, and then top it off with a layer placed with the grass side uppermost. This will grow together into a compacted mat that covers the liner and edges the pond.

Firmly fixed boulders
Use plenty of mortar to secure the boulders

6 When you come to the stone edging, first bed the split sandstone in the mortar, using the club hammer and the two trowels, then top it off with limestone boulders and mortar. Add additional courses of stone and mortar to suit the levels of your particular pond.

Mortar
Scrape away and reshape the mortar joints until they look good

Work carefully
Remember that pond liners are fragile, so when you are moving stones be extra careful not to let them fall in the pond

Inspirations: Natural ponds

The creation of a healthy, natural pond involves bringing together a complex mix of water, plants, bugs, bacteria and animals, to create a well-balanced whole. The animals use oxygen and give out carbon dioxide, the plants absorb carbon dioxide and give out oxygen, the animals eat the plants, the plants and bacteria absorb sunlight – and so the eco-circle keeps turning.

ABOVE **A raised formal courtyard pond, built out of brick and edged with concrete slabs. This could be described as a "natural" pond, in the sense that** it provides a suitable environment for plants and animals. If a pond can be maintained without the need for fountains and filters, it is natural. When stocking a pond with plants, do it in stages, so the individual plants gradually acclimatize to the water temperature and each other.

ABOVE AND LEFT **A** beautiful example of a natural pond. Bright, clear water, thriving plants, the presence of fish, frogs, gnats, water snails and dragonflies, all suggest that the ecosystem of the pond is well balanced. If you can look down into the water and see colonies of animals and plants, you can be sure that the pond is healthy.

Glossary

Aggregate
A mix of sand and crushed stone used with cement to make concrete.

Algae
Minute, non-flowering water plant which resembles a film of green slime on the water surface.

Aligning
Setting one piece of wood against another (or one part of a structure against another) in order to obtain a good alignment or fit.

Aquatic
A general term for plants that thrive in water, or in waterlogged soil.

Backfilling
To fill a hole around a foundation or wall with earth.

Bedding
The process of pressing a stone into a bed or layer of wet mortar and ensuring that it is level.

Bog garden
An area – in a container or garden – where the soil is permanently wet.

Buttering
The act of using a trowel to cover a piece of stone with wet mortar just prior to setting it in place on the bed of mortar.

Butting
The action of pushing one piece of wood hard up against another in order to obtain a good flush fit, with both faces touching.

Centring
Setting a measurement or component part on the centre of another, or measuring a length or width to find the centre.

Circuit breaker
Also called a residual current device (RCD) – an automatic cut-out – used in conjunction with electrical pumps and tools as a safety measure.

Cladding
The procedure of clothing a frame with a covering of wood (such as a sheet of plywood, or a pattern of individual boards) as with the shed projects. Also the name for the wood used to cover the frame.

Colourwashing
The technique of mixing paint with water and brushing the resultant wash on wood in order to achieve a delicate, stained finish.

Compacting

Using a hammer or the weight of your body to press down and compact a layer of sand, earth or hardcore.

Course

A term describing the horizontal lines or layers of stone that make a wall or structure.

Coursing

A general term describing the process of bedding a number of stones in mortar in order to build a course.

Curing time

The time taken for mortar or concrete to become firm and stable. Part-cured mortar or concrete is firm enough to take a small amount of weight.

Damping

Wetting the stone just prior to bedding in on mortar.

Delivery pipe

The pipe that runs from the delivery side of the pump – the pipe from which the water flows.

Dressing

The act of using a hammer, chisel or trowel to trim a stone to a level, smooth, or textured finish.

Dry run

Putting all the parts of a project together without glue, nails or screws, in order to see whether or not the components are going to fit. The procedure can also be used to check that the design is going to work. See also Trial Run.

Filter

A piece of foam in a submersible pump that filters mud, grit and algae from water. A filtration unit (connected to a pump) for cleaning water.

Finishing

The procedure of sanding, painting, staining and fitting hardware (wheels, latches, handles and hinges) in order to complete the project.

Flexible armoured pipe

A heavy-duty pipe used to protect a power cable.

Flexible liner

A sheet of reinforced rubber or thick plastic used for waterproofing ponds and other water features.

Floating

The procedure of using a metal, plastic or wooden float to skim wet concrete or mortar to a smooth and completely level finish.

Hardcore

Broken stone, brick or builder's rubble used to create a firm base.

Hinging

Fixing one part to another by means of a hinge, pivot, or rotating part.

Levelling

Using a spirit level to decide whether or not a structure or component part is perfectly horizontal or vertical, and then going on to make the necessary adjustments to bring the component into line.

Log roll

Edging made from logs and wire – good for edging borders and water features.

Marking out

Using a string, pegs and tape measure to set out the size of a project on the ground, also to mark out an individual stone in readiness for cutting to size or to draw lines on a piece of wood in readiness for cutting.

Oxygenator

A water plant that releases oxygen into the water.

Pea gravel

A fine pea-sized gravel used as a decorative feature or as a levelling layer.

Pointing

Using a trowel, stick, or an alternative tool of your choice to bring the mortar joints to the desired finish.

Pre-formed unit

A factory-made concrete or plastic moulding used in water features – it might be a whole pond, a sump, or part of a waterfall.

Preserving

The procedure of painting wood with preservative in order to protect it against mould and rot. Preservative may be purchased as a colourless liquid, or it can form part of a paint or stain treatment. Some wood is pre-treated with preservative.

Raking out

Using a trowel to rake out part of the mortar, so that the edges of the stone are clearly revealed.

Reservoir pool

A pool or tank of water at the lowest point of the feature – the pool in which the pump sits.

Rubber matting

A sheet of thick rubber used to protect the pond liner – from a heavy block or slab, for example.

Sawing to size

In the context of this book, the term mostly refers to the procedure of taking the sawn wood – meaning wood that has been purchased pre-cut to width and thickness – and cutting it to length.

Sealant

A soft plastic or liquid compound used as a waterproofing material – for holes, seams, and porous surfaces.

Sighting

To judge by eye. Also to look down a tool or down a length of wood or along a wall in order to determine whether or not a particular cut, joint or structure is level or true.

Siting

The act of walking around the garden and taking all the factors into consideration in order to decide whereabouts a structure or water feature is going to be placed.

Sourcing

The process of making enquiries in order to ascertain the best source for materials within your price range.

Squaring

The technique of marking out with a set square or spirit level, and cutting and fixing wood so that surfaces or structures are at right angles to each other.

Submersible pump

A pump that is positioned underwater.

Sump

A small pond or pool into which the water drains – the pool that contains the pump.

Tamping

The act of using a length of wood to compact and level wet concrete.

Trial run

Running through a procedure of setting out all the materials and fittings of a structure – without using concrete or mortar – in order to ascertain whether or not the envisaged project or technique is feasible.

Trimming

Using a cutting tool or hammer or chisel to bring a piece of wood or the edge of a piece of stone to a good finish; also the act of using short lengths of wood to brace or strengthen a frame.

Underlay

A cushioning layer underneath a flexible pond liner used as a protection from sharp stones – it could be a specialist pond underlay or roof insulation.

Wedging

Using small slivers of stone to bring larger pieces up to the desired level.

Wire brushing

The act of using a wire brush to remove dry mortar from the face of the stone.

Suppliers

WOOD

UK

Tool manufacturers

Black & Decker
210 Bath Road
Slough
Berks SL1 3YD
Tel: (01753) 567055

Stanley UK Ltd
The Stanley Works
Woodside
Sheffield
Yorks S3 9PD
Tel: (0114) 276 8888

Tool retailers

Tilgear
Bridge House
69 Station Rd
Cuffley
Herts EN6 4TG
Tel: (01707) 873434

S J Carter Tools Ltd
Gloucester House
10 Camberwell New Rd
London SE5 0TA
Tel: (020) 7587 1222

Sawmills & timberyards

Copford Farm Sawmill
Copford Farm
Dern Lane
Waldron
Heathfield
East Sussex TN21 0PN
Tel: (01435) 813472

Edward Hodgson & Son
   (Timber) Ltd
Silverdale Works
Silverdale Avenue
Liverpool
Merseyside L13 7EZ
Tel: (0151) 228 6328

Helmdon Sawmills Ltd
Weston Road
Helmdon
Brackley
Northamptonshire
NN13 5QB
Tel: (01295) 760305

Herriard Sawmills Ltd
The Sawmill
Herriard
Basingstoke
Hants RG25 2PH
Tel: (01256) 381585

General DIY Outlets
(branches nationwide)

B & Q plc
Head Office:
Portswood House
1 Hampshire Corporate Park
Chandlers Ford
Eastleigh
Hants SO53 3YX
Tel: (01703) 256256

Focus Do-It-All Group Ltd
Head Office:
Gawsworth House
Westmere Drive
Crewe
Cheshire CW1 6XB
Tel: (01384) 456456

Homebase Ltd
Beddington House
Railway Approach
Wallington
Surrey SM6 0HB
Tel: (020) 8784 7200

SOUTH AFRICA

Timber

DIY Superstar
11 Hornbee Street
Bloemfontein, 9301
Tel: (051) 430 4694

Cape Town Timber
86 Fitz Maurice Avenue
2 Eppingindustria
Epping, 7460
Cape Town
Tel: (021) 534 7201

Coleman Timbers (Pty) Ltd
Unit 3, 7 Willowfield Crescent
Springfield Park, 4091
Durban
Tel: (031) 579 1565

H & S Timbers
14 Wilstead Street
Benoni, 1501
Johannesburg
Tel: (011) 422 3223

Uitenhage Sawmills
148 Durban Road
Uitenhage, 6229
Port Elizabeth
Tel: (041) 922 9920

Tools and Hardware

Wardkiss Paint &
   Hardware Centre
329 Sydney Road
Durban, 4001
Tel: (031) 205 1551
(Outlets nationwide)

J & J Sales
38 Argyle Street
East London, 5201
Tel: (043) 743 3380

AUSTRALIA

DIY stores

Mitre 10
319 George Street
Sydney NSW 2000
Tel: (02) 9262 1435
(Outlets nationwide)

BBC Hardware &
   Hardwarehouse
Head Office, Bldg A
Cnr. Cambridge &
   Chester Streets
Epping NSW 2121
Tel: (02) 9876 0888
(Outlets nationwide)

Timber

ABC Timbers and
   Building Supplies Pty Ltd
46 Auburn Road
Regents Park NSW 2143
Tel: (02) 9645 2511

Finlayson's
135 Wellington Road
East Brisbane QLD 4169
Tel: (07) 3393 0588

Bowens Timber and
Building Supplies
Support Office
48 Hallam South Road
Hallam VIC 3803
Tel: (03) 9796 3003

NEW ZEALAND

DIY stores

Mitre 10
Head Office:
182 Wairau Rd
Glenfield, Auckland
Tel: (09) 443 9900
(Outlets nationwide)

Placemakers Support Office
150 Marua Rd
Private Bag 14942, Panmure
Auckland
Tel: (09) 525 5100

Timber

South Pacific Timber
Cnr. Ruru and Shaddock Streets
Auckland City
Tel: (09) 379 5150

Lumber Specialties
117 Main South Road
Upper Riccarton
Christchurch
Tel: (03) 348 7002

Wilson Bros Timber
71 Foremans Road
Hornby
Tel: (03) 688 2336

STONE

UK

Consult the telephone directory for details of your local builder's yard or stone merchant.

The Brick Warehouse
18–22 Northdown Street
London N1 9BG
Tel: (020) 7833 9992

Buffalo Granite (UK) Ltd
The Vestry
St. Clement's Church
Treadgold Street
London W11 4BP
Tel: (020) 7221 7930

Clayax Yorkstone Ltd
Derry Hill
Menston
Ilkley
Leeds
West Yorkshire
LS29 6AZ
Tel: (01943) 878351
Fax: (01943) 870801

The Natural Stone Co
35 Bedford Road
Clapham
London SW4 7SG
Tel: (020) 7733 4455
Fax: (020) 7737 2427
Stonecraft
Burgh Road
Aylsham
NR11 6AR
Tel: (020) 8242 9017 ext. 25

General DIY Outlets
(branches nationwide)

B & Q plc
Head Office:
Portswood House
1 Hampshire Corporate Park
Chandlers Ford
Eastleigh, Hants
SO53 3YX
Tel: (01703) 256256

Focus Do-It-All Group Ltd
Head Office:
Gawsworth House
Westmere Drive
Crewe
Cheshire
CW1 6XB
Tel: (01384) 456456

Homebase Ltd
Beddington House
Railway Approach
Wallington
Surrey
SM6 0HB
Tel: (020) 8784 7200

SOUTH AFRICA

Consult your telephone directory for your local branch of Mica Hardware or Federated Timbers.

Dunrobin Garden Pavilion
Old Main Road
Bothas Hill, Durban
Tel: (031) 777 1855
Fax: (031) 777 1893

Lifestyle Garden Centre
DF Malan Drive
Randpark Ridge
Northcliff, Johannesburg
Tel: (011) 792 5616
Fax: (011) 792 5332

Radermachers Garden &
Home Centre
Kraaibosch, National Road
George
Tel: (044) 889 0075/6
Fax: (044) 889 0071

Safari Garden Centre
Lynwood Road
Pretoria
Tel: (012) 807 0009
Fax: (012) 807 0350

Showgrounds Nursery
Showgrounds
Currie Avenue
Bloemfontein
Tel: (051) 447 5523
Fax: (051) 447 5523

Starke Ayres
322 Kempston Road
Sydwill, Port Elizabeth
Tel: (041) 451 0389
Fax: (041) 451 0393

Stodels
Eversdal Road
Bellville, Cape Town
Tel: (021) 99 1106
Fax: (021) 919 9324

Stoneage Concrete
Industries cc
126 Crompton Street
Pinetown, Durban
Tel: (031) 701 2411
Fax: (031) 701 6842

AUSTRALIA

General building equipment

ABC Timbers and Building
   Supplies Pty Ltd
46 Auburn Road
Regents Park NSW 2143
Tel: (02) 9645 2511

BBC Hardware
Building A
Cnr. Cambridge &
   Chester Streets
Epping
NSW 2121
Tel: (02) 9876 0888
(Branches throughout Australia)

BBC Hardware
Niangala Close
Belrose NSW 2085
Tel: (02) 9450 0799
(Can also order in stone)

Bowens Timber and
   Building Supplies
135–173 Macaulay Road
North Melbourne 3051
Tel: (03) 9328 1041

Mitre 10
319 George Street
Sydney 2000
Tel: (02) 9262 1435
Customer service: 1800 777 850
Outlets nationwide including:
Greens Hardware
cnr Maryvale and Peel Street
South Brisbane
Queensland 4101
Tel: (07) 3844 3341

Cleveland Mitre 10
25–31 Shore Street West
Cleveland
Queensland 4163
Tel: (07) 3821 1153

Stone suppliers

Kellyville Landscape Supplies
Lot 25
Windsor Road
Kellyville NSW 2155
Tel: (02) 9629 4167

Sydney Stone Yard
1/3a Stanley Road
Randwick NSW 2031
Tel: (02) 9326 4479

NEW ZEALAND

Firth Industries Limited
Auckland Regional Office
102 Lunn Ave
Mt Wellington
Auckland
Information Freephone:
   0800 800 576
(Branches nationwide)

Mitre 10
Head Office:
182 Wairau Road
Glenfield
Auckland
Tel: (09) 443 9900
(Branches nationwide)

Placemakers Support Office
150 Marua Road
Private Bag 14942
Panmure
Auckland
Tel: (09) 525 5100

WATER

UK

*Consult the telephone directory for
details of your local water garden
specialist and DIY store.*

Blagdon Water Gardens
Bath Road
Upper Langford
Somerset
BS18 7DN
Tel: (01934) 852973

Hozelock Ltd
Waterslade House
Thame Road
Haddenham
Aylesbury
Buckinghamshire
HP17 8JD
Tel: (01844) 291881

Interpet
Interpet House
Vincent Lane
Dorking
Surrey
RH4 3YX
Tel: (01306) 881033

Lotus Water Garden Products
Junction Street
Burnley
Lancashire
BB12 0NA
Tel: (01282) 420771
Fax: (01282) 412719
*(Manufacturers of self-contained
water features and fountain
ornaments)*

Oases
3 Telford Gate
Whittle Road
West Portway Industrial Estate
Andover
Hampshire
SP10 3SF
Tel: (01264) 333225
(Pumps)

The Traditional Garden
   Supply Co
Scotts of Stowe
Unit 1, Corinium Centre
Lovelane Ind. Estate
Cirencester
Gloucestershire
GL7 1YJ
Orderline: (0870) 600 3366

Trident Water Garden Products
Folehill
Coventry
Warwickshire
CV6 7FL
Tel: (01203) 638802

SOUTH AFRICA

*Consult the telephone directory for
details of your local water garden
specialist and DIY store.*

Dunrobin Garden Pavilion
Old Main Road
Bothas Hill, Durban
Tel: (031) 777 1855
Fax: (031) 777 1893

Lifestyle Garden Centre
DF Malan Drive
Randpark Ridge
Northcliff
Johannesburg
Tel: (011) 792 5616
Fax: (011) 792 5332

Radermachers Garden
  and Home Centre
Kraaibosch
National Road
George
Tel: (044) 889 0075/6
Fax: (044) 889 0071

Safari Garden Centre
Lynwood Road
Pretoria
Tel: (012) 807 0009
Fax: (012) 807 0350

Showgrounds Nursery
Showgrounds
Currie Avenue
Bloemfontein
Tel: (051) 447 5523
Fax: (051) 447 5523

Starke Ayres (Pty) Ltd
322 Kempston Road
Sydwill
Port Elizabeth
Tel: (041) 451 0389
Fax: (041) 451 0393
and
Liesbeek Road
Rosebank
Cape Town
Tel: (021) 685 4120
Fax: (021) 685 3837
(Branches nationwide)

AUSTRALIA

ABC Timbers and Building
Supplies Pty Ltd
46 Auburn Road
Regents Park
NSW 2143
Tel: (02) 9645 2511

BBC Hardware
Building A
Cnr. Cambridge and
  Chester Streets
Epping
NSW 2121
Tel: (02) 9876 0888
(Branches throughout Australia)

Bowens Timber and
  Building Supplies
135–173 Macaulay Road
North Melbourne 3051
Tel: (03) 9328 1041

Mitre 10
319 George Street
Sydney 2000
Tel: (02) 9262 1435
Customer service: 1800 777 850
(Outlets nationwide)

Garden Magic
Harrington Park
Cnr. Northern Road and
  Porrende Street
Narellan
NSW 2567
Tel: (02) 4647 4332

Above the Earth
70 Ben Boyd Road
Neutral Bay
NSW 2089
(02) 9904 0577
(Design and installation of
ponds, fountains and other
water features; can source any
materials required)

Fantasy Fountains
Unit 2/8 Auburn Street
Hunters Hill
NSW 2110
(02) 9651 1154
(Outlets nationwide)

Garden Art Fountains
269 Parramatta Road (cnr.
  Wolseley Street)
Haberfield
NSW 2045

Bambuzit
13 Erith Street
Botany
NSW 2019
(02) 9666 5703
(Bamboo supplier)

NEW ZEALAND

Firth Industries Ltd
Auckland Regional Office
102 Lunn Ave
Mt Wellington
Auckland
Information Freephone:
0800 800 576
(Branches nationwide)

Carine Garden Centre and
  Water World
Cnr. SH2 and Te Karaka Drive
Te Puna
Tauranga
Tel: (07) 552 4949

Jansen's Pet and Aquatic Centre
985 Mt Eden Road
Three Kings
Auckland
Tel: (09) 625 7915
Website: www.jansens.co.nz

Palmers Garden Centres
Head Office:
182 Wairau Road
Glenfield
Auckland
Tel: (09) 443 9910
(Branches nationwide)

Placemakers Support Office
150 Marua Road
Private Bag 14942
Panmure
Auckland
Tel: (09) 525 5100

Index

Conversion chart

To convert the metric measurements used in this book to imperial measurements, simply multiply the figure given in the text by the relevant number in the table alongside. Bear in mind that conversions will not necessarily work out exactly, and you will need to round the figure up or down slightly. (Do not use a combination of metric and imperial measurements – for accuracy, keep to one system.)

To convert	Multiply by
millimetres to inches	0.0394
metres to feet	3.28
metres to yards	1.093
sq millimetres to sq inches	0.00155
sq metres to sq feet	10.76
sq metres to sq yards	1.195
cu metres to cu feet	35.31
cu metres to cu yards	1.308
grams to pounds	0.0022
kilograms to pounds	2.2046
litres to gallons	0.22

Acknowledgments

AG&G Books would like to thank *Dennis Davis Photography Design* for contributing the pictures used on pages 192, 218 top, 218 bottom and 289 right; *Garden and Wildlife Matters Photographic Library* for contributing the pictures used on pages 52, 53, 76, 77, 108, 109, 170 bottom, 193 inset and 321 and *John Glover Photography* for contributing the pictures used on pages 170 top, 288, 289 right and 320.

First published in 2003 by New Holland Publishers (UK) Ltd
London • Cape Town • Sydney • Auckland

Garfield House, 86–88 Edgware Road, London W2 2EA, United Kingdom
www.newhollandpublishers.com

80 McKenzie Street, Cape Town, 8001, South Africa

Level 1, Unit 4, 14 Aquatic Drive, Frenchs Forest, NSW 2086, Australia

218 Lake Road, Northcote, Auckland, New Zealand

ISBN 1 84330 138 5

1 3 5 7 9 10 8 6 4 2

Editorial Direction: Rosemary Wilkinson
Project Editor: Clare Sayer
Production: Hazel Kirkman

Designed and created for New Holland by AG&G BOOKS
Designer: Glyn Bridgewater
Illustrator: Gill Bridgewater
Project design: Alan and Gill Bridgewater
Photography: AG&G Books and Ian Parsons *unless otherwise credited (see page 383)*
Editor: Fiona Corbridge
Woodwork: Alan and Gill Bridgewater, William Del Tufo and Richard Cope
Stonework: Alan and Gill Bridgewater
Water feature project makers: Alan, Gill and Glyn Bridgewater

AG&G Books would like to thank Anglian Timber Ltd for their help.

Reproduction by Pica Digital, Singapore
Printed and bound in Malaysia by Times Offset (M) Sdn. Bhd.